Poetry Focus **2022**

Leaving Certificate poems and notes for **English Higher Level**

Martin Kieran & Frances Rocks

Gill Education
Hume Avenue
Park West
Dublin 12
www.gilleducation.ie

Gill Education is an imprint of M.H. Gill & Co.

ISBN: 978-0-7171-86693

Design: Graham Thew
Print origination: Carole Lynch

At the time of going to press, all web addresses were active and contained information relevant to the topics in this book. Gill Education does not, however, accept responsibility for the content or views contained on these websites. Content, views and addresses may change beyond the publisher or author's control. Students should always be supervised when reviewing websites.

For permission to reproduce photographs, the authors and publisher gratefully acknowledge the following:

© Alamy: 20, 23, 36, 62, 68, 71, 72, 75, 79, 80, 83, 92, 95, 96, 106, 123, 171, 175, 178, 199, 207, 210, 218, 272, 281, 320, 329, 336, 338, 344, 346, 348, 353, 373, 376, 386, 399, 402, 409; © The Art Archive: 364; © Bridgeman Images: 132, 134, 332, 340, 342; © Collins Photo Agency: 154; © E+: 277, 280, 296, 309, 310; © Getty Images: 5, 7, 11, 16, 19, 40, 43, 45, 48, 51, 64, 86, 194, 198, 253, 256, 293, 369, 370, 383, 395, 398, 413; © Imagefile: 366, 391; © iStock: 31, 34, 76, 78, 89, 113, 116, 118, 138, 160, 162, 167, 169, 190, 203, 220, 224, 230, 232, 233, 237, 240, 242, 244, 246, 250, 251, 257, 258, 260, 262, 274, 285, 288, 290, 300, 305, 323, 326, 422; © The Josef and Yaye Breitenbach Charitable Foundation, New York: 2; © Minden Pictures: 25, 29; © National Monuments Service. Dept. of Arts, Heritage, Regional, Rural and Gaeltacht Affairs: 185, 189; © PD Smith: 406, 408; © RTÉ Archives: 152; © Saint Patrick's Cathedral: 403; © Shutterstock: 108, 110, 128, 141, 144; © Topfoto: 377, 380.

The authors and publisher have made every effort to trace all copyright holders, but if any have been inadvertently overlooked we would be pleased to make the necessary arrangement at the first opportunity.

The paper used in this book is made from the wood pulp of managed forests. For every tree felled, at least one tree is planted, thereby renewing natural resources.

Contents

Introduction   v

Elizabeth Bishop

- 'The Fish' (OL)   4
- 'The Bight'   10
- 'At the Fishhouses'   14
- 'The Prodigal' (OL)   20
- 'Questions of Travel'   24
- 'The Armadillo'   30
- 'Sestina'   35
- 'First Death in Nova Scotia'   39
- 'Filling Station' (OL)   44
- 'In the Waiting Room'   49
- Revision Overview   61

Emily Dickinson

- '"Hope" is the thing with feathers'   64
- 'There's a certain Slant of light'   68
- 'I felt a Funeral, in my Brain' (OL)   72
- 'A Bird came down the Walk'   76
- 'I heard a Fly buzz–when I died' (OL)   79
- 'The Soul has Bandaged moments'   82
- 'I could bring You Jewels–had I a   86
  mind to'
- 'A narrow Fellow in the Grass'   89
- 'I taste a liquor never brewed'   92
- 'After great pain, a formal feeling   96
  comes'
- Revision Overview   105

John Keats

- 'To One Who Has Been Long in   108
  City Pent'
- 'Ode to a Nightingale'   111
- 'On First Looking into   118
  Chapman's Homer' (OL)
- 'Ode on a Grecian Urn'   122
- 'When I Have Fears That I May   128
  Cease to Be'
- 'La Belle Dame Sans Merci' (OL)   131
- 'To Autumn'   137

- 'Bright Star, Would I Were   141
  Steadfast as Thou Art'
- Revision Overview   151

Brendan Kennelly

- 'Begin'   154
- 'Bread'   158
- '"Dear Autumn Girl"'   162
- 'Poem from a Three Year Old'   166
- 'Oliver to His Brother'   171
- 'I See You Dancing, Father'   175
- 'A Cry for Art O'Leary'   179
- 'Things I Might Do'   190
- 'A Great Day'   193
- 'Fragments'   199
- 'The soul's loneliness'   203
- 'Saint Brigid's Prayer'   207
- Revision Overview   217

D. H. Lawrence

- 'Call into Death'   220
- 'Piano'   224
- 'The Mosquito'   228
- 'Snake'   235
- 'Humming-Bird' (OL)   242
- 'Intimates'   246
- 'Delight of Being Alone'   250
- 'Absolute Reverence'   251
- 'What Have They Done to You?'   252
- 'Baby-Movements II: "Trailing   257
  Clouds"' (OL)
- 'Bavarian Gentians'   260
- Revision Overview   271

Adrienne Rich

- 'Aunt Jennifer's Tigers' (OL)   274
- 'The Uncle Speaks in the Drawing   277
  Room' (OL)
- 'Power'   281
- 'Storm Warnings'   284
- 'Living in Sin'   288
- 'The Roofwalker'   292

(OL) indicates poems that are also
prescribed for the Ordinary Level course.

○ 'Our Whole Life'   296
○ 'Trying to Talk with a Man'   299
○ 'Diving into the Wreck'   303
○ 'From a Survivor'   309
○ Revision Overview   319

William Wordsworth

○ 'To My Sister'   322
○ 'A slumber did my spirit seal'   326
○ 'She dwelt among the untrodden   329
   ways' (OL)
○ 'Composed Upon Westminister   332
   Bridge'
○ 'It is a beauteous evening, calm   336
   and free' (OL)
○ 'The Solitary Reaper'   339
○ from *The Prelude*: 'The Stolen Boat'   343
○ from *The Prelude*: 'Skating' (OL)   347
○ 'Tintern Abbey'   350
○ Revision Overview   363

W. B. Yeats

○ 'The Lake Isle of Innisfree' (OL)   366
○ 'September 1913'   369
○ 'The Wild Swans at Coole' (OL)   373
○ 'An Irish Airman Foresees his   377
   Death' (OL)

○ 'Easter 1916'   381
○ 'The Second Coming'   386
○ 'Sailing to Byzantium'   390
○ from 'Meditations in Time of   395
   Civil War': 'The Stare's Nest By
   My Window'
○ 'In Memory of Eva Gore-Booth   399
   and Con Markiewicz'
○ 'Swift's Epitaph'   403
○ 'An Acre of Grass'   406
○ from 'Under Ben Bulben'   409
○ 'Politics'   413
○ Revision Overview   421

The Unseen Poem

○ 'Autumn'   424
○ 'Roller-Skaters'   427
○ 'At Cider Mill Farm'   430
○ 'Lipstick'   433
○ 'Stalled Train'   436

Acknowledgements   437

(OL) indicates poems that are also
prescribed for the Ordinary Level course.

Introduction

Poetry Focus is a modern poetry textbook for Leaving Certificate Higher Level English. It includes all the prescribed poems for the 2022 exam as well as succinct commentaries on each one. Well-organised study notes allow students to develop their own individual responses and enhance their skills in critical literacy. **There is no single 'correct' approach to answering the poetry question.** Candidates are free to respond in any appropriate way that shows good knowledge of and engagement with the prescribed poems.

- **Concise poet biographies** provide context for the poems.
- **List of prescribed poems** gives a brief introduction to each poem.
- **Personal response** questions follow the text of each poem. These allow students to consider their first impressions before any in-depth study or analysis. These questions provide a good opportunity for written and/or oral exercises.
- **Critical literacy** highlights the main features of the poet's subject matter and style. These discussion notes will enhance the student's own critical appreciation through focused group work and/or written exercises. Analytical skills are developed in a coherent, practical way to give students confidence in articulating their own personal responses.
- **Analysis (writing about the poem) is provided using graded sample paragraphs** which aid students in fluently structuring and developing valid points, using fresh and varied expression. These model paragraphs also illustrate effective use of relevant quotations and reference.
- **Class/homework exercises** for each poem provide focused practice in writing personal responses to examination-style questions.
- **Points to consider** provide a memorable snapshot of the key aspects to remember about each poem.
- **Full sample Leaving Certificate essays** are accompanied by marking-scheme guidelines and examiner's comments. These show the student exactly what is required to achieve a successful top grade in the Leaving Cert. The examiner's comments illustrate the use of the PCLM marking scheme and are an invaluable aid for the ambitious student.
- **Sample essay plans** on each poet's work illustrate how to interpret a question and recognise the particular nuances of key words in examination questions. Student evaluation of these essay plans increase confidence in developing and organising clear response to exam questions.
- **Sample Leaving Cert questions** on each poet are given at the end of their particular section.
- **Revision Overviews** provide a concise and visual summary of each poet's work, through highlighting and interlinking relevant themes.
- **Unseen Poetry** provides guidelines for this 20-mark section of the paper. Included are numerous sample questions and answers, which allow students to practise exam-style answers.

The FREE eBook contains:

- **Investigate Further** sections which contain **useful weblinks** should you want to learn more.
- **Pop-up key quotes** to encourage students to select their own individual combination of references from a poem and to write brief commentaries on specific quotations.
- Additional sample graded paragraphs called '**Developing your personal response**'.
- Audio of a selection of the poetry as read by the poets, including audio of all Brendan Kennelly poetry.

Further material can also be found on GillExplore.ie:

- **A glossary of common literary terms** provides an easy reference when answering questions.
- **A critical analysis checklist** offers useful hints and tips on how to show genuine engagement with the poetry.

How is the Prescribed Poetry Question Marked?

Marking is done (ex. 50 marks) by reference to the PCLM criteria for assessment.
- Clarity of purpose (P): 30% of the total (15 marks)
- Coherence of delivery (C): 30% of the total (15 marks)
- Efficiency of language use (L): 30% of the total (15 marks)
- Accuracy of mechanics (M): 10% of the total (5 marks)

Each answer will be in the form of a response to a specific task requiring candidates to:
- Display a clear and purposeful engagement with the set task (P)
- Sustain the response in an appropriate manner over the entire answer (C)
- Manage and control language appropriate to the task (L)
- Display levels of accuracy in spelling and grammar appropriate to the required/chosen register (M)

General

'Students at Higher Level will be required to study a representative selection from the work of eight poets: a representative selection would seek to reflect the range of a poet's themes and interests and exhibit his/her characteristic style and viewpoint. Normally the study of at least six poems by each poet would be expected.' (DES English Syllabus, 6.3)

The marking scheme guidelines from the State Examinations Commission state that in the case of each poet, the candidates have **freedom of choice** in relation to the poems studied. In addition, there is **not a finite list of any 'poet's themes and interests'**.

Note that in responding to the question set on any given poet, the candidates must refer to the poem(s) they have studied but are not required to refer to **any specific poem(s), nor are they expected to discuss or refer to all the poems they have chosen to study**.

In each of the questions in **Prescribed Poetry**, the underlying nature of the task is the invitation to the candidates to **engage with the poems themselves**.

Exam Advice

- **You are not expected to write about any set number of poems** in the examination. You might decide to focus in detail on a small number of poems, or you could choose to write in a more general way on several poems.

- Most candidates write one or two well-developed **paragraphs** on each of the poems they have chosen for discussion. In other cases, a paragraph will focus on one specific aspect of the poet's work. When discussing recurring themes or features of style, appropriate cross-references to other poems may also be useful.

- Reflect on central **themes** and viewpoints in the poems you discuss. Comment also on the use of language and the poet's distinctive **style**. Examine imagery, tone, structure, rhythm and rhyme. Be careful not to simply list aspects of style, such as alliteration or repetition. There's little point in mentioning that a poet uses sound effects or metaphors without discussing the effectiveness of such characteristics.

- Focus on **the task** you have been given in the poetry question. Identify the key terms in the wording of the question and think of similar words for these terms. This will help you develop a relevant and coherent personal response in keeping with the PCLM marking scheme criteria.

- Always root your answers in the text of the poems. Support the points you make with **relevant reference and quotation**. Make sure your own expression is fresh and lively. Avoid awkward expressions, such as 'It says in the poem that ...'. Look for alternatives: 'There is a sense of ...', 'The tone seems to suggest ...', 'It's evident that ...', etc.

- Neat, **legible handwriting** will help to make a positive impression on examiners. Corrections should be made by simply drawing a line through the mistake. Scored-out words distract attention from the content of your work.

- Keep the emphasis on why particular poets **appeal to you**. Consider the continuing relevance or significance of a poet's work. Perhaps you have shared some of the feelings or experiences expressed in the poems. Avoid starting answers with prepared biographical sketches. Brief reference to a poet's life are better used when discussing how the poems themselves were shaped by such experiences.

- Remember that the examination encourages **individual engagement** with the prescribed poems. Poetry can make us think and feel and imagine. It opens our minds to the wonderful possibilities of language and ideas. Your interaction with the poems is what matters most. **Commentary notes and critical interpretations are all there to be challenged.** Read the poems carefully and have confidence in expressing your own personal response.

Elizabeth Bishop
1911–1979

'The armored cars of dreams, contrived to let us do so many a dangerous thing.'

Elizabeth Bishop was born in Worcester, Massachusetts, in 1911. She spent part of her childhood with her Canadian grandparents following her father's death and mother's hospitalisation. She then lived with various relatives who, according to Bishop, took care of her because they felt sorry for her. These unsettling events, along with the memories of her youth, inspired her to read poetry – and eventually to write it. After studying English at university, she travelled extensively and lived in New York, Florida and, for 17 years, Brazil. She also taught at several American colleges. Throughout her life she suffered from ill health and depression. As a poet, she wrote sparingly, publishing only five slim volumes in 35 years. However, her work received high acclaim. 'I think geography comes first in my work,' she told an interviewer, 'and then animals. But I like people, too. I've written a few poems about people.' Bishop died suddenly in her Boston apartment on 6 October 1979. She was 68 years old. Her poetry continues to gain widespread recognition and study.

Investigate Further

To find out more about Elizabeth Bishop, or to hear readings of her poems, you could search some useful websites, such as YouTube, BBC poetry, poetryfoundation.org and poetryarchive.org, or access additional material on this page of your eBook.

Prescribed Poems

Note that Bishop uses American spellings and punctuation in her work.

○ **1 'The Fish' (OL)**
Based on an actual experience from her time in Florida during the 1930s, the central notion of the poem is that both nature and human nature share admirable qualities of strength and endurance. **Page 4**

○ **2 'The Bight'**
In describing the small, untidy bight (bay), the poet displays a naturally keen observation and an expert use of metaphor. **Page 10**

○ **3 'At the Fishhouses'**
Bishop travels back to her childhood home in Nova Scotia and notes some of the changes that have taken place. Detailed description leads to intense reflection and introspection. **Page 14**

○ **4 'The Prodigal' (OL)**
This poem is based on the biblical parable of the Prodigal Son. Bishop imagines the squalor and degradation brought about by alcoholism. However, determination, hope and human resilience eventually triumph. **Page 20**

○ **5 'Questions of Travel'**
The striking Brazilian landscape encourages the poet to consider people's interests in foreign places. **Page 24**

○ **6 'The Armadillo'**
Bishop describes the beautiful – but dangerous – fire balloons that light up the darkness during an annual religious festival in Rio de Janeiro. **Page 30**

○ **7 'Sestina'**
In this deeply personal poem, Bishop remembers a painful childhood. Faced with her grandmother's sadness, she retreats to the kitchen of her family home and its familiar comforts. **Page 35**

○ **8 'First Death in Nova Scotia'**
Vividly recalling the death of her young cousin Arthur, the poet explores the innocence and bewilderment of childhood. Many of her memories are dominated by the Canadian winter landscape. **Page 39**

○ **9 'Filling Station' (OL)**
The description of a run-down filling station leads to other discoveries. Despite the grease and oily dirt, Bishop finds signs of family love and beauty in this unlikely place. Some critics see the poem as an allegory of all human life. **Page 44**

○ **10 'In the Waiting Room'**
Set in Worcester, Massachusetts in 1918, the poet returns to the theme of childhood and the loss of innocence. **Page 49**

(OL) indicates poems that are also prescribed for the Ordinary Level course.

1 The Fish

I caught a tremendous fish
and held him beside the boat
half out of water, with my hook
fast in a corner of his mouth.
He didn't fight.   5
He hadn't fought at all.
He hung a grunting weight,
battered and venerable
and homely. Here and there
his brown skin hung in strips   10
like ancient wallpaper,
and its pattern of darker brown
was like wallpaper:
shapes like full-blown roses
stained and lost through age.   15
He was speckled with barnacles,
fine rosettes of lime,
and infested
with tiny white sea-lice,
and underneath two or three   20
rags of green weed hung down.
While his gills were breathing in
the terrible oxygen
—the frightening gills,
fresh and crisp with blood,   25
that can cut so badly—
I thought of the coarse white flesh
packed in like feathers,
the big bones and the little bones,
the dramatic reds and blacks   30
of his shiny entrails,
and the pink swim-bladder
like a big peony.
I looked into his eyes
which were far larger than mine   35
but shallower, and yellowed,
the irises backed and packed
with tarnished tinfoil
seen through the lenses
of old scratched isinglass.   40

tremendous: huge, startling, fearsome.

venerable: ancient, worthy of respect.
homely: comfortable, easy-going, unpretentious, plain.

rosettes: rose-shaped decorations made of ribbon, often awarded as prizes.

sea-lice: small parasites that live on the skin of fish.

gills: breathing organs of fish.

entrails: internal organs.

peony: large, flamboyant flower, usually pink.

irises: coloured parts of an eye.

isinglass: gelatine-like substance obtained from the bodies of fish, opaque.

They shifted a little, but not
to return my stare.
—It was more like the tipping
of an object toward the light.
I admired his sullen face,   45
the mechanism of his jaw,
and then I saw
that from his lower lip
—if you could call it a lip—
grim, wet, and weaponlike,   50
hung five old pieces of fish-line,
or four and a wire leader
with the swivel still attached,
with all their five big hooks
grown firmly in his mouth.   55
A green line, frayed at the end
where he broke it, two heavier lines,
and a fine black thread
still crimped from the strain and snap
when it broke and he got away.   60
Like medals with their ribbons
frayed and wavering,
a five-haired beard of wisdom
trailing from his aching jaw.
I stared and stared   65
and victory filled up
the little rented boat,
from the pool of bilge
where oil had spread a rainbow
around the rusted engine   70
to the bailer rusted orange,
the sun-cracked thwarts,
the oarlocks on their strings,
the gunnels—until everything
was rainbow, rainbow, rainbow!   75
And I let the fish go.

sullen: bad-tempered, sulky.
mechanism: workings.

leader: wire connecting fishhook and line.

crimped: pressed into ridges.

frayed: unravelled, worn.

bilge: dirty water that collects in the bottom of a boat.

bailer: bucket that scoops water out of a boat.
thwarts: rowers' benches.

oarlocks: metal devices for holding oars.
gunnels: upper edges of the side of a boat.

'He hung a grunting weight'

👤 Personal Response

1. List two details that appealed to you in the description of the fish in lines 1–15. Why did they make an impact on you? Were they unusual or did they appeal to your senses? Support your response with quotation from the poem.

2. What is the poet's attitude towards the fish? Where does it change as the poem progresses? Give a reason for this change. Refer closely to the poem in your response.

3. Who had the 'victory' in this situation – the fish or Bishop? Why did you come to this conclusion? Support your discussion with clear references to the poem.

👁 Critical Literacy

'The Fish' is from Elizabeth Bishop's first published collection, *North and South* (1946). She lived in Florida during the 1930s and the poem is based on her experience of catching a large jewfish at Key West. Bishop once said, 'I like painting probably better than I like poetry' and 'The Fish' is certainly a very visual poem. Bishop uses the fish as a way of exploring a 'green' awareness, the respect for nature and all living things.

The poem's opening line is direct and forceful ('I caught a tremendous fish'). Bishop's use of the personal pronoun 'I' gives a sense of immediacy and intimacy. The adjective 'tremendous' reflects the **poet's breathless excitement and awe at this magnificent specimen of fish**. The act of catching the fish is described in a personal, down-to-earth way. Bishop once said, 'I always tell the truth in my poems ... that's exactly how it happened.' The fish is 'half out of water', no longer in its natural habitat.

In line 5, the focus shifts from the person who caught the fish to the fish itself. **It is now given a personality**: 'He didn't fight.' The onomatopoeic 'grunting' allows us to be part of this scene, as we hear the distressed noises from the gasping, ugly ('homely'), exhausted ('battered') fish. Then another aspect of the fish is presented to us: it is 'venerable', ancient and worthy of reverence. Bishop the participant is giving way to Bishop the observer. While in college, Bishop met Marianne Moore, a famous American poet whose focus was on the accurate description of a particular thing. This poetic movement was known as **imagism**. We can see the similarity of style between the two poets in Bishop's description of the fish: 'Here and there/ his brown skin hung in strips/like ancient wallpaper'.

The surface **detail is painstakingly and imaginatively described** ('like full-blown roses'). There seems to be an attempt to domesticate the creature, but the sordid reality of the blotches on the skin is also noted ('stained and lost through age'). The texture of the fish is described

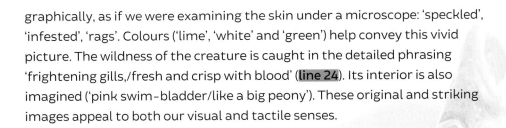

graphically, as if we were examining the skin under a microscope: 'speckled', 'infested', 'rags'. Colours ('lime', 'white' and 'green') help convey this vivid picture. The wildness of the creature is caught in the detailed phrasing 'frightening gills,/fresh and crisp with blood' (line 24). Its interior is also imagined ('pink swim-bladder/like a big peony'). These original and striking images appeal to both our visual and tactile senses.

Bishop's delight in catching this fine specimen soon gives way to an **emotional involvement with the fish** and his struggle for survival (line 34). She compares his eyes to her own ('far larger'). She notes the wear and tear from a long, hard life ('yellowed'). The irises are 'backed and packed/with tarnished tinfoil'. Here, assonance and alliteration give emphasis to the image. However, the fish's eyes are unresponsive, so there seems to be no interplay between creature and poet. This suggests both the independence and the vulnerability of the fish.

Progression in the poem is shown in the verbs: 'I caught', 'I thought', 'I looked' and, in line 45, 'I admired'. The **poet admires the resolute nature of the fish** ('his sullen face'). This fish has survived previous battles ('five big hooks/grown firmly in his mouth'). Precise detail emphasises the severity of these battles ('A green line, frayed at the end/where he broke it'). Military language highlights the effort the fish has made to survive: 'weaponlike', 'medals'. Bishop's sympathy is clear as she notes the fish's 'aching jaw'. For the fish, it is clear that the pain of battle remains.

Line 65 shows the poet transfixed ('I stared and stared'). Now the scene expands from a single fisher in a 'little rented boat' to something of **universal significance** ('victory' fills up the boat). Ordinary details (the 'bilge', the 'thwarts' and the 'gunnels') are transformed. The oil has 'spread a rainbow'. Everything is coloured and Bishop's relationship with the fish changes. She exercises mercy. A moment of epiphany occurs and she lets 'the fish go'. All the tension in the poem is finally released. The underlying drama contained between the opening line ('I caught a tremendous fish') and the closing line ('And I let the fish go.') has been resolved. **Victory belongs to both the poet and the fish**. The fish is free; the poet has seen and understood.

This poem is a long narrative with a clear beginning, middle and end. Bishop has chosen a suitably unrhymed form. The metre is appropriate for the speaking voice: dimeter (two stresses) and trimeter (three stresses). Short run-on lines suggest the poet excitedly examining her catch and the recurring use of dashes indicates her thought process as she moves from delight to wonder, empathy and, finally, comprehension. The concluding rhyming couplet brings a definite and satisfying resolution to the dramatic tension.

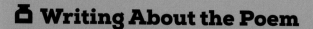

✒ Writing About the Poem

Elizabeth Bishop has been praised for her 'painterly eye'. Discuss this aspect of her style in 'The Fish'. Support your views with close reference to the poem.

Sample Paragraph

An artist looks, re-creates and leads both themselves and us to a new insight. I think Bishop accomplishes all this in her poem 'The Fish'. The poet looks at the event ('I caught a tremendous fish') and then moves to describe the fish, using striking images ('brown skin hung in strips/like ancient wallpaper'). Like a camera, she pans this way and that, making us see also 'its pattern of darker brown' with 'shapes like full-blown roses'. She leads us to imagine the interior of the fish, its 'coarse white flesh/packed in like feathers'. If Bishop were painting this fish, I could imagine it in glistening oil colours. In her poem, she paints with words: 'the pink swim-bladder/like a peony'. She engages with her subject: 'I looked into his eyes'. She acknowledges this veteran as she notes the 'five big hooks/grown firmly in his mouth'. Just like a painter, Bishop orders her picture so that we can see the 'five-haired beard of wisdom/trailing' from the fish. The poem concludes with a burst of colour ('rainbow, rainbow, rainbow!'). The rainbow from the oil-soaked bilge water has transformed the poet's relationship with the fish. Like Bishop, we now see the proper relationship between people and nature – one of respect. So the 'painterly eye' has led us to see the drama, the fish and what it really was to her and finally our correct response to the earth and its creatures.

EXAMINER'S COMMENT

A mature and interesting interpretation of the question. This top-grade response is very well focused and there is a sustained personal perspective throughout. Judicious use of quotations rounds off the answer. With the exception of the last sentence, expression is generally fluent and assured.

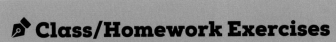 Class/Homework Exercises

1. Bishop often structures her poems like a mini-drama. Examine the poem 'The Fish' and comment on how a dramatic effect is achieved. Consider setting, characterisation, conflict, the interior debate, tension building to climax and resolution. Refer closely to the text of the poem in your response.

2. 'Elizabeth Bishop has commented that she simply tried "to see things afresh" in her poetry.' To what extent is this true of her poem 'The Fish'? Support your answer with reference to the text.

⊙ Points to Consider

- **Themes include endurance and the relationship between nature and human nature.**

- **Observational details, vibrant language, personification, striking comparisons.**

- **Engaging first-person narrative voice.**

- **Varying tones – joyful, admiring, celebratory.**

- **Memorable sound effects – assonance, alliteration, sibilance, repetition.**

- **Dramatic development that ends in a moment of insight.**

2

The Bight

Title: refers to a wide bay or inlet.

On my birthday

At low tide like this how sheer the water is.
White, crumbling ribs of marl protrude and glare
and the boats are dry, the pilings dry as matches.
Absorbing, rather than being absorbed,
the water in the bight doesn't wet anything,   5
the color of the gas flame turned as low as possible.
One can smell it turning to gas; if one were Baudelaire
one could probably hear it turning to marimba music.
The little ocher dredge at work off the end of the dock
already plays the dry perfectly off-beat claves.   10
The birds are outsize. Pelicans crash
into this peculiar gas unnecessarily hard,
it seems to me, like pickaxes,
rarely coming up with anything to show for it,
and going off with humorous elbowings.   15
Black-and-white man-of-war birds soar
on impalpable drafts
and open their tails like scissors on the curves
or tense them like wishbones, till they tremble.
The frowsy sponge boats keep coming in   20
with the obliging air of retrievers,
bristling with jackstraw gaffs and hooks
and decorated with bobbles of sponges.
There is a fence of chicken wire along the dock
where, glinting like little plowshares,   25
the blue-gray shark tails are hung up to dry
for the Chinese-restaurant trade.
Some of the little white boats are still piled up
against each other, or lie on their sides, stove in,
and not yet salvaged, if they ever will be, from the last bad storm, 30
like torn-open, unanswered letters.
The bight is littered with old correspondences.
Click. Click. Goes the dredge,
and brings up a dripping jawful of marl.
All the untidy activity continues,   35
awful but cheerful.

marl: rich clay soil.

pilings: heavy beams supporting a jetty.

Baudelaire: Charles Baudelaire (1821–67), French symbolist poet.

marimba: wooden instrument similar to a xylophone, played by African and Central American jazz musicians.

ocher: ochre; orange-brown colour.

claves: clefs; musical keys.

impalpable drafts: slight air currents.

frowsy: shabby, foul-smelling.

retrievers: hunting dogs.

bristling: shining.

jackstraw gaffs: splinters used as hooks on fishing rods.

bobbles: trimmings.

plowshares: ploughing blades.

stove in: storm-damaged.

salvaged: repaired.

dredge: a machine for digging underwater.

'and the boats are dry'

 **Personal Response**

1. Using close reference to the text, describe the atmosphere in the first six lines of the poem.
2. Choose one simile that you think is particularly effective in the poem. Briefly explain your choice.
3. Although the poem is not directly personal, what does it suggest to you about Elizabeth Bishop herself? Refer to the text in your answer.

👁 Critical Literacy

'The Bight' showcases Elizabeth Bishop's aesthetic appreciation of the world around her. The setting for this poem is Garrison Bight in Florida. In describing the small, untidy harbour, Bishop displays a characteristically keen eye for observation and an expert use of metaphor. The subtitle, 'On my birthday', suggests a special occasion and, perhaps, a time for reflection and reappraisal of life.

The poem begins with an introduction to the bight at 'low tide' and gradually constructs a **vivid picture of an uninviting place**: 'White, crumbling ribs of

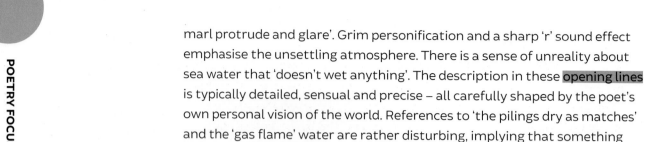

marl protrude and glare'. Grim personification and a sharp 'r' sound effect emphasise the unsettling atmosphere. There is a sense of unreality about sea water that 'doesn't wet anything'. The description in these opening lines is typically detailed, sensual and precise – all carefully shaped by the poet's own personal vision of the world. References to 'the pilings dry as matches' and the 'gas flame' water are rather disturbing, implying that something dangerous might be about to happen.

Bishop's mention of the French poet Charles Baudelaire (line 7) would suggest that she shares his belief in expressing human experience through objects and places around us. The poet imagines Baudelaire being able to 'hear' the water 'turning to marimba music'. She also finds an unexpected jazz rhythm ('perfectly off-beat claves') coming from the machine that is dredging 'off the end of the dock'. In lines 11–19, Bishop depicts the 'outsize' birds through a series of vigorous images. They seem awkward and out of place in this busy, built-up location. **Figurative language illustrates their mechanical movements**: pelicans 'crash' into the sea 'like pickaxes', while man-of-war birds 'open their tails like scissors'. An underlying sense of disquiet can be detected in the detailed observations of these 'tense' birds as they 'tremble' in flight.

The poet's portrayal of the bight is quite realistic: 'frowsy sponge boats keep coming in' to harbour. With wry humour, she acknowledges their unlikely beauty, 'bristling with jackstraw gaffs' and 'decorated with bobbles of sponges'. The cluttered dockside is a busy working environment where 'blue-gray shark tails are hung up to dry' (line 26). The 'little white boats' are a reminder of the local fishing community and its dependence on the sea. Bishop compares the small fishing boats to 'torn-open, unanswered letters'. The bight suddenly reminds her of a cluttered writing-desk – her own, presumably – 'littered with old correspondences'.

This metaphor is developed in lines 33–36. Bishop returns to sharp sounds: the 'Click. Click.' noise of the dredger (compared to an animal unearthing the wet clay) as it 'brings up a dripping jawful of marl'. The ending is highly symbolic of the poet's own impulse to dig deep into personal memories. Drawing a close comparison between her own life and the 'untidy activity' of the bight, she concludes that both are 'awful but cheerful'. **The matter-of-fact tone of these closing lines is derisive but good humoured**. It reflects her realistic approach to the highs and lows of human experience – and the thoughts that are likely to have crossed her mind as she celebrated yet another birthday.

✒ Writing About the Poem

'Closely observed description and vivid imagery are striking features of Elizabeth Bishop's poems.' Discuss this statement in relation to 'The Bight'. Refer to the poem in support of your views.

Sample Paragraph

I think 'The Bight' is a good example of how Elizabeth Bishop slowly builds up a picture of a fairly inhospitable place. At first, she describes the 'sheer' water and the 'crumbling ribs of marl', personifying the soil as an emaciated body. This vivid image suggests that the bay is bleak and unattractive. We get a sense of the sounds she hears – the 'dredge at work' pounding away in the background. Bishop uses dramatic imagery to bring the birds to life – particularly the vicious man-of-war birds whose tails are 'like scissors' and 'tense' as wishbones. We also see the poet's eye for detail in her description of the damaged fishing boats on the shore 'like torn-open, unanswered letters'. Bishop uses colour imagery very effectively – 'blue-gray shark tails' are hanging out to dry for the local restaurant. Her descriptions appeal to other senses, particularly sound. The poem ends with the rasping sound of the dredger – 'Click. Click.' digging up 'a dripping jawful of marl'. This remarkable image suggests how the bight keeps bringing back memories to the poet, both pleasant and unpleasant. It is an impressive way of rounding off the poem, as she associates the untidy harbour with her own life – 'awful but cheerful'.

EXAMINER'S COMMENT

A very well-focused, high-grade response, making excellent use of numerous accurate quotations. The various elements of the question are addressed and there is evidence of good personal engagement with the text. Expression throughout is also fluent and controlled.

✒ Class/Homework Exercises

1. 'Elizabeth Bishop's poetry is both sensuous and reflective.' To what extent is this true of 'The Bight'? Support the points you make with suitable reference to the text of the poem.
2. 'In many of her poems, Elizabeth Bishop begins with vivid visual and aural details which lead to moments of intense understanding.' Discuss this statement with reference to 'The Bight'.

⊙ Points to Consider

- **Descriptive details give a clear picture of the littered bay at low tide.**
- **Enduring personal upheavals and disappointments are central themes.**
- **Bishop relates to the untidy location as she reappraises her own disorderly life.**
- **Striking metaphorical language, memorable patterns of unusual imagery.**
- **Contrasting tones – pessimistic, reflective, insightful, upbeat.**

3

At the Fishhouses

Although it is a cold evening,
down by one of the fishhouses
an old man sits netting,
his net, in the gloaming almost invisible,
a dark purple-brown,   5
and his shuttle worn and polished.
The air smells so strong of codfish
it makes one's nose run and one's eyes water.
The five fishhouses have steeply peaked roofs
and narrow, cleated gangplanks slant up   10
to storerooms in the gables
for the wheelbarrows to be pushed up and down on.
All is silver: the heavy surface of the sea,
swelling slowly as if considering spilling over,
is opaque, but the silver of the benches,   15
the lobster pots, and masts, scattered
among the wild jagged rocks,
is of an apparent translucence
like the small old buildings with an emerald moss
growing on their shoreward walls.   20
The big fish tubs are completely lined
with layers of beautiful herring scales
and the wheelbarrows are similarly plastered
with creamy iridescent coats of mail,
with small iridescent flies crawling on them.   25
Up on the little slope behind the houses,
set in the sparse bright sprinkle of grass,
is an ancient wooden capstan,
cracked, with two long bleached handles
and some melancholy stains, like dried blood,   30
where the ironwork has rusted.
The old man accepts a Lucky Strike.
He was a friend of my grandfather.
We talk of the decline in the population
and of codfish and herring   35
while he waits for a herring boat to come in.
There are sequins on his vest and on his thumb.
He has scraped the scales, the principal beauty,
from unnumbered fish with that black old knife,
the blade of which is almost worn away.   40

gloaming: twilight, evening.

shuttle: tool used for weaving and mending fishing nets.

cleated: wooden projections nailed to a ladder to prevent slipping.
gangplanks: removable ramps used for boarding or leaving boats.

opaque: murky, dark; difficult to see through.

translucence: semi-transparent, light shining partially through.

iridescent: glittering, changing colours.
coats of mail: armour made of metal rings.

capstan: round machine used for winding or hauling rope.

Lucky Strike: American cigarette.

sequins: small, shiny discs used for decorating clothes.

Down at the water's edge, at the place
where they haul up the boats, up the long ramp
descending into the water, thin silver
tree trunks are laid horizontally
across the gray stones, down and down   45
at intervals of four or five feet.

Cold dark deep and absolutely clear,
element bearable to no mortal,
to fish and seals . . . One seal particularly
I have seen here evening after evening.   50
He was curious about me. He was interested in music;
like me a believer in total immersion,
so I used to sing him Baptist hymns.
I also sang 'A Mighty Fortress Is Our God.'
He stood up in the water and regarded me   55
steadily, moving his head a little.
Then he would disappear, then suddenly emerge
almost in the same spot, with a sort of shrug
as if it were against his better judgment.
Cold dark deep and absolutely clear,   60
the clear gray icy water . . . Back, behind us,
the dignified tall firs begin.
Bluish, associating with their shadows,
a million Christmas trees stand
waiting for Christmas. The water seems suspended   65
above the rounded gray and blue-gray stones.
I have seen it over and over, the same sea, the same,
slightly, indifferently swinging above the stones,
icily free above the stones,
above the stones and then the world.   70
If you should dip your hand in,
your wrist would ache immediately,
your bones would begin to ache and your hand would burn
as if the water were a transmutation of fire
that feeds on stones and burns with a dark gray flame.   75
If you tasted it, it would first taste bitter,
then briny, then surely burn your tongue.
It is like what we imagine knowledge to be:
dark, salt, clear, moving, utterly free,
drawn from the cold hard mouth   80
of the world, derived from the rocky breasts
forever, flowing and drawn, and since
our knowledge is historical, flowing, and flown.

total immersion: completely covered in liquid; a form of baptism.

associating: linking.

transmutation: changing shape.

briny: very salty.

'in the gloaming'

👤 Personal Response

1. In your opinion, what is the role of the old fisherman in the poem? Is he a link with the past, a person in harmony with his environment or something else? Refer closely to the text in your response.

2. Bishop uses a chilling maternal image at the conclusion of the poem. What effect has this startling metaphor on the poem's tone? Support your discussion with clear references from the text.

3. Did you find 'At the Fishhouses' thought-provoking? What questions did the poem raise about the poet and her attitudes? Refer to the text in your answer.

👁 Critical Literacy

'At the Fishhouses' comes from Elizabeth Bishop's award-winning second collection, *A Cold Spring* (1965). What Bishop sees is never quite what the rest of us see. She challenges us to look again. She gives us poetry as 'normal as sight … as artificial as a glass eye'. An ordinary sight of an old fisherman 'in the gloaming' mending nets in Nova Scotia becomes a strange, exact hallucination examining the essence of knowledge. Bishop saw; now we see. She changes the view.

The poem's opening section (lines 1–40) gives us a **detailed, sensuous description** of a scene from Nova Scotia. Bishop has an unerring sense of place. The fishhouses are described so vividly that we can almost smell the fish ('it makes one's nose run and one's eyes water'), see the fish tubs ('completely lined/with layers of beautiful herring scales') and hear the sea ('swelling slowly as if considering spilling over'). The poet draws us right into the scene with microscopic detail, making us pore over the surface of 'benches', 'lobster pots' and 'masts'. We experience the 'apparent translucence' of the weathered, silvered wood, which matches the cold, opaque, silver sea. Musical language lends beauty to this timeless scene. The long 'o' sound in 'Although' (in the opening line) is echoed in 'cold', 'old' and 'gloaming'. All is harmonious. The colours of the fisherman's net, 'dark purple-brown', become 'almost invisible'. Nothing jars. The rhythmic work is conveyed in the pulsating phrase 'for the wheelbarrows to be pushed up and down on'. Physical effort is suggested by the assonance of 'u' and 'o'. In lines 23–25, the wheelbarrows are described in minute detail ('plastered/with creamy iridescent coats of mail'). The small, circular fish scales are like the metal rings on a medieval knight's coat of armour. Bishop moves in closer to show us similarly coloured little flies, also 'iridescent', moving on the scales.

The poet's eye focuses on 'the little slope behind the houses' and an 'ancient wooden capstan'. Here is a **forlorn reminder of the tough physical work** of the past. The discarded cylinder is 'cracked' and has 'melancholy stains, like dried blood'; the ironwork has also 'rusted'. In line 32, a human connection is made when the 'old man accepts a Lucky Strike' cigarette. The personal detail ('a friend of my grandfather') gives a surface intimacy to this chilling poem. But there are hidden depths. The man is described as having 'sequins on his vest and on his thumb'. This decorative detail is more usually associated with glamorous ball gowns than an old fisherman's jersey. Does the image of the man's black knife, 'almost worn away', suggest an ebbing life?

In the poem's short second section (lines 41–46), we are at the water's edge and the repetition of 'down' draws us nearer the element of water as we note the 'long ramp/descending'. **The movement seems symbolic of Bishop's own descent into her subconscious mind**. As before, the graceful fish scales have transformed the wooden ramp into 'thin silver/tree trunks'.

The third section (lines 47–83) **changes the view**. We are now not merely looking, but seeing. We are **entering the interior**. We journey with Bishop to examine an element that is 'bearable to no mortal', yet is home 'to fish and seals'. No human can survive in the icy waters of the North Atlantic Sea: 'Cold dark deep and absolutely clear'. Another figure, a seal, appears in this bleak, surreal sequence. In this compelling episode, seal and poet are linked by a shared belief in 'total immersion'. For the seal, this is into water. Is it some form of baptism for Bishop? The poet, however, finds no comfort in religion, despite singing hymns for the seal ('A Mighty Fortress Is Our God'). Religion, like the distant fir trees, is behind her, waiting to be cut down.

The sea now takes on a nightmarish aspect as Bishop describes it 'indifferently swinging above the stones' (line 68). It is becoming a sea of knowledge. The poet warns us against it, telling us that we will be hurt if we delve in: wrists 'would ache immediately' and hands 'would burn'. Just as in the Garden of Eden, knowledge came with a terrible price. Mother Nature is depicted with a 'cold hard mouth' and 'rocky breasts'. Here is no warm, comforting, maternal presence. Instead, Bishop's own dark life is suggested. These final lines – filled with harsh sea imagery – are insightful. Place has receded and insight is present. We, together with the poet, realise that knowledge is like water ('flowing'). It is also 'drawn', just like waves are moved by the power of the moon. As we recognise that the mysterious waves pass into the past, so we realise that knowledge is 'historical' and ends up 'flown'. **All are part of the flux of nature**. In the end, Bishop seems to accept that the vast ocean – like life itself – defies understanding.

Writing About the Poem

'Bishop gives us facts and minute details, sinking or sliding giddily off into the unknown.' Discuss this statement with reference to the poem 'At the Fishhouses'. Support your views with close reference to the text.

Sample Paragraph

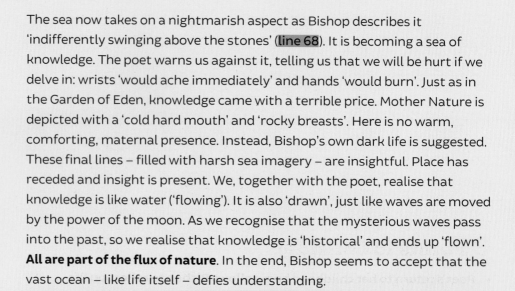

EXAMINER'S COMMENT

A precise discussion that deals directly with both aspects of the statement: 'facts and minute details' and 'sliding ... into the unknown'. Some good personal engagement and a clear understanding of the poem are evident in this top-grade response. There is also effective use of apt quotation.

I certainly agree that Elizabeth Bishop gives us 'facts and minute details'. The 'five fishhouses' are clearly described, with their 'steeply peaked roofs' and their walkways, 'narrow, cleated' to enable the wheelbarrows to move smoothly. The exchange between the poet and the old man ('a friend of my grandfather') is realistically shown, with even the brand of cigarette identified ('Lucky Strike'). We not only see the fish scales, 'coats of mail', but we also note the 'crawling' flies on the scale-splattered wheelbarrows. Then the poem turns from this scrutiny of the actual to an abstract meditation. Here, the poet is 'sliding giddily off into the unknown'. From observing the Atlantic Sea ('Cold dark deep and absolutely clear'), Bishop starts to explore the essence of knowledge – and even of life itself. Knowledge is not comfortable; the world is not a nice place, with its 'cold hard mouth'. Experience and knowledge come with an expensive price tag. The last two lines are dreamlike and surreal. I imagine a sea of knowledge that has been gained in the past ('historical'). This knowledge is always changing and 'flowing' as new discoveries are made.

✒ Class/Homework Exercises

1. How does Bishop's style contribute to the communication of her themes? Refer to two literary techniques used by the poet in 'At the Fishhouses' and comment on their effectiveness in each case. Refer closely to the text in your response.

2. 'Elizabeth Bishop is known for her skill at creating an authentic sense of place.' To what extent is this true of her poem 'At the Fishhouses'? Support your answer with reference to the text.

◉ Points to Consider

- Poet's return to her childhood home allows Bishop to reflect on life.

- Conversational language, descriptive details and sensuous imagery add authenticity.

- Assonant effects echo the deeply reflective mood.

- Alliterative and sibilant sounds evoke a realistic sense of the sea.

- Surreal, nightmarish view of nature.

- Visionary conclusion that the ocean – like life itself – is beyond understanding.

4

The Prodigal

Title: the biblical parable of the Prodigal Son is about a young man who wasted his inheritance on drunkenness and ended up working as a swineherd. The word 'prodigal' refers to a spendthrift or wastrel.

The brown enormous odor he lived by
was too close, with its breathing and thick hair,
for him to judge. The floor was rotten; the sty
was plastered halfway up with glass-smooth dung.
Light-lashed, self-righteous, above moving snouts, 5
the pigs' eyes followed him, a cheerful stare—
even to the sow that always ate her young—
till, sickening, he leaned to scratch her head.
But sometimes mornings after drinking bouts
(he hid the pints behind a two-by-four), 10
the sunrise glazed the barnyard mud with red;
the burning puddles seemed to reassure.
And then he thought he almost might endure
his exile yet another year or more.

But evenings the first star came to warn. 15
The farmer whom he worked for came at dark
to shut the cows and horses in the barn
beneath their overhanging clouds of hay,
with pitchforks, faint forked lightnings, catching light,
safe and companionable as in the Ark. 20
The pigs stuck out their little feet and snored.
The lantern—like the sun, going away—
laid on the mud a pacing aureole.
Carrying a bucket along a slimy board,
he felt the bats' uncertain staggering flight, 25
his shuddering insights, beyond his control,
touching him. But it took him a long time
finally to make his mind up to go home.

odor: odour, smell.

sty: pig-shed.

snouts: pigs' noses.

bouts: sessions.

companionable: comfortable.

the Ark: Noah's Ark. In the Bible story, Noah built a boat to save animals from a great flood.

aureole: circle of light.

'the pigs' eyes followed him'

👤 Personal Response

1. In your opinion, is Elizabeth Bishop sympathetic to the central character in this poem? Give reasons for your answer, using close reference to the text.
2. Choose two images that you found particularly memorable in the poem. Comment briefly on the effectiveness of each.
3. Write your personal response to the poem, referring to the text in your answer.

👁 Critical Literacy

In 'The Prodigal', published in 1951, Elizabeth Bishop returns to the well-known Bible parable of the Prodigal Son. She imagines the squalor and degradation this wayward youth endured when he was forced to live among the pigs he looked after. The poet herself had experienced depression and alcoholism in her own life and could identify with the poem's marginalised central figure. Bishop uses a double-sonnet form to trace the prodigal's struggle from wretchedness to eventual recovery.

The poem's opening lines present the repugnant living conditions of the exiled prodigal's everyday life: 'The brown enormous odor' engulfs him. The abhorrent stench and filth of the pig-sty is the only life he knows. Immersed in this animal-like state, he has lost all sense of judgement. Even the odour, 'with its breathing and thick hair', is beyond his notice. **Bishop's graphic imagery is typically precise**, describing the foul-smelling sty's shiny walls as 'plastered halfway up with glass-smooth dung'.

In lines 5–8, the 'Light-lashed' pigs are given human traits ('self-righteous', 'a cheerful stare'). The poet conveys a **disturbing sense of the young man's confused and drunken grasp on reality**. In his sub-human state, overwhelmed by nausea and isolation, he now seems almost at home among the pigs. Although he is 'sickening', he can still show odd gestures of affection towards them – 'even to the sow that always ate her young'.

Bishop delves deeper into the alcoholic's secretive world in lines 9–14. Ironically, the morning hangovers are not entirely without their compensations: 'burning puddles seemed to reassure'. Despite the ugliness and deprivation of his diminished existence, **he can occasionally recognise unexpected beauty in nature**, such as when 'the sunrise glazed the barnyard mud with red'. It is enough to give him hope: 'then he thought he almost might endure/his exile'. Emphatic broad vowel sounds add a further dimension of pathos to this line.

The poem's second section begins on a more startling note: 'But evenings the first star came to warn' (line 15). There is a suggestion that the **prodigal is finally confronting his personal demons**. For the first time, he seems to realise that he is out of place among the orderly routine of farm work that is going on around him. Unlike the sleeping animals ('safe and companionable as in the Ark'), the unfortunate young man is now intensely aware of his dismal alienation. He is poised on the brink of coming to his senses.

For the frustrated prodigal, a defining moment occurs when he finally disassociates himself from the snoring pigs. Yet ironically, it seems as though he almost envies their simple comfort and security 'beneath their overhanging clouds of hay'. Vivid images of routine farm life, such as 'The lantern – like the sun, going away' (line 22), take on a new symbolic significance for the unhappy exile. Is he finally considering the transience of life? Is there still a possibility of regaining his humanity? For an instant, **the young man seems to find a vague kind of hope** in the beautiful 'pacing aureole' of lamplight reflected on the mud.

A renewed vigour and purpose mark the poem's final lines. Bishop identifies exactly when the prodigal experiences 'shuddering insights'. This defining instant is symbolised by his acute awareness of 'the bats' uncertain staggering flight'. Taking his cue from nature, **he slowly accepts responsibility for his own destiny**: 'But it took him a long time/finally to make his mind up to go home'. This crucial decision to return from exile is a powerful illustration of human resilience. The poem's affirmative ending is emphasised by the importance placed on 'home' (the only unrhymed end word in the poem). Bishop's reworking of the well-known Biblical tale carries a universal message of hope, offering the prospect of recovery not just from alcoholism, but from any form of human debasement.

✒ Writing About the Poem

'Elizabeth Bishop's mood can vary greatly – from deep depression to quiet optimism.' Discuss this statement, with particular reference to 'The Prodigal'.

Sample Paragraph

Bishop's poem 'The Prodigal' is extremely grim. The early mood, describing the 'brown enormous odor' is clearly meant to capture the terrible living conditions of the young alcoholic son who had left his home, partied non-stop and fallen on hard times. The description of the outhouse is extremely repulsive. Bishop's tone is one of despair. The prodigal has fallen as low as any person, living among the pigs he looks after. The images are negative – 'rotten', 'sickening', 'barnyard mud'. The stench makes him queasy. But the mood changes when the alcoholic becomes more aware of himself and dares to hope that he will get it together and return to a decent life. Images of light and beauty suggest this – 'catching light', 'a pacing aureole'. The turning point is when the prodigal stumbles on 'shuddering insights' – which refers to his belief that he can regain his dignity and humanity if he really wants to. Although this is extremely difficult and 'took him a long time', he succeeds in the end. The last line emphasises his optimistic mood – as he decides to 'make his mind up to go home'.

✍ Class/Homework Exercises

1. 'Bishop's poetry often goes beyond description to reveal valuable insights about people's courage and resilience.' Discuss this statement with particular reference to 'The Prodigal'. Refer to the poem in your response.
2. 'While Elizabeth Bishop's poems can appear deceptively simple, they often contain underlying themes of universal significance.' Discuss this view with close reference to 'The Prodigal'.

⊙ Points to Consider

- **Themes include the alcoholic's alienation, human determination and resilience.**
- **Odd glimpses of beauty exist in the most unexpected of circumstances.**
- **Effective descriptive details, personification and startling metaphorical language.**
- **Vivid picture of the prodigal's unhappy life and living conditions.**
- **Striking images of light and darkness.**
- **Varying tones, contrasting moods – despair and hope.**

5 Questions of Travel

There are too many waterfalls here; the crowded streams
hurry too rapidly down to the sea,
and the pressure of so many clouds on the mountaintops
makes them spill over the sides in soft slow-motion,
turning to waterfalls under our very eyes.   5
—For if those streaks, those mile-long, shiny, tearstains,
aren't waterfalls yet,
in a quick age or so, as ages go here,
they probably will be.
But if the streams and clouds keep travelling, travelling,   10
the mountains look like the hulls of capsized ships,
slime-hung and barnacled.

Think of the long trip home.
Should we have stayed at home and thought of here?
Where should we be today?   15
Is it right to be watching strangers in a play
in this strangest of theatres?
What childishness is it that while there's a breath of life
in our bodies, we are determined to rush
to see the sun the other way around?   20
The tiniest green hummingbird in the world?
To stare at some inexplicable old stonework,
inexplicable and impenetrable,
at any view,
instantly seen and always, always delightful?   25
Oh, must we dream our dreams
and have them, too?
And have we room
for one more folded sunset, still quite warm?

But surely it would have been a pity   30
not to have seen the trees along this road,
really exaggerated in their beauty,
not to have seen them gesturing
like noble pantomimists, robed in pink.
—Not to have had to stop for gas and heard   35
the sad, two-noted, wooden tune

here: Brazil.

hulls: main sections of ships.

capsized: overturned in the water.

barnacled: covered with small shellfish.

the sun the other way around: the view of the sun in the southern hemisphere.

inexplicable: incomprehensible; mysterious.

pantomimists: people taking part in a pantomime, a slapstick comedy.

of disparate wooden clogs
carelessly clacking over
a grease-stained filling-station floor.
(In another country the clogs would all be tested.   40
Each pair there would have identical pitch.)
—A pity not to have heard
the other, less primitive music of the fat brown bird
who sings above the broken gasoline pump
in a bamboo church of Jesuit baroque: 45
three towers, five silver crosses.

—Yes, a pity not to have pondered,
blurr'dly and inconclusively,
on what connection can exist for centuries
between the crudest wooden footwear   50
and, careful and finicky,
the whittled fantasies of wooden cages.
—Never to have studied history in
the weak calligraphy of songbirds' cages.
—And never to have had to listen to rain   55
so much like politicians' speeches:
two hours of unrelenting oratory
and then a golden silence
in which the traveller takes a notebook, writes:

'Is it lack of imagination that makes us come   60
to imagined places, not just stay at home?
Or could Pascal have been not entirely right
about just sitting quietly in one's room?

Continent, city, country, society:
the choice is never wide and never free.   65
And here, or there ... No. Should we have stayed at home,
wherever that may be?'

disparate: *very different, separate.*

church of Jesuit baroque: *ornately decorated 17th-century churches, often found in Brazil.*

finicky: *excessively detailed, elaborate.*

whittled: *carved.*

fantasies: *amazing creations.*

calligraphy: *decorative handwriting (in this case, the swirling design of the carved birdcages).*

unrelenting: *never stopping, endless.*

Pascal: *Blaise Pascal, a 17th-century mathematician and philosopher who wrote that 'man's misfortunes spring from the single cause that he is unable to stay quietly in his room'.*

'the pressure of so many clouds on the mountaintops'

👤 Personal Response

1. From your reading of lines 1–12, describe Bishop's reaction to the landscape spread before her. How does she feel about this abundance of nature? Is she delighted, unhappy, awestruck? Support your response with quotation from the text.

2. Choose two examples of repetition in the poem. Briefly explain what each example contributes to Bishop's treatment of the poem's theme.

3. Would you consider the ending of the poem conclusive or inconclusive? How does Bishop really feel about travel? Refer closely to the text in your response.

👁 Critical Literacy

This is the title poem of Elizabeth Bishop's 1965 collection *Questions of Travel*. Bishop herself was a great traveller, aided by an inheritance from her father. In this poem, she questions the need for travel and the desire that people have to see the world for themselves. The poet provokes the reader by posing a series of questions about the ethics of travel. She places her original observations of Brazil before us and wonders whether it would be better if we simply imagined these places while sitting at home. Finally, she challenges us to consider where our 'home' is.

The poem's opening line is an **irritable complaint** about Brazil: 'There are too many waterfalls here'. In the first section (lines 1–12), Bishop observes the luxuriant, fertile landscape spread out before her. She finds fault with the 'crowded streams' that 'hurry too rapidly' and the 'pressure of so many clouds'. The richness of the misty equatorial landscape is caught in a series of soft sibilant 's' sounds ('spill', 'sides', 'soft slow-motion'). Clouds melt into the 'mile-long, shiny, tearstains'. Everything is on the move, changing position and shape. Both Bishop and the water are 'travelling, travelling'. **Repetition emphasises this restless movement**. The circular motion suggests that neither traveller nor clouds have any real purpose or direction. An original and striking image of a mountain range ('like the hulls of capsized ships') catches our attention. The vegetation is 'slime-hung'; the outcrops of rocks are like the crustaceans of shellfish ('barnacled'). As always, the poet's interest lies in the shape and texture of the words.

A more **reflective mood is found in the poem's second section (lines 13–29)**. Bishop presents readers with a **series of challenging questions** for consideration. In all, eight 'questions of travel' are posed. Should we remain 'at home' and imagine 'here'? Bishop is uneasy at the prying scrutiny of tourists 'watching strangers in a play'. She is aware that this is how people live; it is not a performance for public consumption. The emphasis here is on the 'childishness' of the tourists as they rush around, greedily consuming sights, viewing the sun from its other side in southern countries, such as

Brazil. But as far as Bishop is concerned, historic ruins and 'old stonework' do not speak to the visitor. The repetition of 'inexplicable' stresses the inaccessibility of foreign cultures. The bland, unknowing response of tourists is captured in the conversational phrase 'always delightful'. Their selfish desire for more and more experiences is vividly shown in the image of the traveller nonchalantly packing views, as if they were clothes or souvenirs being placed in a bag at the end of a trip: 'And have we room/for one more folded sunset, still quite warm?' Perhaps Bishop is asking whether any famous sight ever actually touched the traveller, or was it skimmed over in a frenzy to pack in as much as possible?

Justification for travel is the dominant theme of the third section (lines 30–59): 'But surely it would have been a pity/not to have seen'; '– A pity not to have heard'; 'a pity not to have pondered'; '– Never to have studied'; 'never to have had to listen'. The repetition of 'pity' beats out a tense rhythm as the poet seeks to condone travel. Bishop's well-known 'painterly eye' provides the evidence, as she presents a series of fresh, first-hand illustrations, e.g. the trees 'gesturing/like noble pantomimists, robed in pink'. The flowing movement of the trees, their flamboyant colour and their suggestion of Brazil's mime plays would be hard to imagine if not really experienced. The sound of this easy-going, carefree society is conveyed in the hard 'c' sound of 'carelessly clacking', which evokes the slovenly walk of local peasants. The Brazilian love of music is evident in 'clacking', a sound usually associated with the rhythmic castanets. The difference in cultures is wryly noted: 'In another country the clogs would all be tested./Each pair there would have identical pitch.' Elsewhere, all would be sanitised uniformity.

Are these the experiences the traveller would miss by not being in another country? The locals' casual attitude to functionality is shown in the contrasting images of the 'broken gasoline pump' and the intricate construction of a 'bamboo church' with 'three towers, five silver crosses'. **The spirit of the people soars in 'Jesuit baroque'.** A similar contrast is seen in wooden carving – the 'crudest wooden footwear' does not have the same importance for these free-spirited people as the 'careful and finicky … fantasies of wooden cages' (line 51). Another unstoppable force, that of equatorial rainstorms, is likened to the endless rant of a politician bellowing out his 'unrelenting oratory'. Could any of this be imagined from afar?

Lines 58–67 begin in 'golden silence', as Bishop attempts to clarify her own thinking on the value of travel. In the final lines, she **wonders if we travel because we lack the imagination to visualise these places**. However, in the previous section, the poet has graphically shown that nothing can surpass a person **actually hearing and seeing** a place and its people. A reference is made to the 17th-century philosopher Blaise Pascal, who preferred to remain at home. The poet feels that he was not 'entirely right' about this, and by sharing her whimsical images of Brazil with us, she has led us to agree with her. Another interesting question is posed: How free are we to go where we wish? Bishop states that the choices are 'never wide and never free'; there are always constraints on the traveller. But an emphatic 'No' tells us that this does not take away from the authenticity of the experience.

In the poem's concluding lines, Bishop returns to the question of whether or not people should stay at home. She then teases the reader with the follow-up, 'wherever that may be?' (line 67). This is a much deeper, philosophical reflection, which reverberates in our minds. **Home is a place of belonging**, from which travellers set out and to which they return. The visited countries are not secure bases; the tourist does not belong there, but is merely a visitor en route to somewhere else. In short, the traveller's role is one of an outsider – observing, but not participating. Bishop's own life experience is revealed here. Perhaps she travelled so extensively because she never felt truly at home in any single place.

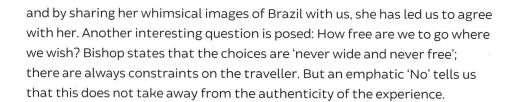

✒ Writing About the Poem

'Elizabeth Bishop's poems are not only delightful observations, but are also considered meditations on human issues.' Discuss this statement with reference to the poem 'Questions of Travel'. Support your views with close reference to the text.

Sample Paragraph

Elizabeth Bishop was a tireless traveller and in 'Questions of Travel', she presents the reader with evocative images from the misty equatorial landscape of Brazil, where clouds 'spill over the sides' of mountains 'in soft slow-motion'. The giant mountain ranges are imaginatively compared to upturned ships, and their vegetation likened to the 'slime-hung and barnacled' appearance of the bottoms of these ships. The sounds of the people intrude – disparate clogs 'carelessly clacking'. The harsh alliteration mimics the sound of wood hitting floor. No detail is too minute to escape her famous 'eye': 'the broken gasoline pump', 'the 'three towers' and 'five silver crosses' of the small bamboo church. These are Bishop's delightful observations. But the poet also addresses moral questions surrounding travel, particularly relevant in our times. What right have we to watch people's private lives, as if they were performing in public? Why are we rushing around, 'travelling, travelling'? Why do we not 'just stay at home'? These issues have a modern resonance, as we are aware nowadays of the effect of our carbon footprint on the environment. The poem concludes with a curious question on the meaning of 'home'. Bishop asks us to consider where it is ('home,/wherever that may be'). Suddenly an accepted certainty becomes as hard to define as the disintegrating clouds at the start of the poem.

✒ Class/Homework Exercises

1. Comment on the different tones in 'Questions of Travel'. Refer closely to the text in your response.
2. 'Elizabeth Bishop's poetry explores interesting aspects of home and belonging.' To what extent do you agree with this statement? Support your answer with suitable reference to 'Questions of Travel'.

⊙ Points to Consider

- The stunning Brazilian landscape prompts Bishop to reconsider the value of travel.

- Other themes include the natural world, home, and the creative imagination.

- Memorable onomatopoeic effects – assonance, alliteration, sibilance.

- Descriptive language, effective use of powerful metaphors and similes.

- Reflective, philosophical tone; inconclusive ending.

6

The Armadillo

Title: An armadillo is a nocturnal burrowing creature found mainly in South America. It rolls up into a ball to protect itself from danger.

For Robert Lowell

This is the time of year
when almost every night
the frail, illegal fire balloons appear.
Climbing the mountain height,

rising toward a saint   5
still honored in these parts,
the paper chambers flush and fill with light
that comes and goes, like hearts.

Once up against the sky it's hard
to tell them from the stars—   10
planets, that is—the tinted ones:
Venus going down, or Mars,

or the pale green one. With a wind,
they flare and falter, wobble and toss;
but if it's still they steer between   15
the kite sticks of the Southern Cross,

receding, dwindling, solemnly
and steadily forsaking us,
or, in the downdraft from a peak,
suddenly turning dangerous.   20

Last night another big one fell.
It splattered like an egg of fire
against the cliff behind the house.
The flame ran down. We saw the pair

of owls who nest there flying up   25
and up, their whirling black-and-white
stained bright pink underneath, until
they shrieked up out of sight.

Dedication: Elizabeth Bishop dedicated 'The Armadillo' to her friend and fellow poet, Robert Lowell.

time of year: St John's Day (24 June).

fire balloons: helium-filled balloons carrying colourful paper boxes.

a saint: St John.

these parts: Rio de Janeiro. Brazil.

chambers: hollow boxes.

tinted: shaded.

the pale green one: probably the planet Uranus.

kite sticks of the Southern Cross: cross-shaped constellation of stars.

The ancient owls' nest must have burned.
Hastily, all alone,   30
a glistening armadillo left the scene,
rose-flecked, head down, tail down,

and then a baby rabbit jumped out,
short-eared, to our surprise.
So soft! – a handful of intangible ash   35
with fixed, ignited eyes.

Too pretty, dreamlike mimicry!
O falling fire and piercing cry
and panic, and a weak mailed fist
clenched ignorant against the sky!   40

intangible: flimsy, insubstantial.

ignited: lit up.

mimicry: imitation.

weak mailed fist: the animal's bony armour (defenceless against fire).

'chambers flush and fill with light'

👤 Personal Response

1. Based on your reading of the first four stanzas, how does the poet present the fire balloons? Are they mysterious, beautiful, threatening? Refer to the text in your answer.
2. Comment on Bishop's use of interesting verbs in the poem.
3. In your view, is this an optimistic or pessimistic poem? Give reasons for your response.

👁 Critical Literacy

'The Armadillo' describes St John's Day (24 June) in Brazil, where Elizabeth Bishop lived for more than 15 years. On this annual feast day, local people would celebrate by lighting fire balloons and releasing them into the night sky. Although this custom was illegal – because of the fire hazard – it still occurred widely.

The opening lines introduce us to an exotic, night-time scene. The sense of drama and excitement is palpable as Bishop observes these 'illegal' balloons 'rising toward a saint'. They are also presented as fragile ('frail') but beautiful: 'the paper chambers flush and fill with light'. There is something magical and majestic about their ascent towards the heavens. **The language is simple and conversational**, reflecting the religious faith of the local people. Bishop compares the flickering light of the 'paper chambers' to 'hearts', perhaps suggesting the unpredictability of human feelings and even life itself.

Lines 9–20 associate the drifting balloons with distant planets, adding to their romantic air of mystery. The unsteady rhythm and alliterative description ('With a wind,/they flare and falter') suggest an irregular, buoyant movement. The poet is **increasingly intrigued by the fire balloons** as they 'wobble' out of sight. She notes that they sometimes 'steer between' the stars. Although she appears to be disappointed that the balloons are 'steadily forsaking us', she also worries about them 'suddenly turning dangerous' as a result of downdrafts buffeting and igniting them.

The tone changes dramatically in line 21, as Bishop recalls the destructive force of one exploding balloon that fell to earth near her house: 'It splattered like an egg of fire'. This characteristically stirring simile and the onomatopoeic verb highlight the sense of unexpected destruction. The shock is immediately felt by humans and animals alike. Terrified owls – desperate to escape the descending flames – 'shrieked up out of sight' (line 28). Contrasting **colour images emphasise the garish confusion**: the 'whirling black-and-white' bodies of the owls are 'stained bright pink underneath'.

The poet suddenly notices 'a glistening armadillo', isolated and alarmed. Determined to escape the fire, it scurries away: 'rose-flecked, head down, tail down' (line 32). Amid the chaos, a baby rabbit 'jumped out', its urgent movement reflecting the lethal atmosphere. Bishop expresses her intense shock at seeing its burnt ears: 'So soft! – a handful of intangible ash'. **This graphic metaphor emphasises the animal's weakness and suffering**. Its 'fixed, ignited eyes' reflect the fire falling from the sky.

Bishop's emotive voice emerges forcefully in the poem's closing lines. She rejects her earlier description of the elegant fire balloons as being 'Too pretty'. Having witnessed the horrifying reality of the tormented animals, she castigates all her earlier romantic notions about the colourful festivities. Such thoughts are suddenly seen as 'dreamlike mimicry'. **The final image of the trapped armadillo is highly dramatic**. Its 'piercing cry' is harrowing. Bishop imagines the terrified creature in human terms ('a weak mailed fist'). Although the armadillo's helpless body is 'clenched ignorant against the sky', it is unlikely that its coat of armour will save it from fire. The irony of this small creature's last futile act is pitiful. Despite its brave defiance, the armadillo is doomed.

Some critics have commented on the **symbolism** in the poem, seeing the victimised creatures as symbols for powerless and marginalised people everywhere. It has been said that the careless fire balloons signify warfare, mindless violence and ignorant destruction. Is Bishop indicating that people's fate is beyond their control? It has also been suggested that the fire balloons signify love ('that comes and goes, like hearts') or even the creative impulse itself – beautiful, elusive and sometimes tragic. As with all poems, readers must decide for themselves.

✒ Writing About the Poem

Describe the tone in 'The Armadillo'. Does it change during the course of the poem? Refer to the text in your answer.

Sample Paragraph

The opening of 'The Armadillo' is dramatic and filled with anticipation. Bishop sets the night-time scene during the noisy Brazilian festival to honour St John. 'This is the time of year' suggests a special occasion. The tone is celebratory as the local community release countless 'illegal fire balloons' which light up the skies. The poet seems in awe of the spectacle, watching the 'paper chambers flush and fill with light'. The tone changes slightly to sadness as she watches the colourful balloons

EXAMINER'S COMMENT

A focused top-grade response that traces the development of tone in the poem. There is a real sense of well-informed engagement with the text. Short, accurate quotations are used effectively to illustrate the different changes in tone. The expression is clear, varied and controlled throughout.

disappear, 'steadily forsaking us'. A more dramatic transformation occurs when the exploding balloons start 'turning dangerous'. Due to careless human activity, fire falls from the air, causing mayhem for the vulnerable animals below. Terrified owls 'shrieked', a young rabbit is burnt to 'intangible ash' and the armadillo is reduced to 'panic'. Bishop's personal voice is filled with anger as she rages against the 'falling fire'. The italics and exclamation marks in the final stanza highlight her frustrated tone as she identifies with the unfortunate armadillo whose 'weak mailed fist/ clenched ignorant against the sky' represents a useless gesture of resistance.

✎ Class/Homework Exercises

1. 'In reading the poetry of Elizabeth Bishop, readers can discover moments of quiet reflection and shocking truth.' Discuss this statement in relation to 'The Armadillo', supporting the points you make with reference to the poem.
2. 'In her poems, Elizabeth Bishop often connects the twin themes of cruelty and vulnerability.' Discuss this view with suitable reference to 'The Armadillo'.

⊙ Points to Consider

- **Both humans and animals are victims of man's thoughtless actions.**
- **Precise sense of place, detailed description of exotic atmospheres and experiences.**
- **Reflective tone reveals the poet's personal feelings and attitudes.**
- **Lack of judgemental comment allows us to find our own interpretation.**
- **Rich visual imagery, striking metaphors, onomatopoeia and end rhyme.**

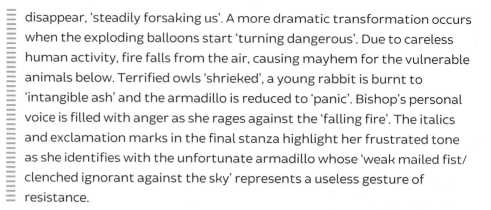

7 Sestina

ELIZABETH BISHOP

Title: a sestina is a traditional poetic form of six six-line stanzas followed by a final stanza of three lines. In Bishop's 'Sestina', the same six words recur at the ends of lines in each stanza: tears, child, almanac, stove, grandmother, house. The final three-line stanza contains all six words.

the Little Marvel Stove: a heater or cooker that burns wood or coal.

almanac: calendar giving important dates, information and predictions.

equinoctial: the time when day and night are of equal length (22 September, 20 March approximately).

September rain falls on the house.
In the failing light, the old grandmother
sits in the kitchen with the child
beside the Little Marvel Stove,
reading the jokes from the almanac,   5
laughing and talking to hide her tears.

She thinks that her equinoctial tears
and the rain that beats on the roof of the house
were both foretold by the almanac,
but only known to a grandmother.   10
The iron kettle sings on the stove.
She cuts some bread and says to the child,

It's time for tea now, but the child
is watching the teakettle's small hard tears
dance like mad on the hot black stove,   15
the way the rain must dance on the house.
Tidying up, the old grandmother
hangs up the clever almanac

on its string. Birdlike, the almanac
hovers half open above the child,   20
hovers above the old grandmother
and her teacup full of dark brown tears.
She shivers and says she thinks the house
feels chilly, and puts more wood in the stove.

It was to be, says the Marvel Stove.   25
I know what I know, says the almanac.
With crayons the child draws a rigid house
and a winding pathway. Then the child
puts in a man with buttons like tears
and shows it proudly to the grandmother.   30

But secretly, while the grandmother
busies herself about the stove,
the little moons fall down like tears
from between the pages of the almanac
into the flower bed the child   35
has carefully placed in the front of the house.

Time to plant tears, says the almanac.
The grandmother sings to the marvellous stove
and the child draws another inscrutable house.

inscrutable: secret;
impossible to understand or
interpret.

'the child draws a rigid house'

👤 Personal Response

1. Describe the atmosphere in the house. Is it happy, unhappy, relaxed, secretive? Support your response with quotation from the text.
2. Choose one image that you find particularly interesting and effective in the poem. Briefly explain your choice.
3. Write your personal response to the poem, supporting your views with reference to the text.

👁 Critical Literacy

'Sestina' was written between 1960 and 1965. For Elizabeth Bishop, the creative act of writing brought shape and order to experience. This poem is autobiographical, as it tells of a home without a mother or father. It is one of Bishop's first poems about her childhood and she was in her fifties, living in Brazil, when she wrote it. The complicated, restrictive structure of the poem can be seen as the poet's attempt to put order on her early childhood trauma.

The poem's opening stanza paints a domestic scene, which at first seems cosy and secure. The child and her grandmother sit in the evening light beside a stove. They are reading 'jokes from the almanac' and 'laughing and talking'. However, on closer observation, sadness is layered onto the scene with certain details: 'September rain', 'failing light' and the old grandmother hiding 'her tears'. Bishop adopts the point of view of adult reminiscence. She recollects; she is an observer of her own childhood and the poem's **tone is disturbing and challenging**. We are introduced to someone who is concealing deeply rooted feelings of sorrow. The six end-words echo alarmingly throughout the poem. This is a house full of tears with a grandmother and child together, alone.

In stanza two the grandmother believes that her autumn tears and the rain were 'foretold by the almanac'. There is a sense of inevitability and tired resignation in the opening lines. But normality enters: 'The iron kettle sings on the stove'. Homely domesticity is seen when the grandmother cuts some bread and says to the child: 'It's time for tea now'. **Bishop suddenly switches from being an observer to being an interpreter**, as she lets the reader see the workings of the child's mind in the third stanza: 'but the child/is watching the teakettle's small hard tears'. The child interprets sorrow everywhere; even droplets of steam from a kettle are transformed into the unwept tears of the grandmother. The phrase 'dance like mad' strikes a poignant note as we remember that Bishop's own mother was committed to a psychiatric hospital when Bishop was just five years old; they never met again. A cartoon-like image of the almanac ends this stanza. We view it through the child's eyes, as 'the clever almanac'.

Stanza four focuses closely on the almanac. It is a **sinister presence**, personified as a bird of ill-omen: 'Birdlike' it hovers, suspended 'half open'. This mood of misgiving is heightened when we are told that the grandmother's cup is not full of tea, but of 'dark brown tears'. However, normality asserts itself again – the grandmother 'shivers' and puts wood on the fire.

Stanza five opens with the eerie personification of the Marvel Stove and the almanac. A **sense of inevitability** ('It was to be') and hidden secrets ('I know what I know') is absorbed by the child. Just as the older Bishop puts order on her traumatic childhood experiences by arranging them into the tightly knit form of the sestina, the child in the poem attempts to order her experiences by drawing houses. But the house is tense, 'rigid', inflexible. The unhappy history of this childhood cannot be changed; the situation was as it was. This house can only be reached by a 'winding pathway'. Does this echo Bishop's later travels, as she searches for home? The sadness of Bishop's situation focuses on the drawing now, as the child sketches a man with 'buttons like tears'.

In stanza six, the tears continue to fall, now 'into the flower bed' in the child's drawing. **Fantasy and reality are mixed** in the innocent perception of the child, who feels but does not understand. The final three lines contain all six key words as the almanac instructs that it is 'Time to plant tears'. Is the time for regret over? Is the child planting tears that will be wept in the future? Should the grandmother and child be shedding tears now? The 'child draws another inscrutable house'. The secrecy continues. Nothing is as it seems. The future looks chilling.

✒ Writing About the Poem

Elizabeth Bishop's poetry is an emotional journey. To what extent do you agree with this? Support your views with close reference to 'Sestina'.

Sample Paragraph

I agree that the reader goes on an emotional journey in the poem 'Sestina' as Bishop struggles to come to terms with her traumatic childhood. Our hearts go out to the motherless and fatherless little girl, caught in an almost nightmare scenario, as the almanac hangs 'Birdlike' above her. The child senses, but does not comprehend the awful tragedy in the house. Bishop allows us to see the workings of the little mind as the child blends reality and fantasy, as stoves and books talk. Everything seems to know except the child. The chaotic experiences of Bishop's childhood are strictly contained in the formal structure of the sestina, with six stanzas, each of six lines ending with the same six end-words: house, grandmother, child, stove, almanac and tears. This mirrors the 'rigid' house of the little girl's drawings. Both the older and the younger Bishop are trying desperately to put order on this overwhelming situation. The reader experiences the poignancy through the details of the 'failing light', 'the rain that beats on the roof of the house' and the teacup 'full of dark brown tears'. Finally, the reader, like Bishop, is not left comforted, but is faced with one last mystery as yet another 'inscrutable' house is drawn.

EXAMINER'S COMMENT

A top-grade, insightful answer focusing on the emotional journey undertaken by both the poet and reader. There is a clear sense of engagement with the poem. Quotations are used effectively throughout.

✎ Class/Homework Exercises

1. Some critics have said that 'Sestina' is a sentimental poem. Do you agree with this? Support your views with close reference to the poem.
2. 'Elizabeth Bishop's most compelling poems often address painful memories of the poet's childhood.' To what extent is this true of her poem 'Sestina'? Support your answer with reference to the text.

⊙ Points to Consider

- **Adult poet reflects on troubled childhood and the desire for security of home.**
- **Disturbing sinister tone, sense of inevitability.**
- **Ominous personification and surreal imagery blur reality.**
- **Tear imagery patterns emphasise sorrow-filled scene.**
- **Strict form of sestina contains and controls overflowing emotions.**
- **Vivid imagery, powerful metaphorical language.**

8 First Death in Nova Scotia

In the cold, cold parlor
my mother laid out Arthur
beneath the chromographs:
Edward, Prince of Wales,
with Princess Alexandra,   5
and King George with Queen Mary.
Below them on the table
stood a stuffed loon
shot and stuffed by Uncle
Arthur, Arthur's father.   10

Since Uncle Arthur fired
a bullet into him,
he hadn't said a word.
He kept his own counsel
on his white, frozen lake,   15
the marble-topped table.
His breast was deep and white,
cold and caressable;
his eyes were red glass,
much to be desired.   20

'Come,' said my mother,
'Come and say good-bye
to your little cousin Arthur.'
I was lifted up and given
one lily of the valley   25
to put in Arthur's hand.
Arthur's coffin was
a little frosted cake,
and the red-eyed loon eyed it
from his white, frozen lake.   30

Arthur was very small.
He was all white, like a doll
that hadn't been painted yet.
Jack Frost had started to paint him
the way he always painted   35

parlor: room set aside for entertaining guests.

chromographs: coloured copies of pictures.
Edward: British Royal (1841–1910).
Alexandra: Edward's wife.

King George: King George V (1865–1936).
Queen Mary: wife of King George V (1867–1953).
loon: great crested grebe, an aquatic diving bird.

counsel: opinion.

frosted: iced.

the Maple Leaf (Forever).
He had just begun on his hair,
a few red strokes, and then
Jack Frost had dropped the brush
and left him white, forever.   40

The gracious royal couples
were warm in red and ermine;
their feet were well wrapped up
in the ladies' ermine trains.
They invited Arthur to be   45
the smallest page at court.
But how could Arthur go,
clutching his tiny lily,
with his eyes shut up so tight
and the roads deep in snow?   50

the Maple Leaf: Canadian national emblem.

ermine: white fur.

page: boy attendant.

'the roads deep in snow'

👤 Personal Response

1. With reference to lines 1–20 of the poem, describe the mood and atmosphere in the 'parlor'.
2. The poet uses several comparisons in this poem. Select one that you found particularly interesting and comment on its effectiveness.
3. Write your personal response to this poem, referring to the text in your answer.

👁 Critical Literacy

'First Death in Nova Scotia' was published when Elizabeth Bishop was in her early fifties. Written entirely in the past tense, it is an extraordinarily vivid memory of a disturbing experience. In the poem, Bishop's young narrator recounts the circumstances of an even younger cousin's death.

From the outset, we visualise Cousin Arthur's wake through a child's eyes. Characteristically, Bishop sets the scene in stanza one using **carefully chosen** descriptive details. It is winter in Nova Scotia. The dead child has been laid out in a 'cold, cold parlor'. Above the coffin are old photographs of two deceased royal couples. Fragmented memories of unfamiliar objects add to the dreamlike atmosphere. A stuffed loon sits on the marble-topped table. The young girl is suddenly confronted with strange signs of life and death. In her confusion, she takes refuge in the unfamiliar objects she sees around her.

The dead boy and the 'dead' room soon become real for the reader, as does the dilemma faced by the **living child, who seems increasingly unsettled**. Stanza two focuses on the young narrator's fixation with the stuffed bird. By thinking hard about the death of this 'cold and caressable' loon, she is trying to find a possible explanation for death. She is fascinated by the loon – perhaps an escape mechanism from the unfamiliar atmosphere in the parlour. In any case, the bird – with its spellbinding 'red glass' eyes – might be less threatening than the dead body in the casket. Suddenly, somewhere in the child's imagination, Cousin Arthur and the personified bird become closely associated. Both share an impenetrably cold stillness, suggested by the 'marble-topped table', which is compared to a 'white, frozen lake'.

In stanza three the child's mother lifts her up to the coffin so that she can place a lily of the valley in the dead boy's hand. Her mother's insistent invitation ('Come and say good-bye') is chillingly remote. We sense the young girl's vulnerability ('I was lifted up') as she is forced to place the flower in Arthur's hand. In a poignantly childlike image, she compares her cousin's white coffin to 'a little frosted cake'. **The mood turns progressively surreal** when the apprehensive narrator imagines the stuffed bird as a predator ('the red-eyed loon eyed it'). As always, Bishop's imagery is direct, brisk and to the point.

Bishop continues to explore childhood innocence in stanza four. Using the simplest of language, the child narrator describes her dead cousin: 'He was all white, like a doll'. In a renewed burst of imagination, she creates her own 'story' to explain what has happened to Arthur. His death must be caused by the winter frost that 'paints' the autumn leaves, including the familiar maple leaf. This thought immediately brings to mind the Canadian song 'The Maple Leaf (Forever)'. To the child, it seems that Jack Frost started to paint Arthur, but 'dropped the brush/and left him white, forever'. This creative **stream of consciousness highlights the child's efforts to make sense of death's mysterious reality**.

The imagery of childhood fairytales continues in stanza five when the narrator pictures Arthur in the company of the royal families whose pictures hang on the parlour walls. He is now 'the smallest page at court'. For the first time, the cold has disappeared and the royals are 'warm in red and ermine'. This fantasy, however, is short-lived. Still shaken by the strangeness of the occasion, the young narrator questions how this could have happened – especially as Arthur could not travel anywhere 'with his eyes shut up so tight/and the roads deep in snow'. The poem's final, tender image reflects both the child's naivety and a genuine concern for her cousin. Ironically, all around are symbols of immortality – the heavenly royal images of Arthur's entrance into a new, more glorious life. But the narrator's **enduring uncertainty remains central to the poem**.

✒ Writing About the Poem

'The unknowable nature of life and death is a central concern of Elizabeth Bishop's poetry.' Discuss this statement with reference to 'First Death in Nova Scotia'. Support the points you make by referring to the poem.

Sample Paragraph

EXAMINER'S COMMENT

A focused and sustained answer, showing good engagement with the text. Starting with a succinct overview, the paragraph traces the progress of thought through the poem, using apt and accurate quotations effectively. Clear expression and a convincing personal approach also contribute to this top-grade response.

In several poems I have studied, it's clear that Elizabeth Bishop addresses life's mysteries. Sometimes she does this through the eyes of a child, as in 'First Death in Nova Scotia'. The poem describes her first experience of a death and how she struggled to understand it. It is an elegy for her young cousin, Arthur, and Bishop's memories of his funeral are extraordinarily clear. Everything about it confuses her. The formal, domestic setting is uninviting – a 'cold, cold parlor' has strange chromographs of the British Royal Family on the walls and a stuffed loon bird on the marble table. As a young girl, Bishop recalls being forced to place a lily in her dead cousin's hand. These objects add to her insecurity. Nothing is explained to her and she escapes into her own imaginary world, comparing Arthur's casket to 'a little frosted cake'. In the last verse, she imagines her dead cousin in an afterlife – not in heaven, but in a magical royal castle, 'the smallest page at court'. However, the young Elizabeth is caught between make-believe and reason. Common sense tells her that Arthur, 'with his eyes shut up so tight', could not go out into 'roads deep in snow'. I thought Bishop really captured the uncertainty of a young child's mind in this poem. I also got the impression that she was making the point that life and death can never be fully understood, no matter what age a person is.

✒ Class/Homework Exercises

1. In your opinion, does 'First Death in Nova Scotia' present a realistic view of death? Support your argument with reference to the text of the poem.
2. 'Elizabeth Bishop often makes effective use of simple language and childlike images to convey disturbing childhood experiences.' Discuss this statement with close reference to 'First Death in Nova Scotia'.

⊙ Points to Consider

- Cousin Arthur's death and wake is seen from the point of view of a child.
- Elegy based on vivid memories expressed in simple language.
- Surreal imagery emphasises the deathly cold atmosphere.
- Fairytale element conveys child's attempt to understand the finality of death.
- Effective use of colour, assonance, repetition.

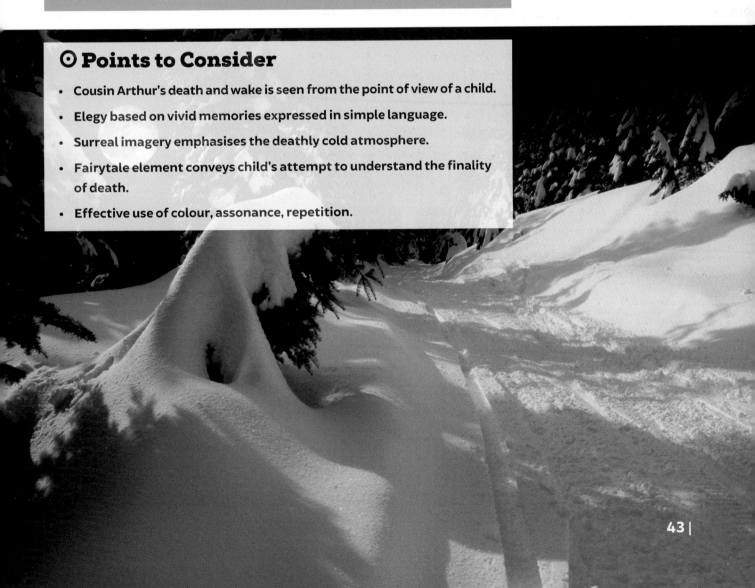

Filling Station

Oh, but it is dirty!
– this little filling station,
oil-soaked, oil-permeated
to a disturbing, over-all
black translucency.   5
Be careful with that match!

Father wears a dirty,
oil-soaked monkey suit
that cuts him under the arms,
and several quick and saucy   10
and greasy sons assist him
(it's a family filling station),
all quite thoroughly dirty.

Do they live in the station?
It has a cement porch   15
behind the pumps, and on it
a set of crushed and grease-
impregnated wickerwork;
on the wicker sofa
a dirty dog, quite comfy.   20

Some comic books provide
the only note of color –
of certain color. They lie
upon a big dim doily
draping a taboret   25
(part of the set), beside
a big hirsute begonia.

Why the extraneous plant?
Why the taboret?
Why, oh why, the doily?   30
(Embroidered in daisy stitch
with marguerites, I think,
and heavy with gray crochet.)

oil-permeated: soaked through with oil.

translucency: shine, glow.

monkey suit: dungarees; all-in-one working clothes.

saucy: cheeky, insolent.

impregnated: saturated.

doily: ornamental napkin.

taboret: drum-shaped low seat; a stool.

hirsute: hairy.

begonia: house plant with large multicoloured leaves.

extraneous: unnecessary, inappropriate.

daisy stitch: stitch pattern used in embroidery.

marguerites: daisies.

crochet: intricate knitting patterns.

Somebody embroidered the doily.
Somebody waters the plant,   35
or oils it, maybe. Somebody
arranges the rows of cans
so that they softly say:
ESSO–SO–SO–SO
to high-strung automobiles.   40
Somebody loves us all.

ESSO–SO–SO: Esso is a brand of oil; reference to the careful arrangement of oil cans.

👤 Personal Response

1. In your opinion, how does Bishop make the opening two stanzas of this poem dynamic and interesting? Comment on her use of punctuation, direct speech and compound words, which draw us into the world of the poem. Support your response with quotation from the text.

2. Trace the development of the poet's attitude to the filling station throughout the poem. Does it change from being critical and patronising to being more positive? Illustrate your answer with close reference to the text.

3. Comment on the effectiveness of Bishop's use of repetition in lines 34–41. Refer to the text in your response.

👁 Critical Literacy

Elizabeth Bishop was strongly influenced by a poetic movement called imagism, which was concerned with the accurate description of a particular thing. In this poem, she gives us an iconic description of a familiar American scene, the small-town gas station. Bishop found the new culture in 1960s California bewildering and it is noteworthy that the voice in this poem is that of an outsider trying to make sense of what is observed.

'it's a family filling station'

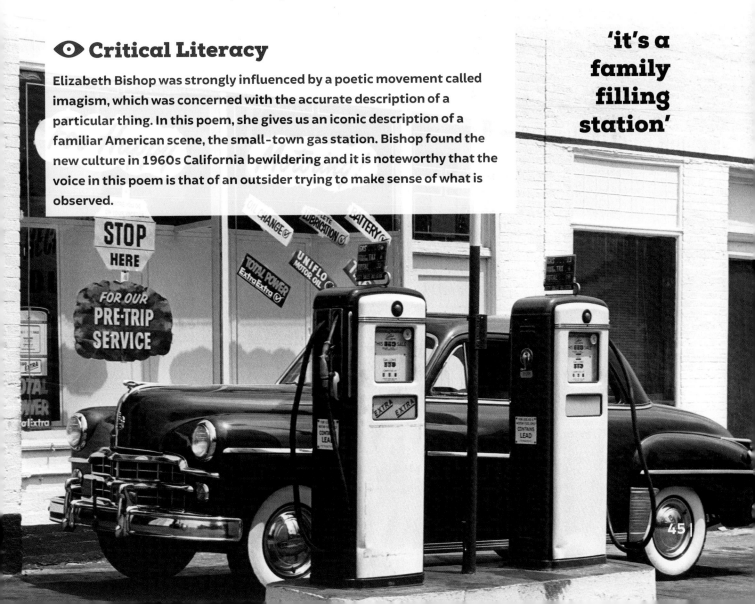

The prosaic title of the poem sets the mood for this commonplace scene. The poem opens with a **highly strung comment, disparaging the lack of hygiene** at the little station: 'Oh, but it is dirty!' The compound words ('oil-soaked', 'oil-permeated') suggest that everything is covered in a fine film of grease. This 'black translucency' has its own particular glow. Bishop's tense, dismissive tone creates a volatile, brittle atmosphere. Another voice interrupts her thoughts: 'Be careful with that match!' In a few lines, the poet has set the scene, established the mood and introduced her characters. She uses a series of intensely descriptive lines that gives the poem a cinematic quality as we observe the details, like close-ups on a big screen.

The busy little station is captured in the second stanza through the poet's critical observations as she watches the family go about their business. The father is wearing a 'dirty,/oil-soaked monkey suit' that is too small for him ('cuts him under the arms'). The sons are described using alliteration of the letter 's', which suggests their fluid movements as well as their oily appearance ('several quick and saucy/and greasy sons assist'). Like the poet, we also become fascinated by this unremarkable spot. Bishop's critical tone becomes more strident as she comments on the sons' insolence ('saucy') and their lack of hygiene ('all quite thoroughly dirty'). **We can hear the contempt in her voice**.

The third stanza questions, in a disbelieving tone, whether anyone could actually reside in such an awful place: 'Do they live in the station?' The poet's eye seems to pan around her surroundings **like a camera, picking up on small details** as she tries to piece the scene into some kind of order. She lingers on the porch and its set of 'crushed and grease-/impregnated wickerwork'. Her disdain is obvious to the reader. The dog is described as a 'dirty dog' – it is almost as if it, too, has been smeared in oil. The repetition of the 'd' sound emphasises the unkempt appearance of everything. Then, suddenly, the poem turns on the homely word 'comfy'. The poet is surprised to note that the dog is quite content here. We are reminded that because of the harrowing circumstances of her own childhood, Bishop never fully knew what home was; we are left wondering if she longed to be 'comfy' too.

In stanzas four and five, she begins to notice evidence of a woman's hand in this place, particularly 'a big dim doily' on the 'taboret'. She notes the colourful 'comic books' and her eye is caught by the incongruous sight of 'a big hirsute begonia'. Even the plant has masculine qualities, being big and hairy. Bishop is observing the extraordinary in the ordinary; **in the most unlikely places, there is beauty and love**. We understand her bemusement as she reflects, almost in exasperation: 'Why, oh why, the doily?' We, like the narrator, have to reassess our initial view of this cluttered gas station. On closer observation, there is care and attention to detail, including artistic embroidery. We are brought up close to examine this marvellous 'daisy stitch'. The critical, conversational tone of the poem clearly belongs to someone who is an observer, someone who does not belong. Is this the role Bishop was forced to adopt in her own life?

The poet's disturbed tone gives way in the final stanzas to one of comfort. The lines whisper softly with sibilant 's' sounds. 'Somebody' cares for things, arranging the cans in order 'so that they softly say: ESSO–SO–SO–SO'. Bishop commented that 'so–so–so' was a phrase used to calm highly strung horses. It is used here to calm herself, just as the oil in the cans is used to make the engines of 'high-strung automobiles' run smoothly. The tone relaxes and a touch of humour creeps in: she notes that 'Somebody waters the plant,/or oils it, maybe'. The use of repetition is also soothing as we, like Bishop, come to realise that there is 'Somebody' who cares. **The poem concludes on a quiet note of assurance that everybody gets love from somewhere: 'Somebody loves us all'**. This is a particularly poignant ending when we consider that Elizabeth Bishop's parents were both absent from her childhood.

✒ Writing About the Poem

'Elizabeth Bishop's poems are often described as deceptively casual.' Discuss this view of the poet's work, with particular reference to 'Filling Station'. Support your response with close reference to the text.

Sample Paragraph

'Filling Station' deals with a central concern of all human beings, the need to feel cared for, the need to belong. Bishop adopts a casual tone from the start, with its conversational opening: 'Oh, but it is dirty!' However, the phrases ('oil-soaked, oil-permeated') show a carefully crafted poem. The use of repetition of 'why' to suggest the puzzlement of the poet as she tries to make sense of this scene also convinces me that Bishop is a craftsperson. Similarly, the repetition of 'Somebody' leaves a sense of reassurance not only for the high-strung cars and their drivers, but also for us, as the poet states that 'Somebody loves us all'. The tone is that of a parent soothing a child who won't sleep. The word 'comfy' is also casual as, suddenly, the critical tone changes when the poet realises that the dog is content to be living there. I thought it was clever of the poet to use such a homely word as 'comfy' to totally change the mood of the poem. Finally, I think that Bishop shows her skill in the use of the sibilant 's'. Just as the oil stops the gears in a car from making noise, the carefully arranged oil cans in the filling station send their message of comfort: 'Somebody loves us all'.

EXAMINER'S COMMENT

This is a solid mid-grade answer, which competently addresses the question. There is some very good engagement with the poem and effective use is made of apt references. The expression is reasonably well-controlled, although slightly repetitive at times, leaving this short of being a high-grade standard.

✎ Class/Homework Exercises

1. 'A sense of homelessness pervades Bishop's poetry'. Comment on this statement, referring to both the content and stylistic techniques used in 'Filling Station'. Support your discussion with reference to the poem.

2. 'Elizabeth Bishop succeeds in conveying her themes through effective use of striking visual imagery and powerful aural effects.' Discuss this view with reference to 'Filling Station'.

⊙ Points to Consider

- Bishop attempts to comprehend the significance of a run-down filling station.

- Vivid picture of homely petrol station through closely observed visual detail.

- Cinematic techniques, conversational and colloquial language, flashes of humour.

- Contemptuous tone gives way to a concluding note of reassurance.

- Realisation that love and beauty can be found anywhere.

10 In the Waiting Room

In Worcester, Massachusetts,
I went with Aunt Consuelo
to keep her dentist's appointment
and sat and waited for her
in the dentist's waiting room.   5
It was winter. It got dark
early. The waiting room
was full of grown-up people,
arctics and overcoats,
lamps and magazines.   10
My aunt was inside
what seemed like a long time
and while I waited I read
the *National Geographic*
(I could read) and carefully   15
studied the photographs:
the inside of a volcano,
black, and full of ashes;
then it was spilling over
in rivulets of fire.   20
Osa and Martin Johnson
dressed in riding breeches,
laced boots, and pith helmets.
A dead man slung on a pole
—'Long Pig,' the caption said.   25
Babies with pointed heads
wound round and round with string;
black, naked women with necks
wound round and round with wire
like the necks of light bulbs.   30
Their breasts were horrifying.
I read it right straight through.
I was too shy to stop.
And then I looked at the cover:
the yellow margins, the date.   35
Suddenly, from inside,
came an *oh!* of pain
—Aunt Consuelo's voice—
not very loud or long.
I wasn't at all surprised;   40

Worcester: much of the poet's childhood was spent here.

arctics: waterproof overshoes.

National Geographic: international geography magazine.

Osa and Martin Johnson: well-known American explorers.

pith helmets: sun helmets made from dried jungle plants.

'Long Pig': term used by Polynesian cannibals for human flesh.

even then I knew she was
a foolish, timid woman.
I might have been embarrassed,
but wasn't. What took *me*
completely by surprise   45
was that it was *me*:
my voice, in my mouth.
Without thinking at all
I was my foolish aunt,
I—we—were falling, falling,   50
our eyes glued to the cover
of the *National Geographic*,
February, 1918.

I said to myself: three days
and you'll be seven years old.   55
I was saying it to stop
the sensation of falling off
the round, turning world
into cold, blue-black space.
But I felt: you are an *I*,   60
you are an *Elizabeth*,
you are one of *them*.
Why should you be one, too?
I scarcely dared to look
to see what it was I was.   65
I gave a sidelong glance
—I couldn't look any higher—
at shadowy gray knees,
trousers and skirts and boots
and different pairs of hands   70
lying under the lamps.
I knew that nothing stranger
had ever happened, that nothing
stranger could ever happen.
Why should I be my aunt,   75
or me, or anyone?
What similarities—
boots, hands, the family voice
I felt in my throat, or even
the *National Geographic*   80
and those awful hanging breasts –
held us all together
or made us all just one?
How—I didn't know any
word for it—how 'unlikely' ...   85

Elizabeth: the poet is
addressing herself.

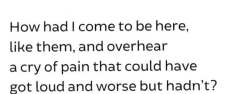

How had I come to be here,
like them, and overhear
a cry of pain that could have
got loud and worse but hadn't?

The waiting room was bright   90
and too hot. It was sliding
beneath a big black wave,
another, and another.

Then I was back in it.
The War was on. Outside,   95
in Worcester, Massachusetts,
were night and slush and cold,
and it was still the fifth
of February, 1918.

The War: World War I (1914-18).

'then it was spilling over'

👤 Personal Response

1. In your view, what image of women is presented in the poem? Support your answer with reference to the text.
2. Select two images that have a surreal or dreamlike impact in the poem. Comment on the effectiveness of each image.
3. Write your personal response to the poem, using textual reference.

◉ Critical Literacy

'In the Waiting Room' describes a defining coming-of-age experience for the poet when she was just six years old. While her aunt receives dental treatment, the child narrator browses through the pages of a *National Geographic* magazine and observes what is happening around her. In the powerful and provocative moments that follow, she begins to acknowledge her individual sense of being female.

The poem opens with a specific setting recalled in vivid detail by the child narrator. She flicks through a *National Geographic* magazine in the dentist's office while her aunt is in the patients' surgery. Familiar images of 'grown-up people,/arctics and overcoats' seem to convey a sense of wellbeing. It is the winter of 1918 in Worcester, Massachusetts. **The language is direct and uncomplicated, mirroring the candid observations of a young girl** as filtered through the adult poet's mature interpretation. Short sentences establish the fragmented flashback, allowing the reader to identify immediately with the narrative: 'It was winter. It got dark/early'. In addition to the unguarded tone, Bishop's short lines give the poem a visual simplicity, even though the first stanza is composed of 54 lines.

The mood changes from line 18 onwards, as the young girl studies the dramatic magazine photographs of an active volcano 'spilling over/in rivulets of fire'. For the first time, **she recognises the earth's destructive force**. In contrast to the earlier feeling of security in the waiting room, the atmosphere becomes uneasy. Disturbing pictures ('A dead man slung on a pole' and 'Babies with pointed heads') are as intriguing as they are shocking. The child is drawn further into an astonishingly exotic scene of cannibalism and violence. Graphic images of ornamental disfigurement seem horrifying: 'naked women with necks/wound round and round with wire'. The repetition of 'round and round' emphasises the young girl's spiralling descent into an enthralling world. Caught between fascination, repulsion and embarrassment ('too shy to stop'), she concentrates on the magazine's cover in an effort to regain control of her feelings.

The child is unexpectedly startled by a voice 'from inside' (line 36). At first, she presumes that the sound ('an *oh!* of pain') has been made by her aunt. But then something extraordinary happens and she realises that she has made the sound herself: 'it was *me*'. This sudden awareness that the cry has come from within herself prompts a **strange, visionary experience** in which she identifies closely with her 'foolish aunt'. The scene is dramatic and dreamlike: 'I – we – were falling, falling'.

In the surreal sequence that follows, the child focuses on her approaching birthday as she tries to resist the sensation of fainting: 'three days/and you'll be seven years old' (line 54). Ironically, it is at this crucial point (on the edge of 'cold, blue-black space') that she gains an astonishing insight into her own sense of self: 'you are an *Elizabeth,*/you are one of *them*'. The idea of sharing a common female identity with her aunt and the unfamiliar women in the magazine is overwhelming: 'nothing stranger/had ever happened' (line 72). It seems as though **all women have lost their individuality and have merged into a single female identity**. Although she attempts to stay calm, she is plagued by recurring questions and confusion: 'Why should I be my aunt,/or me, or anyone?' The young Elizabeth's awakening to adulthood is obviously painful. In attempting to come to terms with her destiny as both an individual and also as part of a unified female gender, she makes this hesitant statement: 'How – I didn't know any/word for it – how "unlikely" …'.

Before she can return to reality, the young girl must endure further discomfort. Her surroundings feel 'bright/and too hot' (line 90) and she imagines being submerged 'beneath a big black wave', a startling metaphor for helplessness and disorientation. In the final stanza, she regains her composure in the waiting room's apparent safety, where she lists the certainties of place and time. But there is a distinct sense of life's harshness: 'The War was on' and Massachusetts is encountering 'slush and cold' (line 97). Such **symbols are central to our understanding of this deeply personal poem**. Just as the image of the erupting volcano seemed to signify Bishop's development, the waiting room itself marks a transition point in her self-awareness.

✒ Writing About the Poem

'An unsettling sense of not being fully in control is a central theme in the poetry of Elizabeth Bishop.' To what extent is this true of 'In the Waiting Room'? Support your answer with reference to the text of the poem.

Sample Paragraph

The theme of growing up is central to 'In the Waiting Room'. It's unlike nostalgic poems. They often describe childhood in a sentimental way. The atmosphere is relaxed as the child passes time reading the magazine. However, the photographs of cannibals carrying a dead man ('Long Pig') are upsetting. Photographs of native women terrify the child as some wear wire necklaces. The poet compares them to 'light bulbs' – an image which frightens her. The outside world is so violent that she goes into a trance-like state. Her experience is more unsettled as she struggles to keep a grip on reality. Instead, she faints into 'cold, blue-black space'. However, what really unsettles her is the discovery that she herself is a young woman and she shares this with every other female. Her uneasy feelings are summed up when she describes being overcome by the heat, 'beneath a big black wave'. This leaves me feeling sympathy for this girl who is unsure about life and her future.

✒ Class/Homework Exercises

1. 'Bishop's reflective poems combine precise observation with striking imagery.' Discuss this view with reference to 'In the Waiting Room'.
2. 'In many of her poems, Elizabeth Bishop offers interesting insights into how children struggle to make sense of the adult world.' Discuss this statement with reference to 'In the Waiting Room'.

⊙ Points to Consider

- Themes include loss of innocence, coming-of-age experience, lack of belonging.
- Realisation of unique individuality and common female identity.
- Conversational language relays candid observations of young girl.
- Contrasting tones of alarm, dismay and disgust.
- Unnerving imagery used to explore comprehension of the wider world.
- Dreamlike atmosphere – surreal, nightmarish.

Sample Leaving Cert Questions on Bishop's Poetry

1. 'Bishop's reflective poetry is defined largely by tranquil observation, precise descriptive language and deep compassion.' Discuss this view, supporting your answer with reference to both the thematic concerns and poetic style in the poetry of Elizabeth Bishop on your course.

2. 'Bishop's powerful portrayal of the world of nature is conveyed through vibrant imagery and energetic expression.' To what extent do you agree or disagree with this view? Support your answer with reference to Bishop's subject matter and writing style in her prescribed poems.

3. From your study of the poetry of Elizabeth Bishop on your course, select the poems that, in your opinion, best show her effective use of specific places to communicate a sense of separation and loss. Justify your selection by showing how Bishop's effective use of specific places communicates a sense of separation and loss.

How do I organise my answer?

(Sample question 1)

'Bishop's reflective poetry is defined largely by tranquil observation, precise descriptive language and deep compassion.' Discuss this view, supporting your answer with reference to both the thematic concerns and poetic style of the poetry of Elizabeth Bishop on your course.

Sample Plan 1

Intro: (*Stance: agree with viewpoint in the question*) Bishop's poetry is distinguished by her position as the outsider. Poems thinly conceal her estrangement as orphan, woman and troubled adult. Recurring themes of identity, endurance and man's relationship with nature explored through detailed language and tones of care and concern.

Point 1: (*Endurance/epiphany – visual details*) 'The Fish' explores themes of endurance and hope through the precise description of a caught fish. Striking imagery conveys the unique wonder of the fish ('brown skin hung in strips', 'pink swim-bladder'). Details reveal the fish's astonishing beauty and tenacity; compels compassion from poet and reader.

Understanding the Prescribed Poetry Question

Marks are awarded using the PCLM Marking Scheme:
P = 15; C = 15; L = 15; M = 5
Total = 50

- **P** (Purpose = 15 marks) refers to the set question and is the launch pad for the answer. This involves engaging with all aspects of the question. Both theme and language must be addressed, although not necessarily equally.

- **C** (Coherence = 15 marks) refers to the organisation of the developed response and the use of accurate, relevant quotation. Paragraphing is essential.

- **L** (Language = 15 marks) refers to the student's skill in controlling language throughout the answer.

- **M** (Mechanics = 5 marks) refers to spelling and grammar.

- Although no specific number of poems is required, students usually discuss at least 3 or 4 in their written responses.

- Aim for at least 800 words, to be completed within 45–50 minutes.

NOTE

In keeping with the PCLM approach, the student has to take a stance – agreeing, disagreeing or partially agreeing – with the statement that:

- **Bishop's reflective observation** (childhood, loss of innocence, coming-of-age experiences, belonging/alienation, endurance, man's relationship with nature, etc.)

... is defined through:

- **precise descriptive language and deep compassion** (observational detail, startling personification, striking comparisons, surreal imagery, sound effects, sympathetic tones, etc.)

Point 2: (*Alienation – comparisons*) 'The Prodigal' captures squalor ('enormous odor'). Unexpected beauty in nature ('the sunrise glazed the barnyard mud'). Sense of empathy towards central character in this dehumanised setting ('comfortable as in the Ark').

Point 3: (*Childhood experience – striking imagery*) 'First Death in Nova Scotia' is a powerful observation of coming-of-age. Startling dreamlike imagery ('Arthur's coffin was a little frosted cake') and fairy-tale language suggest an understanding of child's terrifying experience ('Jack Frost had dropped the brush/and left him white, forever').

Point 4: (*Identity – surreal imagery*) 'In the Waiting Room' also uses bizarre imagery ('Babies with pointed heads') to show child's struggle with nature's destructive forces. Dramatic otherworldly sequence signals the end of childhood. Sensitive tone, realisation of common identity ('you are one of them').

Conclusion: Poems reveal hidden beauty found in ordinary places. Bishop succeeds in 'making the familiar strange' through her carefully crafted poetry and sympathetic point of view.

Sample Paragraph: Point 1

'The Fish' is a detailed description of a close encounter between man and nature. It is full of vivid imagery and figurative language. A first-person narrative enables Bishop to bring the reader with her, 'I looked', 'I stared'. Through her well-known painterly language, the poet conveys the patterns on the fish's skin, 'shapes like full-blown roses'. The sibilant sounds and compound word emphasise its lush markings. Tranquil observation shows a deeply felt regard for the battle-scarred creature, 'I admired his sullen face'. The fish's admirable endurance is detailed, 'five big hooks grown firmly in his mouth'. He has earned his 'medals'. Bishop's compassionate eye notes his 'aching jaw'. We share the poet's reflective moment of heightened awareness with the description of the universal symbol of hope, 'a rainbow'. The excitement is captured in short run-on lines. However, the rhyming couplet brings the poem to a harmonious conclusion – a respectful relationship between human beings and nature is expressed in the simple final line, 'And I let the fish go'.

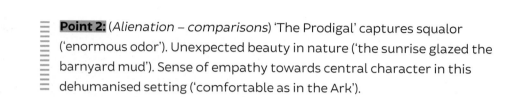

EXAMINER'S COMMENT

This well-written top-grade response carefully considers all the main aspects of the question. There is a clear sense of engagement with the poem, particularly in the succinct analysis of how Bishop's themes are communicated through stylistic features, such as the first-person narrative, vivid imagery and sound effects. Textual support is excellent throughout and the final point on the use of rhythm is impressive.

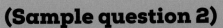

(Sample question 2)

'Bishop's powerful portrayal of the world of nature is conveyed through vibrant imagery and energetic expression.' To what extent do you agree or disagree with this view? Support your answer with reference to Bishop's subject matter and writing style in her prescribed poems.

NOTE

In keeping with the PCLM approach, the student has to take a stance by agreeing and/ or disagreeing that Bishop's poetry conveys:

– **a powerful portrayal of the world of nature** (relationship between nature and human nature, beauty, power, vulnerability of nature, etc.)

… conveyed through:

– **vibrant imagery and energetic expression** (vivid details, sensuous imagery, striking comparisons, strong verbs, energetic sound effects, dramatic encounters, engaging conversational language, evocative tones, etc.)

Sample Plan 2

Intro: (*Stance: partially agree with viewpoint in the question*) Bishop not only provides a powerful portrayal of nature, but also examines people and their circumstances through vigorous imagery and lively language.

Point 1: (*Nature – coastal scene at low tide*) 'The Bight' gives a vivid view of a compelling scene that stimulates Bishop's imagination. Vibrant details and rich metaphors describe the small coastal bay's dilapidated scenery ('crumbling ribs of marl', 'frowsy sponge boats').

Point 2: (*Human nature – child, grandmother*) 'Sestina' examines childhood trauma through ominous personification ('birdlike, the almanac/hovers') and surreal imagery ('a man with buttons like tears'). Poem's structure mirrors child's drawing of 'rigid' house, both trying to contain tremendous grief.

Point 3: (*Nature – Brazilian landscape*) 'Questions of Travel' is a painterly description of the luxuriant, equatorial landscape. Bishop wonders why people are so interested in foreign places. Effective use of emphatic verbs ('hurry', 'spill'), surreal simile of exotic trees ('gesturing/like noble pantomimists robed in pink').

Point 4: (*Nature – environment, animals*) 'The Armadillo' details tragic consequences for nature of man's unthinking actions. Oral and descriptive imagery reflect the poet's frustration and compassion ('piercing cry/and panic').

Conclusion: Bishop makes 'the familiar strange' in her portrayals of both people and nature through her 'forever flowing' precise imagery and powerful language use.

Sample Paragraph: Point 4

Bishop's dramatic portrayal of nature is vivid and precise. 'The Armadillo' highlights her ecological outlook, exploring the tragic consequences of man's thoughtless actions. The damaging effects of the 'fragile' fire balloons, lit as celebrations for a Brazilian festival, are shown through a powerful simile – one balloon 'splattered like an egg of fire'. The poem slows down to focus on the beauty of each animal. The rabbit is described in the sibilant phrase, 'so soft'. Individual animals' responses are carefully noted. The owls 'shrieked', the 'baby rabbit jumped out'. The poet is compelling readers to be aware of the unique beauty under threat. The rabbit has been 'ignited' into 'intangible ash', only its eyes remain, red and fixed. The horrific danger of the lanterns is depicted in the alliterative phrase, 'falling fire'. This results in the 'glistening' armadillo scurrying 'head down, tail down' to find safety. The concluding lines force us to see just how vulnerable nature is – its 'weak mailed fist' raised against the powerful forces of destruction.

EXAMINER'S COMMENT

Excellent response that focuses on all elements of the question. The 'powerful portrayal' aspect is effectively tackled ('dramatic', 'highlights', 'force us'). Informed and insightful views are presented in an argument seamlessly interwoven with textual support, employing critical terms with skill. Impressive expression throughout. Top-grade standard.

MARKING SCHEME GUIDELINES

Candidates are free to agree and/or disagree with the statement, but they should engage with how various stylistic features effectively communicate compelling insights into the harshness and cruelty of life. Reward responses that include clear analysis of both themes and language use (though not necessarily equally) in Bishop's poetry.

INDICATIVE MATERIAL

- **Bishop uses a range of stylistic features** (dramatic settings, precise detail, vivid contrasts, diverse poetic forms, powerful imagery, striking aural effects, evocative tones, energetic language, etc.)

... to confront:

- **uncertainties and harsh realities of life** (alienation, grief, death, violence, addiction, suffering, troubling rites of passage, thought-provoking moments of epiphany, etc.)

Leaving Cert Sample Essay

'Elizabeth Bishop uses a range of stylistic features to confront the uncertainties and harsh realities of life.' To what extent do you agree or disagree with this view? Support your answer with reference to the poetry of Bishop on your course.

Sample Essay

1. Elizabeth Bishop often brings order to the chaotic experiences of life. In 'The Prodigal', the issue of addiction is addressed through vivid imagery. Elsewhere, the poet uses her controlled writing skill using the sestina form in the poem of the same name to discuss loss. She examines the disturbing subject of death in 'First Death in Nova Scotia' through the perspective of a child. Bishop can be a sympathetic observer who quietly gets our attention while she confronts the uncertainties and challenges of life.

2. 'Filling Station' is a graphic description of a run-down garage in which loneliness and belonging are explored. A driver observes a greasy station, irritated by its 'oil-soaked, oil-permeated' atmosphere which she dismisses with a patronising comment, 'Oh, but it is dirty!' Sibilant sound effects portray the owner in his 'dirty oil-soaked monkey suit' accompanied by his 'several quick and saucy and greasy sons'. The lady's

contemptuous tone is very evident. But Bishop notices 'a dirty dog, quite comfy'. A moment of epiphany occurs. This is an environment of nurturing and belonging, 'Somebody waters the plant'. The driver has discovered that love and happiness exist even in the most run-down places.

3. In 'Sestina', the adult poet examines the searing loss of her painful childhood. A cosy, domestic scene, a grandmother making tea, her granddaughter drawing, is filled with surreal imagery. Not everything is as it seems. The almanac book, with its facts about the cycles of the moon, transforms into a kind of mystery movie – 'Birdlike, the almanac/ hovers half open above the child'. The buttons in the child's drawing become 'like tears' and the 'little moons that fall down like tears' into the flowerbed. Magic realism has steeped the scene with sadness. The young child is trying to create order with the 'carefully placed' flowerbed in her drawing. But the almanac suggests that life is hard, 'Time to plant tears'. The poem concludes with the child drawing 'another inscrutable house'. Life's uncertainties and harshness will not disappear.

4. The poet herself also attempts to control the painful memories of childhood herself by using the strict form of the sestina. The child's pencil drawing of an inflexible house mirrors this rigid poetic structure of six 6-line stanzas, all with the same end words, 'house', 'grandmother', 'child', 'stove', 'almanac' and 'tears'. Unlike 'Filling Station', this poem does not end on a reassuring note. Instead, it ends in a worried tone and points towards a troubling time ahead, 'Time to plant tears'. Bishop faces up to the confusion and harshness of real life.

5. 'First Death in Nova Scotia' also uses the perspective of a child, rather than that of an adult, to tackle loss and death. Childlike language, 'In the cold, cold parlor' is used to bring us inside the innocent mind. She regards her dead cousin Arthur's coffin as 'a little frosted cake' and Arthur as 'a doll that hadn't been painted yet'. The child's attempt to grasp the reality of death is portrayed through a vivid stream of consciousness, 'Jack Frost had dropped his brush and left him white, forever'. The child retreats into the comforting world of fairy tales, imagining her little cousin as 'the smallest page at court'. But the fantasy is disrupted by the final question. How could he go 'with his eyes shut up so tight and the roads deep in snow?' Bishop accepts the uncertainty of death, leaving the unanswered question. Is there a possibility of an afterlife or not?

6. The bleak topic of alcohol addiction is addressed in 'The Prodigal' through a retelling of the Biblical story. Detailed description sets the degrading farmyard scene where the unhappy youth is living with the pigs. Broad assonant sounds emphasise the horrific stench, 'The brown enormous odor he lived by/was too close'. His shame is evoked by the telling detail that 'he hid the pints behind the two-by-four'. However, the poet then changes the viewpoint. The alcoholic can still recognise a flash of beauty, 'sunrise glazed the barnyard mud with red'. He has not become completely dehumanised. There is a possibility of redemption from life with the pigs 'safe and companionable as in the Ark'. He is starting to realise, 'shuddering insights', that he can regain his humanity, but only 'if he wants to'. Redemption is possible, although it won't be easy, 'But it took him a long time/finally to make his mind up to go home'.

7. Bishop is a disruptive poet who succeeds in making the familiar strange. She uses a greasy filling station, a homely domestic scene, a family ritual and a squalid farmyard to confront bitter aspects of life. The meticulous attention to detail in her imagery, use of tone, poetic form and aural effects slowly alters our perception of reality so that we too can face the unpredictable and difficult realities of life.

(803 words)

EXAMINER'S COMMENT

A confident critical response to the question, showing good engagement with Bishop's poetry – both subject matter and style (especially sound effects, tone and imagery). Focused discussion supported by accurate quotation ranges widely over several key poems. A little more emphasis on how the poet 'confronts' harsh truths would have secured full marks. Overall, however, points are generally well-developed – despite some repetition in paragraph 4. Expression is clear and varied, adding to the essay's top-grade standard.

GRADE: H2
P = 14/15
C = 13/15
L = 14/15
M = 5/5
Total = 46/50

Revision Overview

'The Fish'
Nature is a central theme. After surviving previous struggles against adversity, the fish gains Bishop's respect.

'The Bight'
A beautifully conceived poem that reflects on the chaotic nature of everyday existence.

'At the Fishhouses'
Detailed observation of the relationship between people and nature leads to insight and a sense of belonging.

'The Prodigal'
Compelling presentation of the power of the human spirit to endure hardship and to retain hope.

'Questions of Travel'
Reflective poem raises issues about the meaning and necessity of travel – and the morality of tourism.

'The Armadillo'
Powerful depiction of man-made disasters and careless violence signified by the suffering of defenceless animals.

'Sestina'
Unsettling story of a grandmother and a child living with loss addresses poignant themes of grief and coming-of-age.

'First Death in Nova Scotia'
In this recollection of childhood and loss of innocence, Bishop transforms the child's uncertainty into a dynamic poetic vision.

'Filling Station'
Closely observed description of a small family filling station where the nurturing influence of women is evident.

'In the Waiting Room'
Recalls a dramatic scene that highlights the difficult transition from childhood to adulthood.

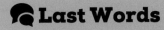 Last Words

'Bishop was spectacular at being unspectacular.'
Marianne Moore

'Bishop disliked the swagger and visibility of literary life.'
Eavan Boland

'The sun set in the sea ... and there was one of it and one of me.'
Elizabeth Bishop

 NATURE   TRAVEL/ JOURNEYS   IDENTITY   MEANING OF LIFE   CONFICT   SUFFERING   HISTORY/ MEMORY   DEATH   LOVE   BEAUTY

Emily Dickinson
1830–86

'Forever is composed of nows.'

Emily Dickinson was born on 10 December 1830 in Amherst, Massachusetts. Widely regarded as one of America's greatest poets, she is also known for her unusual life of self-imposed social seclusion. An enigmatic figure with a fondness for the macabre, she was a prolific letter-writer and private poet, though fewer than a dozen of her poems were published during her lifetime. It was only after her death in 1886 that her work was discovered. It is estimated that she wrote about 1,770 poems, many of which explored the nature of immortality and death, with an almost mantric quality at times. Ultimately, however, she is remembered for her distinctive style, which was unique for the era in which she wrote. Her poems contain short lines, typically lack titles and often ignore the rules of grammar, syntax and punctuation, yet she expressed far-reaching ideas within compact phrases. Amidst paradox and uncertainty, her poetry has an undeniable capacity to move and provoke.

Investigate Further

To find out more about Emily Dickinson, or to hear readings of her poems, you could do a search of some of the useful websites available such as YouTube, BBC Poetry, poetryfoundation.org and poetryarchive.org, or access additional material on this page of your eBook.

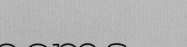

Prescribed Poems

○ 1 '"Hope" is the thing with feathers'
In this optimistic poem, Dickinson addresses the experience of hope and imagines it as having some of the characteristics of a small bird. **Page 64**

○ 2 'There's a certain Slant of light'
A particular beam of winter light puts the poet into a depressed mood in which she reflects on human mortality and our relationship with God. **Page 68**

○ 3 'I felt a Funeral, in my Brain' (OL)
Dickinson imagines the experience of death from the perspective of a person who is about to be buried. **Page 72**

○ 4 'A Bird came down the Walk'
The poet observes a bird and tries to establish contact with it, revealing both the beauty and danger of nature. **Page 76**

○ 5 'I heard a Fly buzz— when I died' (OL)
Another illustration of Dickinson's obsession with the transition of the soul from life into eternity. **Page 79**

○ 6 'The Soul has Bandaged moments'
This intricate poem explores the soul's changing moods, from terrified depression to delirious joy. **Page 82**

○ 7 'I could bring You Jewels— had I a mind to'
In this short love poem, Dickinson celebrates nature's simple delights and contrasts the beauty of an everyday flower with more exotic precious gifts. **Page 86**

○ 8 'A narrow Fellow in the Grass'
Using a male perspective, the poet details the fascination and terror experienced in confronting a snake. **Page 89**

○ 9 'I taste a liquor never brewed'
Dickinson uses an extended metaphor of intoxication in this exuberant celebration of nature in summer-time. **Page 92**

○ 10 'After great pain, a formal feeling comes'
A disturbing examination of the after-effects of suffering and anguish on the individual. **Page 96**

(OL) indicates poems that are also prescribed for the Ordinary Level course.

1

'Hope' is the thing with feathers

'Hope' is the thing with feathers—
That perches in the soul—
And sings the tune without the words—
And never stops—at all—

And sweetest—in the Gale—is heard—   5
And sore must be the storm—
That could abash the little Bird
That kept so many warm—

I've heard it in the chillest land—
And on the strangest Sea—   10
Yet, never, in Extremity,
It asked a crumb—of Me.

And sweetest—in the Gale—is heard: hope is most comforting in times of trouble.
abash: embarrass; defeat.

in Extremity: in terrible times.

'And sweetest—in the Gale—is heard—'

👤 Personal Response

1. What are the main characteristics of the bird admired by Dickinson?
2. Would you consider Dickinson to be an optimist or a pessimist? How does the poem contribute to your view?
3. In your view, what is the purpose of the poem – to instruct, to explain, to express a feeling? Support your response by reference to the text.

👁 Critical Literacy

Few of Emily Dickinson's poems were published during her lifetime and it was not until 1955, 69 years after her death, that an accurate edition of her poems was published, with the original punctuation and words. This didactic poem explores the abstraction: hope. It is one of her 'definition' poems, wherein she likens hope to a little bird, offering comfort to all.

The dictionary definition of hope is an expectation of something desired. The Bible refers to hope, saying, 'Hope deferred maketh the heart sick', while the poet Alexander Pope (1688–1744) declares that 'Hope springs eternal in the human breast'. In stanza one, Dickinson explores hope by using the **metaphor of a little bird** whose qualities are similar to those of hope: non-threatening, calm and powerful. Just like the bird, hope can rise above the earth with all its troubles and desperate times. Raised in the Puritan tradition, Dickinson, although rejecting formal religion, would have been aware of the religious symbolism of the dove and its connection with divine inspiration and the Spirit or Holy Ghost, as well as the reference to doves in the story of Noah's Ark and the Flood. Hope appears against all odds and 'perches in the soul'. But this hope is not easily defined, so she refers to it as 'the thing', an inanimate object.

This silent presence is able to **communicate** beyond reason and logic and far **beyond the limitations of language**: 'sings the tune without the words'. Hope's permanence is highlighted by the unusual use of dashes in the punctuation: 'never stops—at all—.' This effective use of punctuation suggests the ongoing process of hope.

Stanza two focuses on the tangible qualities of hope (sweetness and warmth) and shows the spiritual, emotional and psychological **comfort found in hope**. The 'Gale' could refer to the inner state of confusion felt in the agony of despair. The little bird that comforts and shelters its young offers protection to 'so many'. The vigour of the word 'abash' suggests the buffeting wind of the storm against which the little bird survives. The last two lines, which run on, convey the welcoming, protective circle of the little bird's wing.

A **personal experience of hope in times of anguish** ('I've heard') is referred to in stanza three. Extreme circumstances are deftly sketched in the phrases 'chillest land' and 'strangest Sea'. This reclusive poet, who spent most of her life indoors in her father's house, deftly catches an alien, foreign element. She then explains that hope is not demanding in bad times; it is generous, giving rather than taking: 'Yet, never, in Extremity,/It asked a crumb—of Me.' The central paradox of hope is expressed in the metaphor of the bird, delicate and fragile, yet strong and indomitable. The tiny bird is an effective image for the first stirring of hope in a time of despair. In the solemn ending, the poet gives hope the dignified celebration it deserves.

Dickinson is a unique and original talent. She used the metre of hymns. She also uses their form of the four-line verse. Yet this is not conventional poetry, due to Dickinson's use of the dash to slow the line and make the reader pause and consider. Ordinary words like 'at all' and 'is heard' assume a tremendous importance and their position is to be considered and savoured. **Her unusual punctuation has the same effect, as it highlights the dangers ('Gale', 'Sea')**. The alliteration of 's' in 'strangest Sea' and the run-on line to suggest the circling comfort of the little bird all add to the curious music of Dickinson's poems. The buoyant, self-confident tone of the poem is in direct contrast to the strict Puritanical tradition of a severe, righteous God, with which she would have been familiar in her youth and which she rejected, preferring to keep her Sabbath 'staying at home'.

✒ Writing About the Poem

'Emily Dickinson's poetry contains an intense awareness of the private, inner self.' Discuss this view with particular reference to '"Hope" is the thing with feathers'.

Sample Paragraph

Everyone has experienced moments of depression when it seems that nothing is ever going to go right again. Dickinson, with her simple image of the bird singing, provides an optimistic response to this dark state of mind. She then develops this metaphor, comforting us with the thought that the bird (symbolising hope) can communicate with us without the need for language, 'sings the tune without words'. There is no end to hope. It 'never stops—at all—'. Dickinson understands the darkness of despair, 'in the Gale', 'the strangest Sea'. The use of capital letters seems to emphasise the terror of the individual. But the bird of hope provides comfort and warmth ('sweetest'). The poet uses enjambment effectively in the lines 'That could abash the little Bird/That kept so many warm'. The run-on rhythm suggests the protection of hope encircling us, just as the wing of the bird protects her young in the nest. This is an upbeat poem in which Dickinson is instructing the reader that one should never give up. The phrase 'perches in the soul' suggests to me that the poet regards hope as coming of its own choice. Hope is generous, always giving, 'Yet, never, in Extremity,/It asked a crumb—of Me'.

✒ Class/Homework Exercises

1. 'Dickinson is a wholly new and original poetic genius.' Do you agree or disagree with this statement? Support your response with reference to '"Hope" is the thing with feathers'.
2. 'Emily Dickinson often uses concrete language to communicate abstract ideas in her unusual poems.' Discuss this view, with reference to '"Hope" is the thing with feathers'.

⊙ Points to Consider

- **The poem explores the concept of hope and its impact on human life.**

- **Effective use of the extended metaphor of 'the little Bird'.**

- **Symbols represent the challenges people face in life.**

- **Variety of tones – assured, personal, reflective, optimistic, etc.**

2 There's a certain Slant of light

There's a certain Slant of light,
Winter Afternoons—
That oppresses, like the Heft
Of Cathedral Tunes—

Heavenly Hurt, it gives us—   5
We can find no scar,
But internal difference,
Where the Meanings, are—

None may teach it—Any—
'Tis the Seal Despair—   10
An imperial affliction
Sent us of the Air—

When it comes, the Landscape listens—
Shadows—hold their breath—
When it goes, 'tis like the Distance   15
On the look of Death—

Slant: incline; fall; interpretation.

oppresses: feels heavy; overwhelms.
Heft: strength; weight.

Any: anything.

Seal Despair: sign or symbol of hopelessness.
imperial affliction: God's will for mortal human beings.

'Heavenly Hurt, it gives us—'

👤 Personal Response

1. Describe the mood and atmosphere created by the poet in the opening stanza.
2. Comment on Dickinson's use of personification within the poem.
3. Write your own personal response to the poem, supporting your views with reference or quotation.

⊙ Critical Literacy

Dickinson was a keen observer of her environment, often dramatising her observations in poems. In this case, a particular beam of winter light puts the poet into a mood of depression as the slanting sunlight communicates a sense of despair. The poem typifies her creeping fascination with mortality. But although the poet's subject matter is intricate and disturbing, her own views are more difficult to determine. Ironically, this exploration of light and its effects seems to suggest a great deal about Dickinson's own dark consciousness.

From the outset, Dickinson creates an uneasy atmosphere. The setting ('Winter Afternoons') is dreary and desultory. Throughout stanza one, there is an underlying sense of time weighing heavily, especially when the light is compared to solemn cathedral music ('Cathedral Tunes'). We usually expect church music to be inspirational and uplifting, but in this case, its 'Heft' has a burdensome effect which simply 'oppresses' and adds to the **downcast mood**.

In stanza two, the poet considers the significance of the sunlight. For her, its effects are negative, causing pain to the world: 'Heavenly Hurt, it gives us.' The paradoxical language appears to reflect Dickinson's ironic attitude that **human beings live in great fear of God's power**. Is there a sense that deep down in their souls ('Where the Meanings, are'), people struggle under the weight of God's will, fearing death and judgement?

This feeling of humanity's helplessness is highlighted in stanza three: 'None may teach it' sums up the predicament of our limitations. Life and death can never be fully understood. Perhaps this is our tragic fate – our 'Seal Despair'. Dickinson presents **God as an all-powerful royal figure** associated with suffering and punishment ('An imperial affliction'). Is the poet's tone critical and accusatory? Or is she simply expressing the reality of human experience?

Stanza four is highly dramatic. **Dickinson personifies a terrified world** where 'the Landscape listens'. The earlier sombre light is now replaced by 'Shadows' that 'hold their breath' in the silence. The poet imagines the shocking moment of death and the mystery of time ('the Distance'). While the poem's ending is open to speculation, it seems clear that Dickinson is exploring the transition from life into eternity, a subject that is central to her writing. The only certain conclusion is an obvious one – that death is an inescapable reality beyond human understanding, as mysterious as it is natural. The poet's final tone is resigned, almost relieved. The 'Slant of light' offers no definitive answers to life's questions and the human condition is as inexplicable as death itself.

Throughout the poem, Dickinson's fragmented style is characterised by her **erratic punctuation and repeated use of capital letters**. She uses the dash at every opportunity to create suspense and drama. For the poet, the winter light is seen as an important sign from God, disturbing the inner 'Landscape' of her soul. In the end, the light (a likely metaphor for truth) causes Dickinson to experience an inner sadness and a deep sense of spiritual longing.

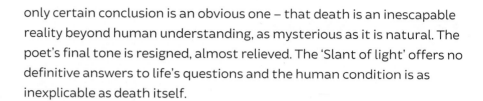

✒ Writing About the Poem

In your view, what is the central theme in this poem? Support the points you make with suitable reference to the text.

Sample Paragraph

I think that death is the main theme in all Dickinson's poems. The poem is atmospheric, but the light coming through the church window can be interpreted as a symbol of God, hope for the world. However, Dickinson's language is quite negative and it could be argued that our lives are under pressure and that fear of eternal damnation is also part of life. The phrases 'Heavenly Hurt' and 'imperial affliction' suggest that we are God's subjects, trying to avoid sin in this life in order to find salvation after death. I believe that the central message is that death comes to us all and we must accept it. The mood is oppressive, just like the sunlight coming in through the church window and the depressing 'Cathedral Tunes'. The poet's punctuation, using dashes and abrupt stops, is part of the tense mood of the poem. Dickinson's theme is quite distressing and images such as 'Seal Despair' and 'Shadows' add to the uneasiness of the reality that death is unavoidable.

EXAMINER'S COMMENT

A well-written, top-grade response that shows good engagement with both the poem and the question. References and succinct quotations used effectively to illustrate the poet's startling consideration of death. Confident and varied discussion of the poet's style throughout.

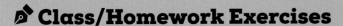

✒ Class/Homework Exercises

1. How would you describe the dominant mood of the poem? Is it positive in any way? Explain your response, supporting the points you make with suitable reference to the text.

2. Identify the dramatic elements of 'There's a certain Slant of light', commenting on their impact.

⊙ Points to Consider

- **The relationship between God and human beings is a central theme.**

- **Dickinson also explores the mystery of death.**

- **Dramatic atmosphere created by dynamic imagery and fragmented rhythm.**

- **Variety of moods – unease, fear, pessimism, etc.**

3 I felt a Funeral, in my Brain

I felt a Funeral, in my Brain,
And Mourners to and fro
Kept treading—treading—till it seemed
That Sense was breaking through—

And when they all were seated,   5
A Service, like a Drum—
Kept beating—beating—till I thought
My Mind was going numb—

And then I heard them lift a Box
And creak across my Soul   10
With those same Boots of Lead, again,
Then Space—began to toll,

As all the Heavens were a Bell,
And Being, but an Ear,
And I, and Silence, some strange Race   15
Wrecked, solitary, here—

And then a Plank in Reason, broke,
And I dropped down, and down—
And hit a World, at every plunge,
And Finished knowing—then—   20

treading: crush by walking on.
Sense: faculty of perception; the senses (seeing, hearing, touching, tasting, smelling); sound, practical judgement.

toll: ring slowly and steadily, especially to announce a death.

As all: as if all.

And Being, but an Ear: all senses, except hearing, are now useless.

'And then a Plank in Reason, broke'

👤 Personal Response

1. Do you find the images in this poem frightening, gruesome or coldly realistic? Give reasons for your answer, supported by textual reference.
2. Where is the climax of the poem, in your opinion? Refer to the text in your answer.
3. Write a short personal response to the poem, highlighting the impact it made on you.

👁 Critical Literacy

This poem is thought to have been written in 1861, at a time of turbulence in Dickinson's life. She was having religious and artistic doubts and had experienced an unhappy time in a personal relationship. This interior landscape paints a dark picture of something falling apart. It is for the reader to decide whether it is a fainting spell, a mental breakdown or a funeral. That is the enigma of Dickinson.

The startling perspective of this poem in stanza one can be seen as the view experienced by a person in a coffin, if the poem is read as an **account of the poet imagining her death**. Alternatively, it could refer to the suffocating feeling of the breakdown of consciousness, either through fainting or a mental breakdown. Perhaps it is the death of artistic activity. Whichever reading is chosen, and maybe all co-exist, the **interior landscape of awareness is being explored**. The use of the personal pronoun 'I' shows that this is a unique experience, although it has relevance for all. The relentless pounding of the mourners walking is reminiscent of a blinding migraine headache. The repetition of the hard-sounding 't' in the verb 'treading—treading' evocatively describes this terrible experience. The 'I' is undergoing an intense trauma beyond understanding: 'Sense was breaking through.' This repetition and disorientation are synonymous with psychological breakdown.

Stanza two gives a **first-person account of a funeral**. The mourners are seated and the service has begun. Hearing ('an Ear') is the only sense able to perceive. All the verbs refer to sound: 'tread', 'beat', 'heard', 'creak', 'toll'. The passive 'I' receives the experience, hearing, not listening, which is an active process. The experience is so overwhelming that 'I' thought the 'Mind was going numb', unable to endure any more. The use of the past tense reminds the reader that the experience is over, so is the first-person narrative told from beyond the grave? Is this the voice of someone who has died? Or is it the voice of someone in the throes of a desperate personal experience? The reader must decide.

The reference to 'Soul' in stanza three suggests a **spiritual dimension** to the experience. The 'I' has started to become disoriented as the line dividing an external experience and an internal one is breaking. The mourners 'creak across my Soul'. The oppressive, almost suffocating experience is captured in the onomatopoeic phrase 'Boots of Lead' and space becomes filled with the tolling bell. Existence in stanza four is reduced totally to hearing. The fearful transitory experience of crossing from awareness to unconsciousness, from life to death, is being imagined. The 'I' in stanza four is now stranded, 'Wrecked', cut off from life. The person is in a comatose state, able to comprehend but unable to communicate: 'solitary, here.' The word 'here' makes the reader feel present at this awful drama.

Finally, in stanza five, a new sensation takes over, **the sense of falling uncontrollably**. The 'I' has finished knowing and is now no longer aware of surroundings. Is this the descent into the hell of the angels in 'Paradise Lost'? Is it the descent of the coffin into the grave? Or is it the descent into madness or oblivion? The 'I' has learned something, but it is not revealed. The repetition of 'And' advances the movement of the poem in an almost uncontrollable way, mimicking the final descent. The 'I' is powerless under the repetitive verbs and the incessant rhythm punctuated by the ever-present dash. This poem is extraordinary, because before the study of psychology had defined it, it is a step-by-step description of mental collapse. Here is 'the drama of process'.

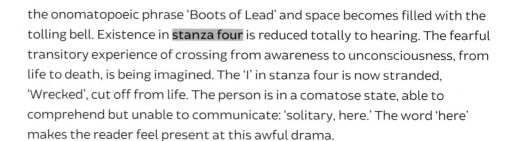

Writing About the Poem

'"I felt a Funeral, in my Brain" is a detailed and intense exploration of the experience of death.' Discuss this statement, using references from the text to support your views.

Sample Paragraph

Dickinson's imagined funeral suggests the losing of the grip on life by the individual 'I'. The noise ('treading', 'beating') induces an almost trance-like state as the brain cannot function anymore, and so becomes numb. The poet suggests that awareness is reduced to a single sense – hearing – 'an Ear'. I also find the poetic voice chilling. The idea that this is the view of someone lying in the coffin observing their own funeral is macabre. But the most compelling line in the poem is 'And then a Plank in Reason, broke'. This conveys the snap of reason as the 'I' loses consciousness, hurtling away into another dimension. Even the punctuation, with the use of commas, conveys this divided reality. But the most unnerving word is yet to come – 'then'. What exactly does the poet know? As always, Dickinson leaves us with unanswered questions.

EXAMINER'S COMMENT

A sustained personal response which attempts to stay focused throughout. The intensity within the poem is conveyed through a variety of expressions ('compelling', 'unnerving') and there is some worthwhile discussion on how features of the poet's style advance the theme of death. A solid high-grade answer.

✒ Class/Homework Exercises

1. 'She seems as close to touching bottom here as she ever got.'
   Discuss this view of Emily Dickinson with reference to the poem
   'I felt a Funeral, in my Brain'.
2. Comment on the conclusion of the poem. Did you think it is
   satisfactory? Or does it leave unanswered questions?

⊙ Points to Consider

- Themes include the imagined experience of loss of control and death.

- Vivid imagery depicts funeral scene.

- Introspective tones of uncertainty, shock and terror.

- Insistent rhythms, anguished tone, abrupt syntax all create dramatic impact.

- Striking use of onomatopoeia – assonance, repetition, etc.

4 A Bird came down the Walk

A Bird came down the Walk—
He did not know I saw—
He bit an Angleworm in halves
And ate the fellow, raw,

And then he drank a Dew   5
From a convenient Grass—
And then hopped sidewise to the Wall
To let a Beetle pass—

He glanced with rapid eyes
That hurried all around—   10
They looked like frightened Beads, I thought—
He stirred his Velvet Head

Like one in danger, Cautious,
I offered him a Crumb
And he unrolled his feathers   15
And rowed him softer home—

Than Oars divide the Ocean,
Too silver for a seam—
Or Butterflies, off Banks of Noon
Leap, plashless as they swim.   20

Angleworm: small worm used as fish bait by anglers.

the Ocean: Dickinson compares the blue sky to the sea.
silver: the sea's surface looks like solid silver.
a seam: opening; division.
plashless: splashless; undisturbed.

👤 Personal Response

1. In your view, what does the poem suggest about the relationship between human beings and nature?
2. What is the effect of Dickinson's use of humour in the poem? Does it let you see nature in a different way? Support the points you make with reference to the text.
3. From your reading of the poem, what impression of Emily Dickinson herself is conveyed? Refer to the text in your answer.

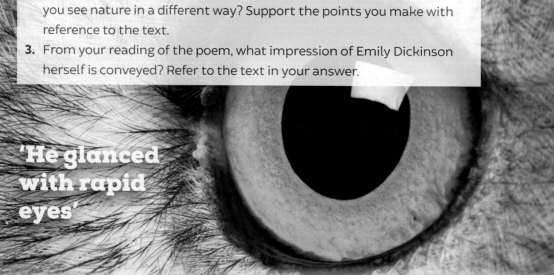

'He glanced with rapid eyes'

⊙ Critical Literacy

In this short descriptive poem, Dickinson celebrates the beauty and wonder of animals. While the bird is seen as a wild creature at times, other details present its behaviour and appearance in human terms. The poem also illustrates Dickinson's quirky sense of humour as well as offering interesting insights into nature and the exclusion of human beings from that world.

The poem begins with an everyday scene. Because the bird is unaware of the poet's presence, it behaves naturally. Stanza one demonstrates the **competition and danger of nature**: 'He bit an Angleworm in halves.' Although Dickinson imagines the bird within a human context, casually coming 'down the Walk' and suddenly eating 'the fellow, raw', she is amused by the uncivilised reality of the animal kingdom. The word 'raw' echoes her self-deprecating sense of shock. Despite its initial elegance, the predatory bird could hardly have been expected to cook the worm.

The poet's comic portrayal continues in stanza two. She gives the bird certain social qualities, drinking from a 'Grass' and politely allowing a hurrying beetle to pass. The tone is relaxed and playful. The slender vowel sounds ('convenient') and soft sibilance ('sidewise', 'pass') add to the seemingly refined atmosphere. However, the mood changes in stanza three, reflecting the bird's cautious fear. Dickinson observes the rapid eye movement, 'like frightened Beads'. Such **precise detail increases the drama of the moment**. The details of the bird's prim movement and beautiful texture are wonderfully accurate: 'He stirred his Velvet Head.' The simile is highly effective, suggesting the animal's natural grace.

The danger becomes more explicit in stanza four. Both the spectator and the observed bird are 'Cautious'. The crumb offered to the bird by the poet is rejected, highlighting the **gulf between their two separate worlds**. The description of the bird taking flight evokes the delicacy and fluidity of its movement: 'And he unrolled his feathers/And rowed him softer home.' The confident rhythm and emphatic alliteration enrich our understanding of the harmony between the creature and its natural environment. The sensual imagery captures the magnificence of the bird, compared to a rower moving with ease across placid water.

Stanza five develops the metaphorical description further, conveying the bird's poise and mystery: 'Too silver for a seam.' Not only was its flying seamless, it was smoother than that of butterflies leaping 'off Banks of Noon' and splashlessly swimming through the sky. The **breathtaking image and onomatopoeic language** remind us of Dickinson's admiration for nature in all its impressive beauty and is one of the most memorable descriptions in Dickinson's writing.

✒ Writing About the Poem

In your view, does Dickinson have a sense of empathy with the bird? Support your response with reference to the poem.

Sample Paragraph

It is clear from the start of the poem that Dickinson is both fascinated and amused by the appearance of a small bird in her garden. She seems almost honoured that out of nowhere 'A Bird came down the Walk'. When it suddenly swallows a worm 'raw', she becomes even more interested. The fact that she admits 'He did not know I saw' tells me that she really has empathy for the bird. Her tone suggests she feels privileged to watch and she certainly doesn't want to disturb it in its own world. The poet also finds the bird's antics funny. Although it devours the snail, it behaves very mannerly towards the beetle. Dickinson shows her feelings for the bird when it becomes frightened and she notices its 'rapid eyes'. She sees that it is 'in danger'. The fact that she offered it a crumb also shows her empathy. At the very end, she shows her admiration for the beauty of the bird as it flies off to freedom – to its 'softer home'. The descriptions of it like a rower or a butterfly suggest that she admires its grace.

EXAMINER'S COMMENT

Apt references and short quotations are effectively used to illustrate the poet's regard for the bird. The answer ranges well over much of the poem and considers various tones (including fascination, amusement, reverence, concern and admiration). A confident top-grade response.

✎ Class/Homework Exercises

1. Comment on Dickinson's use of imagery in 'A Bird came down the Walk'. Support the points you make with the aid of suitable reference.
2. In your opinion, what does the poem suggest about the differences (or similarities) between animals and humans? Support your response with reference to the text.

⊙ Points to Consider

- **Exploration of the wonder of nature.**
- **Interesting use of personification gives the bird social graces.**
- **Impact of sensuous imagery, metaphorical language, sibilant effects.**
- **Contrasting tones – bemused, concerned, surprised, upbeat, etc.**

The poem address us beyond the ~~grave~~ grave
Atmosphere of tension and expectation
ABAB rhyming scheme
4 ~~stan~~ line stanza

regular rhythm until final stanza (becomes irregular) mirror what happens in the poem

5 I heard a Fly buzz— when I died

EMILY DICKINSON

I heard a Fly buzz—when I died—
The Stillness in the Room
Was like the Stillness in the Air—
Between the Heaves of Storm—

Heaves: lift with effort.

metaphor : the eye is compared to a spongy substance

The Eyes around—had wrung them dry—   5
And Breaths were gathering firm
For that last Onset—when the King
Be witnessed—in the Room—

Onset: beginning.
the King: God.

I willed my Keepsakes—Signed away
What portion of me be   10
Assignable—and then it was
There interposed a Fly—

Keepsakes: gifts treasured for the sake of the giver.

interposed: inserted between or among things.

light = afterlife / window / concias

With Blue—uncertain stumbling Buzz—
Between the light—and me—
And then the Windows failed—and then   15
I could not see to see—

'And then the Windows failed–'

👤 Personal Response

1. How would you describe the atmosphere in the poem? Pick out two phrases which, in your opinion, are especially descriptive and explain why you chose them.
2. Do you think Dickinson uses contrast effectively in this poem? Discuss one contrast you found particularly striking.
3. Write a brief personal response to the poem, highlighting its impact on you.

◉ Critical Literacy

Dickinson was fascinated by death. This poem examines the moment between life and death. At that time, it was common for family and friends to be present at deathbed vigils. It was thought that the way a person behaved or looked at the moment of death gave an indication of the soul's fate.

The last moment of a person's life is a solemn and often sad occasion. The perspective of the poem is that of the person dying and this significant moment is dominated by the buzzing of a fly in the room in the first stanza. This is **absurdly comic and strangely distorts** this moment into something grotesque. Surely the person dying should be concerned with more important matters than an insignificant fly: 'I heard a Fly buzz—when I died.' The room is still and expectant as the last breaths are drawn, a stillness like the moments before a storm. All are braced for what is to come. The word 'Heaves' suggests the force of the storm that is about to break.

The second stanza shows us that the mourners had now stopped crying and were holding their breath as they awaited the coming of the 'King' (God) into the room at the moment of death. The phrase 'Be witnessed' refers to the dying person and the mourners who are witnessing their faith, and it conjures up all the solemnity of a court. The word 'firm' also suggests these people's steadfast religious beliefs. The third stanza is concerned with putting matters right. The dying person has made a will – 'What portion of me be/Assignable' – and what is not assignable belongs to God. The person is awaiting the coming of his/her Maker, 'and then it was/There interposed a Fly' – the symbol of decay and corruption appeared. Human affairs cannot be managed; real life intervenes. The **fly comes between ('interposed') the dying person and the moment of death, which trivialises** the event.

The fractured syntax of the last stanza shows the **breakdown of the senses** at the moment of death: 'Between the light—and me.' Sight and sound are blurring. The presence of the fly is completely inappropriate, like a drunken person at a solemn ceremony, disturbing and embarrassing and interrupting proceedings. The fly is now between the dying person and the source of light. Does this suggest that the person has lost concentration on higher things, distracted by the buzzing fly? The sense of sight then fails: 'And then the Windows failed.' The moment of death had come and gone, dominated by the noisy fly. Has the fly prevented the person from reaching another dimension? Is death emptiness, just human decay, as signified by the presence of the fly, or is there something more? Do we need comic relief at overwhelming occasions? Is the poet signalling her own lack of belief in an afterlife with God? Dickinson, as usual, intrigues, **leaving the reader with more questions than answers**, so that the reader, like the dying person, is struggling to 'see to see'.

🖋 Writing About the Poem

'Dickinson's poems on mortality often lead to uncertainty or despair.' Discuss this statement with particular reference to 'I heard a Fly buzz—when I died'.

Sample Paragraph

The view of this deathbed scene is from the dying person's perspective. The problem is that everyone is distracted by the arrival of a noisy fly! Dickinson seems to be saying that life and death are random – and this goes against the human desire for order and control, 'Signed away/ What portion of me be/Assignable'. I feel the poet may be suggesting that the dying person, distracted by the fly is, therefore, cheated in some way. The momentous occasion has passed, dominated by a buzzing fly. Dickinson's voice is far from reassuring. Instead, she dispassionately draws a deathbed scene and lets us 'see to see'. Are we – like the dying person – distracted and unable to achieve greater wisdom? The divided voice, that of the person dying and that of the person after death leaves us with a question – is death just the final absurd stage in the meaningless cycle of life? In the end, this poem leaves me with bleak uncertainties about the human condition and our ability to exercise control.

EXAMINER'S COMMENT

This solid, high-grade response includes interesting and thought-provoking ideas on a challenging question. Comments show some good personal engagement with the poem and the issues raised by Dickinson. Expression is impressive and apt quotations are used effectively throughout the answer. References to the dramatic style and tone would have improved the standard.

🖋 Class/Homework Exercises

1. Comment on how Dickinson's style contributes to the theme or message in this poem. Refer closely to the text in your response.
2. Is there any suggestion that the speaker in this poem believes in a spiritual afterlife? Give a reason for your response, supporting your views with reference to the text.

⊙ Points to Consider

- **Dickinson raises questions about death and the possibility of an afterlife.**
- **Surreal sense of the absurd throughout.**
- **Dramatic elements – the deathbed scene, still atmosphere, observers, noises, etc.**
- **Contrasting tones include disbelief, confusion, resignation and helplessness.**
- **Effective use of contrast and symbols (light, the fly) and repetition.**

6 The Soul has Bandaged moments

The Soul has Bandaged moments—
When too appalled to stir—
She feels some ghastly Fright come up
And stop to look at her—

Salute her—with long fingers— 5
Caress her freezing hair—
Sip, Goblin, from the very lips
The Lover—hovered—o'er—
Unworthy, that a thought so mean
Accost a Theme—so—fair— 10

The soul has moments of Escape—
When bursting all the doors—
She dances like a Bomb, abroad,
And swings upon the Hours,

As do the Bee—delirious borne— 15
Long Dungeoned from his Rose—
Touch Liberty—then know no more,
But Noon, and Paradise—

The Soul's retaken moments—
When, Felon led along, 20
With shackles on the plumed feet,
And staples, in the Song,

The Horror welcomes her, again,
These, are not brayed of Tongue—

Bandaged moments: painful experiences.
appalled: shocked, horrified.
stir: act; retaliate.

Accost: address.

Escape: freedom.

like a Bomb: dramatically.
abroad: in unusual directions.

Dungeoned: imprisoned in the hive.

Felon: criminal.

shackles: chains, ropes.
plumed: decorated.
staples: fastenings.

brayed: inarticulate.

👤 Personal Response

1. What details in the poem evoke the feelings of 'ghastly Fright' experienced by the soul? Support your answer with quotation or reference.
2. Choose one comparison from the poem that you find particularly effective. Explain your choice.
3. Comment on Dickinson's use of dashes in this poem, briefly explaining their effectiveness.

⊙ Critical Literacy

Throughout much of her poetry, Dickinson focuses on the nature of consciousness and the experience of being alive. She was constantly searching for meaning, particularly of transient moments or changing moods. This search is central to 'The Soul has Bandaged moments', where the poet takes us through a series of dramatic images contrasting the extremes of the spirit and the conscious self.

Stanza one introduces the soul as being fearful and vulnerable, personified as a terrified female who 'feels some ghastly Fright', with the poem's stark

'As do the Bee—delirious borne—'

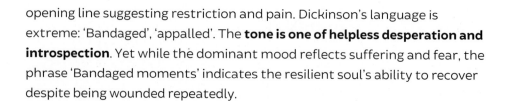

opening line suggesting restriction and pain. Dickinson's language is extreme: 'Bandaged', 'appalled'. The **tone is one of helpless desperation and introspection**. Yet while the dominant mood reflects suffering and fear, the phrase 'Bandaged moments' indicates the resilient soul's ability to recover despite being wounded repeatedly.

Stanza two is unnervingly dramatic. The poet creates a mock-romantic scene between the victimised soul and the 'ghastly Fright' figure, now portrayed as a hideous goblin and her would-be lover, their encounter depicted in terms of gothic horror. The soul experiences terrifying fantasies as the **surreal sequence becomes increasingly menacing** and the goblin's long fingers 'Caress her freezing hair'. The appearance of an unidentified shadowy 'Lover' is unexpected. There is a sense of the indecisive soul being caught between two states, represented by the malevolent goblin and the deserving lover. It is unclear whether Dickinson is writing about the choices involved in romantic love or the relationship between herself and God.

The stanza ends inconclusively, juxtaposing two opposites: the 'Unworthy' or undeserving 'thought' and the 'fair' (worthy) 'Theme'. The latter might well refer to the ideal of romantic love. If so, it is confronted by erotic desire (the 'thought'). Dickinson's disjointed style, especially her frequent use of dashes within stanzas, isolates key words and intensifies the overwhelmingly **nightmarish atmosphere**.

The feeling of confused terror is replaced with ecstatic 'moments of Escape' in stanzas three and four. The soul recovers in triumph, 'bursting all the doors'. This **explosion of energy** ('She dances like a Bomb') evokes a rising mood of riotous freedom. Explosive verbs ('bursting', 'dances', 'swings') and robust rhythms add to the sense of uncontrollable excitement. Dickinson compares the soul to a 'Bee—delirious borne'. After being 'Long Dungeoned' in its hive, this bee can now enjoy the sensuous delights of 'his Rose'.

The mood is short-lived, however, and in stanzas five and six, 'The Horror' returns. The soul becomes depressed again, feeling bound and shackled, like a 'Felon led along'. **Dickinson develops this criminal metaphor** – 'With shackles on the plumed feet' – leaving us with an ultimate sense of loss as 'The Horror welcomes her, again'. Is this the soul's inevitable fate? The final line is unsettling. Whatever horrible experiences confront the soul, they are simply unspeakable: 'not brayed of Tongue.'

As always, Dickinson's poem is open to many interpretations. Critics have suggested that the poet is dramatising the turmoil of dealing with the loss of creativity. Some view the poem's central conflict as the tension between romantic love and sexual desire. Others believe that the poet was exploring the theme of depression and mental instability. In the end, readers must find their own meaning and decide for themselves.

🖋 Writing About the Poem

Comment on the dramatic elements that are present in the poem, supporting the points you make with reference to the text.

Sample Paragraph

'The Soul has Bandaged moments' is built around a conflict between two opposing forces, the 'Soul', or spirit, and its great enemy, 'Fright'. Dickinson sets the dramatic scene with the Soul still recovering – presumably from the last battle. It is 'Bandaged' after the fight with its arch enemy. The descriptions of the soul's opponent are startling. Fright is 'ghastly', a 'Horror' and a sleazy 'Goblin' who is trying to seduce the innocent soul. Dickinson's images add to the dramatic tension. In the seduction scene, the goblin is described as having 'long fingers'. His intended victim is petrified with fear. The goblin uses its bony claws to 'Caress her freezing hair'. The drama continues right to the end. The soul is compared to a 'Felon' being led away in 'shackles'. Such images have a distressing impact in explaining the pressures on the soul to be free. Finally, Dickinson's stop-and-start style is unsettling. Broken rhythms and her condensed language increase the edgy atmosphere throughout this highly dramatic poem.

EXAMINER'S COMMENT

An assured and focused top-grade response, showing a clear understanding of the poem's dramatic features. The answer addressed both subject matter and style, using back-up illustration and integrated quotes successfully. Expression throughout was also excellent.

✒ Class/Homework Exercises

1. How would you describe the dominant tone of 'The Soul has Bandaged moments'? Use reference to the text to show how the tone is effectively conveyed.
2. Identify the poem's surreal aspects and comment on their impact.

⊙ Points to Consider

- **An intense exploration on the nature of spiritual awareness.**

- **Dickinson focuses on a series of traumatic experiences.**

- **Effective use of dramatic verbs and vivid imagery.**

- **The soul is personified to convey various states – fear, joy, terror, etc.**

A, B, C, B rhyme scheme
style of writing: very ~~concise~~ concise, Laconic (very economic on words)

7 I could bring You Jewels—had I a mind to

I could bring You Jewels—had I a mind to—
But You have enough—of those—
I could bring You Odors from St. Domingo—
Colors—from Vera Cruz—   — assonance.

Odors: fragrances, perfumes.
St. Domingo: Santo Domingo in the Caribbean.
Vera Cruz: city on the east coast of Mexico.

alliteration —

Berries of the Bahamas—have I—   5
But this little Blaze   — metaphor
Flickering to itself—in the Meadow—
Suits Me—more than those—

Bahamas: group of islands south-east of Florida.
Blaze: strong fire or flame; very bright light.

assonance —

Never a Fellow matched this Topaz—
And his Emerald Swing—   10
Dower itself—for Bobadilo—   hyperbole
Better—Could I bring?

Dower: part of her husband's estate allotted to a widow by law.
Bobadilo: braggart; someone who speaks arrogantly or boastfully.

assonance/alliteration = adds musical qaulity to the poem/theme/beautiful things

use of imagery =

'Never a Fellow matched this Topaz—'

👤 Personal Response

1. Does the poet value exotic or homely gifts? Briefly explain your answer.
2. Write your own personal response to the poem, highlighting its impact on you.
3. What is the tone in this poem: arrogant, humble, gentle, strident, confident? Quote in support of your opinion.

👁 Critical Literacy

Although described as a recluse, Dickinson had a wide circle of friends. She wrote letter-poems to them, often representing them as flowers, 'things of nature which had come with no practice at all'. This poem is one without shadows, celebratory and happy, focusing out rather than in as she concentrates on a relationship.

In the first stanza, the poem opens with the speaker **considering the gift she will give** her beloved, 'You'. The 'You' is very much admired, and is wealthy ('You have enough'), so the gift of jewels is dismissed. The phrase 'had I a mind to' playfully suggests that maybe the 'I' doesn't necessarily wish to present anything. There is a certain coquettish air evident here. A world of privilege and plenty is shown as, one after another, expensively exotic gifts are considered and dismissed. These include perfumes and vibrant colours from faraway locations, conjuring up images of romance and adventure: 'Odors from St. Domingo.'

The second stanza continues the list, with 'Berries of the Bahamas' being considered as an option for this special gift, but they are not quite right either. The tense changes to 'have I' and the laconic listing and dismissing stops. A small wildflower 'in the Meadow', 'this little Blaze', is chosen instead. This 'Suits Me'. Notice that it is not that this suits the other person. **This gift is a reflection of her own unshowy personality**. The long lines of considering exotic gifts have now given way to shorter, more decisive lines.

In the third stanza, the speaker has a definite note of conviction, as she confidently states that 'Never a Fellow matched' this shining gift of hers. No alluring, foreign gemstone, be it a brilliant topaz or emerald, shines as this 'little Blaze' in the meadow. The gift glows with colour; it is natural, inexpensive and accessible. The reference to a dower might suggest a gift given by a woman to a prospective husband. This **gift is suitable** for a Spanish adventurer, a 'Bobadilo'. The assured tone is clear in the word 'Never' and the jaunty rhyme 'Swing' and 'bring'. The final rhetorical question suggests that this is the best gift she could give. The poem shows that **the true value of a present cannot be measured in a material way.**

✒ Writing About the Poem

'Dickinson is fascinated by moments of change.' Discuss this statement with reference to 'I could bring You Jewels—had I a mind to'.

Sample Paragraph

In this lively poem, the speaker considers what present would be most suitable to give to her arrogant lover. The first change occurs when this confident woman dismisses expensive, exotic gifts, 'But You have enough' and chooses something which is natural and simple – and, more importantly – which is to her liking: 'Suits Me –' The simple flower she offers is unexpectedly beautiful – this 'little Blaze' suggests the hidden passion of the woman herself. The unpretentious meadow flower is free and easily picked, but it shines! The changing breathless tone reflects the love she feels. The flower is brighter than any precious stone of 'Topaz' or 'Emerald'. Short lines express the self-belief of a woman who knows best. Even the rhyme changes from where she is considering her options ('those'/'Cruz') in the first stanza, to the more definite jaunty rhyme of 'Swing' and 'bring' in the final stanza. I enjoyed how Dickinson explored the feminine trait of considering everything, and then finally deciding, after humorous hesitation. Dickinson is fascinated by the spontaneity of life.

EXAMINER'S COMMENT

A confident top-grade response to the question, backed up with a convincing use of quotation. Good discussion about changes in thought and tone. The point about the change in line length was particularly interesting. Assured, varied vocabulary is controlled throughout and the paragraph is rounded off impressively.

✎ Class/Homework Exercises

1. 'Dickinson disrupts and transforms our accepted view of things.' What is your opinion of this statement? Refer to 'I could bring You Jewels—had I a mind to' in support of your response.
2. Comment on the impact of Dickinson's use of sound effects in the poem.

◉ Points to Consider

- Central themes include the wonder and beauty of nature.
- Celebratory mood conveyed by powerful visual imagery and lively rhythm.
- Simplicity of the wildflower contrasted with extravagant glamour.
- Confident, optimistic tone contrasts with the poet's downbeat poems.

8 A narrow Fellow in the Grass

EMILY DICKINSON

A narrow Fellow in the Grass
Occasionally rides—
You may have met Him—did you not
His notice sudden is—

The Grass divides as with a Comb—   5
A spotted shaft is seen—
And then it closes at your feet
And opens further on—

a spotted shaft: patterned skin of the darting snake.

He likes a Boggy Acre
A Floor too cool for Corn—   10
Yet when a Boy, and Barefoot—
I more than once at Noon
Have passed, I thought, a Whip lash
Unbraiding in the Sun
When stooping to secure it   15
It wrinkled, and was gone—

Whip lash: sudden, violent movement.
Unbraiding: straightening out, uncoiling.

Several of Nature's People
I know, and they know me—
I feel for them a transport
Of cordiality—   20

transport: heightened emotion.

cordiality: civility, welcome.

But never met this Fellow
Attended, or alone
Without a tighter breathing
And Zero at the Bone—

Zero at the Bone: cold terror.

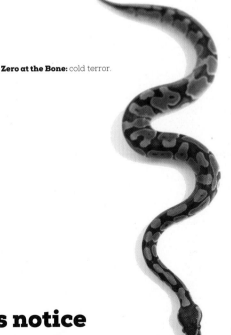

👤 Personal Response

1. Select two images from the poem that suggest evil or menace. Comment briefly on the effectiveness of each.
2. How successful is the poet in conveying the snake's erratic sense of movement? Refer to the text in your answer.
3. Outline your own feelings in response to the poem.

'His notice sudden is—'

89 |

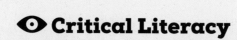 Critical Literacy

In this poem, one of the few published during her lifetime, Dickinson adopts a male persona remembering an incident from his boyhood. Snakes have traditionally been seen as symbols of evil. We still use the expression 'snake in the grass' to describe someone who cannot be trusted. Central to this poem is Dickinson's own portrayal of nature – beautiful, brutal and lyrical. She seems fascinated by the endless mystery, danger and unpredictability of the natural world.

The opening lines of stanza one casually introduce a 'Fellow in the Grass'. (Dickinson never refers explicitly to the snake.) The **conversational tone immediately involves readers** who may already 'have met Him'. However, there is more than a hint of warning in the postscript: 'His notice sudden is.' This underlying wariness now appears foreshadowed by the menacing adjective 'narrow' and by the disjointed rhythm and slightly awkward word order.

Dickinson focuses on the volatile snake's dramatic movements in stanza two. The verbs 'divide', 'closes' and 'opens' emphasise its dynamic energy. The snake suddenly emerges like a 'spotted shaft'. The poet's **comparisons are particularly effective**, suggesting a lightning bolt or a camouflaged weapon. Run-on lines, a forceful rhythm and the repetition of 'And' contribute to the vivid image of the snake as a powerful presence to be treated with caution.

Stanza three reveals even more about the snake's natural habitat: 'He likes a Boggy Acre.' It also divulges the speaker's identity – an adult male remembering his failed boyhood efforts to capture snakes. The memory conveys something of the intensity of childhood experiences, especially of dangerous encounters with nature. The boy's innocence and vulnerability ('Barefoot') contrasts with the 'Whip lash' violence of the wild snake. **Dickinson's attitude to nature is open to interpretation**. Does the threat come from the animal or the boy? Did the adult speaker regard the snake differently when he was young? The poet herself clearly appreciates the complexities found within the natural world and her precisely observed descriptions ('Unbraiding', 'It wrinkled') provide ample evidence of her interest.

From the speaker's viewpoint in stanza four, nature is generally benign. This positive image is conveyed by the affectionate tribute to 'Nature's People'. The familiar personification and personal tone underline the mutual 'cordiality' that exists between nature and human nature. Despite this, **divisions between the two worlds cannot be ignored**. Indeed, the focus in stanza five is on the sheer horror people experience when confronted by 'this Fellow'. The poet's sparse and chilling descriptions – 'tighter breathing', 'Zero at the Bone' – are startling expressions of stunned terror.

As in other poems, Dickinson attributes human characteristics to nature – the snake 'Occasionally rides', 'The Grass divides' and the bogland has a 'Floor'. One effect of this is to highlight the **variety and mystery of the**

natural environment, which can only ever be glimpsed within limited human terms. The snake remains unknowable to the end, dependent on a chance encounter, a fleeting glance or a trick of light.

✒ Writing About the Poem

Comment on the effectiveness of Dickinson's use of the male persona voice in 'A narrow Fellow in the Grass'. Support the points you make with reference to the poem.

Sample Paragraph

In some poems, Dickinson chose to substitute her own voice with that of a fictional narrator. This is the case in 'A narrow Fellow in the Grass', where she uses a country boy to tell the story of his experiences trying to catch snakes when he was young. It is obvious that he has a great love for nature, but neither is he blind to the cold fear he felt when he came face to face with the 'spotted shaft'. Dickinson's language emphasises youthful terror. She lets him remember his encounter as it happened. The images are disturbing: 'a tighter breathing.' The boy remembers shuddering with uncontrollable fright, 'Zero at the Bone'. The description is dramatic and I could relate to the boy's horror. The poem is all the more effective for being centred around one terrified character, the young boy. I can visualise the child in his bare feet trying to catch a frightened snake in the grass. It is only later that he realises the danger he was in and this has taught him a lifelong lesson about nature. By using another persona, Dickinson explores the excitement and danger of nature in a wider way that allows readers to imagine it more clearly.

EXAMINER'S COMMENT

A well-written and sustained response that includes some good personal engagement and a great deal of insightful discussion – particularly regarding the conflict between the boy and the snake. References and quotations are well used throughout the answer to provide a very interesting high-grade standard.

✐ Class/Homework Exercises

1. In your opinion, how does Dickinson portray nature in 'A narrow Fellow in the Grass'? Support your points with reference to the poem.
2. Identify the dramatic moments in this poem and comment on their impact.

⊙ Points to Consider

- **Dickinson explores contrasting aspects of the natural world.**
- **Effective use of everyday conversational language.**
- **The poet adopts the persona of a young boy who encounters a snake.**
- **Dramatic atmosphere concludes on a note of terror.**

theme = love of nature and natural beauty

9 I taste a liquor never brewed

Dominated by images of intoxication

_its a paradox —
precious nature of
the liquid_

I taste a liquor never brewed—
From Tankards scooped in Pearl—
Not all the Vats upon the Rhine
Yield such an Alcohol!

_regular dashes are used
to invoke an ongoing sense
of delight_

drunk on air
Inebriate of Air—am I—
And Debauchee of Dew— _alliteration_   5
Reeling—thro endless summer days— _assonance_
From inns of Molten Blue—

_intoxicated
really bad_

When 'Landlords' turn the drunken Bee _— too much pollen_
Out of the Foxglove's door—– _assonance_   10
When Butterflies—renounce their 'drams'—
I shall but drink the more!

_completely devoted
to drinking
foxglove = flower_

sibilance
Till Seraphs swing their snowy Hats—
And Saints—to windows run—
To see the little Tippler   15
Leaning against the—Sun—

_assonance and alliteration
adds a joyous mood
Euphonic sounds_

Tankards: one-handled mugs, usually made of pewter, used for drinking beer.
Vats: large vessels used for making alcohol.

Debauchee: someone who has overindulged and neglected duty.

Seraphs: angels who are of the highest spiritual level.

Tippler: a person who drinks often, but does not get drunk.

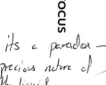

'Not all the Vats upon the Rhine/ Yield such an Alcohol!'

👤 Personal Response

1. What is the mood in this poem? Does it intensify or change? Use references from the text in your response.
2. Which stanza appeals to you most? Discuss both the poet's style and content in your answer.
3. Write a brief personal response to the poem, highlighting its impact on you.

👁 Critical Literacy

This 'rapturous poem about summer' uses the metaphor of intoxication to capture the essence of this wonderful season. Dickinson's family were strict Calvinists, a religion that emphasised damnation as the consequence of sin. Her father supported the Temperance League, an organisation that warned against the dangers of drink.

This poem is written as a **joyful appreciation of this wonderful life**. The tone is playful and exaggerated from the beginning, as the poet declares this drink was never 'brewed'. The reference to 'scooped in Pearl' could refer to the great, white frothing heads of beer in the 'Tankards'. The poet certainly conveys the merriment of intoxication, as the poem reels along its happy way. The explanation for all this drunkenness is that the poet is drunk on life ('Inebriate', 'Debauchee'). The pubs are the inns of 'Molten Blue', i.e. the sky (stanza two). It is like a cartoon, with little drunken bees being shown the door by the pub owners as they lurch about in delirious ecstasy. The drinkers of the natural world are the bees and butterflies, but she can drink more than these: 'I shall but drink the more!' This roots the poem in reality, as drunken people always feel they can manage more.

But this has caused uproar in the heavens, as the angels and saints run to look out at this little drunk, 'the little Tippler'. She stands drunkenly leaning against the 'Sun', a celestial lamppost. The final dash suggests the crooked stance of the little drunken one. **There is no heavy moral at the end of this poem. In fact, there seems to be a slight note of envy for the freedom and happiness being experienced by the intoxicated poet.** Are the angels swinging their hats to cheer her on in her drunken rebellion? Is this poem celebrating the reckless indulgence of excess? Or is the final metaphor of the sun referring to Christ or to the poet's own arrival in heaven after she indulgently enjoys the beauty of the natural world?

Nature is seen as the spur for high jinks and good humour. The riddle of the first line starts it off: how was the alcohol 'never brewed'? The exaggerated imagery, such as the metaphor of the flower as a pub and the bee as the drunk, all add to the fantasy land atmosphere. The words 'Inebriate', 'Debauchee' and 'renounce' are reminiscent of the language which those disapproving of the consumption of alcohol might use for those who do indulge. Is the poet having a sly laugh at the serious Temperance League to which her father belonged? The ridiculous costumes, 'snowy Hats', and the uproar in heaven ('swing' and 'run') all add to the impression of this land of merriment. The juxtaposition of the sacred ('Seraphs') and the profane ('Tippler') in stanza four also adds to the comic effect. However, it is the verbs that carry the sense of mad fun most effectively: 'scooped', 'Reeling', 'drink', 'swing', 'run' and 'Leaning'. The poem lurches and flows in an almost uncontrollable way as the ecstasy of overindulging in the delirious pleasure of nature is vividly conveyed.

There are two different types of humour present in this irrepressible poem – the broad humour of farce and the more **subversive humour of irony**. She even uses the steady metre of a hymn, with eight syllables in lines one and three and six syllables in lines two and four. Dickinson seems to be standing at a distance, smiling wryly, as she gently deflates.

✒ Writing About the Poem

'Dickinson was always careful to avoid expressing excessive emotion, even of joy.' Discuss this statement with reference to 'I taste a liquor never brewed'.

Sample Paragraph

I don't agree about the question. This is a funny poem and the poet is enjoying herself. She is drunk on nature and it is humourous when the angels are waving their caps, egging her on. I think this is really a very happy go lucky poem, unlike Dickenson's disturbing poems we studied about death, funerals and souls. It goes to show she also writes happier poetry when she wants. Dickenson is an excentric writer who hardly ever uses normal punctuation. Her poems are hard as they don't have normal sentences but use capital letters for the words. There is a comparison for drinking all through this poem to describe being drunk on nature. The poem is definately full of joy, eg the story about the bee. The lines describing the tippler against the paling post are also really joyful. I think everyone should be able to enjoy Emily's brilliant poem as it has happy images.

EXAMINER'S COMMENT

This note-like answer shows limited engagement with the poem. While there is a recognition of the poem's joyful tone and some supportive reference, the lack of substantial analysis is noticeable. Language use is repetitive, expression is flawed and there are several mechanical mistakes. The over-enthusiastic ending is not convincing. Closer study of the poem and greater care in writing the response would raise the standard from a basic grade.

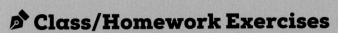

✒ Class/Homework Exercises

1. 'Hypersensitivity to natural beauty produced Dickinson's poetry.' Do you agree or disagree with this statement? Refer to the poem 'I taste a liquor never brewed' in your response.
2. Identify the childlike elements of the poem and comment on their impact.

⊙ Points to Consider

- **The poem highlights Dickinson's close relationship with nature.**

- **Exuberant mood conveyed by sibilant sounds, vivid images, lively rhythm, etc.**

- **Extended metaphor of intoxication used effectively throughout.**

- **Dominant sense of delight, celebration and good humour.**

10 After great pain, a formal feeling comes

After great pain, a formal feeling comes—
The Nerves sit ceremonious, like Tombs—
The stiff Heart questions was it He, that bore,
And Yesterday, or Centuries before?

The Feet, mechanical, go round—   5
Of Ground, or Air, or Ought—
A Wooden way
Regardless grown,
A Quartz contentment, like a stone—

This is the Hour of Lead—   10
Remembered, if outlived,
As Freezing persons, recollect the Snow—
First—Chill—then Stupor—then the letting go—

formal: serious; exact.

ceremonious: on show.

He: the stiff Heart, or possibly Christ.
bore: endure; intrude.

Ought: anything.

Quartz: basic rock mineral.

Hour of Lead: traumatic experience.

Stupor: numbness; disorientation.

👤 Personal Response

1. Comment on the poet's use of personification in the opening stanza.
2. How does the language used in the second stanza convey the condition of the victim in pain?
3. Write your own short personal response to the poem.

'First—Chill—then Stupor'

◉ Critical Literacy

Dickinson wrote 'After great pain, a formal feeling comes' in 1862, at a time when she was thought to have been experiencing severe psychological difficulties. The poet addresses the effects of isolation and anguish on the individual. Ironically, the absence of the personal pronoun 'I' gives the poem a universal significance. The 'great pain' itself is never fully explained and the final lines are ambiguous. Like so much of Dickinson's work, this dramatic poem raises many questions for consideration.

From the outset, Dickinson is concerned with the emotional numbness ('a formal feeling') that follows the experience of 'great pain'. The poet's authoritative tone in stanza one reflects a first-hand knowledge of trauma, with the adjective 'formal' suggesting self-conscious recovery from some earlier distress. Dickinson personifies the physical response as order returns to body and mind: 'The Nerves sit ceremonious, like Tombs.' The severe pain has also shocked the 'stiff Heart', which has become confused by the experience. Is the poet also drawing a parallel with the life and death of Jesus Christ (the Sacred Heart), crucified 'Centuries before'? The images certainly suggest timeless suffering and endurance. This **sombre sense of loss** is further enhanced by the broad vowel assonance of the opening lines.

The feeling of stunned inertia continues into stanza two. In reacting to intense pain, 'The Feet, mechanical, go round'. It is as if the response is unfocused and indifferent, lacking any real purpose. Dickinson uses two **analogies to emphasise the sense of pointless alienation**. The reference to the 'Wooden way' might be interpreted as a fragile bridge between reason and insanity, or this metaphor could be associated with Christ's suffering as he carried his cross to Calvary. The level of consciousness at such times is described as 'Regardless grown', or beyond caring. Dickinson's second comparison is equally innovative: 'A Quartz contentment' underpins the feeling of complete apathy that makes the victims of pain behave 'like a stone'. Is she being ironic by suggesting that the post-traumatic state is an escape, a 'contentment' of sorts?

There is a disturbing sense of resignation at the start of stanza three: 'This is the Hour of Lead'. The dull weight of depression is reinforced by the insistent monosyllables and solemn rhythm, but the devastating experience is not 'outlived' by everyone. Dickinson outlines the aftermath of suffering by using one final comparison: 'As Freezing persons.' This shocking simile evokes the unimaginable hopelessness of the victim stranded in a vast wasteland of snow. The poem's last line traces the tragic stages leading to oblivion: 'First—Chill—then Stupor—then the letting go—.' The inclusion of the dash at the end might indicate a possibility of relief, though whether it is through rescue or death is not revealed. In either case, **readers are left with an acute awareness of an extremely distraught voice**.

✒ Writing About the Poem

One of Dickinson's great achievements is her ability to explore the experience of deep depression. To what extent is this true of her poem 'After great pain, a formal feeling comes'? Refer closely to the text in your answer.

Sample Paragraph

'After great pain, a formal feeling comes' is a good example of Dickinson's skill in addressing distressing subjects, such as mental breakdown. Although she never really explains the 'pain' referred to in the first line, she deals with the after–effects of suffering. What Dickinson does very well is to explain how depression can lead to people becoming numb, beyond all emotion. I believe this is what she means by 'a formal feeling'. She uses an interesting image of a sufferer's nerves sitting quietly in a church at a funeral service. They 'sit ceremonious'. This same idea is used to describe the mourners following the hearse – 'Feet mechanical'. I get the impression that grief can destroy people's confidence. Dickinson's images are compelling and suggest the coldness experienced by patients who have suffered depression. They are 'like a stone'. The best description is at the end, when she compares sufferers to being lost in the snow. They will slowly fade into a 'stupor' or death wish. Dickinson is very good at using images and moods to explore depression.

EXAMINER'S COMMENT

Although the expression is slightly awkward in places, there are a number of interesting points in the response – particularly the discussion of 'a formal feeling' and the exploration of key images in the poem. Expression is controlled throughout and supportive references are used effectively. A solid high-grade standard.

✒ Class/Homework Exercises

1. In your opinion, what is the dominant mood in 'After great pain, a formal feeling comes'? Is it one of depression, sadness or acceptance? Refer closely to the text in your answer.
2. In your view, which metaphor in the poem best conveys a sense of deep depression? Briefly explain your choice.

⊙ Points to Consider

- **Intense exploration of depression and psychological suffering.**
- **Effective use of vivid imagery, personification and serious tone.**
- **Disturbing mood throughout is solemn and sombre.**
- **Ambiguous, open-ended conclusion.**

Sample Leaving Cert Questions on Dickinson's Poetry

1. 'Emily Dickinson's unique poetic style is perfectly suited to the extraordinary experiences which she explores in her poems.' Do you agree with this assessment of Dickinson's poetry? Support your answer with suitable reference to the poems by Dickinson on your course.

2. 'Dickinson's exploration of profound life experiences is effectively conveyed through her innovative style.' Discuss this statement, supporting your answer with reference to the poetry of Emily Dickinson on your course.

3. 'A dark, eccentric vision is at the heart of Emily Dickinson's most dramatic poems.' Discuss this view, supporting the points you make with reference to the poems by Dickinson on your course.

How do I organise my answer?

(Sample question 1)

'Emily Dickinson's unique poetic style is perfectly suited to the extraordinary experiences which she explores in her poems.' Do you agree with this assessment of Dickinson's poetry? Support your answer with suitable reference to the poems by Dickinson on your course.

Sample Plan 1

Intro: *(Stance: agree with viewpoint in the question)* Dickinson is an original voice who addresses abstract subject matter, such as states of consciousness, hope, death and the relationship between nature and human nature. Her energetic style is in keeping with the intensity of her experiences.

Point 1: *(Positive approach in keeping with spontaneous enthusiastic tone)* '"Hope" is the thing with feathers' – metaphorical language reflects the small bird's presence to illustrate and highlight various aspects of hope and human resilience.

Point 2: *(Evocative language matches startling sense of self-awareness)* Dramatic atmospheres in 'I felt a Funeral, in my Brain' and 'I Heard a Fly buzz—when I died'. Surreal imagery, haunting aural effects and fragmented rhythms effectively convey disorientation and powerlessness.

Understanding the Prescribed Poetry Question

Marks are awarded using the PCLM Marking Scheme: P = 15; C = 15; L = 15; M = 5 Total = 50

- **P** (Purpose = 15 marks) refers to the set question and is the launch pad for the answer. This involves engaging with all aspects of the question. Both theme and language must be addressed, although not necessarily equally.

- **C** (Coherence = 15 marks) refers to the organisation of the developed response and the use of accurate, relevant quotation. Paragraphing is essential.

- **L** (Language = 15 marks) refers to the student's skill in controlling language throughout the answer.

- **M** (Mechanics = 5 marks) refers to spelling and grammar.

- Although no specific number of poems is required, students usually discuss at least 3 or 4 in their written responses.

- Aim for at least 800 words, to be completed within 45–50 minutes.

NOTE

In keeping with the PCLM approach, the student has to take a stance by agreeing, disagreeing or partially agreeing with the statement that:

– **Dickinson's unique poetic style** (condensed poetic forms, compressed language, unconventional punctuation, broken rhythms, haunting aural effects, unsettling humour, intriguing perspectives, insightful reflection, vivid dramatization, surreal imagery, quirky precise details, etc.)

… is perfectly suited to the exploration of:

– **her extraordinary experiences** (hope/despair, loss, death/afterlife, consciousness/disorientation, profound reactions to the natural world, etc.)

Point 3: *(Unusual view of the natural world in line with off-beat dramatization)* The poet's strangely realistic view of nature evident in 'A Bird came down the Walk'. Use of odd, precise details, onomatopoeic language and comic moments enhance the reader's understanding of Dickinson's attitude.

Point 4: *(Playful poetic voice enhances the ecstatic portrayal of nature)* Extended metaphor of drunkenness to reflect the poet's celebration of nature in 'I taste a liquor never brewed' reveals an idiosyncratic sense of humour. Strikingly imaginative images, forceful rhythms and enthusiastic tones all echo the poet's response to natural beauty.

Conclusion: Condensed poetic forms, compressed syntax and daring language use is entirely appropriate to Dickinson's insightful reflections and dramatisations. Readers can engage more immediately with the intensity of the poet's heightened experiences.

Sample Paragraph: Point 2

In both 'I felt a Funeral, in my Brain' and 'I heard a Fly buzz—when I died', Dickinson creates a disturbing account of the sensation of dying. The two poems are dramatic, with a central speaker experiencing death through terrifying images. I thought the poet's style is perfectly in keeping with this alarming subject in 'I felt a Funeral', especially her presentation of the 'Mourners' who keep 'treading' as the coffin is lowered – ' I dropped down, and down'. Repetition – the unreal drum 'beating—beating' – and short, broken phrasing emphasised the feeling of helplessness. Dickinson's vivid imagery and sounds add to the feeling of being overpowered. There is a more absurd atmosphere in 'I heard a Fly buzz'. The exaggerated scene seems distorted, particularly when the insignificant insect became the centre of attention, an 'uncertain stumbling Buzz'. The broken sentences also conveyed the confusion of the scene. The ending stops abruptly, 'I could not see to see', a line suggesting the dreadful frustration and struggle, a desperation for clarity.

EXAMINER'S COMMENT

As part of a full examination essay, this is a clear personal response that addresses the question directly. The sustained focus on Dickinson's language use is aptly supported with very effective use of quotation. Both poems were treated succinctly and included some thoughtful discussion. Well-controlled expression added to the quality of the response. Grade H1.

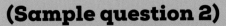

(Sample question 2)

'Dickinson's exploration of profound life experiences is effectively conveyed through her innovative style.' Discuss this statement, supporting your answer with reference to the poetry of Emily Dickinson on your course.

NOTE

In keeping with the PCLM approach, the student has to take a stance by agreeing, disagreeing or partially agreeing with the statement that:

- **Dickinson's exploration of profound life experiences** (loneliness/ depression, death, mental anguish, joy, appreciation of life/ relationships, deep response to the world of nature, etc.)

... is conveyed through:

- **her innovative style** (disruptive perspectives, innovative syntax, surreal sequences, dynamic verbs, colloquial language, memorable sound effects, unusual imagery, extended metaphor, dramatic personification, subversive humour.)

Sample Plan 2

Intro: *(Stance: agree with viewpoint in the question)* Dickinson – looks to understand death, mental anguish and intensely vivid moments of joy. Through her inventive approach to language, she invites readers to join her as she tells 'the truth, but tells it slant'.

Point 1: *(The shock of intense self-consciousness – powerful language use)* 'After great pain, a formal feeling comes' – surreal sequence, alliteration, unusual syntax and monosyllabic words create a vivid exploration of disorientation.

Point 2: *(Original, vibrant poetic voice – deep appreciation of nature)* 'I could bring You Jewels—had I a mind to' – unusual appreciation of nature's simple joys. Chooses a simple, modest meadow flower ('But this little Blaze/Flickering to itself'). Alliteration, onomatopoeia, a run-on line and the monosyllabic broad vowel sound describe the strong impact of the flower. The dynamic verb 'Flickering' suggests its lively movement.

Point 3: *(Intensity of emotion – fresh comparative effects)* 'I taste a liquor never brewed' – another poem delighting in the natural world's everyday delights. Startling extended metaphor of stages of intoxication irrepressibly conveys the delirious pleasures of nature, ('When landlords turn the drunken Bee/out of the Foxglove's door'). Unconventional use of capital letters evokes a fantastical landscape.

Point 4: *(Unique poetic style – confronting fear and intrigue)* 'A narrow Fellow in the Grass' – contrasting description of the brutal, unpredictable aspects of nature. Personification increases the surreal unnerving quality, 'the Grass divides', the bogland has a 'Floor'. The discomforting experience and extreme fright conveyed in the cryptic phrase, 'Zero at the Bone', alarming readers.

Conclusion: Dickinson's disconcerting use of humour, unconventional punctuation, dramatic use of personification coupled with unusual imagery disrupt the reader's conventional awareness of life experiences.

Sample Paragraph: Point 1

Dickinson's poem, 'After great pain, a formal feeling comes', uses a surreal series of images to examine how emotional numbness, 'a formal feeling', often follows a difficult experience, 'great pain'. Emphatic alliteration ('formal feeling') underlines the paralysis of emotion into which a person sinks after trauma. There is a disturbing sense of losing control as the 'Feet, mechanical, go round'. The line suggests a complete lack of purpose in the body's movements. Unusual syntax mimics the awkward movement of an inanimate puppet figure. The bridge between sanity and insanity, 'A Wooden way', is breaking, leaving the helpless individual incapable of rational thought – 'regardless grown'. Monosyllables describe this nightmarish experience of sinking into inertia, 'First—Chill'. The poet creates a vivid sense of the descent into despair ('then the letting go—). The final dash marks the disorientating awareness of the swirling 'Snow'. By this stage, all sense of direction has been lost. Dickinson is exploring the numbing effects of tragedy.

EXAMINER'S COMMENT

As part of a full essay answer to question 2, this is an impressive top-grade standard that shows close engagement with Dickinson's poetry. Incisive discussion of the poet's curious style (sound effects, syntax, punctuation, etc.) is also commendable. Excellent use of quotations and the expression is exceptionally good throughout (e.g. 'the constrictive paralysis of emotion', 'disorientating awareness').

Leaving Cert Sample Essay

'Emily Dickinson's distinctly eccentric poems explore intense emotions that range from stark desolation to giddy delight.' Discuss this view, supporting your answer with reference to the poetry of Dickinson on your course.

Sample Essay

1. Emily Dickinson writes poems about intense emotions and experiences that everyone has. These can go from stark desolation to giddy delight. She always uses language in a very strange way, especially using capital letters, personification and a weird order of words. Her poems can be very eccentric and depressing, but she also writes with a giddy sense of humour at certain times. I will examine four poems, 'There's a certain Slant of light', 'I felt a Funeral, in my Brain', '"Hope" is the thing with feathers' and 'A narrow Fellow in the Grass'.

2. In writing 'There's a certain Slant of light' she uses a capital letter to draw attention to the word 'Slant'. Dickinson sets the scene in a church in wintertime which is dramatic in itself. Their's a religious setting immediately and this sets the scene for being mainly about death

and how we all have a relationship with God. The low angle of the winter's afternoon sunlight is like a warning from God. It 'oppresses' her just like the 'Cathedral Tunes' (which is also written in capital letters). This is unusual because light and hymns can normally be expected to lift people up, they do not depress them. But Dickinson is really pointing out the fear people sometimes have because God judges them and has great power over them, 'Heavenly Hurt'. God punishes. 'An imperial affliction' means the whole world is afraid, so 'The Landscape listens'. In this poem Dickinson presents a very original way of looking at life and God. She uses dashes to make the poem extremely dramatic and full of dread.

3. 'I felt a Funeral, in my Brain' also deals with terror. Dickinson uses nightmarish images in which she imagines the experience of her own burial, 'mourners to and fro'. She shows her helplessness by making references to their feet, 'threading, threading'. This is a haunting sound affect. She also imagines hearing a funeral drum 'beating, beating'. This is a continuous sound – like a pounding beat. It's also a very sad scene of desolation with the rhythms of sorrowful mourners which just adds to the poet's panic. A stark image of a coffin being put into a grave is described. 'And I dropped down and down'. The poet writes in short bursts of a fragmented style bringing out the nightmare atmosphere. She creates fear, the feeling of being a powerless victim confined in the coffin, 'solitary', lowered down into her own grave. This surreal scene is dramatic. It sends shock waves when we imagine what is happening as Dickinson describes the traumatic protrayal of an actual burial.

4. '"Hope" is the thing with feathers' is a poem full of giddy delight. The bird suggests hope, as a positive symbol high above the world's stark desolation. This is another of Dickinson's eccentric poems. It is like the dove in the bible story of Noah's Ark and the Flood. In this bible story, a dove let Noah know that the waters were going down and people would be able to survive. Therefore, the bird is 'sweetest' because it would of always brought good news.

5. In the poem, 'A Narrow Fellow in the Grass', Dickinson uses the voice of a young boy to tell a story of surprise and fear. She mixes up the order of words in a very eccentric way, 'His sudden notice is'. This shows the effect the unexpected snake had on the boy. This event is dramaticed. The setting is the strange field, the event is the meeting of the snake and the 'Barefoot' boy, the action is the snake 'Unbraiding in the sun'. The boy is 'stooping to secure it'. I thought the image of the snake as 'A spotted shaft' was very unusual. It suggested a bolt of lightning or a hidden weapon, both conveying danger. Nature is filled with mystery. I also thought the personification in the line 'The Grass divides as with a Comb'

EMILY DICKINSON

INDICATIVE MATERIAL

- **Dickinson's distinctly eccentric poems** (inventive style, vivid/surreal imagery, dramatic personification, fragmented syntax, unconventional punctuation, unusual settings, unnerving sense of humour, etc.)

... explore:

- **intense emotions from stark desolation to giddy delight** (mental anguish, death, loneliness and depression, moments of surprise, and joy, love and loss, profound reactions to the natural world, etc.)

was very unusual. I could imagine the snake slithering along, the only movement is the grass parting as if someone was combing their hair. I thought this was surreal but Dickinson is also celebrating nature.

6. Dickinson's poems vary from terror of dying to intense feelings about the natural world. She looks at everything 'Slant', whether it is winter sunshine, hymns, a little bird or a snake. She made me think twice about nature and death. She also writes about the beauty and mystery of nature. Dickinson's language is eccentric. She is by far the most unusual of the poets we have studied.

(760 words)

EXAMINER'S COMMENT

A solid mid-grade standard, with reasonably focused engagement and analysis – particularly in paragraphs 2, 3 and 5. More emphasis on the element of 'giddy delight' would be expected. Paragraph 4 is particularly slight and lacking in developed discussion. Expression varies greatly from fluent to awkward and the essay included several mechanical errors ('Their's', 'affect', 'protrayal', 'would of', 'dramaticed'). Some personal engagement evident at times and the essay was rounded off well in the concluding paragraph.

GRADE: H3
P = 11/15
C = 11/15
L = 10/15
M = 4/5
Total = 36/50

◠◠ Revision Overview

'"Hope" is the thing with feathers'
Theme of hope, extended metaphor, unusual punctuation, reflective, optimistic tones.

'There's a certain Slant of light'
Reflection on human mortality and our relationship with God, personification, fragmented rhythm and style add to unease and pessimism.

'I felt a Funeral, in my Brain'
Shocking introspection on loss and death, first-person perspective, onomatopoeia and repetition.

'A Bird came down the Walk'
Bemused observation of nature, personification, rich imagery and sound effects.

'I heard a Fly buzz—when I died'
Dramatic exploration of death and the afterlife, surreal, use of contrast and symbols add to feeling of helplessness.

'The Soul has Bandaged moments'
Unsettling examination of nature of consciousness, central conflict, changing moods.

'I could bring You Jewels—had I a mind to'
Treatment of relationship, celebration of nature, vivid imagery, optimistic tone.

'A narrow Fellow in the Grass'
Danger and beauty in nature, use of persona, colloquial language, concluding tone of terror.

'I taste a liquor never brewed'
Joyful celebration of nature, extended metaphor, subversive humour.

'After great pain, a formal feeling comes'
Disquieting exploration of depression, rich imagery, sombre tone, ambiguous ending.

🗨 Last Words

'The Dickinson dashes are an integral part of her method and style ... and cannot be translated ... without deadening the wonderful naked voltage of the poems.'
Ted Hughes

(On her determination to hide secrets) 'The price she paid was that of appearing to posterity as perpetually unfinished and wilfully eccentric.'
Philip Larkin

'The Brain—is wider than the Sky—
The Brain is deeper than the sea—'
Emily Dickinson

JOY/HOPE NATURE RELIGION/SPIRITUALITY SUFFERING DEATH MEANING OF LIFE

John Keats
1795–1821

'I have loved the principle of beauty in all things.'

John Keats is one of the most widely recognised and loved English poets. Born in London in 1795, he was not expected to have poetic aspirations, considering his ordinary background. Nevertheless, from his boyhood he had an acute sense of beauty and chose to make a career as a poet.

Keats is best known for his series of odes, filled with lush images of nature. These display an assured poetic instinct and a remarkable ability to appeal powerfully to the senses by the brilliance of his diction. Many of his poems are noted more for their strength of feeling than for thought, often reflecting the poet's intense inner conflicts.

In 1818, Keats met 18-year-old Frances (Fanny) Brawne and a close friendship developed between them. In 1819, they became engaged and he dedicated his sonnet 'Bright Star' to her. However, the relationship was cut short by the effects of the poet's consumption (tuberculosis). As his medical condition worsened, Keats was advised to move to a warmer climate and in November 1820, he arrived in Rome. Unfortunately, his health continued to deteriorate and he died there on 23 February 1821.

Investigate Further

To find out more about John Keats, or to hear readings of his poems, you could do a search some useful websites, such as YouTube, BBC Poetry, poetryfoundation.org and poetryarchive.org, or access additional material on this page of your eBook.

Prescribed Poems

1 'To One Who Has Been Long in City Pent'
This Italian sonnet describes the delights of the English countryside while reflecting poignantly on the passing of time. Keats disliked living in the city and was firmly convinced about nature's restorative power. **Page 108**

2 'Ode to a Nightingale'
Unhappy with the real world, Keats attempts to escape into the ideal by entering the mysterious world of the nightingale's song. The poem begins by describing the song of an actual nightingale, but the bird quickly becomes a symbol of the immortality of nature. In the end, the poet is left with an intense self-awareness and returns to reality. **Page 111**

3 'On First Looking into Chapman's Homer' (OL)
This Petrarchan sonnet conveys the sheer sense of excitement and wonder which Keats found after reading the ancient works of Homer. The poet uses dramatic imagery to describe the revelation of Chapman's English translation comparing it to an astronomer who has discovered a new planet, or to Cortez's first sighting of the Pacific Ocean. **Page 118**

4 'Ode on a Grecian Urn'
Keats's famous ode explores the paradoxical relationship between the immortal world of art and transient reality. The enigmatic Grecian urn excites his imagination. It is a powerful symbol of timeless perfection which provokes by silently posing questions. **Page 122**

5 'When I Have Fears That I May Cease to Be'
In this Shakespearean sonnet, Keats expresses his fear of dying young before he has time to fulfil his potential. He also reflects on the transience of life, love and fame. The poem is a good example of Keats's use of archaic language and his distinctive musical sound effects. **Page 128**

6 'La Belle Dame Sans Merci' (OL)
A highly dramatic ballad set in the medieval era, this mysterious poem tells the tragic tale of a lovesick knight and his 'Beautiful Lady without Mercy'. The haunting story of love and loss in a bleak wintry landscape is dominated by images of death. **Page 131**

7 'To Autumn'
Characteristically filled with wonderful images and sensuous detail, this celebrated poem describes the beauty of nature, highlighting autumn's abundant fruitfulness and ultimate decline. This is achieved through Keats's rich language, personification and evocative sound effects. **Page 137**

8 'Bright Star, Would I Were Steadfast as Thou Art'
Another Shakespearean sonnet focusing primarily on the differences between eternity and mortality. As in many of his well-known odes, Keats is fascinated by the idea of a perfect, unchanging world – but is forced to accept that his dream is impossible. **Page 141**

(OL) indicates poems that are also prescribed for the Ordinary Level course.

1

To One Who Has Been Long in City Pent

Title: closely echoes a line from John Milton's epic poem, 'Paradise Lost': 'As one who long in populous city pent'.

To one who has been long in city pent,
   'Tis very sweet to look into the fair
   And open face of heaven, – to breathe a prayer
Full in the smile of the blue firmament.
Who is more happy, when, with heart's content,   5
   Fatigued he sinks into some pleasant lair
   Of wavy grass, and reads a debonair
And gentle tale of love and languishment?
Returning home at evening, with an ear
   Catching the notes of Philomel, – an eye   10
Watching the sailing cloudlet's bright career,
   He mourns that day so soon has glided by:
E'en like the passage of an angel's tear
   That falls through the clear ether silently.

pent: confined, imprisoned.

firmament: sky.

lair: sheltered hideaway.

debonair: pleasing, sophisticated.
languishment: yearning, desire.

Philomel: legendary nightingale.
cloudlet: small cloud.
career: movement.

ether: upper air, atmosphere.

👤 Personal Response

1. Describe the contrasting moods in the poem's octave and sestet. Support your answer with suitable reference to the poem.
2. Comment on Keats's use of sound effects throughout the sonnet in describing the natural world.
3. In your opinion, how relevant is this poem to modern life? Briefly explain your response.

👁 Critical Literacy

Written in the summer of 1816 when Keats was 21 and a medical student in London, this poem follows the Petrarchan (or Italian) sonnet structure. The octave (first eight lines) describes the delights of the English countryside while the sestet (last six lines) reflects poignantly on the passing day.

The opening section of the octave immediately reveals Keats's preference for nature over city life. Line 1 is marked by an insistent rhythm and a series of heavy monosyllables which echo the dull monotony of urban routine: 'To one who has been long in city pent'. The emphatic verb 'pent' is particularly effective in highlighting Keats's

frustrated sense of confinement. But we soon see his obvious excitement as he considers the 'fair' countryside, personifying its natural beauty as the 'open face of heaven' (**line 3**). The energetic run-on lines and celebratory tone ("Tis very sweet') add to the upbeat mood. For Keats, however, there is more to the unspoilt country than just its beauty and sense of release. He also finds a reverential kind of spiritual peace when he is able to 'breathe a prayer' and reaffirm the joys of existence in such a natural setting. This worshipful tone is reinforced in various religious references to 'heaven' and the 'firmament', a biblical term often used to describe the sky.

Keats continues to praise nature's virtues in **lines 5–8** by appealing directly to the reader's likely sympathy for 'happy' country living and the joy of relaxing to one's 'heart's content'. He illustrates this with the image of finding a 'pleasant lair' and sinking into the 'wavy grass' to read a 'gentle tale of love and languishment'. Characteristically, **Keats's musical language is filled with rich sibilant, assonant and alliterative sounds**. At ease in this tranquil rural landscape, he can enjoy reading a favourite 'tale of love'. This defines his notion of perfect contentment. As always, the most important Romantic qualities of Keats's poetry are the imagination, a love of nature, and the sense of beauty to which a strangeness has been added.

The **sestet**, however, is largely dominated by a **tender sense of loss**. As in so many of his poems, Keats can only escape from the real world for a limited time. Returning home in the evening, he hears the nightingale singing ('the notes of Philomel'). This elevated reference to a tragic mythical figure who was turned into a bird reflects the pervading atmosphere of serenity. The imagery Keats uses is equally mellow. He observes 'the sailing cloudlet's bright career' and 'mourns that day so soon has glided by'. Again, broad assonant vowels enhance the sense of melancholy. Does his brief visit to the countryside symbolise the transience of all human life? **Lines 13–14**, comparing the onset of evening to the falling of 'an angel's tear' are particularly evocative. There is a clear suggestion of some underlying sense of a divine presence existing within nature's mysterious beauty.

Keats's journey from confinement in the city to finding peace in the quiet meadows and finally to **reflective nostalgia** all takes place over a single day. The concise sonnet form is ideally suited to the poet's meditative subject matter. Readers are left with a thought-provoking poem whose deft use of metaphorical language illustrates the poet's heartfelt views on nature's restorative power and human mortality.

✒ Writing About the Poem

'The rejuvenating force of nature is a central theme in many of Keats's poems.' Discuss this statement in relation to 'To One Who Has Been Long in City Pent', using suitable reference to the text.

Sample Paragraph

In 'To One Who Has Been Long in City Pent', the poet describes the experience of a city-dweller who visits the countryside. He is cheered up at once as he breathes in the open atmosphere. Keats uses simple childlike language – ''Tis very sweet'. The sight of the clear blue sky fills his heart with joy. I felt that he almost discovered God in nature which he personifies – 'face of heaven'. This image suggests a personal relationship between Keats and nature. His mood is brighter under the 'blue firmament' where he can lie on a bed of soft 'wavy grass' and reads a sweet romantic story. At that moment he feels as if he is the happiest man on earth. Keats's language is more positive when he describes the rejuvenating force of nature – 'more happy', 'gentle tale of love'. In the end, he must face reality again. But thanks to nature, he is prepared for city life. He has happy memories of a day that has 'glided by'.

EXAMINER'S COMMENT

This is a competent response which includes some worthwhile discussion of the poet's themes and language use. Comments on stylistic features, such as contrast and mood, are well-supported by apt reference: 'Keats's language is more positive when he describes the rejuvenating force of nature'. There is evidence of genuine engagement with the poem, for example in the last sentence. However, the expression is awkward at times: 'His mood is so much brighter under the "blue firmament" where he can lie on a bed of soft "wavy grass" and reads a sweet romantic story'. Overall, however, a solid high-grade standard.

✒ Class/Homework Exercises

1. 'John Keats's poetry focuses some of life's mysterious elements.' Discuss this view, with particular reference to the poem 'To One Who Has Been Long in City Pent'.

2. 'Keats often makes effective use of metaphors and personification in his poems.' To what extent is this true of 'To One Who Has Been Long in City Pent'? Support your answer with suitable reference to the poem.

⊙ Points to Consider

- **Nature's power to delight, life's transience, the joy of literature.**
- **Varying moods and atmospheres.**
- **Effective personification, vivid images and metaphors.**
- **Musical sound effects, alliteration, broad assonant vowels.**
- **Complementary use of octave and sestet creates unity.**

2 Ode to a Nightingale

Title: the nightingale has always been considered a secretive bird known for singing very beautifully. It is also associated with romantic love.

I

My heart aches, and a drowsy numbness pains
  My sense, as though of hemlock I had drunk,
Or emptied some dull opiate to the drains
  One minute past, and Lethe-wards had sunk:
'Tis not through envy of thy happy lot,   5
  But being too happy in thine happiness, –
    That thou, light-winged Dryad of the trees,
      In some melodious plot
Of beechen green, and shadows numberless,
  Singest of summer in full-throated ease.   10

hemlock: poisonous plant.

opiate: sleep-inducing drug.
Lethe-wards: forgetfulness. (In Greek mythology, the dead drank from the River Lethe to forget their human lives.)

Dryad: beautiful woodland maiden; tree nymph.

II

O, for a draught of vintage! that hath been
  Cooled a long age in the deep-delved earth,
Tasting of Flora and the country green,
  Dance, and Provençal song, and sunburnt mirth!
O for a beaker full of the warm South,   15
  Full of the true, the blushful Hippocrene,
    With beaded bubbles winking at the brim,
      And purple-stained mouth;
That I might drink, and leave the world unseen,
  And with thee fade away into the forest dim: 20

draught of vintage: drink of good wine.

Flora: Roman goddess of flowers.
Provençal: south-eastern France.
South: the warm Mediterranean.
blushful Hippocrene: red wine of the Greek gods, associated with inspiration.

III

Fade far away, dissolve, and quite forget
  What thou among the leaves hast never known,
The weariness, the fever, and the fret
  Here, where men sit and hear each other groan;
Where palsy shakes a few, sad, last gray hairs,   25
  Where youth grows pale, and spectre-thin, and dies;
    Where but to think is to be full of sorrow
      And leaden-eyed despairs,
Where Beauty cannot keep her lustrous eyes,
  Or new Love pine at them beyond tomorrow.   30

palsy: wasting disease.

spectre-thin: ghostly.

lustrous: radiant, bright.

pine: yearn for.

IV

Away! away! for I will fly to thee,
　　Not charioted by Bacchus and his pards,
But on the viewless wings of Poesy,
　　Though the dull brain perplexes and retards:
Already with thee! tender is the night,　　　　　　　　　35
　　And haply the Queen-Moon is on her throne,
　　　Clustered around by all her starry Fays;
　　　　But here there is no light,
　　Save what from heaven is with the breezes blown
　　　Through verdurous glooms and winding mossy ways.　　40

V

I cannot see what flowers are at my feet,
　　Nor what soft incense hangs upon the boughs,
But, in embalmed darkness, guess each sweet
　　Wherewith the seasonable month endows
The grass, the thicket, and the fruit-tree wild;　　　　　45
　　White hawthorn, and the pastoral eglantine;
　　　Fast fading violets covered up in leaves;
　　　　And mid-May's eldest child,
　　The coming musk-rose, full of dewy wine,
　　　The murmurous haunt of flies on summer eves.　　　50

VI

Darkling I listen; and, for many a time
　　I have been half in love with easeful Death,
Called him soft names in many a mused rhyme,
　　To take into the air my quiet breath;
Now more than ever seems it rich to die,　　　　　　　55
　　To cease upon the midnight with no pain,
　　　While thou art pouring forth thy soul abroad
　　　　In such an ecstasy!
　　Still wouldst thou sing, and I have ears in vain –
　　　To thy high requiem become a sod.　　　　　　　60

VII

Thou wast not born for death, immortal Bird!
　　No hungry generations tread thee down;
The voice I hear this passing night was heard
　　In ancient days by emperor and clown:
Perhaps the self-same song that found a path　　　　　65
　　Through the sad heart of Ruth, when, sick for home,
　　　She stood in tears amid the alien corn;
　　　　The same that oft-times hath
　　Charmed magic casements, opening on the foam
　　　Of perilous seas, in faery lands forlorn.　　　　　70

Bacchus: god of wine in Roman legend.
pards: leopards were used to draw Bacchus's chariot.
Poesy: poetry.

Queen-Moon: Diana, the Roman moon-goddess.
Fays: fairy attendants.

verdurous: grassy green.

incense: pleasant fragrance.

embalmed: heavy-scented.

endows: enriches.

eglantine: sweet briar, a beautiful wild rose.

Darkling: in the darkness.

mused: bemused, uncertain.

requiem: liturgical funeral song.
sod: clump of earth; grassy soil.

emperor and clown: the highest and lowest in society.

Ruth: Biblical character who was exiled.

casements: windows.
faery: fairy (early spelling).
forlorn: abandoned, despondent.

VIII

Forlorn! the very word is like a bell
  To toll me back from thee to my sole self!
Adieu! the fancy cannot cheat so well
  As she is fam'd to do, deceiving elf.
Adieu! adieu! thy plaintive anthem fades   75
  Past the near meadows, over the still stream,
    Up the hillside; and now 'tis buried deep
      In the next valley-glades:
Was it a vision, or a waking dream?
    Fled is that music: – Do I wake or sleep?   80

toll: call.
sole self: personal loneliness.
fancy: imagination.

plaintive anthem: bittersweet song.

'in faery lands forlorn'

Personal Response

1. Comment on the effectiveness of Keats's language throughout the second stanza in conveying his longing to escape from reality.
2. Select two memorable images from the poem that you find particularly effective. Explain your choice in each case.
3. Describe Keats's mood in the poem's final stanza.

Critical Literacy

'Ode to a Nightingale' is considered one of the finest poems in English literature and reveals John Keats's highest imaginative powers. The beautiful song of the nightingale fills him with a desire to escape from the cares of life. This highly passionate ode illustrates Keats's intense perception of human experience. Written in a single day in May 1819, the poem explores themes of transience, mortality and nature. It is a typical Romantic ode which emphasises powerful emotions and the importance of imagination. Keats also makes effective use of synaesthesia (the mixing of sense impressions) which is a characteristic of his rich imagery.

The ode begins with an expression of the poet's acute self-awareness and his deep desire to escape. The initial mood of the opening stanza combines ecstatic joy and pain – almost to the point of completely dulling the senses. Keats declares his own brooding heartache. He feels 'a drowsy numbness' that he associates with hemlock or opium. Sibilant sounds echo this wistful trance-like feeling. Overwhelmed by the rich music of the nightingale's song, **he appears to be in a meditative dream**, attempting to identify himself with the bird. Heavy alliterative 'd' and 'n' sounds add to the weary tone. Monosyllables ('pains', 'drunk', 'drains') create a slow, deliberate rhythm, reflecting the poet's dejected mood. Lines 9–10 focus directly on the nightingale and are less lethargic. The mood lightens here, in contrast to the earlier exhausted atmosphere. Vowel sounds sharpen and the sibilance becomes noticeably more energetic ('Singest of summer', 'full-throated ease').

In stanza two, Keats longs for the oblivion of alcohol, calling for 'a draught of vintage' that tastes of 'the country green'. The exclamatory 'O' emphasises his sense of yearning. In his wildly imaginative state, the wine tastes of the French Mediterranean 'Dance, and Provençal song'. But the poet longs for more than just being carefree. He also wishes the wine to inspire him when he refers to the 'Hippocrene', a sacred fountain that was said to bring poetic inspiration to those who drank from it. There is **an abundance of vigorous imagery** throughout these lines and an atmosphere of warmth predominates. The phrase 'sunburnt mirth' combines the idea of sunshine with the joy of young people celebrating. Repeated references to dancing and the 'blushful' wine with its 'beaded bubbles winking at the brim' are enriched by vibrant onomatopoeic sounds. Keats's compressed images often overlap. The senses of sight, hearing and touch are closely associated with tasting the wine as a pleasurable escape from harsh reality.

Ironically, the poet's awareness of the real world makes it impossible for him to 'Fade far away'. Much of the third stanza is preoccupied with the human condition at its worst: the 'weariness, the fever, and the fret' of everyday life is illustrated with a **graphic image of physical suffering** where 'youth grows pale, and spectre-thin, and dies'. Assonance emphasises this tragic view of illness and decay. Keats sees time itself as the greatest of all sorrows, worse than any terrible disease. Everything decays and 'Beauty cannot keep her lustrous eyes'. Only the nightingale's singing transcends mortality.

In stanza four, the poet orders the nightingale to fly away, and he will follow, not through being intoxicated ('Not charioted by Bacchus'), but through poetry, which will give him 'viewless wings'. As Keats imagines himself joining the nightingale's magical world, the **atmosphere becomes dreamlike**: 'tender is the night'. The personified 'Queen-Moon' is surrounded by 'her starry Fays'. This majestic image is typical of the exaggerated senses which heighten the poet's fantasy. An underlying air of excitement pervades the darkness. The imaginary woodland setting is mysterious with the heavenly breeze blowing through 'verdurous glooms and winding mossy ways'. Soft sibilance and consonant 'm' sound effects are used here to further invigorate the poet's ecstatic mood.

Stanza five consists of a single flowing sentence describing Keats's close union with the nightingale. A vivid impression of smell is created to serve his exuberant imagination. The poet becomes acutely aware of the sweet fragrances around him. Yet even here, it is impossible to avoid the presence of death within the 'embalmed darkness'. He lists the intoxicating forest smells of fresh grass, fruit-trees and flowers. **Aural imagery enhances the magical quality of the visual details**. Recurring sibilant effects emphasise the beauty of 'White hawthorn', 'pastoral eglantine' and 'Fast fading violets'. In his visionary journey, Keats makes remarkable use of sensory language – and particularly elegant assonance – to create a truly languid atmosphere: 'The murmurous haunt of flies on summer eves.'

Much of the focus in the sixth stanza is on **escaping painful reality through death**. Keats again addresses the nightingale directly: 'Darkling I listen'. He then makes a somewhat unsettling revelation that he has often been 'half in love' with the idea of dying. His use of personification ('Called him soft names') implies that death has seemed like a friend, offering comfort to the poet. He feels that the present moment would be the ideal time to ease into a new spiritual life now that the bird is singing in 'such an ecstasy'. The enthusiastic tone suddenly changes, however, as Keats realises the irony that the bird would continue singing while the poet's lifeless body lies buried in the earth.

Throughout stanza seven, he continues to contrast the nightingale (as a symbol of immortality) with his own mortal self. **The forceful tone seems almost celebratory**: 'Thou wast not born for death'. Indeed, the bird's stirring voice has always been heard, by ancient 'emperor and clown'. He considers how such birdsong once consoled the lonely biblical figure of Ruth when she 'stood in tears amid the alien corn'. Always the Romantic poet, Keats traces the nightingale's comforting song back to 'faery lands', both magical and tragic. For him, the beauty of nature has fascinated humanity throughout generations.

At the start of stanza eight, the emphatic word 'Forlorn' rings like a bell to wake Keats from his deep preoccupation back to his 'sole self'. The nightingale has ceased to be a symbol and is again the actual bird the poet heard at the outset. As Keats emerges from his hypnotic state to say farewell, he realises that the bird's song (even if it is immortal) will not always be within his range of hearing: 'thy plaintive anthem fades/Past the near meadows, over the still stream'. This marks a crucial development for the poet, who until now has yearned to leave the physical world and follow the nightingale into a higher realm. The bird flies farther away from him, however, becoming a faint memory and **Keats laments that his imagination has failed him**. In the last two lines, he wonders whether he has had a true insight or whether he has been daydreaming: 'Was it a vision, or a waking dream?'

Throughout the ode, Keats has been caught between a yearning to escape into a permanent ideal world and an acceptance of transient reality. But has he been changed by his visionary experience? Critics have disagreed about the poem's ending, so readers are left to interpret the final tone for themselves. Is it happy, hopeful, sad, excited, despairing or resigned? Only the individual reader can decide.

✒ Writing About the Poem

'Tensions and contrasts are central elements of Keats's poetry.' To what extent is this true of 'Ode to a Nightingale'? Support your answer with reference to the text of the poem.

Sample Paragraph

'Ode to a Nightingale' is structured around the poet, who is aware of his own mortality. Keats's mood is of longing, but 'not through envy'. The tension is within the poet himself. He is caught between celebrating the nightingale's 'happy lot' and wishing to be part of this ideal existence. His tone reflects this yearning – 'That I might drink ... And with thee fade away'. Keats admits to being 'half in love with easeful Death'. The mood keeps changing throughout, at times deliriously joyful when enjoying the bird singing 'In such an ecstasy'. But the poet is often downbeat – 'to think is to be full of sorrows'. While Keats returns to reality at the end and accepts that his imagination will not provide a lasting escape from life's suffering, he never seems truly at ease as the nightingale's 'plaintive anthem fades'. For me, this was the most heartbreaking moment in the poem. The last lines summed up Keats's dilemma, as if he was stranded between longing and disappointment, not even sure if the nightingale was 'a vision or a waking dream'.

EXAMINER'S COMMENT

A very assured and controlled answer that addressed both elements of the task, 'tensions' and 'contrasts'. Supportive points made excellent use of accurate quotation and reference ranging over the poem. Expression was also very impressive – fluent and varied: 'The mood keeps changing throughout, at times deliriously joyful'. The brief personal engagement, 'For me this was the most heartbreaking moment in the poem', also enhanced this successful top-grade answer.

✒ Class/Homework Exercises

1. 'A deep and disturbing sense of unhappiness often pervades Keats's poetry.' To what extent do you agree with this view of 'Ode to a Nightingale'? Support your answer with reference to the poem.
2. 'Sensuous imagery is a key feature of Keats's distinctive language use.' Discuss this statement with close reference to 'Ode to a Nightingale'.

⊙ Points to Consider

- **Themes include the conflicted nature of human life, imagination, the natural world and escapism.**
- **Contrasting tones and moods: sorrow and joy, the real and ideal.**
- **Keats's sensuous language and symbols are characteristic of the ode.**
- **Dense concentration of sense impressions and use of synaesthesia.**
- **Memorable sound effects – alliteration, assonance, sibilance.**

3

On First Looking into Chapman's Homer

Chapman: the writer George Chapman (1559–1634) who translated Homer's epic poems into English.
Homer: Greek epic poet (circa 750–650 BC); author of *The Iliad* and *The Odyssey*.

Much have I travell'd in the realms of gold,
   And many goodly states and kingdoms seen;
   Round many western islands have I been
Which bards in fealty to Apollo hold.
Oft of one wide expanse had I been told   5
   That deep-brow'd Homer ruled as his demesne;
   Yet did I never breathe its pure serene
Till I heard Chapman speak out loud and bold:
Then felt I like some watcher of the skies
   When a new planet swims into his ken;   10
Or like stout Cortez when with eagle eyes
   He star'd at the Pacific – and all his men
Looked at each other with a wild surmise –
   Silent upon a peak in Darien.

realms of gold: majestic worlds of the imagination and poetry.
goodly states: wonderful works of literature.
western islands: poems from the British Isles and Ireland.
bards in fealty to Apollo: poets dedicate their work to the Greek god of the arts.
wide expanse: undiscovered world of great literature.
deep-browed: wise; scholarly.
demesne: private kingdom.
serene: clear air.

watcher of the skies: astronomer.
ken: knowledge; understanding.
stout: fearless.
Cortez: The explorer Cortez reached Mexico in 1518. Another Spaniard, Balboa, was the first European to glimpse the Pacific Ocean in 1513.
surmise: surprise; wonder.
Darien: old name for the narrow stretch of land (now called Panama).

'He stared at the Pacific'

👤 Personal Response

1. In your opinion, what is the central theme of this poem? Support your response with reference to the text.
2. There are several striking metaphors in the octave (first eight lines) of the poem. Choose one that you consider particularly interesting and comment on its effectiveness.
3. Explain how Keats uses language to convey his feelings in the sestet (final six lines).

👁 Critical Literacy

Written in October 1816, this famous sonnet expresses the intensity of John Keats's experience while reading the translated works of Homer. For the 20-year-old Keats, there was nothing to equal the excitement of Greek poetry. To show how deeply Homer's genius affected him, Keats uses dramatic images of exploration and discovery. In a sense, the reading experience itself becomes a great voyage, leading to creative writing both for the poet and the reader.

Keats's intense love of poetry is evident from the start. He addresses the reader directly, comparing himself to a traveller who enjoys visiting exotic places. For him, reading is an adventure. The exclamatory opening lines establish his enthusiasm for literature. **Keats makes effective use of vivid comparisons, travel imagery and a vigorous tone to express his feelings**. The vivid phrase 'realms of gold' implies world riches – the power of creativity and the imagination.

Keats develops the metaphor of exploration, reflecting on the many wonderful poems ('goodly states' and 'western islands') that he has already read. In the second quatrain, he identifies the 'wide expanse' of Homer's epic works with a vast ocean. Throughout the octave, there is **an unmistakable impression of restlessness** and eager anticipation. The poet is heartfelt in his praise of Chapman whose 'loud and bold' translation of Homer's poetry allows him to enjoy its invigorating atmosphere ('pure serene').

The sense of fresh discovery brings the reader to the sonnet's volta (or change in the train of thought): 'Then felt I …' (line 9). Keats uses two similes that are both beautiful and appropriate to convey the astonishment of finally reading Homer: 'Then felt I like some watcher of the skies/When a new planet swims into his ken'. Just as the astronomer is excited to discover a newly found world among the stars, Keats is similarly thrilled to finally read the poems of Homer. The swimming metaphor is part of the many **recurring water images which add to the poem's cohesive structure**.

The second comparison used by Keats is also in keeping with the language of travel and gives the sonnet a unity of imagery that intensifies the poet's experience. He likens his reading of Chapman's translation to the Spanish conquistador Cortez and his crew first setting eyes on the Pacific Ocean. Keats emphasises Cortez's 'eagle eyes' (line 11). **This alliterative phrase emphasises the visual experience**, reflecting the wonder felt by the explorer who is stunned by a vast landscape of beauty.

Cortez's men stand in silent amazement, looking 'at each other with a wild surmise'. The emotion is carefully controlled, with a sureness of diction and sound. The sense of openness to a wide sea of wonder is suggested by long vowels ('wild', 'surmise', 'silent'), tapering off to hushed astonishment in the weak syllables of the final words, 'upon a peak in Darien'. There is no need for overstatement as Keats's **restrained ending** leaves the reader with a lingering sense of breathtaking exhilaration.

All through the sestet, run-on lines intensify the rhythm to convey a wide-sweeping sense of movement – of planets circling the heavens, and ships circumnavigating the earth. In this way, Keats makes the subtle point that discovery is part of what makes us all human. The **poem typifies much of his Romantic style**. Internal rhymes and sibilant sound effects give it a rich, sensuous, musical quality. But primarily, this dramatic sonnet expresses the power of Keats's personal experience and reveals his passion for poetry.

✒ Writing About the Poem

'Keats makes effective use of the Petrarchan sonnet form in "On First Looking into Chapman's Homer".' Discuss this view, using suitable reference to the poem.

Sample Paragraph

'On First Looking into Chapman's Homer' is a Petrarchan sonnet, divided into an octave and a sestet, with a controlled rhyme scheme. In the first eight lines, Keats presents the idea of his lifelong desire to read the poetry of 'deep-brow'd Homer'. The tone is emphatic: 'Much have I travell'd in the realms of gold'. He uses various travel images to explain his love of books, such as 'Round many western islands have I been'. In line nine, the word 'Then' marks the break or turn in his thought and the sestet records his delight after discovering Chapman's English version of Homer's poems. This is a characteristic of sonnets and Keats develops the subject of his response to Homer through the use of vibrant imagery and similes which convey his surprise. Comparing himself to a successful astronomer who finds 'a new planet' and the explorer Cortez adds energy.

The sensation of joy is evident in the final image, 'Silent upon a peak in Darien'. Keats uses the condensed sonnet form very effectively to convey the intensity of his feelings – and I could relate to this.

JOHN KEATS

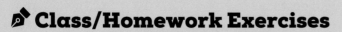 Class/Homework Exercises

1. Trace the progress of thought in 'On First Looking into Chapman's Homer', using suitable reference to the poem.
2. Comment on the changes of tone between the octave and sestet, supporting your points with apt reference to the text.

⊙ Points to Consider

- **Central themes include the excitement of literature and the power of imagination.**

- **Superbly sustained metaphors of exploration.**

- **Petrarchan or Italian sonnet form (octave and sestet).**

- **Sensuous language, vivid imagery patterns, contrasting tones.**

- **Powerful sound effects, run-on lines, contrasting rhythms and moods.**

4

Ode on a Grecian Urn

Ode: celebratory poem addressed to a person or a thing.
Urn: tall vase with stem and base used for storing a person's cremated ashes.

I

Thou still unravish'd bride of quietness,
    Thou foster-child of silence and slow time,
Sylvan historian, who canst thus express
    A flowery tale more sweetly than our rhyme:
What leaf-fring'd legend haunts about thy shape   5
    Of deities or mortals, or of both,
      In Tempe or the dales of Arcady?
    What men or gods are these? What maidens loth?
What mad pursuit? What struggle to escape?
    What pipes and timbrels? What wild ecstasy?   10

still: as yet, unmoving.
unravish'd: untouched.

Sylvan historian: storyteller from the woods.

legend: myth, tale.

Tempe: Greek valley.
Arcady: rural district in Greece.
loth: unwilling.

timbrels: tambourines.

II

Heard melodies are sweet, but those unheard
    Are sweeter; therefore, ye soft pipes, play on;
Not to the sensual ear, but, more endear'd,
    Pipe to the spirit ditties of no tone:
Fair youth, beneath the trees, thou canst not leave   15
    Thy song, nor ever can those trees be bare;
      Bold Lover, never, never canst thou kiss,
Though winning near the goal – yet, do not grieve;
    She cannot fade, though thou hast not thy bliss,
      For ever wilt thou love, and she be fair!   20

sensual: physical.

spirit ditties of no tone: poems from another dimension which have no earthly sound.

Bold: confident, fearless.

III

Ah, happy, happy boughs! that cannot shed
    Your leaves, nor ever bid the Spring adieu;
And, happy melodist, unwearied,
    For ever piping songs for ever new;
More happy love! more happy, happy love!   25
    For ever warm and still to be enjoyed,
      For ever panting, and for ever young;
All breathing human passion far above,
    That leaves a heart high-sorrowful and cloyed,
      A burning forehead, and a parching tongue.   30

cloyed: overfull.

parching: dried up, thirsty.

JOHN KEATS

IV

Who are these coming to the sacrifice?
    To what green altar, O mysterious priest,
Lead'st thou that heifer lowing at the skies,
    And all her silken flanks with garlands dresst?
What little town by river or sea shore,   35
    Or mountain-built with peaceful citadel,
        Is emptied of this folk, this pious morn?
And, little town, thy streets for evermore
    Will silent be; and not a soul to tell
        Why thou art desolate, can e'er return.   40

V

O Attic shape! Fair attitude! with brede
    Of marble men and maidens overwrought,
With forest branches and the trodden weed;
    Thou, silent form, dost tease us out of thought
As doth eternity: Cold Pastoral!   45
    When old age shall this generation waste,
        Thou shalt remain, in midst of other woe
Than ours, a friend to man, to whom thou say'st,
    'Beauty is truth, truth beauty' – that is all
        Ye know on earth, and all ye need to know.   50

heifer: young cow.

citadel: stronghold protecting a city.
pious: God-fearing.

desolate: deserted.

Attic: from Athens.
brede: decoration, embroidery.
overwrought: frantic, overworked.

tease: provoke, tantalise.

Cold Pastoral: passionless story of idealised rural life.

'What wild ecstasy?'

👤 Personal Response

1. In your opinion, what is the main theme of this poem?
2. Select one image from the poem that you found particularly effective. Briefly explain your choice.
3. Comment on the final two lines of the poem.

👁 Critical Literacy

Keats's famous ode explores the paradoxical relationship between the permanent world of art and transient reality. The poet believed that despite being mortal, human beings must strive to make themselves immortal. The mysterious Grecian urn enables the imagination to operate. It is a symbol of timeless perfection that provokes by silently posing questions. This symbol of eternal beauty is in eternal repose.

The poet stands before an ancient Grecian vase and addresses it in a series of vivid metaphors – 'bride of quietness … foster-child of silence'. Keats is immediately engrossed in the artistic images which are frozen in time. Respectfully, he considers the **meaning of the urn**. The word 'still' establishes an atmosphere of ambiguity ('as yet' or 'not moving'). This 'unravish'd' urn has not been affected by the destructive power of time. Although it does not speak, this 'Sylvan historian' clearly tells a story. Indeed, it can relate a tale from the countryside much better than the poet – 'thus express/A flowery tale more sweetly than our rhyme'. Keats wonders about the scene that is depicted on the side of the vase: 'What leaf-fring'd legend haunts about thy shape.' He speculates that it is an ancient saga about groups of men – or possibly gods – enjoying themselves in the scenic Greek countryside. Several rapid questions close the **first stanza** capturing all the frenzied excitement associated with lovers. The 'mad pursuit' involves unwilling maidens who 'struggle to escape'. This headlong dash is accompanied by wild music on 'pipes and timbrels' and concludes with the climactic phrase, 'wild ecstasy'. In this stanza, Keats has drawn a sharp contrast between the dynamic pursuit portrayed on the urn and the stillness of its own form.

Stanza two opens quietly. The poet makes effective use of a memorable paradox to argue that music heard on earth is 'sweet' but that the music of the imagination is 'sweeter'. He urges the musicians on the urn to 'play on' – even though their other-worldly music cannot be experienced in the mortal world: 'Pipe to the spirit ditties of no tone'. Keats directly addresses one particular young man, 'Fair youth, beneath the trees, thou canst not leave/ Thy song'. The breathless run-on lines suggest suspended time – the immediacy of being preserved at a precise moment, forever singing to his beloved. In this idyllic place, the trees will never shed their leaves. **Keats has become deeply engrossed in the urn's images**. Paradoxically, all the characters are immortal, but not living. Although the young lover is very near to the girl he loves, she is just out of reach: 'never, never canst thou kiss'. The double negative reinforces the poignant reality. Nonetheless, the poet offers a consoling insight. Even though the youth cannot embrace his beloved, she can never grow old. Within the permanent reality of art, their love and beauty will live on: 'For ever wilt thou love, and she be fair'.

In the **third stanza**, Keats focuses on the sublime joy of the pastoral scene pictured on the urn where nothing is subject to transience. The poet's mood is ecstatic and he evidently delights in the 'happy, happy boughs' that will not lose their leaves with the passing seasons. Repetition and vibrant rhythm echo his enjoyment. Within the ideal artistic world, it will always be springtime. The 'unwearied' musician will constantly play songs which will stay 'for ever new'. **Time does not exist here**. The pace of the stanza becomes more urgent as the poet immerses himself in the urn's narrative. Emphatic alliteration conveys the joy of escaping the tyranny of ageing: 'More happy love! more happy, happy love!' In contrast to this blissful state of endless 'warm' and 'panting' emotion on the beautiful vase, Keats acknowledges the stark truth of everyday human feeling with its 'burning forehead' and 'parching tongue'. In the real world, people suffer the pain of unreturned love which leaves them with 'a heart high-sorrowful and cloyed'. Is the poet suggesting that romantic love between human beings is always flawed?

Stanza four describes another of the urn's dramatic images – the ritual sacrifice of an animal. Keats inquires about the images of people approaching a 'green altar': 'Who are these coming to the sacrifice?' Readers are also drawn into the scene by the poet's fascination with the festivities recorded on the urn. Keats's **imagery is characteristically sensuous**. A 'mysterious priest' leads in a ceremonial heifer – 'her silken flanks with garlands dresst'. Meanwhile, the nearby village remains strangely deserted, its silent streets desolate 'for evermore'. Like everything else on the urn, its inhabitants are frozen in time and will never return home.

In the **final stanza**, the poet steps back from his close observation and looks at the vase in its entirety, 'O Attic shape'. He is completely in awe at its beauty, 'Fair attitude'. Keats acknowledges that the urn confuses mere mortals with its intriguing narrative – 'tease us out of thought'. Human beings cannot ever comprehend the concept of 'eternity'. He refers to the urn as a 'Cold Pastoral' which tells its inanimate story of romance and religious rites. It is eternal and far removed from the living, breathing, imperfect world of those on earth. The urn remains 'in midst of other woe/ Than ours'. Others will look at it. It is a 'friend to man' showing beautiful images on its exquisite form which contains the ashes of the dead.

The concluding two lines have long been debated. The urn seems to be addressing man, 'Beauty is truth, truth beauty'. What is beautiful is real and genuine. Keats clearly seems to be celebrating the transcendent powers of art which can offer a glimpse of the unchanging happiness to be realised in eternity. Like all great works of art, the Greek vase will always be 'a friend to man'. Did the sculptor who created it recognise the limited capabilities of humans to comprehend the mysteries of life and death? While we must make up our own minds about the poet's meaning, at the very least, Keats has made us consider these important questions through his reflections on the beautiful urn and its enigmatic images.

✍ Writing About the Poem

'Keats explores the transient and immortal through striking and sensual imagery.' Discuss this view, with reference to 'Ode on a Grecian Urn'.

Sample Paragraph

'Ode on a Grecian Urn' illustrates Keats's imaginative use of vivid imagery. The cold marble of this 'Attic shape' was originally used to store ashes. Yet it is decorated with dynamic images of a 'mad pursuit' of maidens by 'men or gods'. Rapid-fire questions mimic the frantic chase, 'What pipes and timbrels? What wild ecstasy?' Keats captures young love, 'For ever panting'. Sensuality is conveyed through the assonance of the long 'a', almost like a young lover's sigh. Yet this is not human love, there is no 'For ever'. Human love is subject to change, whereas the urn shows a love yet to be enjoyed where the 'Bold lover' will always love and his beloved will always be fair, 'She cannot fade'. The immortality of the urn is depicted by the 'desolate' image of the little town which will never know where its inhabitants have gone because they will never return and the town will remain 'silent'. The 'Cold Pastoral' will puzzle its viewers throughout time with its idealised pictures of rural life. Through the use of sensuous imagery, Keats effectively explores the transience of human life, which he contrasts with the permanence of art.

EXAMINER'S COMMENT

This is a very assured response, engaging closely with the poem's main themes of mortality and immortality. Quotations are effectively interwoven to support discussion points: 'Rapid-fire questions mimic the frantic chase, "What pipes and timbrels? What wild ecstasy?"' The expression throughout is both varied and controlled, ensuring the top grade.

✒ Class/Homework Exercises

1. Keats becomes deeply involved in the story told on the urn. What questions does he consider? Support your response with close reference to the poem.

2. How does Keats create a mood of excitement in 'Ode on a Grecian Urn'? Comment on his use of questions, the exclamation marks, sentence length and use of repetition in your answer.

⊙ Points to Consider

- Key themes include transience, immortality, art, reality and the desire to escape.

- Innovative use of the ode enables readers to reflect on the subject matter.

- Distinctive moods – contrasting images of the lovers and little town.

- Sensuous language, metaphors, paradoxes, recurring questions, emphatic repetition.

- Variety of tones; effective use of assonance, alliteration, sibilance.

5 When I Have Fears That I May Cease to Be

When I have fears that I may cease to be
Before my pen has gleaned my teeming brain,
Before high-piled books, in charactery,
Hold like rich garners the full ripen'd grain;
When I behold, upon the night's starr'd face,   5
Huge cloudy symbols of a high romance,
And think that I may never live to trace
Their shadows, with the magic hand of chance;
And when I feel, fair creature of an hour,
That I shall never look upon thee more,   10
Never have relish in the faery power
Of unreflecting love; – then on the shore
Of the wide world I stand alone, and think
Till love and fame to nothingness do sink.

gleaned: gathered; made use of.
teeming: full (of ideas).
charactery: print; writing.
garners: granaries; stores.

high romance: noble poetic themes.

relish: pleasure.
faery: magical.

unreflecting: spontaneous, natural.

'the wide world'

👤 Personal Response

1. In your opinion, what are the main fears expressed by Keats in the poem?
2. Choose one image from the poem that you found particularly interesting. Briefly explain your choice.
3. Comment on the change of tone and mood in lines 12–14.

👁 Critical Literacy

In this carefully crafted Shakespearean sonnet, consisting of a long single sentence, Keats describes his fear of dying young before he has time to fulfil his artistic potential. He is also fearful of never experiencing the joy of being truly in love. This makes him feel that he is utterly alone in the world. However, he finally resolves his anxiety in the poem's concluding lines by asserting the unimportance of romance and literary fame.

The sombre tone reflecting Keats's fear of failure is evident from the start. Striking images convey the poet's personal confession about his deepest concerns. Throughout the first quatrain, he emphasises the dreadful possibility that he may never achieve his full creative potential. His anxiety is typical of dissatisfied artists throughout time. The **extended autumn harvest imagery** – 'gleaned', 'garners', 'full ripen'd grain'– suggests the fertility of Keats's youthful mind and reinforces his heightened sense of frustration. The adjectives, 'high-piled' and 'rich', clearly indicate how acutely aware he is of his own poetic power ('teeming brain').

In the second quatrain, Keats reveals that he is also anxious about not having sufficient time to explore more of life's great mysteries. The strange beauty of creation is symbolised by his **dramatic personification** of the sky – 'night's starr'd face'. Sadly, there is a suggestion of the unattainable in the poet's dreamlike desire to sit under the stars hoping for inspiration. He recognises the wonders of the natural world and its countless mysteries ('Huge cloudy symbols') masking undiscovered delights. If he is fortunate enough, then such 'shadows' might well prompt him to be creative – depending on the 'magic hand of chance'.

The focus throughout the poem, however, is on **the unstoppable passing of time**, emphasised by Keats's repetitive use of 'When' and 'never'. Its corrosive effects are further considered in the third quatrain where the poet is clearly saddened by the thought of losing his lover – 'fair creature of an hour'. Characteristically, he is likely to be using personification here as a poetic technique to highlight the effects of time. For Keats, all of human experience is beautiful but short-lived. Romantic love is also transient, but has 'faery power' or some curious magical quality because it is 'unreflecting' and allows lovers to momentarily escape reality.

As the sonnet builds to a climax in the rhyming couplet, Keats achieves some distancing from his own feelings and this enables him to reach a resolution. He considers his own solitary destiny ('I stand alone') and the more general reality of human insignificance. The stark image of being stranded on the shore of 'the wide world' (a traditional image of eternity) signifies an important development of thought from his initial terrors to an acceptance of life's unimportance. **He ceases to fear and yearn**. Some critics have interpreted Keats's view of death as finding freedom from suffering and dread. However, the concluding tone includes both submission and despair – echoed by broad assonant vowels and the final word 'sink'. The slow, deliberate rhythm further reflects the poet's stark realisation that neither love nor poetry can ever challenge mortality.

Overall, this sonnet offers readers **an interesting insight into Keat's personal perspective on transience and death**. There is a remarkable contrast between the poet's early energetic mood and his eventual acknowledgment of life's brevity. The poem is distinguished by Keats's characteristic archaic language and by his distinctive style, which is marked by melodious sound effects.

✒ Writing About the Poem

'John Keats's poems often portray the conflict between the poet's personal feelings and the stark realities of life.' Discuss this view, with reference to 'When I Have Fears That I May Cease to Be'.

Sample Paragraph

The title of 'When I Have Fears That I May Cease to Be' brings us into Keats's private world which is filled with anxiety. Time is seen as the great enemy of his 'teeming brain'. The poet's urgent tone reflects his sense of panic about death. The disturbing awareness of his own mortality is seen in the repetition of key words, such as 'When', 'before' and 'never'. Keats compares his potential for producing new poems to a farmer harvesting 'the full-ripen'd grain'. He uses metaphorical language to describe the mysterious universe – 'the night's starr'd face' which he 'may never live to trace'. This inner conflict is expressed in the final lines where Keats imagines himself alienated between the land and the sea in transition from this life to the next. He is on the edge 'of the wide world'. The poet's troubled self-analysis has been resolved as he now sees himself as insignificant – 'I stand alone'. In accepting the truth about how short life is, Keats has come to terms with the fact that his fears about missing out on 'love and fame' are unimportant.

EXAMINER'S COMMENT

This impressive top-grade response makes effective use of apt quotations to address the question directly. The conflict between Keats's feelings and the growing awareness of his mortality is central to the answer. There is also some very good discussion of the poet's language use in developing key themes: 'The poet's troubled self-analysis has been resolved as he now sees himself as insignificant – "I stand alone"'. Controlled fluent expression confirms the high standard.

✐ Class/Homework Exercises

1. Outline the central themes in 'When I Have Fears', carefully tracing the progress of thought in the poem.
2. Comment on the effectiveness of Keats's vibrant language in this sonnet. Refer to the text in your answer.

⊙ Points to Consider

- **Transience, immortality, poetry and love are central themes.**
- **Concise Shakespearean sonnet form intensifies Keats's feelings.**
- **Effective use of language – extended harvest metaphor.**
- **Vivid imagery, recurring personification, contrasting tones.**

6 La Belle Dame Sans Merci

JOHN KEATS

Title: the lovely lady without mercy (translated from a medieval ballad).

I

O what can ail thee, knight-at-arms,
   Alone and palely loitering?
The sedge has withered from the lake
   And no birds sing.

ail: make you unwell.

sedge: marsh plant (resembling coarse grass).

II

O what can ail thee, knight-at-arms,   5
   So haggard and so woe-begone?
The squirrel's granary is full,
   And the harvest's done.

haggard: looking exhausted and unwell.
woe-begone: miserable in appearance.
granary: storehouse for grain.

III

I see a lily on thy brow,
   With anguish moist and fever-dew,   10
And on thy cheeks a fading rose
   Fast withereth too.

IV

I met a lady in the meads,
   Full beautiful – a faery's child,
Her hair was long, her foot was light,   15
   And her eyes were wild.

meads: flat grassland meadows.

V

I made a garland for her head,
   And bracelets too, and fragrant zone;
She looked at me as she did love,
   And made sweet moan.   20

fragrant zone: flower-filled belt.

VI

I set her on my pacing steed
   And nothing else saw all day long.
For sidelong would she bend, and sing
   A faery's song.

steed: horse.

131 |

VII

She found me roots of relish sweet,   25
   And honey wild, and manna-dew,
And sure in language strange she said –
   'I love thee true.'

relish: delight.

manna: food (God's food to the Israelites in the wilderness).

VIII

She took me to her elfin grot,
   And there she wept and sighed full sore,   30
And there I shut her wild wild eyes
   With kisses four.

elfin: small and delicate.
grot: cave, grotto.

IX

And there she lulled me asleep,
   And there I dreamed – Ah! woe betide!
The latest dream I ever dreamt   35
   On the cold hill side.

X

I saw pale kings and princes too,
   Pale warriors, death-pale were they all;
They cried – 'La Belle Dame sans Merci
   Hath thee in thrall!'   40

in thrall: in another's power, enslaved.

XI

I saw their starved lips in the gloam,
   With horrid warning gaped wide,
And I awoke and found me here,
   On the cold hill's side.

gaped: open-mouthed.

XII

And this is why I sojourn here,   45
   Alone and palely loitering,
Though the sedge is withered from the lake,
   And no birds sing.

sojourn: remain.

'And there I dreamed'

👤 Personal Response

1. How does Keats establish a dreamlike or eerie atmosphere in this poem? In your response consider the effect of medieval references, the use of archaic words and the supernatural elements.
2. How effective is Keats in conveying the message of doomed love? Support your answer with suitable reference to the poem.
3. In your opinion, what moral lesson can be learned from this poem? Briefly explain your answer.

👁 Critical Literacy

Keats has set his dramatic ballad in the medieval era. This mysterious poem can be interpreted in several ways. Is it a tale of human yearning for eternal love? Is Keats warning against the seductive physical attractions of the deadly femme fatale who loves only to destroy? Does the storyline demonstrate the loss of freedom that comes with falling in love? The Romantic poets, such as Keats, were interested in nature, art, freedom, love and equality. They usually wrote about these themes in lyrical, descriptive language.

This ballad plunges the reader into a conversation between an unidentified speaker and a dying knight. The first three stanzas contain the sequence of questions which the speaker puts to the knight. The next nine stanzas are the knight's reply. He is unlike the stereotypical heroic figures who appear in legends. This is no chivalrous warrior intent on overcoming enormous challenges to win his fair lady. Instead, the knight is 'alone and palely loitering'. From the start, he is portrayed as vulnerable, 'O what can ail thee, knight-at-arms'? **The desolate autumn setting is sketched in a few well-chosen details**. The land is arid and the birds have already flown away: 'The sedge has withered from the lake'. The emphatic monosyllables of 'And no birds sing' reinforce the dismal scene. Throughout stanza one, Keats makes effective use of pathetic fallacy – almost personifying the bleak landscape – to underline the plight of the unfortunate knight.

Stanza two focuses on the knight's bedraggled appearance: 'So haggard and so woe-begone'. Nature has completed its annual cycle, 'The squirrel's granary is full,/And the harvest's done'. This natural world is in order, and is one of plenty and ease, unlike the disordered predicament of the distraught knight. In stanza three, Keats continues to use descriptive imagery to paint a vivid picture of the lonely, listless knight. **Broad vowel sounds ('brow', 'anguish moist') echo his despondent mood**. The lily is a flower which is traditionally associated with death and even the rose – usually a symbol of beauty and passion – is 'fading'. The onomatopoeic verb 'withereth' also suggests that the helpless knight is trembling in his death throes.

In stanza four, the knight remembers how he met a beautiful and enchanting lady: 'a faery's child'. He describes her **alluring appeal**: 'Her hair was long, her foot was light'. But this mysterious woman's 'wild' eyes suggest a creature not of this world. He courts her in the time-honoured tradition and she appears to return his ardour: 'She looked at me as she did love'. He is completely obsessed and 'nothing else saw all day long' (stanza six). He helps her onto his 'pacing steed', seemingly placing her on a pedestal to be worshipped while she holds him spellbound by her 'faery's song'.

Almost immediately, this enigmatic lady seduces him with exotic food: 'relish sweet', 'honey wild' and 'manna-dew'. The focus is on the intense physical attraction between the couple and she cannot hide her feelings – "I love thee true". But once again, a note of disquiet appears when she begins to speak in 'language strange' – another suggestion of her otherworldliness. **The suspense increases** further in stanza eight when the couple arrive at her 'elfin grot'. Suddenly the lady indulges in an uncontrolled outburst of emotion: 'there she wept and sighed full sore'. Was this because she knew what she was about to do, but was unable to reverse it? The knight attempts to calm her: 'I shut her wild wild eyes/With kisses four'. Repetition and run-on line give emphasis to the turbulent scene.

However, the romantic mood seems dimmed by her weeping and the knight is 'lulled' to sleep in stanza nine. His **dreams instantly descend into nightmares** as a haunting procession of 'pale kings, and princes too' utter dire warnings: "La Belle Dame sans Merci/Hath thee in thrall". The horrific state of these unfortunates is emphasised by the compound word, 'death-pale'. Their grotesque appearance of 'starved lips' that 'gaped wide' show the consequences of becoming involved with this merciless creature.

The poem concludes as it began beside the remote lake. Keats's use of the present tense raises interesting questions. Can the knight ever really escape the dire consequences of his passionate romance with 'La Belle Dame'? The repetition of details from the opening lines give a sense of finality. **An ominous aura of mystery lingers**. Keats has composed a thought-provoking poem which cautions against the risks of being carried away by impulsive desire.

The Romantic poets revived the medieval ballad genre, a form of poetry which simply tells its tale largely through dialogue. The hypnotic alternating rhythm of four and three beats to a line weaves its spell on readers. This unsettling story slowly and deliberately moves to its inevitable tragic ending. The deluded knight who invested so much in pursuing ideal love is left trapped on the 'cold hill's side' (stanza eleven). Is Keats issuing a stark warning about the dangers of obsessive love?

✒ Writing About the Poem

Keats explores themes of transience and death in richly emotional and symbolic poetry. Discuss this statement in relation to 'La Belle Dame Sans Merci', supporting your points with suitable reference to the poem.

Sample Paragraph

The poet explores the divide between human mortality and eternity in the ballad, 'La Belle Dame Sans Merci'. In this puzzling narrative of the knight and his lady, Keats examines the difficulties of seeking never-ending romantic love. Various voices are heard, the unidentified speaker, 'O what can ail thee knight-at-arms', the lovesick knight, 'I met a lady in the meads', and the bewitching woman, "I love thee true". The timeless landscape is dramatised with a few well-chosen details, 'The sedge has withered' and 'no birds sing'. I thought this was symbolic of the knight's predicament, facing up to a life without hope. The description of his physical and mental state was conveyed through the image of flowers, the lily a symbol of death and the decaying rose. How different this was to the lovely garlands he had given to his love. The nightmarish consequences of his doomed affair is detailed in the procession of former lovers of this beautiful creature, 'pale warriors, death-pale were they all'.

EXAMINER'S COMMENT

A mature and insightful reaction to a challenging question, addressing both the poet's subject matter and language use. Quotations are used to effectively support key discussion points: 'The nightmarish consequences of his doomed affair is explicitly detailed in the procession of former lovers of this creature, "pale warriors, death-pale were they all".' Worthwhile personal engagement and fluently expressed ideas contribute to this successful top-grade paragraph.

Readers are left wondering if this strange lady will continue to captivate other unsuspecting men with her dangerous promise of perfect love.

✒ Class/Homework Exercises

1. Comment on the effectiveness of Keats's imagery in this ballad. Refer closely to the text in your answer.

2. 'Keats's use of contrast in "La Belle Dame Sans Merci" is an important part of the poem's fascination.' Discuss this view, supporting your points with suitable reference to the text.

⊙ Points to Consider

- **Reality, the supernatural, and romantic love are key themes.**

- **Archaic language adds to the mysterious world of the poem.**

- **Evocative imagery intensifies the timeless scene.**

- **The ballad form is effectively used to relate the story of the knight and his lady.**

- **Effective use of setting, contrasting atmospheres, onomatopoeia and repetition.**

7   **To Autumn**

JOHN KEATS

I

Season of mists and mellow fruitfulness,
    Close bosom-friend of the maturing sun;
Conspiring with him how to load and bless
    With fruit the vines that round the thatch-eaves run;
To bend with apples the moss'd cottage-trees,   5
    And fill all fruit with ripeness to the core;
      To swell the gourd, and plump the hazel shells
    With a sweet kernel; to set budding more,
And still more, later flowers for the bees,
Until they think warm days will never cease,   10
    For Summer has o'er-brimm'd their clammy cells.

II

Who hath not seen thee oft amid thy store?
    Sometimes whoever seeks abroad may find
Thee sitting careless on a granary floor,
    Thy hair soft-lifted by the winnowing wind;   15
Or on a half-reaped furrow sound asleep,
    Drowsed with the fume of poppies, while thy hook
      Spares the next swath and all its twined flowers:
And sometimes like a gleaner thou dost keep
    Steady thy laden head across a brook;   20
    Or by a cider-press, with patient look,
      Thou watchest the last oozings, hours by hours.

III

Where are the songs of Spring? Ay, where are they?
    Think not of them, thou hast thy music too, –
While barred clouds bloom the soft-dying day,   25
    And touch the stubble-plains with rosy hue;
Then in a wailful choir the small gnats mourn
    Among the river sallows, borne aloft
      Or sinking as the light wind lives or dies;
And full-grown lambs loud bleat from hilly bourn;   30
    Hedge-crickets sing, and now with treble soft
    The red-breast whistles from a garden-croft;
      And gathering swallows twitter in the skies.

mellow: pleasantly smooth, soft to taste and in colour.

Conspiring: making secret plans.
thatch-eaves: overhanging roof of straw.

core: centre.

gourd: large fleshy fruit.

kernel: soft part of nut.

clammy: unpleasantly damp.

abroad: over a large expanse.
sitting careless: seated unconcerned.
winnowing: removing chaff (the dry outer covering of grain).

poppies: flower, cutter.

swath: strip of corn cut by scythe.
twined: twisted around.
gleaner: gatherer of leftover grain after harvest has been cut.

bloom: give a glow to.
stubble-plains: field after harvest is cut.
gnats: small flies.

sallows: young willows.

bourn: small stream.

Hedge-crickets: shrill, chirping insect.
garden-croft: cultivated area near to country cottage.

POETRY FOCUS

'Season of mists'

👤 Personal Response

1. In your opinion, what is the main theme of the poem?
2. Choose one image from the poem which appealed to you and comment on its effectiveness.
3. How does Keats create a mood of peace and calm in this poem? Refer to aspects of his content and style in your response.

👁 Critical Literacy

In a letter written in September 1819, Keats says: 'How beautiful the season is now – How fine the air … I never liked stubble-fields so much as now – Aye better than the chilly green of the spring. Somehow, a stubble-field looks warm – in the same way that some pictures look warm. This struck me so much in my Sunday's walk that I composed upon it.' What he composed was the ode, 'To Autumn'. This was written at a time when Keats knew he was seriously ill. Yet, in this poem, he achieves a great serenity. Acutely aware that moments of intense pleasure do not last, he sets his love of the beautiful against the uncontrollable reality of suffering and death.

This is Keats's final ode in his celebrated sequence of 'Great Odes'. It is a valediction, a farewell to the season of abundance and fruition. The poet absents himself from this poem, unlike his very obvious presence in his other two odes. There is no use of the personal pronoun, 'I'. Nonetheless, the reader is very much aware of the presence of the poet who is delighting in this rich 'Season of mists and mellow fruitfulness'. Keats does not even include the term 'ode' in the title. Indeed, a low-key invocation begins the poem. He is enabling us to enter into the season itself' thanks to his rich description of its pleasures.

Stanza one concentrates on the imagery of touch. In stanza two, he focuses on the visual while the third stanza appeals to the ear. Over the course of the poem, Keats examines various aspects of the season – including vegetation, human activity, animals, birds and insects. The ode moves slowly from the ripeness just before the harvest to the activities associated with harvest-time and its aftermath. In its broad structure, the poem follows the pattern of a typical autumn day, progressing from the 'maturing sun' to the actual harvesting to the evening's 'soft-dying day'.

Lines 1–11 invite us to experience the season directly, through concrete images of ripeness and fulfilment, 'fruit the vines', 'bend with apples'. The **wonderful excess of the season** is represented through repetition – 'budding more,/And still more'. The endless pleasure of the season is vividly conveyed by the soft alliterative 'm', 'For Summer has o'er-brimm'd their clammy cells'. Even the bees are deceived into thinking this warm atmosphere will last. Personification of autumn as a co-conspirator with the sun adds to the season's enigmatic image. Precise and onomatopoeic verbs ('load', 'bend', 'fill', 'swell', 'plump', 'o'er-brimm'd') trace the ongoing quiet activity of growth and maturity. There is even a sacred quality (implied by the word 'bless') to this creative world of nature. Keats's tactile imagery focuses on this seemingly endless abundance, 'swell'. The essence of the season is conveyed in one long sentence and there is little to suggest that this season is going to end.

Stanza two personifies the season as several youthful workers engaged in bringing in the harvest. A beautiful picture of a young girl with her hair blowing softly in the autumn breeze is portrayed in the phrase 'soft-lifted by the winnowing wind'. Even the breeze is busy harvesting. The image of the exhausted granary labourer is suggestive of a lingering season, work as yet incomplete, 'half-reaped furrow sound asleep'. Keats skilfully conjures up an air of lethargy in the deep peace of this rich time of year. The gleaner is described as balancing a load on her head as she crosses the brook unhurried. Finally, autumn is portrayed as the patient watcher, the cider-maker who ensures that he gets the 'last oozings' of the apples. The slow movement is caught in the sibilant 's' sounds, reminding us that autumn is indeed a season of **sensuous profusion**.

Somewhat surprisingly, stanza three does not proceed directly to winter, but instead returns to spring: 'Where are the songs of Spring?' The poet is untroubled by that and listens to the mournful sounds of autumn. Its **melancholic music** is wistfully relayed in the 'wailful choir' of gnats who 'mourn', as they rise and fall on the 'light wind'. We can imagine hearing the grown lambs in the onomatopoeic 'bleat', adding to the mood of nostalgia. The chirping of the hedge-crickets joins the melodic ensemble. Finally, the robin 'whistles', contributing its distinctively shrill tone to the choir – and suddenly the reality of autumn is upon us. Robins are usually associated with winter. The migrating swallows 'twitter', but will soon be heard no more – it is a 'soft-dying day'. This final stanza – with its many suggestions of death contrasts sharply with the vitality and excess of the first. But even the poem's open and closing rhyme scheme reinforces the natural symmetry and sense of finality. In his mature ode, Keats has succeeded in blending 'beauty' and 'truth'. This magnificent season must end because the world is governed by time and mortality. Having experienced the delights of autumn, the poet is now quietly resigned to the cycle of nature.

📖 Writing About the Poem

'Keats explores the beauty of the world with sensuous passion, but he also views it honestly.' Discuss this view, with reference to the subject matter and style of 'To Autumn'.

Sample Paragraph

Keats appealed to the senses with a dazzling display of imagery in 'To Autumn'. He combines a picture into both tactile and visual imagery, 'touch the stubble-plains with rosy hue'. I could feel the sharp bristles of the cut corn in the harvested field. The image of 'Thy hair soft-lifted by the winnowing wind' is portrayed in sensuous detail. But it is not just poetic imagery, there is the reality of the actual harvesting and the exhaustion of cutting, 'on a half-reaped furrow sound asleep'. Similarly, Keats does not shy away from the reality of the dying year. In the last stanza, he faces the transience of the season unlike the bees who 'think warm days will never cease'. There are many melancholy words and phrases, 'wailful', 'soft-dying', 'sinking', all contributing to the truth that winter inevitably follows autumn. There is also an inherent sadness which cannot be denied in the long vowel sounds of 'mourn', 'borne' and 'bourn'. The sumptuousness of autumn, its 'mellow fruitfulness', is slowly receding into the mists.

EXAMINER'S COMMENT

An assured personal response engaging closely with the question. Quotations are well-integrated into the commentary to support discussion points. A highly commendable detailed analysis of aural effects and tone: 'There is also an inherent sadness which cannot be denied in the long vowel sounds of "mourn", "borne" and "bourn"'. Expression throughout is varied, fluent and controlled: 'the lavish sumptuousness of autumn, its "mellow fruitfulness" is slowly receding into the mists'. An excellent top-grade paragraph.

✒ Class/Homework Exercises

1. The first eight lines deal with the process of watching and contemplating. How do you think Keats watches and contemplates the season in this poem? Support your response with close reference to the poem 'To Autumn'.
2. How does Keats create a mood of serenity in the poem? Refer to his use of imagery and sound effects in your answer.

⊙ Points to Consider

- Key themes of this great ode include rich abundance of the season, the reality of transience.
- Sensuous visual, tactile and aural imagery.
- Sound effects – alliteration, assonance, sibilance, repetition, rhyme.
- Distinctive moods – elation, melancholy.

8 Bright Star, Would I Were Steadfast as Thou Art

JOHN KEATS

Bright star, would I were steadfast as thou art –
 Not in lone splendour hung aloft the night
And watching, with eternal lids apart,
 Like nature's patient, sleepless Eremite,
The moving waters at their priestlike task   5
 Of pure ablution round earth's human shores,
Or gazing on the new soft-fallen mask
 Of snow upon the mountains and the moors –
No – yet still steadfast, still unchangeable,
 Pillow'd upon my fair love's ripening breast,   10
To feel for ever its soft fall and swell,
 Awake for ever in a sweet unrest,
Still, still to hear her tender-taken breath,
And so live ever – or else swoon to death.

steadfast: steady, unswerving, resolute.
aloft: above.

lids: eyelids.

Eremite: hermit, recluse.

ablution: the act of cleansing.

Pillowed: cushioned.

tender: youthful, warm, romantic.
swoon: faint, pass out.

'still steadfast, still unchangeable'

👤 Personal Response

1. Outline the contrasts that Keats draws between himself and the star. Illustrate your answer with close reference to the poem.
2. Keats uses repetition extensively throughout this poem. In your opinion, what is its effect on the reader? Support your answer with reference to the text.
3. Choose one image from the poem that you found particularly effective. Briefly explain your choice.

👁 Critical Literacy

In 1820 when Keats was setting sail to Italy to find a cure for his worsening ill-health, he inscribed this sonnet into a book of Shakespearean poetry belonging to a friend. It is thought to be one of the last poems he ever composed. The poet focuses primarily on the differences between eternity and mortality.

This well-known poem consists of a single sentence and is divided into an octet and sestet from the Italian sonnet form. Line 1 begins with the arresting exclamation, 'Bright star'. Keats is startled by the brilliance of a distant star's 'splendour'. A heartfelt wish swiftly follows and he desires to be as dependable as the faraway star, 'hung aloft the night'. But in line 2, the emphatic 'Not' conveys his misgivings about the star's detached situation. Its isolation is implicit in its solitary occupation which consists of 'watching', 'gazing' on the earth. But the poet does not wish to be 'lone'. Personification emphasises the star's solitary existence. It observes, but does not participate. Existing on the periphery, there is no rest for this star because it continually views the ocean 'with eternal lids apart'. However, its sleeplessness is non-human, so the poet's wishes seem already to be futile.

Line 4 adds to the reclusive image of the star which Keats likens to 'nature's patient, sleepless Eremite'. The sea's restless stirrings are presented as a stately religious ceremony, a 'priestlike' ritual. It cleanses 'earth's human shores'. The poet's focus has now changed from contemplating the permanence of the star to the flux and flow of life here on earth. The rise and fall of the sea is beautifully expressed in the gentle run-on lines 5–6. Broad 'u' and 'o' vowels create a serene, flowing movement which is in contrast to the still star. Line 7 reveals another transient image of life on earth. The blanket of snow covering all in its white purity is regarded as a temporary 'mask'. It conceals – but only for a time. Keats uses the compound word, 'soft-fallen' to mimic the snowfall's silent arrival. The tranquillity of the newly transformed landscape is suggested by the alliterative phrase, 'the mountains and the moors', diverse places encased in a harmonious covering. The octet concludes with positive suggestions of life on earth – 'pure', 'new' and 'soft'.

However, the sharp monosyllabic negative, 'No', marks the turning-point of this sonnet. Is Keats rejecting the cold, eternal life of the star? Or is he refusing to accept the transience of human life? The adverb 'still' is repeated, announcing his desire to spend eternity frozen in a special moment, 'Pillow'd upon my fair love's ripening breast'. He clearly desires the permanence of the star's life, but not its cold, isolated existence. He also wants the warmth of a human relationship. This is evocatively conveyed in the rich imagery and sound effects of line 11. The intimate sensuality of human love is shown in the rise and fall of his lover's breath: 'To feel for ever its soft fall and swell'. This is reminiscent of an incoming, outgoing tide. A sharp contrast with the passive star is evident with the poet's wish to be 'Awake for ever in a sweet unrest'. More than anything, he wants to be constantly aware of his blessed state.

Unfortunately what he desires is impossible. All moments on this earth end. They will not last 'for ever' (line 12). His lover's mortality is conveyed in her even breathing which resonates in the compound word 'tender-taken'. This personal search for an ideal ('And so live ever') cannot be achieved by a human being whose world is one of change and ending. The poem's final phrase accepts this inescapable inevitability. If Keats cannot live forever, he will have to 'swoon to death' and pass into another kind of eternity. The sonnet's couplet provides a conclusive finish to the poem: 'breath' ceases on 'death'.

✒ Writing About the Poem

'John Keats often expresses profound concern for life's deepest questions in poetry of rich description and sensual language.' Discuss this view, with reference to 'Bright Star, Would I Were Steadfast as Thou Art'.

Sample Paragraph

In 'Bright Star', Keats explores the unobtainable, but much sought-after goal of enjoying the pleasures of this life. The permanence of the star is admired by Keats as he addresses important questions about human existence. He quickly rejects the star's solitary existence, not once but twice, 'Not', 'No'. Keats paints dynamic pictures of life on earth, 'the moving waters', 'the mask/Of snow'. Although these are temporary, the poet glorifies the tides which cleanse 'round earth's human shores'. The broad vowels, 'u' and 'o', create

EXAMINER'S COMMENT

This is an excellent response to a challenging question. There is close engagement with the viewpoint and language in the poem: 'The snow is a unifying influence on "mountains and the moors".' Points are clearly expressed and supported by useful and accurate quotation. The analysis of the poet's technique in using aural imagery is particularly impressive: 'The explosive "p" and "b" together with the lyrical "l" sounds suggest a sensual picture of warmth.' A top-grade answer.

a mood of calmness. The snow is a unifying influence on 'mountains and the moors'. Keats also presents us with the significance of human intimacy where the lovers embrace: 'Pillow'd upon my fair love's ripening breast'. The explosive 'p' and 'b' together with the lyrical 'l' sounds suggest a sensual picture of warmth. The soft rise and fall of his lover's breathing is heard in the alliterative word, 'tender-taken'. Keats wishes to remain in this moment endlessly. But that is not human destiny. So he accepts reality and death, but even here he conveys a graceful, sensual action – he will 'swoon to death'.

✒ Class/Homework Exercises

1. 'Tensions between the transient and the immortal are often found in Keats's poetry.' Discuss this view, using suitable reference to 'Bright Star, Would I Were Steadfast as Thou Art'.

2. Keats led a 'life of sensation' and also a 'life of thoughts'. Discuss this statement in relation to the poem. Support your points with close reference to the text in your answer.

⊙ Points to Consider

- **Eternity and mortality are central themes.**

- **Precise descriptions convey contrasts between the star and transient human life.**

- **Distinctive imagery patterns reinforce the tensions within the poem.**

- **Sonnet forms frame Keats's intense feelings.**

- **Repetition, musical language and personification enhance the sensual experience.**

Sample Leaving Cert Questions on Keats's Poetry

1. **From your study of the poetry of John Keats on your course, select the poems that, in your opinion, best show his effective use of sensuous language to convey his preoccupation with transience and mortality. Justify your response by discussing Keats's effective use of sensuous language to convey his preoccupation with transience and mortality.**

2. **'Keats makes effective use of a variety of stylistic features to express an intense awareness of both the joys and sorrows of human experience.' To what extent do you agree or disagree with this statement? Support your answer with reference to the poetry of John Keats on your course.**

3. **'Keats's poetry is defined largely by rich imagery, striking symbolism and a deeply felt belief in the importance of the imagination.' Discuss this statement, supporting your answer with reference to the poetry of John Keats on your course.**

Understanding the Prescribed Poetry Question

Marks are awarded using the PCLM Marking Scheme: P = 15; C = 15; L = 15; M = 5 Total = 50

- **P** (Purpose = 15 marks) refers to the set question and is the launch pad for the answer. This involves engaging with all aspects of the question. Both theme and language must be addressed, although not necessarily equally.
- **C** (Coherence = 15 marks) refers to the organisation of the developed response and the use of accurate, relevant quotation. Paragraphing is essential.
- **L** (Language = 15 marks) refers to the student's skill in controlling language throughout the answer.
- **M** (Mechanics = 5 marks) refers to spelling and grammar.
- Although no specific number of poems is required, students usually discuss at least 3 or 4 in their written responses.
- Aim for at least 800 words, to be completed within 45–50 minutes.

How do I organise my answer?

(Sample question 1)

From your study of the poetry of John Keats on your course, select the poems that, in your opinion, best show his effective use of sensuous language to convey his preoccupation with transience and mortality. Justify your response by discussing Keats's effective use of sensuous language to convey his preoccupation with transience and mortality.

Sample Plan 1

Intro: (*Stance: agree with viewpoint in the question*) Keats explores the paradoxical relationship between immortal worlds of art and nature and the transience of human life through language that appeals to the senses.

Point 1: (*Immortality/transience – visual and aural imagery*) 'Ode to a Nightingale' contrasts human suffering and death with immortal world of nature. Vivid visual and aural imagery show the difference between man ('youth grows pale, and spectre-thin, and dies') and bird ('Singest of summer', 'full-throated ease').

Point 2: (*Immortality/transience – questions, repetition, paradox*) 'Ode on a Grecian Urn' conveys the immortal world of art through a powerful symbol of silence ('unravish'd bride of quietness') posing enigmatic questions ('Who are these coming to the sacrifice?'). Repetition depicts joyful pastoral scene ('happy, happy love').

Point 3: (*Immortality/transience – symbol, paradox*) 'Ode on a Grecian Urn' explores troubling mortal life through compound words and onomatopoeia ('heart high sorrowful and cloyed'). 'Cold Pastoral' of romance and religious rites shows beautiful images, yet contains ashes of dead.

Point 4: (*Immortality/transience – metaphor, personification, sonnet*) 'When I Have Fears That I May Cease to Be' portrays poet's fears of dying young and not achieving potential. Reversal of viewpoint in concluding couplet expresses acceptance of human fate through assonance vowels and a stark monosyllable ('Till love and fame to nothingness do sink').

Conclusion: Rich, powerful poetry connects two opposing views – the immortal worlds of nature and art and the transient mortal world of human beings. Submission to the reality of human fate.

Sample Paragraph: Point 4

The sonnet, 'When I Have Fears That I May Cease to Be', uses its first quatrain to reveal the poet's concerns about the future. Using characteristically sensual language, Keats compares his creative potential as a poet to the natural world through several harvest images ('garners', 'full ripen'd grain'). His 'teeming brain' is shown through vivid adjectives 'high-piled', 'rich'. The second quatrain symbolises life's wonders, using dramatic personification, 'night's starr'd face'. The poet expresses his frustration that he 'may never live to trace' these wonders because he may 'cease to be' too soon. A memorable image of his isolation 'on the shore/Of the wide world I stand alone' exposes his realisation that he is unimportant in the vast universe. The poem is filled with rich sound effects – and the concluding assonance adds a poignant quality to Keats's sense of reality that human existence is brief, 'love and fame to nothingness do sink'.

EXAMINER'S COMMENT

Well-written top-grade response addresses both aspects of the question (transience and sensual language). There is close engagement with the poem, particularly in the analysis of how Keats's concerns are conveyed through stylistic features, including rich imagery and evocative sound effects. Supportive accurate quotations are carefully integrated into the discussion throughout.

(Sample question 2)

'Keats makes effective use of a variety of stylistic features to express an intense awareness of both the joys and sorrows of human experience.' To what extent do you agree or disagree with this statement? Support your answer with reference to the poetry of John Keats on your course.

Sample Plan 2

Intro: (*Stance: agree with viewpoint in the question*) Keats explores the joys and sorrows of the human experience through an effective use of sensuous language, rich imagery, personification, vivid contrasts and the use of various poetic forms.

Point 1: (*Joy/sorrow – sonnet, personification, musical imagery*) 'To One Who Has Been Long in City Pent' uses the sonnet's octet to compare the frustration of confined urban lifestyle ('long in city pent') to delight of the open countryside ('look into the fair/And open face of heaven') using dynamic personification.

Point 2: (*Joy – imagery, run-on lines*) 'On First Looking into Chapman's Homer' expresses the joy and richness of imagination in reading. Effective use of vivid imagery ('realms of gold'). Exhilarated sense of discovery compared to awe of astronomer ('When a new planet swims into his ken') or the shock of an explorer ('He star'd at the Pacific').

Point 3: (*Joy/sorrow/romantic love – ballad, imagery*) 'La Belle Dame Sans Merci' is a dramatic ballad using dialogue and haunting imagery to trace the dire consequences of unrequited love ('the sedge has withered'). Nightmare consequences of doomed love depicted through shocking procession of former lovers ('starved lips in the gloom').

Point 4: (*Joy/sorrow – visual, tactile, aural imagery, personification*) 'To Autumn' is a farewell to the season of abundance evoked though alliteration and sibilance ('Season of mists and mellow fruitfulness'). Dynamic images of ripeness ('fruit the vines') contrasts with the passing evening ('soft-dying day'). Vivid personification of the transient season as a young girl ('Thy hair soft-lifted by the winnowing wind'). Long vowels capture the sad reality of the transient season ('mourn', 'bourne').

Conclusion: Keats presents the wonder and sadness of the human experience through contrasting views of urban and rural life, the joy of the imagination, the reality of transience and death, the consequences of doomed love and the celebration of the paradoxical nature of autumn, both its abundance and inevitable decline.

NOTE

In keeping with the PCLM approach, the student has to take a stance by agreeing or disagreeing that Keats expresses:

– **an intense awareness of both the joys and sorrows of human experience** (restorative power of nature contrasted with confinement of city life, the power of the imagination and literature, the joy and sorrow of romantic love, beauty and transience of the human world, etc.)

... through an effective use of:

– **a variety of stylistic features** (visual, aural and tactile imagery, personification, varying moods, contrasts, archaic language, setting, repetition, run-on lines, ballad, ode and sonnet forms, etc.)

Sample Paragraph: Point 1

In 'To One Who Has Been Long in City Pent', Keats uses sonnet form effectively. The octet and sestet are skilfully unified to create a satisfying poem that glorifies nature and the open landscape. The oppressiveness of city life is described in the heavy monosyllables of the first line, concluding in the verb 'pent'. In contrast, lively personification and dashing run-through lines reveal Keats's enthusiastic reaction to the countryside, 'in the smile of the blue firmament'. The sestet strikes a poignant note, however, as he accepts that all this beauty will pass. Despondent broad-vowelled verbs list the inevitable change, 'mourns', 'glided by'. An evocative image of 'an angel's tear' which 'falls through the clear ether silently' acknowledges the mystery behind nature's beauty. The changing tone from confinement in the city to contentment in nature is echoed by various poetic devices that reveal the joy and sorrow of the human world.

EXAMINER'S COMMENT

An insightful response that tackles the question directly and shows excellent understanding of the sonnet form. Discussion of Keats's skilful use of sound effects and tone are well developed. Confident expression throughout. Suitable references and quotes are skilfully worked into the answer. A well-deserved top grade.

Leaving Cert Sample Essay

'Keats's frequent desire for an imaginary dream world is expressed through his effective use of evocative language and dramatic moments.' Discuss this statement, supporting your answer with reference to the poetry of John Keats on your course.

Sample Essay

1. John Keats longs for an attractive imaginary world. He often expresses a deep desire to escape the reality of suffering, transience and human mortality. He creates moving odes, intense ballads and forceful sonnets using sensuous language. However, I believe that it is not the fantasies which make most impact, but the poet's acceptance of reality despite its imperfections. The world of nature seems to represent a kind of paradise in Keats's imagination. His wish to find joy and fulfillment clearly reflects his experience of a real-life existence filled with pain. His poetry is characterised by intense feelings – often reflecting the inner tensions in his own life. But Keats never fully escapes into this ideal world of beauty and perfection.

2. In 'Ode to a Nightingale' Keats is torn between wanting to free himself from the suffering of this world, graphically portrayed in the image of youth 'pale and spectre thin', and the desire for the perfection of an ideal dream world. But it is the real world's pleasures that are most memorably described – 'a beaker full of the warm South ... With beaded bubbles winking at the brim'. Sultry summer evenings are brought to life through echoing assonance – 'The murmurous haunt of flies'.

Keats considers the various limitations of eternity. He would be deprived of the natural world's beauty, unable to see the flowers. He would be prevented from hearing the nightingale's song, 'Still wouldst thou sing, and I have ears in vain'. The poet also includes many dramatic images associated with death, such as 'embalmed' and 'requiem'. For him, death clearly has some positive associations. It is 'easeful', a 'rich' experience which might free Keats into an eternity without suffering. At the end, however, he wakes up from his dream to face actual life on its terms. He discovers that the imagination created through his poetry is not permanent, so he abandons the fantasy of 'charmed magic casements' and admits that the dream world 'cannot cheat so well/As she is fam'd to do'.

3. The melodramatic story of unhappy love in the ballad, 'La Belle Dame Sans Merci', explores the longing for eternal romance. An extraordinary encounter occurs between a medieval knight and a beautiful woman, 'I met a lady in the meads'. Graphic descriptive details suggest the lady's appeal, 'Her hair was long, her foot was light', and the lovers' passionate relationship, 'I shut her wild, wild eyes/With kisses four'. However, it is the nightmarish procession of 'pale kings, and princes' which are really haunting. The repetition of 'pale' adds to the dramatic atmosphere. The horrific sight of 'starved lips' which 'gaped wide' shows the terrible consequences of helplessly falling in love with this bewitching, merciless creature who eventually abandons her lover and breaks his heart. Surrendering to a vision of perfect love is seen as being the cause of tragedy. Once more, the poet's desire for a visionary dream is misleading.

4. Keats explores immortality in 'Ode on a Grecian Urn'. He desires escape from transient reality of this life into the changeless world of art that is permanent. The graphic drawings on the beautiful vase capture perfection and permanence. The 'Sylvan' urn symbolizes a changeless world frozen in time in graphic detail. Through vibrant imagery, repetition and run-on lines, Keats creates an ideal scene, 'Ah, happy, happy boughs'. The lovers will be 'for ever young'. The musicians will be 'piping songs for ever new'. He can leave troublesome reality, 'burning forehead', 'parching tongue', behind. Yet, the illusion is revealed in the ironic phrase used – 'Cold Pastoral'. In eternity, there is no warm life. The 'Bold Lover' will always be disappointed, 'never canst thou kiss'. The little town will always be silent. Imperfect human beings can only through the perfection of the urn glimpse beauty. They are left longing for the best of both worlds, the permanence of art and transient life.

5. An extended metaphor of discovery suggests the wonderful moment when Keats first read Chapman's translation of Homer's writing, 'Then felt I like some watcher of the skies'. The graphic image of the explorer, 'stout Cortez' staring at the Pacific 'with eagle eyes', symbolises artistic

INDICATIVE MATERIAL

- **Keats's desire for an imaginary dream world** (escaping painful reality into imagination and ideal world, timeless artistic perfection and permanence, longing for happiness and release, etc.)

... is expressed through:

- **effective use of evocative language and dramatic moments** (sensuous aural/visual imagery, evocative tones, striking symbolism, archaic language, vivid flights of fancy, powerful odes, melodramatic ballads, intense narratives scenes, etc.)

perfection. Keats, like the explorer, also struggles with his new discovery when a new planet 'swims into his ken'. This vast sea of astonishment is suggested by assonant vowels, 'wild', 'surmise'. The sailors are also fascinated, 'Silent upon a peak in Darien'. People long to escape but often struggle to understand these new environments. This is similar to the conclusion in 'When I Have Fears That I May Cease to Be' when the poet stands 'on the shore/Of the wide world' alone and thinks 'Till love and fame to nothingness do sink'.

6. So many of Keats's poems show him as a dreamer whose astounding imagination allows us to share his desire to escape reality. Yet, in all of his visionary poems, he comes to accept and value the real world, with all its wonder.

(820 words)

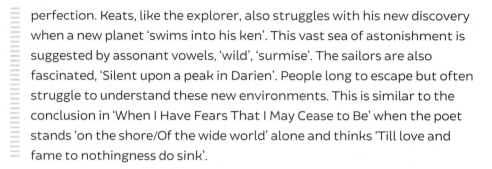

EXAMINER'S COMMENT

A commendable top-grade essay, addressing both elements of the question (theme and style) in detail and with enthusiasm. The clear stance set out in the introductory paragraph is followed by some excellent critical discussion on Keats's odes. However, a little more focus on 'dramatic moments' would have been welcome. There is a refreshing overview of two poems in paragraph 5. Expression, overall, is well-managed, although there is occasional awkwardness (e.g. in paragraph 4) and the adjective 'graphic' is over-used. Excellent use of accurate quotations throughout, often impressively integrated into the commentary.

GRADE: H1
P = 14/15
C = 14/15
L = 13/15
M = 5/5
Total = 46/50

👀 Revision Overview

'To One Who Has Been Long in City Pent'
Nature's beauty and its powers of regeneration are central themes in this Petrarchan (Italian) sonnet.

'Ode to a Nightingale'
Keats tries to free himself from suffering and the world of change by identifying with the nightingale's song.

'On First Looking into Chapman's Homer'
Celebrates the imaginative vision of great literature which Keats experienced when he first read a translation of Homer's *The Iliad*.

'Ode on a Grecian Urn'
Addresses the complexities of art and its impact on people's lives. Keats claims that the most powerful truths are to be found in art.

'When I Have Fears That I May Cease to Be'
Fearful about the inevitability of death, Keats feels anxious about his own poetic achievement and reputation.

'La Belle Dame Sans Merci'
In this haunting ballad, romantic love is entangled with pain, and pleasure is intertwined with death.

'To Autumn'
Keats celebrates the beauty of autumn by focusing on its passing and the transitory nature of human existence.

'Bright Star, Would I Were Steadfast as Thou Art'
In this compelling sonnet, Keats reflects on romantic love and the appreciation of things that are unchanging.

💬 Last Words

'Keats's poetry is "an ark of the covenant between language and sensation".'
Seamus Heaney

'Keats's important poems are related to, or grow directly out of ... inner conflicts.'
Douglas Bush

'I am certain of nothing, but of the holiness of the Heart's affections and the truth of Imagination.'
John Keats

NATURE   ART   JOY/HOPE   TRANSIENCE   SUFFERING   DEATH   LOVE   BEAUTY

Brendan Kennelly

1936–

'Everything has a voice. The poet is used only to let the voices speak.'

Brendan Kennelly is one of Ireland's most important poets. His prolific output extends to over 20 books of poetry (as well as plays, novels and literary criticism) since the publication of his first collection in 1959.

He was born in Ballylongford, Co. Kerry, on 17 April 1936. He studied at the local national school and then at St Ita's College in Tarbert before reading English and French at Trinity College, Dublin. Among his early influences were Patrick Kavanagh and the American 'Beat poets', particularly Allen Ginsberg. As a writer, teacher and social commentator, Kennelly has produced work that explores the legacy of Ireland's colonial past, the place of religion in contemporary culture and politics, gender, language and the role of poets and artists. At its best, Kennelly's work reflects the complexity of Irish life and provides a wonderful model for addressing it with curiosity, creativity and compassion.

Investigate Further

To find out more about Brendan Kennelly, or to hear readings of his poems not already available in your eBook, you could search some useful websites, such as YouTube, BBC Poetry, poetryfoundation.org and poetryarchive.org, or access additional material on this page of your eBook.

Prescribed Poems

○ **1 'Begin'(OL)**
Written after recovering from serious illness, Kennelly expresses a renewed enthusiasm to live every moment to the full. **Page 154**

○ **2 'Bread'(OL)**
Based on a memory of watching his grandmother baking, Kennelly's poem is written in the 'voice' of the bread and explores the natural cycle, creativity and continuity. **Page 158**

○ **3 '"Dear Autumn Girl"'**
This beautiful sonnet addresses the subject of artistic creativity. Kennelly reflects on some of the characters and personae he has created in his poetry. **Page 162**

○ **4 'Poem from a Three Year Old'**
Kennelly's exuberance – his love of the sense of newness, wonder and his endless enthusiasm for the essential strangeness of people and things – is central to the poem. **Page 166**

○ **5 'Oliver to His Brother'**
Using the letter format, Kennelly allows readers to hear Oliver Cromwell's actual words as he reveals conflicting aspects of his character. **Page 171**

○ **6 'I See You Dancing, Father'**
Kennelly's fond memory of his father dancing in the kitchen of the family home leads the poet to reflect on several universal themes. **Page 175**

○ **7 'A Cry for Art O'Leary'**
Famous Irish lament is told in the voice of a young widow, Eibhlín Dubh Ní Chonaill (Eileen O'Connell). It is a cry of grief and of a deep, frustrated passion for justice. **Page 179**

○ **8 'Things I Might Do'**
Kennelly addresses the subject of the 'heart' and finding possible ways to express emotion. **Page 190**

○ **9 'A Great Day'**
This stream of consciousness portrait of an Irish wedding raises thought-provoking questions about the challenges presented by modern marriage. **Page 193**

○ **10 'Fragments'**
In this poignant, introspective poem, Kennelly reflects on the individual's attempts to understand the past while at the same time facing an uncertain future. **Page 199**

○ **11 'The soul's loneliness'**
This poem explores Kennelly's belief in animism and the sense of being part of a universal spirit. **Page 203**

○ **12 'Saint Brigid's Prayer'(OL)**
Adapted from the Irish version and narrated in the saint's 'voice', the poem is structured around the extended metaphor of social drinking as a symbol for glorifying God in prayer. **Page 207**

(OL) indicates poems that are also prescribed for the Ordinary Level course.

1 🔊 **Begin**

Begin again to the summoning birds
to the sight of light at the window,
begin to the roar of morning traffic
all along Pembroke Road.
Every beginning is a promise   5
born in light and dying in dark
determination and exaltation of springtime
flowering the way to work.
Begin to the pageant of queuing girls
the arrogant loneliness of swans in the canal   10
bridges linking the past and future
old friends passing though with us still.
Begin to the loneliness that cannot end
since it perhaps is what makes us begin,
begin to wonder at unknown faces   15
at crying birds in the sudden rain
at branches stark in the willing sunlight
at seagulls foraging for bread
at couples sharing a sunny secret
alone together while making good.   20
Though we live in a world that dreams of ending
that always seems about to give in
something that will not acknowledge conclusion
insists that we forever begin.

'linking the past and future'

👤 Personal Response

1. Briefly trace the development of thought throughout the poem. Support your answer with suitable reference to the text.
2. Comment on the effectiveness of the poet's use of repetition in the poem.
3. Write a short paragraph (at least 100 words) contrasting the images Kennelly uses of sunlight and intimacy with those of darkness and loneliness. Support your answer with suitable reference to the poem.

👁 Critical Literacy

Kennelly wrote 'Begin' in his fifties while recovering from heart surgery. He had radically changed his lifestyle after a series of health and personal problems. His renewed enthusiasm to live every moment to the full is evident in the poem's celebratory tone, which makes singing sense out of life's confusing experiences. Through sound, rhyme and contrast, the music of the language expresses not only actual reality but also possible reality.

The emphatic verb 'Begin' introduces an immediate uplifting movement. Nature calls through birdsong, 'the summoning birds', and sunrise, 'the sight of the light'. The adverb 'again' suggests that this need to start afresh must happen repeatedly. Kennelly skilfully employs characteristics of old Gaelic verse to add a **jaunty lilt** to the rhythm. The ecstatic opening four lines are filled with playful half rhyme, 'begin again', and internal rhyme (rhyming of words not at the end of the line), 'the sight of the light', to announce the wonder of the morning. This co-exists with the rush of the traffic as commuters speed to work, captured through the onomatopoeic verb 'roar'. Four steady beats mark the ballad's rhythm as the early morning rush strives headlong 'all along Pembroke Road' in Dublin.

Description gives way to reflection in lines 5–8: 'Every beginning is a promise'. The poet is setting out what might be, the opportunity for something better in our lives. The optimism is 'born in light' but its failure is signalled by the deadening alliteration: 'dying in dark/determination'. The mood recovers, however, rising again in acknowledgement of the new season – 'exaltation of springtime'. Kennelly was educated in a formal Roman Catholic ethos. The religious connotations of this echoes in his use of 'exaltation' to express such high praise. It is further amplified by the personification of spring, 'flowering' the route to work. The energy and dynamism of the new year blooms. The city workers no longer trudge along on their daily routine, but move through an avenue of spring blossom. Run-on lines convey the forward movement of the young season, the rush towards hope. Through his intent gaze, **the ordinary has become extraordinary**. The overwhelming sense of delight pays homage to another Irish poet, Patrick Kavanagh, who had also written about celebrating the wonder of creation through innocent eyes.

Line 9 invites the reader once more to start again. Literal observation captures the **familiar images** of early morning Dublin. The common sight of female workers queuing for buses is re-defined by the descriptive noun 'pageant'. Their beauty is transformed into something elaborate and dramatic. It's as though a public entertainment is taking place, an elegant procession in elaborate costume. This theatrical image is matched by nature, 'the arrogant loneliness of swans' – the broad vowel assonance highlighting the aloof character of the birds as they glide under canal bridges. For a moment, the intense stillness reminds Kennelly of the sad 'passing' of 'old friends'. This adult experience of death and loss now replaces the joyful wonder of earlier lines. Yet the poet feels these friends remain 'with us still' in memory. Kennelly has said: 'When we write of loneliness, even of what might feel like despair, we discover that there is in language a kind of resilience, a surging hopeful energy that is redemptive and reassuring'.

In line 13, the poet advises: 'Begin to the loneliness that cannot end/since it perhaps is what makes us begin'. The run-on lines 15–20 convey the spiritual excitement that stimulates and intensifies this sense of wonder. It resurges in a series of urgent images that 'makes us begin'. Subtle internal rhyme ('wonder' and 'unknown') heralds the process of looking at strangers and guessing their story. **Contrast is used to convey the harshness and optimism** of the new season. Harsh-sounding discordant consonants ('crying birds', 'sudden rain', branches stark', 'foraging seagulls') evoke the stridency and competitiveness of nature. Yet these co-exist with images of warmth, expressed through musical language and soft alliteration ('willing sunlight', 'sharing a sunny secret'). Playfully, the poet acknowledges the presence of human nature – 'couples sharing a sunny secret' completely at ease in their own world.

The last four lines conclude with the mature awareness of inevitable endings, 'give in', 'conclusion'. But this dark mood is challenged by the statement 'something … insists that we forever begin'. The assonance of the slender vowel 'i' draws attention to the idea that there is some unknown force that encourages people to keep going. This poem ends as it starts – with the word 'Begin'. To a great extent, Kennelly has addressed the mystery of time itself. All beginnings and endings can be seen as metaphors for birth and death. By its very nature, life is transitional, yet human beings have an innate urge to be resilient and to cherish life.

Writing About the Poem

'Kennelly's poems shape and articulate our most joyous and troubling moments.' To what extent is this true of 'Begin'? Support your answer with reference to the poem.

Sample Paragraph

In 'Begin', Kennelly voices our strongest fears of loneliness and death. However, he places these beside the optimism of nature. Despite its harsh aspects, 'seagulls foraging for bread', nature is always ready to 'begin'. In this carefully crafted poem, Kennelly asks us to acknowledge the reality of life, 'old friends passing', 'a world that dreams of ending'. The alliterative phrase 'dying in dark/determination' suggests life's sorrow. Yet run-on lines capture the force of life. Personification lifts the ordinary sight of girls queuing for a bus into a spectacular 'pageant'. Using old Gaelic poetic techniques, Kennelly creates a poem that conveys joy through the assonance of slender vowels, 'the sight of the light at the window', the repetition of the broad vowel sounds, 'wonder at the unknown faces'. I particularly liked the final lines, which close with the cruel truth of mortal life, 'ending', 'give in' and 'conclusion'. But Kennelly shatters such dark thoughts with the verb 'begin'. Indeed, the repetition of this verb throughout the poem and the steady rhythm of the ballad echo in this life-affirming poem.

EXAMINER'S COMMENT

A clear, focused response that shows a very close understanding of the poem. Impressive awareness of the poet's language use (particularly sound effects) throughout. Quotations are used to support key points and the expression is varied and well controlled. While some further analysis of contrast would have been useful, this is a confident top-grade answer.

🖋 Class/Homework Exercises

1. 'Kennelly's tender lyric poetry evokes a sense of wonder in his reader through his use of imagery and sound.' Discuss this statement with particular reference to 'Begin'.
2. 'Kennelly's adventure in words and rhythms effectively conveys light and dark, hope and despair.' Discuss this view, with reference to the poem 'Begin'.

◉ Points to Consider

- **Kennelly often addresses the essential mystery of existence.**
- **Human resilience and the refusal to give up are central themes.**
- **Natural images carry the poem's contrasting views of life.**
- **Effective use of simple language, everyday sights, intricate sound effects.**
- **Variety of tones – optimistic, realistic, exciting, inspiring, etc.**

2 🔊 Bread

Someone else cut off my head
In a golden field.
Now I am re-created

By her fingers. This
Moulding is more delicate   5
Than a first kiss,

More deliberate than her own
Rising up
And lying down.

I am fine   10
As anything in
This legendary garden.

Yet I am nothing till
She runs her fingers through me
And shapes me with her skill.   15

The form that I shall bear
Grows round and white.
It seems I comfort her

Even as she slits my face
And stabs my chest.   20
Her feeling for perfection is

Absolute.
So I am glad to go through fire
And come out

Shaped like her dream.   25
In my way
I am all that can happen to men.
I came to life at her finger-ends.
I will go back into her again.

Moulding: kneading. contact.

👤 Personal Response

1. In your opinion, is the narrative voice in this poem convincing or unconvincing? Refer to the text in your answer.
2. Choose one image from the poem that you found particularly effective. Briefly explain your choice.
3. Write a short personal response to the poem, referring closely to the text in your answer.

👁 Critical Literacy

There is a tradition in Ireland, England and Wales of giving inanimate objects their own poetic voices. Kennelly's poems are frequently written in a persona, which he explains as a desire to understand by 'becoming someone else'. He has said: 'As a child I would watch my grandmother bake brown bread, and I would wonder, "How does that bread feel at the end of her fingers?" Years later I wrote the poem "Bread"'.

Kennelly has always envisaged poetry as 'a house of voices'. In the poem's dramatic opening lines, he personifies the original sheaf of wheat ('Someone else cut off my head') that was eventually milled into flour and is now being 're-created' as dough for baking. The violence of the image is eased by the matter-of-fact tone. Wheat is grown to be harvested, new life emerges out of death. The poet's **vivid memory** of watching the tantalising precision of his grandmother's fingers is marvellously merged with a very different experience when he describes the physical contact as being: 'more delicate/ Than a first kiss'. The hushed tone and sibilant 's' sounds evoke excited anticipation.

There are **erotic undertones** throughout the poem and it is not easy to separate the persona of the poet – either as child or adult – from the invented personae populating the poem itself. In describing the measured cadence of 'Rising up/And lying down' (lines 8–9), Kennelly conveys a sense of the natural movement that results from human breathing as well as the rhythmic action of handling dough.

Characteristically, the poet sees beyond the surface of everyday existence. Like many other visionary poets, Kennelly senses a **mysterious radiance in life** around him. In line 12, the narrative voice (of the dough his grandmother is kneading) is entirely at ease within 'This legendary garden'. As in many of his early poems, this one is filled with the notion of animism and an awareness of being part of a universal spirit.
Lines 13–18 focus on the idea of changing form: 'She runs her fingers through me/And shapes me with her skill'. The dynamic language and steady rhythm reflect his grandmother's natural talent for making bread. **Kennelly dramatises the baking exercise**, presenting it almost as an artistic

performance or a new birth that 'Grows round and white'. The image – with its pre-natal associations – is further enriched by the feeling of mutual consolation: 'It seems I comfort her'.

In sharp contrast, the violent imagery of lines 19–20 describes the process of baking in terms of necessary suffering: 'she slits my face/And stabs my chest'. The harsh verbs and staccato rhythm express the grandmother's purposeful hand movements. Yet it will all be worth it because the final product – the bread itself – will be 'perfection'. Kennelly imagines the resigned voice of the bread, realising the need to endure the transformation, indeed 'glad to go through fire' in order to fulfil a 'dream' (line 25). On a **metaphorical level**, the poet might well be referring to any act of creation – including procreation. Human beings usually encounter suffering on a variety of levels in their everyday lives and relationships.

Kennelly has always considered this eclectic mixture of experience to be part of his development as a poet. In the final lines, he universalises the process of bread-making, likening it to the changes that occur in every human life: 'I am all that can happen to men'. Teasingly, he finishes on a **sensual note**, merging his vivid childhood memory with adult sensations: 'I came to life at her finger-ends/I will go back into her again'. However, the last line is much more spiritually focused, leaving readers with the belief that all of life eventually returns to become one with the universal soul out of which we were born.

This sense of **imaginative unison** is central to the poem. Elsewhere, Kennelly has written about his inclination to speak in different voices: 'For me, poetry is an entering into the lives of things and people, dreams and events'. He has also remarked that 'the use of a persona can be a liberating agent and reveal more about our existence and our way of life than personal outpourings'.

'She runs her fingers through me'

✒ Writing About the Poem

It has been said that Kennelly's poetry 'moves from the here-and-now to the mystical'. To what extent is this evident in his poem 'Bread'?

Sample Paragraph

The setting in Kennelly's poem 'Bread' is not out of the ordinary. Remembering his grandmother at work in the kitchen would suggest a simple nostalgic poem, but this is not how the poet presents the scene. By giving the bread its own 'voice', Kennelly transcends the ordinary, making it extraordinary. He gives the wheat a consciousness as though it were a living person – 'Now I am re-created'. The poet develops this idea of 'permanent beginning' when the voice of the dough takes over the narration, reacting to the woman's touch as she 'shapes me'. It seems that everything and every person has a spiritual life and that there is a constant state of change in this 'legendary garden' or heavenly existence. The bread will 'go through fire' to reach 'perfection'. Kennelly's memory of bread-making becomes a mystical exploration of the mysteries of the universe. Just as the wheat 'suffered' to become bread, human souls endure pain on earth for spiritual fulfilment. The ending of the poem is optimistic. 'I will go back into her again' suggests the soul's progress as part of the natural cycle.

EXAMINER'S COMMENT

This is a good top-grade attempt at tackling a challenging question, focusing well on how Kennelly uses the domestic scene to explore a spiritual theme. The notion of development and 'permanent beginning' is a very impressive point. Commentary is effectively supported by apt (and accurate) quotations. Expression is clear and very well-controlled throughout.

✏ Class/Homework Exercises

1. 'Brendan Kennelly uses evocative language to create poems that are deeply reflective.' To what extent is this true of 'Bread'? Support your answer with reference to the poem.
2. Comment on the use of contrasts in this poem, referring closely to the text in your answer.

◎ Points to Consider

- **Simple family theme – a woman is making bread and the bread is 'speaking'.**
- **Other themes include: time, change, the natural cycle, creativity and continuity.**
- **Contrasting moods, everyday imagery, use of extended metaphor.**
- **Resonant narrative voice creates a dreamlike atmosphere.**

3 'Dear Autumn Girl'

(*from* Love Cry)

Dear Autumn girl, these helter-skelter days
When mad leaf-argosies drive at my head,
I try but fail to give you proper praise
For the excitement you've created
In my world: an islander at sea,   5
A girl with child, a fool, a simple king,
Garrulous masters of true mockery –
My hugest world becomes the littlest thing

Whenever you walk smiling through a room
And your flung golden hair is still wet   10
Ready for September's homaged rays;
I see what is, I wonder what's to come,
I bless what you remember or forget
And recognise the poverty of praise.

helter-skelter: chaotic, hurriedly.

leaf-argosies: leaves like a fleet of rich merchant ships.

Garrulous: talkative, long-winded.

'Ready for September's homaged rays'

👤 Personal Response

1. In your opinion, is the 'Autumn girl' an effective symbol for poetic inspiration? Briefly explain your answer, referencing the text.
2. Choose two images from the poem that appeal to you and comment on their effectiveness.
3. Write your own personal response to the poem, referring closely to the text in your answer.

👁 Critical Literacy

Brendan Kennelly's poetry collection *Love Cry: The Kerry Sonnets* (1971) contains 48 beautifully composed, affirmative love sonnets, including '"Dear Autumn Girl"'. Kennelly has commented that at the time, the sonnet form got so deeply embedded inside his head that for around three years, he could write nothing but sonnets. In this poem, he addresses the subject of poetic inspiration – something that is very close to his heart.

A buoyant tone is immediately struck in the opening lines with the tender address to 'Dear Autumn girl', the representation of Kennelly's poetic muse. The **chaotic rush** of golden, tumbling autumn leaves is vividly evoked in the run-on lines, 'these helter-skelter days/When mad leaf-argosies drive at my head'. The use of the vibrant compound word, 'helter-skelter', reinforces the glorious, 'mad', haphazard nature of the season. For Kennelly, the falling leaves are as precious as rich merchant ships bearing priceless cargo, spinning rapidly towards the poet's mind. The monosyllabic verb 'drive' catches their relentless descent. Is this the force, the delight, that gives rise to poetry?

In a confessional third line, the poet admits his futile attempt to do justice to the inspiration: 'I try but fail'. While the monosyllabic verb 'try' suggests his effort, the disconsolate word 'fail' trails weakly. Kennelly is aware that mortal man is prone to failure in his attempts to give 'proper praise' to his muse. The alliterative, explosive 'p' effect forces the reader to exert effort in pronouncing the phrase, thereby **mimicking the poet's own struggle to write**. Use of the adjective 'proper' reveals Kennelly's attempts to celebrate his beautiful 'Autumn girl' in an appropriate ladylike fashion. He believes that literature is something to be celebrated rather than criticised and he is grateful for the gift of 'excitement', the thrill and pleasure that literature has produced in his world. Elsewhere, he has described his poetic talent as 'a gift that took me unawares/And I accepted it'.

Lines 5–6 list some of the **characters and personae** brought into existence by Kennelly's poetic muse. First, there is the outsider ('an islander at sea') with whom he shares that experience. As a very young child, Kennelly was sent to live with his aunt for 18 months. He later commented, 'I do think that

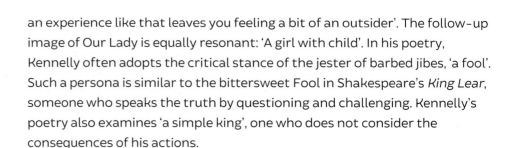

an experience like that leaves you feeling a bit of an outsider'. The follow-up image of Our Lady is equally resonant: 'A girl with child'. In his poetry, Kennelly often adopts the critical stance of the jester of barbed jibes, 'a fool'. Such a persona is similar to the bittersweet Fool in Shakespeare's *King Lear*, someone who speaks the truth by questioning and challenging. Kennelly's poetry also examines 'a simple king', one who does not consider the consequences of his actions.

In line 7, he even **pokes fun at himself** through the onomatopoeic adjective, 'Garrulous'. Kennelly had a reputation as a raconteur and has admitted: 'I want to write poetry that is capable of containing ... this kind of self-critical laughter'. He believed that there was too much self-importance in the world. The comic sense forbids us from taking ourselves too seriously, but it also unleashes scathing utterances against pomp, falsehood and self-regarding ego. It's not surprising that so much of his poetry (which he refers to elsewhere as a 'house of voices') states, pleads, commentates and confesses.

The octet flows seamlessly into the sestet. Kennelly loosens the restricting order of the Petrarchan sonnet in the same way as the flurry of autumn leaves were unleashed by the wind. His 'Autumn girl' has flung her 'golden hair'. Now, when she gifts him with creativity ('Whenever you walk smiling through a room'), he becomes intensely aware, sensitised to 'the littlest thing'. His muse has provided the inspiration and awaits his praise, 'September's homaged rays'. The poet now understands something of the mystery that has occurred, 'I see what is', but even more importantly for the artist, **his sense of astonishment has been stirred**, 'I wonder what's to come'. He is happy to accept any inspiration that might come his way and he is keen to show gratitude for the creative impulse – which he acknowledges in religious terms: 'I bless what you remember or forget'.

In the concluding lines Kennelly comments wryly on his poetic efforts. Although he wished to be more appreciated, he has only been able to achieve 'poverty of praise'. He is deeply self-critical of his inadequate attempts to glorify his 'Dear Autumn girl'. Autumn is the season of maturity and abundance. She has provided plentiful well-developed ideas and stimulus. Yet there is **one final irony**: the romantic outsider has succeeded in creating a tender lyric poem of rhythmical elegance. The poet has displayed his craft in combining its flowing iambic pentameter and abab, cdcd rhyme scheme from the sonnets of Shakespeare, the octet/sestet form of the Petrarchan sonnet and his own unique rhyme scheme in the sestet, efg, efg. His original compound word, 'leaf-argosies' and the image of his dream woman (the 'Autumn girl') all add to the originality of his affectionate tribute to poetic inspiration.

✒ Writing About the Poem

'Brendan Kennelly's poetry is distinctive, memorable and powerful.' To what extent is this true of '"Dear Autumn Girl"'? Support your answer with reference to the poem.

Sample Paragraph

'"Dear Autumn Girl"' is a distinctive sonnet addressed to Kennelly's muse or source of inspiration. He divides his poem on the model of an octet and sestet, yet he allows one to flow into the other, 'My hugest world becomes the littlest thing/Whenever you walk smiling through a room'. Inspiration can strike at any time, it is not confined. His original rhyme scheme for the sestet adds to his unique version of the sonnet form. However, it is the poem's imagery that makes it so memorable. The swirl of dancing autumn leaves, 'mad leaf-argosies', are echoed in the 'flung golden hair ... still wet' of the 'Autumn girl'. The poem's power lies in the ability of the poet to be self-critical, 'I try but fail', 'Garrulous', 'I ... recognise the poverty of praise'. We can empathise with his self-deprecation because we all wish we could have done better in meeting life's challenges. Through his viewpoint, style and content, Kennelly has created a distinctive and powerful poem that reveals inner vitality.

> ### EXAMINER'S COMMENT
>
> *A successful top-grade response that explores interesting aspects of a challenging poem, with some well-focused discussion about Kennelly's 'unique version' of the sonnet form. Other effective points deal with imagery and the poet's self-criticism. Some good use of quotation reflects a close knowledge of the text. Expression is impressive throughout.*

✎ Class/Homework Exercises

1. Comment on the effectiveness of Kennelly's use of rhyme in this poem, referring closely to the text in your answer.
2. 'Kennelly's poetry has been described as an adventure in words and rhythms, in images and dreams.' In your opinion, how true is that view in relation to the poem '"Dear Autumn Girl"'? Support your response with reference to the text.

⊙ Points to Consider

- **Innovative adaptation of the sonnet form.**
- **The mysterious power of artistic inspiration is a central theme.**
- **Startling visual imagery and use of an extended metaphor.**
- **Rhythmic iambic pentameter and distinctive rhyme patterns.**
- **Varied tones: upbeat, reflective, self-critical, appreciative, etc.**

4 🔊 Poem From A Three Year Old

And will the flowers die?

And will the people die?

And every day do you grow old, do I
grow old, no I'm not old, do
flowers grow old?   5

Old things – do you throw them out?

Do you throw old people out?

And how you know a flower that's old?

The petals fall, the petals fall from flowers,
and do the petals fall from people too,   10
every day more petals fall until the
floor where I would like to play I
want to play is covered with old
flowers and people all the same
together lying there with petals fallen   15
on the dirty floor I want to play
the floor you come and sweep
with the huge broom.

The dirt you sweep, what happens that,
what happens all the dirt you sweep   20
from flowers and people, what
happens all the dirt? Is all the
dirt what's left of flowers and
people, all the dirt there in a
heap under the huge broom that   25
sweeps everything away?

Why you work so hard, why brush
and sweep to make a heap of dirt?
And who will bring new flowers?
And who will bring new people? Who will   30
bring new flowers to put in water
where no petals fall on to the

broom: sweeping brush.

floor where I would like to
play? Who will bring new flowers
that will not hang their heads   35
like tired old people wanting sleep?
Who will bring new flowers that
do not split and shrivel every
day? And if we have new flowers,
will we have new people too to   40
keep the flowers alive and give
them water?

And will the new young flowers die?

And will the new young people die?

And why?   45

shrivel: wither and shrink.

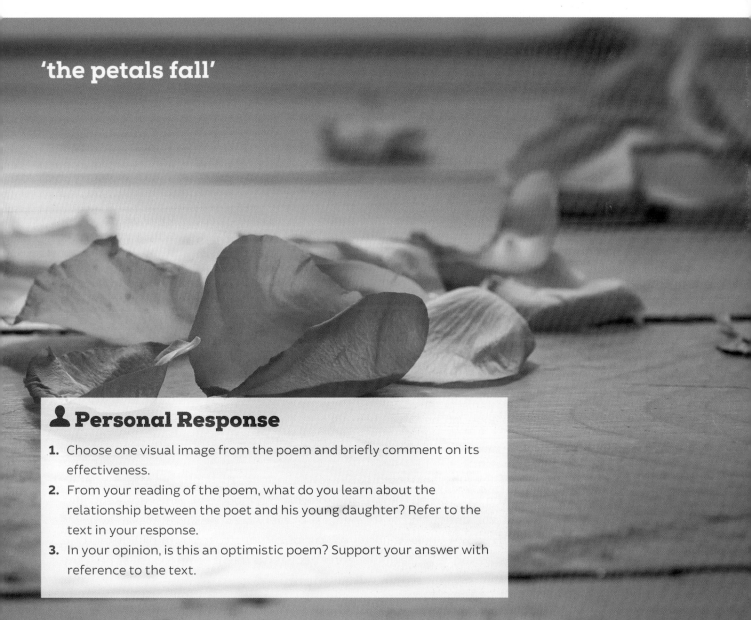

'the petals fall'

👤 Personal Response

1. Choose one visual image from the poem and briefly comment on its effectiveness.
2. From your reading of the poem, what do you learn about the relationship between the poet and his young daughter? Refer to the text in your response.
3. In your opinion, is this an optimistic poem? Support your answer with reference to the text.

167 |

⊙ Critical Literacy

Kennelly's love of the sense of newness and his enthusiasm for the essential strangeness of people and things are central to 'Poem from a Three Year Old' in which he paraphrases a child's intimations of mortality. He has commented: 'One night, my three-year-old daughter was noisily refusing to sleep, screaming her little head off, in fact. I brought her downstairs to the living-room and tried to have a chat with her. A vase of flowers stood on the table. Petals were falling from the flowers. She said, "What are these?" "Petals," I replied. "Why are they falling?" she asked. "Because the flowers are dying," I answered. She was quiet for a while and then the questions began to pour out of her.'

This poem begins in the voice and language of a very young child: 'And will the flowers die?' While the direct simplicity of the stand-alone first line is characteristic of **childhood wonder**, the follow-up question strikes a more startling note: 'And will the people die?' The line-break with its in-built pause emphasises the actual thought process. This is the moment when the infant is coming into contact with the grown-up world, raising a universal reality that is likely to be more disquieting to her adult father than it is to her.

The directness of the child's language seems to fascinate Kennelly. Her additional series of questions in **lines 3-5** are couched in a highly animated personal tone: 'do you grow old, do I/grow old, no I'm not old'. The **broken syntax and insistent rhythm** reflect the intense activity of her young mind, eagerly trying to make sense of the real world. Three further questions (lines 6-8) indicate a new train of thought about what happens to 'Old things' and – even more puzzling for her – 'old people'. Innocence and reason come together in the impatient pursuit of answers: 'And how do you know a flower that's old?'

Lines 9-18 dramatise the spirit of play, the incessant questioning, and the moments of wonder intrinsic to childhood. The infant's innately chaotic thoughts and feelings are expressed in a **dreamlike internal monologue** characterised by an absence of regular punctuation. In the middle of the torrential questioning about decaying flowers, the child suddenly returns to her natural state of cheerfulness. Random syntax and diction ('flowers and people all the same/together lying there') create a surreal mood. Yet the central idea is repeatedly stated: 'I want to play'.

The **exuberant interrogative tone** continues through lines 19-26 – but with the focus on 'all the dirt'. In exploring childhood consciousness, Kennelly reminds us that the strangeness of everyday life is usually taken for granted by adults. Unlike children, our curiosity is destroyed by familiarity and experience. While his daughter's concerns might seem foolish at first, she is much more aware of what is going on around her, regardless of how trivial her observations might appear.

Throughout lines 27-42, the child turns her attention to the future: 'And who will bring new flowers?' She reveals an **intuitive compassion** not just for the vulnerability of nature, but for human nature: 'And who will bring new people?' In her engaging vision of an ideal existence, she imagines being able to play forever in a timeless world where flowers 'will not hang their heads/ like tired old people wanting sleep'. Such an ingenuous dream unleashes her profound vitality with its emphasis on freshness – 'new flowers', 'new people'.

Despite her instinctive optimism, the child is still aware that she has touched on more serious aspects concerning life and death. The resonant tone of the last three lines makes it clear that she retains some of her earlier unease about the cycle of life: 'And will the new young people die?' The poem ends as it began – with a much more general, **fundamental question** ('And why?') that gets straight to the heart of the mystery and wonder of creation.

Many of Kennelly's early poems address **the strange sensation of being alive** and an awareness of being part of a universal spirit. The poet has stated: 'I like to write about children, especially about their talk because they say very wise things and ask very strange and wonderful questions. And also they love to play in the middle of it all frequently. So asking questions and loving to play – I sometimes think that's what education should be about'.

✒ Writing About the Poem

In your opinion, how successful is Brendan Kennelly in conveying the authentic voice of a young child in this poem? Support your answer with reference to the text.

Sample Paragraph

The child's innocent voice dominates this poem. The simple diction is exactly the way young children speak. It's not just the endless questions, but the language itself that is so true to life – 'Why you work so hard'. The poet presents readers with the disorganised thoughts of the child who mixes up various topics – age, flowers, playing, work, etc. Kennelly structures the poem effectively to capture the rhythms of the child's voice. Using run-on lines and omitting punctuation marks allows the voice to be heard without interruption. Everything is a mystery for children who are discovering new things all the time. I found it interesting that the child kept comparing flowers with people. She has an understanding of the fragility of flowers – and is saddened when 'petals fall on to/ the floor'. I liked the concluding line, 'And why?', as it summed up every little child's natural inquisitiveness. There was even a sense that she knew she was now the centre of attention and was testing her father's knowledge.

✍ Class/Homework Exercises

1. Trace the changing tones throughout the poem, supporting your answer with close reference to the text.
2. 'Kennelly's poems can sometimes appear simple, but they often have layers of underlying meaning.' Discuss this view, with particular reference to 'Poem from a Three Year Old'.

⊙ Points to Consider

- Key themes include time, the natural cycle and essential mystery of life.

- Effective use of simple language, rhythm, repetition and vivid imagery.

- Conveys the authentic 'voice' of the child throughout.

- Variety of tones – inquisitive, concerned, reflective, playful, bittersweet, etc.

5 🔊 Oliver to His Brother

BRENDAN KENNELLY

Loving brother, I am glad to hear of your welfare
And that our children have so much leisure
They can travel far to eat cherries.
This is most excusable in my daughter
Who loves that fruit and whom I bless.   5
Tell her I expect she writes often to me
And that she be kept in some exercise.
Cherries and exercise go well together.
I have delivered my son up to you.
I hope you counsel him; he will need it;   10
I choose to believe he believes what you say.
I send my affection to all your family.
Let sons and daughters be serious; the age requires it.
I have things to do, all in my own way.
For example, I take not kindly to rebels.   15
Today, in Burford Churchyard, Cornet Thompson
Was led to the place of execution.
He asked for prayers, got them, died well.
After him, a Corporal, brought to the same place
Set his back against the wall and died.   20
A third chose to look death in the face,
Stood straight, showed no fear, chilled into his pride.
Men die their different ways
And girls eat cherries
In the Christblessed fields of England.   25
Some weep. Some have cause. Let weep who will.
Whole floods of brine are at their beck and call.
I have work to do in Ireland.

Loving brother: Extract from letter sent by Oliver Cromwell to his brother, Richard Mayor, Bristol, 19 July 1649.
… I am very glad to hear of your welfare, and that our children have so good leisure to make a journey to eat cherries. I have delivered my Son up to you; and I hope you will counsel him: he will need it; and indeed I believe he likes well what you say, and will be advised by you. I hope I shall have your prayers in the Business to which I am called …
welfare: wellbeing

delivered: entrusted.
counsel: advise.

Burford Churchyard, Cornet Thompson: Three leaders of the rebel soldiers known as the 'Levellers' (including Captain Cornet Thompson) were executed on the orders of Cromwell. Extract from contemporary book, *The Works of Thomas Carlyle*:
This day in Burford Churchyard, Cornet Thompson … was brought to the place of execution, and expressed himself to this purpose: That it was just what did befall him; that God did own the ways he went; that he had offended the General: he desired the prayers of the people; and told the soldiers who were appointed to shoot him, that when he held out his hands, they should do their duty.

work to do in Ireland: The Cromwellian conquest of Ireland, or Cromwellian war in Ireland (1649–53), refers to the conquest of Ireland by the forces of the English Parliament, led by Oliver Cromwell, in order to crush the Royalists who wished to restore an English monarchy and who were allied with the Irish Catholic Confederation. Cromwell landed in Ireland with his New Model Army on 15th August, 1649, promising to carry on 'the great work against the barbarous and blood-thirsty Irish'.

'I have work to do in Ireland'

👤 Personal Response

1. In your opinion, what kind of impact does the poet achieve by using so much of Cromwell's actual correspondence in the poem? Support your answer with close reference to the text.
2. Based on your reading of the poem, were you surprised by any aspects of Cromwell's character? Briefly explain your response.
3. Write a short personal response to the poem, referring closely to the text in your answer.

◉ Critical Literacy

Brendan Kennelly's comic-grotesque epic, *Cromwell* (published in 1983) is a book-length poem comprised of many smaller poems, in various discursive modes (letter, newspaper article, history, legend, folktale and fantasy). Yet all share an angry focus on the nature of human brutality. Kennelly reimagines the complex persona of Cromwell, a man blamed for barbaric violence against the people of Ireland. The poet taunts the reader with the story of the realist statesman against whom hopeless visionaries strike. This bold attempt to dramatise the savage complications of Irish history delighted and scandalised readers. Seamus Heaney chose it as his book of the year (1983), speaking of a 'sense of outbreak' – something that is difficult to pin down.

Brendan Kennelly's poetry often gives a voice to others and otherness. In this poem, closely based on Oliver Cromwell's original letter to his brother, Kennelly reinvents one of Ireland's most reviled figures of hate. Cromwell's affectionate address to his 'Loving brother' seems somewhat unexpected. The poet broadens the traditional Irish view of Cromwell the monster into a multi-dimensional figure – a concerned parent and courteous brother. Indeed, the tone throughout the opening section portrays **a warm and generous character**, 'I am glad to hear of your welfare'. Run-on lines convey the fond father, 'our children have so much leisure/They can travel far to eat cherries'. He is softly indulgent of his young daughter and concerned that she keeps in contact with him, 'Tell her I expect she writes often to me'. Like most fathers, he dotes on his child and is worried about her happiness. A slightly **sterner tone emerges (line 9)** in discussing his son's welfare. Cromwell asks his brother to advise his son, whom he clearly thinks is in need of instruction: 'I choose to believe he believes what you say'. But he is also considerate in wishing his brother's family well: 'I send my affection to all your family'. At this point, the narrative voice changes even more as Cromwell begins to focus on English society at large: 'Let sons and daughters be serious; the age requires it'. These were certainly changing times. The flamboyant and artistic monarch, Charles I, had just been defeated by Cromwell and his Model Army.

Over the course of the next 16 lines, however, a different Cromwell emerges. Here is the methodical, calculating politician and assured leader, 'I have things to do, all in my own way'. The plain monosyllabic line reflects his blunt Protestant mindset. Cromwell had ordered the execution in Burford Churchyard of several leaders of the Levellers movement in 1649: 'I take not kindly to rebels'. The short staccato statement shows his lack of compassion with one of these, Cornet Thompson, the only officer to be named in the poem. Yet Cromwell's detached sense of **military honour** is evident in his obvious regard for an enemy soldier who 'died well'.

The anonymous 'Corporal' mentioned in line 19 also faced death bravely: 'Set his back against the wall and died'. A third rebel was equally prepared to 'look death in the face'. The alliterative phrase, 'Stood straight', emphasises his fearlessness while the verb, 'chilled', reflects his steely composure. We are left in no doubt about Cromwell's cold professionalism when dealing with the rebels. In line 23, he explains his handiwork, 'Men die their different ways'. The pounding alliterative 'd' effect suggests the sound of the executed men falling to the ground.

But Kennelly is realistic about the fleeting nature of military history, reminding us that people get on with their everyday lives, 'And girls eat cherries'. The rich rolling 'r' contrasts the warm pulse of life with the cold finality of death. There is more than a little **irony** in the deeply religious Cromwell's reference to his new English society. The bland compound description, 'Christblessed fields', conveniently glosses over the suffering Cromwell has caused. Apart from the token acknowledgement – 'Some weep. Some have cause', the sense of expediency dominates: 'Let weep who will', and the tears of his countless victims are dismissed as 'floods of brine'. Kennelly makes it clear that the pragmatic Cromwell was intent on solving the problem of his restless military force by distracting them with a campaign in Ireland that would allow them to acquire wealth and land for resettlement, 'I have work to do in Ireland'.

The detached military leader's unsettling statement in the final line is in marked contrast with the loving father's earlier humanity. Throughout this poem, the varied rhythms and tones of Cromwell's voice insinuate themselves into the mind and psyche of readers, so that we are forced to question assumed perceptions of this complex man. As always, Kennelly is the bardic puppet-master controlling not only the performance of his characters onstage, but also the reactions of his audience. He challenges us to question, but provides few answers.

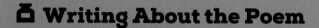 Writing About the Poem

Brendan Kennelly's poetry gives expression to 'voices out of history' to 'deepen and extend the self'. To what extent is this evident in his poem 'Oliver to His Brother'? Support your answer with reference to the text.

Sample Paragraph

Kennelly often speaks even from the mind of hate-filled figures from history such as Oliver Cromwell who was responsible for so much bloodshed in Ireland. The poet captures his authoritative voice, 'I have things to do in my own way'. His lack of empathy is seen in his account of the executions of the leaders of the failed revolt against him, 'Men die their different ways'. But Kennelly also asserts the humanity of this man whom so many regarded as a cold-blooded monster. The loving father is developed in the tender run-on lines, 'This is most excusable in my daughter/ Who loves that fruit and whom I bless'. Through the picture that develops of an anxious father and a polite brother, 'I send my affections to all your family', Kennelly forces us to have a plural response to history. He challenges our complacency of a received image. Cromwell can speak of 'Christblessed lands' and also still remark, 'Whole floods of brine are at their beck and call'.

Class/Homework Exercises

1. 'Kennelly is an investigative poet who wishes to understand the complexity of historical characters.' Discuss this view, with particular reference to the poem 'Oliver to His Brother'.
2. 'Brendan Kennelly's evocative use of language is ideally suited to his disturbing subject matter.' To what extent is this true of 'Oliver to His Brother'? Support your argument with reference to the text.

Points to Consider

- **Private letter format – hearing Cromwell's actual words creates intimacy between reader and subject.**
- **Repetition of first person highlights self-regarding assurance of Cromwell.**
- **Contrasting tones (warm, human, cold, methodical, pragmatic, dismissive) develop the image of this multi-dimensional character.**
- **Reliance on real documentation brings an air of authenticity to this bold endeavour.**

6 🔊 I See You Dancing, Father

BRENDAN KENNELLY

No sooner downstairs after the night's rest
And in the door
Than you started to dance a step
In the middle of the kitchen floor.

And as you danced   5
You whistled.
You made your own music
Always in tune with yourself.

Well, nearly always, anyway.   10
You're buried now
In Lislaughtin Abbey
And whenever I think of you

I go back beyond the old man
Mind and body broken   15
To find the unbroken man.
It is the moment before the dance begins,

Your lips are enjoying themselves
Whistling an air.
Whatever happens or cannot happen
In the time I have to spare   20
I see you dancing, father.

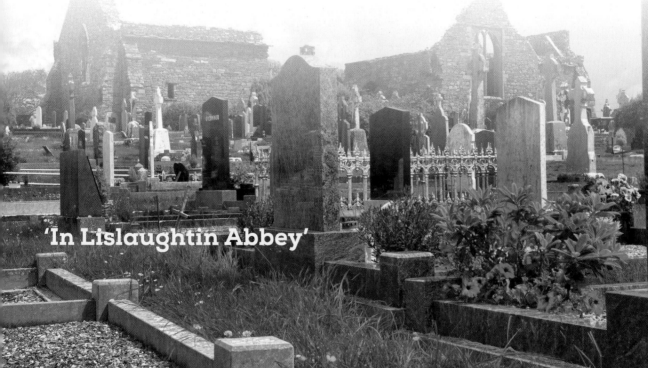

'In Lislaughtin Abbey'

👤 Personal Response

1. What is your impression of the poet's relationship with his father? Support your answer with suitable reference to the poem.
2. Select one visual image from the poem that shows Kennelly's eye for close observation. Comment briefly on the effect of your chosen image.
3. Write a short personal response to the poem, explaining its impact on you.

👁 Critical Literacy

Brendan Kennelly's parents owned a pub at the village crossroads in Ballylongford, where he and his six siblings sang, told stories and exchanged banter with the local men and women. Unsurprisingly, North Kerry resurfaces in many of his most compelling poems. Indeed, the family kitchen – the primal place of familial relationships – was also the home of Kennelly's poetic imagination. 'I See You Dancing, Father' centres around the fragment of the poet's fondest memory of his father. To a great extent, however, this bittersweet tribute is essentially about how we choose to remember the dead.

The poem's title introduces an immediate **sense of celebration**. Kennelly chooses to set aside all morbid thoughts of death and insists on remembering his father in his prime. This note of defiance is developed in the opening stanza as he recalls his extrovert father at his happiest – the centre of attention – dancing 'in the middle of the kitchen floor'. The run-on lines and lively rhythm create a relaxed, playful mood. Kennelly's use of the present tense allows him relive the past. He addresses his father directly: 'You started to dance'. There is little doubt that the poet has made a decision to highlight the positive aspects of his father's happy-go-lucky nature rather than criticise him for sleeping late or behaving irresponsibly. The slightly petulant tone ('No sooner downstairs ...') suggests that Kennelly's father had a habit of behaving like a mischievous child.

The energetic vocabulary of stanza two ('danced', 'whistled', 'music', 'tune') adds to the exuberant atmosphere and helps to define the father's carefree personality. Kennelly's unmistakable sense of awe is present in the easy image of his father naturally breaking into a traditional solo dance (*damhsa ar an sean nós*) and stepping out to his own whistling. The poet cannot hide his feelings of admiration for someone who clearly lived life on his own terms – 'Always in tune with yourself'. The pun seems ideally suited to such a colourful character.

Yet Kennelly is realistic about his father – 'Well, nearly always, anyway' – and checks himself from idealising him as a man without faults. The tone changes in stanza three with the **stark acceptance of mortality and loss**: 'You're buried now/In Lislaughtin Abbey'. In contrast with the earlier lines, the pace becomes sluggish, slowed by the use of commas and half-rhymes. This creates an unsettling sense of pathos. Short lines and broad vowel assonant sounds match the sombre mood, quietly conveying the son's unspoken grief.

But the air of sorrow is soon replaced with an emphatic pledge to acknowledge his father's happy life: 'I go back beyond the old man'. Stanza four reveals the poet's crucial choice to focus on preserving his memory of 'the unbroken man'. Kennelly's determination in catching the timeless image of 'the moment before the dance begins' challenges death and mourning. In this ecstatic instant of anticipation, neither father nor son can ever grow old. Even if it is illusory, it marks a **momentary triumph**, celebrating their close relationship.

Stanza five illustrates the beauty and simplicity of the reminiscence as the poet delights in imagining his father's presence again: 'Your lips are enjoying themselves'. The **detailed personification** has a surreal quality that is both uplifting and unnerving. For Kennelly, all that he can still hold dear is this curious image of his father whistling. The poet communicates his feelings subtly, by suggesting his love for his father rather than stating it directly. In the final three lines, he returns to the present and accepts the poignant reality of coping and grieving 'In the time I have to spare'. Faced with the inevitability of death, he prefers to make the most of life – just as his father did.

Dance is a central motif in this heartfelt love poem – with its distinct echoes of Patrick Kavanagh's elegies. From the start, Kennelly makes characteristic use of a crisp, pared-down language – a distinctive style that is always a model of melodious clarity. The rhythmical elegance of expression captures the movement into dance when the poet's father truly became himself. Throughout 'I See You Dancing, Father', the **uninhibited nostalgia and tender lyricism** typify Brendan Kennelly's extraordinary enthusiasm for life.

✒ Writing About the Poem

'Kennelly's most personal poems are filled with deeply felt sentiment which never lapses into sentimentality.' To what extent is this true of 'I See You Dancing, Father'? Support your answer with reference to the poem.

Sample Paragraph

The title, 'I See You Dancing, Father', sets the tone of this compassionate poem. Kennelly takes a narrative theme to remember the fondest memory he has of his late father and how he must move on after his death. There is nothing false about the poet's feelings. Without being over-emotional, he makes a conscious decision to remember a loved one who celebrated the bright side of life. While the son feels love, he refuses to become sentimental about his father's good behaviour – which was only 'nearly always'. Kennelly does not shy away from the fact that the old man became sick – 'Mind and body broken' – but he will always recall the good times – 'the moment before the dance begins'. The poem is caring, but it is also rooted in the real world. The way the memory was mixed with reality showed that Kennelly is very sincere.

EXAMINER'S COMMENT

This is a reasonably good response that maintains a focus on the poet's attitude and feelings. Quotations are used to support points and the expression is generally controlled. More detailed analysis of tone and language use would have improved the standard from a solid middle grade.

✒ Class/Homework Exercises

1. 'Brendan Kennelly's most heart-rending poems often highlight the twin themes of love and loss.' Discuss this statement with reference to 'I See You Dancing, Father'.
2. 'Kennelly's deceptively simple language in "I See You Dancing, Father" is ideally suited to his emotional subject matter.' Discuss this view, with reference to the poem.

⊙ Points to Consider

- Memory, family love and the celebration of life are central themes.
- Dancing used as a symbol of the father's life and the poet's enduring love.
- Effective use of simple language, energetic verbs and vivid imagery.
- Variety of tones – nostalgic, realistic, reflective, loving, etc.

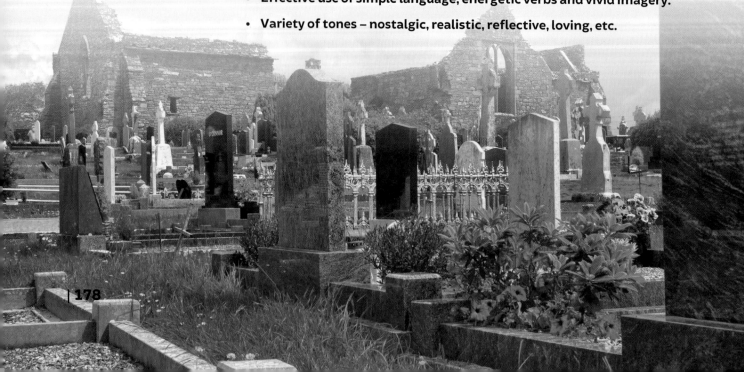

7

A Cry for Art O'Leary

(from the Irish of Eibhlín Dubh Ní Chonaill)

BRENDAN KENNELLY

Title: Art O'Leary (1746-73) from Irish Roman Catholic gentry, captain in Hungarian Hussars regiment of Empress Maria Theresa of Austria. **Eibhlín Dubh Ní Chonaill** (Eileen O'Connell) was the Irish noblewoman wife of Art O'Leary. She was born in 1743 and died in 1800.

My love
The first time I saw you
From the top of the market
My eyes covered you
My heart went out to you   5
I left my friends for you
Threw away my home for you

What else could I do?

You got the best rooms for me
All in order for me   10
Ovens burning for me
Fresh trout caught for me
Choice meat for me

In the best of beds I stretched
Till milking-time hummed for me   15

You made the whole world
Pleasing to me

White rider of love!

I love your silver-hilted sword
How your beaver hat became you   20
With its band of gold
Your friendly homespun suit
Revealed your body
Your pin of glinting silver
Glittered in your shirt   25

My love: lament was composed extempore (as an impromptu lament) by Eibhlin, mourning her young husband's death and calling for revenge.

Threw away my home for you: her parents were opposed to the marriage.

beaver hat: fur hat; Penal laws demanded payment to the British Crown for wearing a gentleman's hat. **homespun:** plain, unpretentious.

On your horse in style
You were sensitive pale-faced
Having journeyed overseas
The English respected you
Bowing to the ground   30
Not because they loved you
But true to their hearts' hate
They're the ones who killed you
Darling of my heart

My lover   35
My love's creature
Pride of Immokelly
To me you were not dead
Till your great mare came to me
Her bridle dragging ground   40
Her head with your startling blood
Your blood upon the saddle
You rode in your prime
I didn't wait to clean it
I leaped across my bed   45
I leaped then to the gate
I leaped upon your mare
I clapped my hands in frenzy
I followed every sign
With all the skill I knew   50
Until I found you lying
Dead near a furze brush
Without pope or bishop
Or cleric or priest
To say a prayer for you   55

Only a crooked wasted hag
Throwing her cloak across you

I could do nothing then
In the sight of God
But go on my knees   60
And kiss your face
And drink your free blood

My man!
Going out the gate
You turned back again   65
Kissed the two children
Threw a kiss at me
Saying 'Eileen, woman, try

Immokelly: reference to Art O'Leary's lineage from lords of Athenry.

bridle: buckled straps used to control horse.

frenzy: turmoil, passion.

To get this house in order,
Do your best for us   70
I must be going now
I'll not be home again.'
I thought that you were joking
You my laughing man

My man!   75
My Art O'Leary
Up on your horse now
Ride out to Macroom
And then to Inchigeela
Take a bottle of wine   80
Like your people before you
Rise up
My Art O'Leary
Of the sword of love

Put on your clothes   85
Your black beaver
Your black gloves
Take down your whip
Your mare is waiting
Go east by the thin road   90
Every bush will salute you
Every stream will speak to you
Men and women acknowledge you

They know a great man
When they set eyes on him   95

God's curse on you Morris,
God's curse on your treachery
You swept my man from me
The man of my children
Two children play in the house   100
A third lives in me

He won't come alive from me

Macroom: Rattleigh House near Macroom, Co. Cork was O'Leary's home.
Inchigeela: small Co. Cork village with beautiful landscapes.

Morris: Abraham Morris, Protestant sheriff of Cork.

A third lives in me: Eibhlin is pregnant with their third child.

My heart's wound
Why was I not with you
When you were shot   105
That I might take the bullet
In my own body?
Then you'd have gone free
Rider of the grey eye
And followed them   110
Who'd murdered me

My man!
I look at you now
All I know of a hero
True man with true heart   115
Stuck in a coffin
You fished the clean streams
Drank nightlong in halls
Among frank-breasted women

I miss you   120

My man!
I am crying for you
In far Derrynane
In yellow-appled Carren
Where many a horseman   125
And vigilant woman
Would be quick to join
In crying for you
Art O'Leary
My laughing man   130

O crying women
Long live your crying
Till Art O'Leary
Goes back to school
On a fateful day   135
Not for books and music

But for stones and clay

Derrynane: Co. Kerry village named after Daniel O'Connell ('Liberator of Irish people') and nephew of Eibhlín Dubh Ní Chonaill. **Carren:** Small region near the Burren, Co. Clare.

crying women: professional keeners who wept at funerals.

My man!
The corn is stacked
The cows are milking   140
My heart is a lump of grief
I will never be healed
Till Art O'Leary
Comes back to me

I am a locked trunk   145
The key is lost
I must wait till rust
Devours the screw

O my best friend
Art O'Leary   150
Son of Conor
Son of Cadach
Son of Lewis
East from wooded glens
West from girlish hills   155
Where rowanberries grow
Yellow nuts budge from branches
Apples laugh like small suns
As once they laughed
Throughout my girlhood   160
It is no cause for wonder
If bonfires lit O'Leary country
Close to Ballingeary
Or holy Gougane Barra
After the clean-gripping rider   165
The robust hunter
Panting towards the kill
Your own hounds lagged behind you
O horseman of the summoning eyes
What happened you last night?   170
My only whole belief
Was that you could not die
For I was your protection

My heart! My grief!

My man! My darling!   175

rowanberries: red berries
from rowan trees.

Ballingeary: village in the
Co. Cork mountains.

In Cork
I had this vision
Lying in my bed:
A glen of withered trees
A home heart-broken   180
Strangled hunting-hounds
Choked birds
And you
Dying on a hillside
Art O'Leary   185
My one man
Your blood running crazily
Over earth and stone

Jesus Christ knows well
I'll wear no cap   190
No mourning dress
No solemn shoes
No bridle on my horse
No grief-signs in my house
But test instead   195
The wisdom of the law
I'll cross the sea
To speak to the King
If he ignores me
I'll come back home   200
To find the man
Who murdered my man

Morris, because of you
My man is dead

Is there a man in Ireland   205
To put a bullet through your head

Women, white women of the mill
I give my love to you
For the poetry you made
For Art O'Leary   210
Rider of the brown mare
Deep women-rhythms of blood
The fiercest and the sweetest
Since time began
Singing of this cry I womanmake   215
For my man

bullet through your head:
Morris was eventually shot
by Art O'Leary's brother.

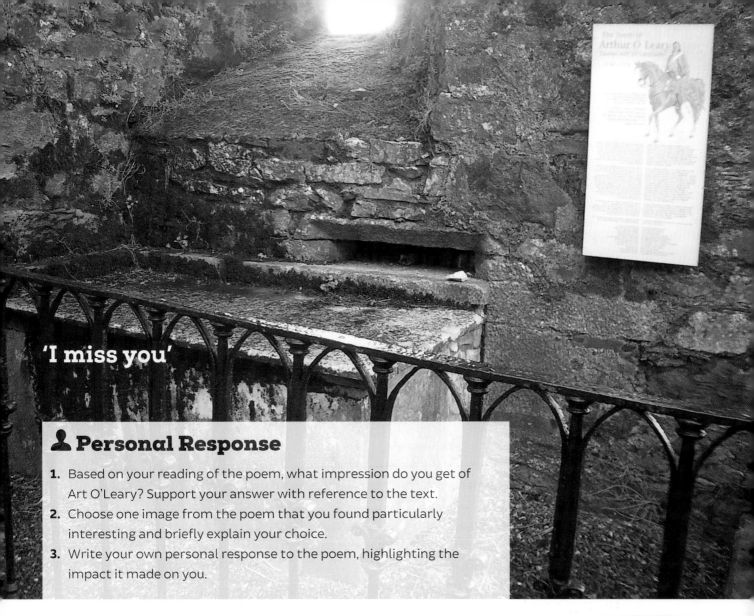

'I miss you'

👤 Personal Response

1. Based on your reading of the poem, what impression do you get of Art O'Leary? Support your answer with reference to the text.
2. Choose one image from the poem that you found particularly interesting and briefly explain your choice.
3. Write your own personal response to the poem, highlighting the impact it made on you.

👁 Critical Literacy

'A Cry for Art O' Leary' is a translation by Brendan Kennelly of the Irish lament, 'Caoineadh Airt Uí Laoghaire', which was published in his collection Love of Ireland (1989). Kennelly, a native Irish speaker, believed that a good verse translation 'is also a completely new, autonomous poem in English'. The purpose of translation, he felt, was to deconstruct and reconstruct. He regarded himself as a version-maker rather than translator. Frank O'Connor, Thomas Kinsella and Eilis Dillon, among others, have also translated this famous Irish elegy. The hot-tempered Art O'Leary became involved in a feud with an arrogant Englishman, Abraham Morris of Hanover Hall, Macroom, Co. Cork. The Englishman demanded that Art sell to him a beautiful brown mare that he had brought back with him from Austria. The Penal Laws stated that no Catholic could own a horse worth more than five pounds and so could be forced to sell it at that price to any Protestant. When Art refused to sell, Morris used his position as magistrate to proclaim O'Leary an outlaw who could then, legally, be shot on sight. On 4th May, 1773, he tracked O'Leary to Carraig an Ime where one of Morris's soldiers shot and killed Art.

This poem has been called the 'greatest poem written in these islands in the whole of the 18th century' by Peter Levi, Professor of Poetry at Oxford University. It was composed by Art O'Leary's wife (Eileen of the Raven Hair) and recited on the spot where he lay murdered. This lament for her dashing young husband of 26 is a traditional **caoineadh** or keen from the oral tradition of Irish literature, a song of the dead performed by women at a wake. It is divided into three parts: the salutation calls upon the deceased with affection ('My love'); the dirge or keen praises the character ('sensitive'), virtues ('great man'), achievements ('hero'), lineage ('Son of Conor') and dreams ('vision'); and the third section focuses on the declaration of an enemy ('Morris').

The **language** of the keen is clear, direct and plain, 'I miss you'. It is people's poetry. This poem explores one individual's personal loss of a loved one. The young widow's passionate feelings for her flamboyant husband ring with a haunting, time-defying force. The poem's momentum is unimpeded by punctuation marks, except for those conveying her grievous sense of loss, 'My heart! My grief!'

Eibhlín speaks directly to the reader (lines 1-7) reciting her **thrilling first encounter** with her good-looking husband, 'My eyes covered you/My heart went out to you'. It was certainly love at first sight. She refers to the price she paid for this love, forsaking friends and family, but a wistful rhetorical question intones: 'What else could I do?' The young woman was so intoxicated with the handsome Hussar that she had no will of her own. Their idyllic romance is evoked through lines 9-18. The gentle repetitive 'm' sound in 'Till milking-time hummed for me' recalls the harmony of their life together. She obviously worships her young husband, 'White rider of love'.

Lines 19-25 portray in a series of telling details **Art O'Leary in his prime** with his 'silver-hilted sword' and 'beaver hat' with its 'band of gold'. At this time, under Penal Laws, a gentleman's hat could only be worn if a payment was made to the ruling British Crown. Eibhlín refers to Art's impressive army service, 'having journeyed overseas'. The first inclination that the young woman had of her husband's murder was the arrival of his blood-stained horse. This riderless horse is not only a messenger of death, but also an emblem of the political vacuum in a country without a true leader. Her anguished reaction is caught in the explosive verb 'leaped'. From this point onwards, the poem's form is one headlong rush encompassing a single breathless thought – her husband's murder. Tragically, she finds Art 'Dead near a furze bush' without having had any proper funeral rites. Burial in monastic ground was forbidden under Penal Law. Alone and agitated, she performs her own personal funeral rites.

Lines 63-74 poignantly relate the couple's **final meeting**. Art has asked Eibhlín to get 'this house in order', prophetically remarking, 'I'll not be home again'. Ironically, she believed that her 'laughing man' was only joking. In her distress, she now exhorts her dead husband to return to life and ride out where all may greet him: 'Men and women acknowledge you' (line 93). This memory of how great a man he had been causes her to explode with anger and she utters a curse against his enemy, Abraham Morris, who ordered the killing. The brutal finality of Art's death is highlighted in line 98, 'You swept my man from me'. Equally upsetting is the heartbreaking picture of their two children innocently playing, still unaware that they are fatherless. A further tragic consequence is to follow – the loss of their unborn child.

The frantic widow berates herself for not being with Art so that she could have been killed instead of him. Then she would most certainly have been avenged by her husband. But now she has to deal with his murder, its stark reality related in the cacophonous phrase, 'Stuck in a coffin' (line 116). This **dreadful sight** contrasts sharply with what he had once been, 'True man with true heart', someone who lived life to the full. Eibhlín's simple admission, 'I miss you', reaches across the ages to touch the reader. She urges the keeners to mourn Art in the alliterative 'Long live your crying' and she recounts with pride how she has kept their house in order, 'The corn is stacked/The cows are milking' (line 139). But she remains overcome by unhappiness and the powerful metaphor, 'My heart is a lump of grief' palpably communicates her profound sorrow. A second comparison emphasises the sense of resignation, 'I am a locked trunk' – which will heal only through the passing of time, 'I must wait till rust/Devours the screw'.

Lines 150-153 describe Art O'Leary's fine lineage, 'Son of Conor'. The fertile Irish landscape is detailed through internal rhyme of the broad 'ow' ('rowanberries grow') and alliteration ('Yellow nuts budge from branches'). Personification enlivens the simile, 'Apples laugh like small suns'. In the meantime, bonfires continue to mourn Art's passing. Eibhlín still cannot fully understand what has happened. She shares a **nightmare vision** that she had of 'withered trees'. Graphic description transmits the horrific violence and devastation: 'Strangled', 'Choked', 'crazily'. Yet she refuses to mourn, preferring to seek justice, 'I'll cross the sea/To speak to the King'.

This determined widow decides that if she gets no satisfaction, then she alone will hunt whoever 'murdered my man' (line 202). Her desire for vengeance could hardly be clearer as she imagines the single bullet that will end Morris' life. A more formal, dignified tone emerges as she thanks the keening women ('I give my love to you') for their protestations. She reverts to the **strong force within women** that enables them to withstand terrible sorrows, communicated through original compound words, 'women-rhythms' and 'womanmake'. Through this impressive plaintive lament, Eibhlín herself has just created a tremendous elegy for her dead husband.

In translating the work of other writers, Kennelly illuminates people and events by absorbing them and allowing the language of his sources to pass through him to his readers. He offers up these stories for us to interpret and in so doing preserves them for posterity. In this poem, the raw grief and frustration of a young wife is caught in the **tonal complexity**, which ranges widely from misty-eyed remembrances to vivid accounts of action and anger, to scenes of heart-rending sorrow, deep curses and quiet dignity.

Kennelly's version of this 18th-century lament presents all the torment of one woman's personal heartache after the sudden death of the man she loves and whose name continually haunts her. Aching tenderness, a furious wish for retribution, pleas for justice, pride and reassurance in the continuities of family are all expressed through remarkable imagery. The poet has listened to the **voice of the young widow** and conveys her reactions to human cruelty in the subtle interwoven harmonies of alliteration and internal rhyme.

The strength of Eibhlín's feeling is shown by the perfection of the poetic technique. This narrative epic confirms not only confidence in the essential dignity and greatness of man but also **celebrates the feminine ability to love** in all its sublime blossoming, vigour and maturing. The poem succeeds in communicating what it means to grieve over loss in all its sadness and rage. It also proves the ability of woman to suffer and survive, to 'womanmake' and endure.

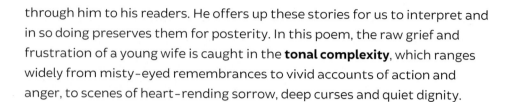

Writing About the Poem

'Brendan Kennelly's translations encompass the spirit of the original work to let it sing.' Discuss this view, with particular reference to 'A Cry for Art O'Leary'.

Sample Paragraph

EXAMINER'S COMMENT

An impressive top-grade response that shows close engagement with the poem. The introductory overview is clearly developed with well-supported discussion points. These include some incisive comments on various poetic techniques, such as rhythm, sound effects and the use of compound words. Reference and quotation are highly effective throughout. Expression is particularly good – varied, lively and controlled.

In this traditional ballad, 'A Cry for Art O'Leary', Kennelly describes the consequences of Art's brutal murder. We see the heroic husband, the beautiful Irish landscape, the warm love between Eibhlín and Art, and a wife's powerful feelings. Through the use of the aural techniques of old Gaelic poetry and the traditional keening chant rhythm, Kennelly's translation has a musical quality. The couple's idyllic marriage is conveyed through assonance, 'You made the whole world/Pleasing to me'. Sweeping rhythm adds to the choral effect of the voices expressing grief at a funeral. Harsh consonants contrast sharply with the detailed description of the Irish landscape in the alliterative line, 'Yellow nuts budge from branches'. Kennelly's use of compound words ('womanmake') shows how women have always survived sorrow and concludes the poem with musical language.

✒ Class/Homework Exercises

1. 'The ferocity of people's feelings is coupled with an awesome control of language in Kennelly's poetry.' Discuss this view, with particular reference to 'A Cry for Art O'Leary'.
2. 'Kennelly's poetry raises disturbing perspectives about the human condition in ways that challenge readers.' To what extent is this true of 'A Cry for Art O'Leary'? Support your answer with reference to the poem.

⊙ Points to Consider

- **Central themes include love, loss, grieving, relationships, memory, anger and acceptance.**

- **Simple direct language, vivid imagery, lack of punctuation.**

- **Hypnotic tone and keening rhythm add to the sense of pathos.**

- **Poem's structure based on the traditional form of the Irish lament.**

- **Varied moods and tones: shock, tenderness, nostalgic reverie, personal outrage, vengeance concluding in immense dignity.**

8 🔊 Things I Might Do

I thought of things I might do with my heart.
Should I make it into a month like October,
A chalice for the sad madness of leaves
That I might raise in homage to the year's end?

Should I make it into a small white church in   5
A country-place where bells are childhood prayers?
Or a backroom of a brothel in Dublin
Where the trade of somethinglikelove endures?

Should I make it a judge to judge itself?
Or a caring face in a memory-storm?   10
Or a bed

For Judas dreaming of the tree:
    'There now, there now, rest as best you can,
    Darling, rest your treacherous head
    And when you've rested, come home to me.'   15

chalice: wine cup used in religious ceremonies.
homage: honour, praise.

treacherous: false, deceptive.

'the sad madness of leaves'

👤 Personal Response

1. Over the course of the poem, Kennelly explores emotions through a series of metaphors. Choose the metaphor that you think is most interesting. Give at least one reason for your choice.
2. Describe the mood in the last three lines of the poem. Refer to the text to support your answer.
3. In your opinion, what is the central theme or message in this poem? Support your answer with suitable reference to the text.

◉ Critical Literacy

Brendan Kennelly's *The Book of Judas* (published in 1991) explores the theme of betrayal at various levels. Many of the poems bring Judas' story to life in a modern context by addressing the failings of Irish society. The central character is an elusive figure who takes numerous forms.

In the poem's opening lines, the unnamed speaker is initially concerned with the 'heart' and finding ways of expressing emotion. The plaintive question: 'Should I make it into a month like October?' has a poignant quality. The month marks the transition from autumn into winter's bitter weather. Kennelly introduces another metaphor for feelings in line 3, using the religious image of lifting up a chalice to give thanks for another year. **The narrative voice is downbeat**, however, focusing on 'the sad madness of leaves'. The wistful description is filled with onomatopoeic effects: internal rhymes echo the chaos in nature while sibilant 's' sounds accentuate the narrator's tone of quiet dejection. Does the 'year's end' offer any good reason for celebration?

Lines 5-9 present a stark contrast between the simple fulfilment of youthful Christian faith (symbolised by 'a small white church') and the loss of innocence in later adult life. The seedy image, 'a backroom of a brothel in Dublin', illustrates the loneliness of people seeking a substitute for genuine human connection. To highlight the irony, Kennelly **experiments with the layout** of the poem. The self-created compound word, 'somethinglikelove', makes an immediate visual impact on the page, simulating the close physical contact of the anonymous sexual encounters endured in 'the trade'.

The efforts to come to terms with the speaker's entangled emotional life continue in line 9 with another pertinent suggestion: 'Should I make it a judge to judge itself?' The **self-critical tone** challenges the 'heart'. Can an individual's own feelings be fully trusted? Are they sometimes selfish or false – even based on self-betrayal? This disturbing possibility is immediately countered with a much more consoling interpretation of human emotions: 'a caring face in a memory storm'.

The poem's final lines envision a disturbing scene featuring **conflicting experiences of guilt and compassion**. The speaker imagines the outcast Judas recalling his crucial role in bringing about Christ's death on the cross. The self-destructive deceiver is 'dreaming of the tree' while another tender voice tries to console him: 'there now, rest as best you can'. Shame, regret, forgiveness and concern amalgamate in the well-worn words of comfort – but the startling inclusion of 'rest your treacherous head' is an unnerving reminder of the consequences of betrayal.

Throughout this reflective poem, moments of tender lyricism have been undermined by Kennelly's bleak vision of modern life. The **bitterly articulate narrative voice** presents readers with a disturbing irony. Just like Judas, every human being is capable of a variety of feelings – both sympathetic and destructive. In the end, individuals have to face up to the reality of their emotional behaviour – 'and when you've rested, come home to me'. They must then live with themselves and the truth about all their relationships. The poem's conclusion offers no hint of salvation, leaving the original question about what to 'do with my heart' almost entirely unresolved.

⌂ Writing About the Poem

'Brendan Kennelly writes hauntingly powerful poems that make an immediate impact on readers.' Discuss this statement, with particular reference to 'Things I Might Do'.

Sample Paragraph

I thought the mood in 'Things I Might Do' was edgy, especially at the end where it seems that Judas, the apostle who betrayed his friend Jesus, is being pampered by someone in his family. The idea of somebody close to Judas being so supportive is disturbing. I was surprised by the paradox, 'Darling, rest your treacherous head'. The whole poem has the sense of a dying person's bucket list. At the start, the imagery is mainly about death, 'madness of leaves' in October and 'the year's end'. Kennelly struggles with his feelings as if he fears the future and is sorry about the past. Everyone experiences a feeling of sadness about something said or about a serious mistake that you have made. Overall, this was a very thought-provoking poem that made me ask questions about how we can hurt other people's feelings.

EXAMINER'S COMMENT

A solid middle-grade response that includes some close personal engagement and good points on imagery. Effective use is made of accurate quotations. More analysis of the poet's use of language (memorable comparisons, introspective tone, etc.) would have raised the standard.

✎ Class/Homework Exercises

1. 'Soul-searching and existential anguish are recurring features of the poetry of Brendan Kennelly.' Discuss this view, with particular reference to the poem 'Things I Might Do'.
2. 'The casual force that energises Kennelly's language use is a key characteristic of his poetry.' To what extent is this true of 'Things I Might Do'? Support your answer with reference to the poem.

⊙ Points to Consider

- **Kennelly raises incisive questions about people's emotional lives and relationships.**
- **Effective use of metaphors, rhetorical questions, contrasts and layout.**
- **Dreamlike atmosphere and sense of timelessness.**
- **Range of tones: inquisitive, reflective, self-critical, confessional, etc.**

⚫ **A Great Day**

BRENDAN KENNELLY

She was all in white.

Snow
Suggests itself as metaphor

But since this has been so often said
I may be justified in considering it dead.   5
Something about snow is not quite right.

Therefore, she was all in white.

He was most elegant too
All dickied up in dignified blue.

They came together, as is habitual   10
In that part of the world,
Through a grave ritual,

Listening
With at least a modicum of wonder –
What God has joined together   15
Let no man put asunder.

Man in woman, woman in man.
Soon afterwards, the fun began.

It was a great day –
Long hours of Dionysiac festivity.   20

Songs poured out like wine.
Praises flowed as they had never done.

The people there
Seemed to see each other in a new way.
This added to the distinction of the day.   25

And all the time she was all in white
Enjoying every song and speech
Enjoying every sip and bite.

metaphor: describing somebody or something using a vivid comparison.

dickied up: well dressed.

habitual: usual, expected, customary.

grave: solemn, ominous.
ritual: ceremony, sacrament.

modicum: small amount.
wonder: surprise, doubt.

asunder: apart, in bits.

Dionysiac: relating to Dionysus, Greek god of wine and fertility.

distinction: special importance, excellence.

Such whiteness seems both beautiful and true
He thought, all dickied up in dignified blue.   30

He looks so good in blue
(This warmed her mind)
Blue suits him
Down to the ground.

At the table where they sat   35
Things seemed to fit.

And the loud crowd sang and danced
The whole day long, the whole night long.
There could never be anything but dance and song.

I must change, she whispered,   40
I must change my dress.

He never saw the white dress again.

In the train, the trees wore their rainy veils
With a reticent air.
                                                     reticent: silent,
                                                     uncommunicative.

It's good to get away, she whispered,   45
Touching her beautiful hair.

She closed her eyes, the trees were silent guests,
A tide of thoughts flowed in her head,
In his head.

'Darling, it was a great day,' she said.   50

'beautiful and true'

👤 Personal Response

1. In your opinion, what expectations does the poet raise in the reader by the use of the title, 'A Great Day', and are these expectations fulfilled? Support your answer with close reference to the poem.
2. Choose one image from the poem that appealed to you and comment on its effectiveness.
3. Write a short personal response to the poem, referring closely to the text in your answer.

👁 Critical Literacy

'A Great Day' forms part of Brendan Kennelly's collection, *Familiar Strangers: New and Collected Poems (1960–2004)*. The poet himself arranged this 'collection of voices' into thematic, rather than chronological, sections. 'Looking back over the poems I've tried to write, they all seemed to be moments, or stabs of memory, or sudden images, and seemed independent of chronological time,' he observed.

Kennelly offers a thought-provoking **portrait of a wedding** in his poem, 'A Great Day'. It takes the form of a stream of consciousness (an uninterrupted flow of thoughts and feelings through the poet's mind). The poem begins with a familiar visual image, 'She was all in white'. White is traditionally worn by brides and suggests purity, innocence, a new beginning. The poet dismisses the familiar cliché of snow as a metaphor to describe this colour, 'since this has been so often said/I may be justified in considering it dead'. Run-on lines and a banal rhyme scheme ('said', 'dead') emphasise the hackneyed reference. 'Poetry,' according to Kennelly, 'is an attempt to cut through the deadening familiarity and repeated mechanical usage' of language.

Suddenly an unrhymed line produces an air of mystery, 'Something about snow is not quite right' (line 6). The poet challenges the reader to consider what is not quite right about the comparison. In a stand-alone line, he chooses to record his simplified solution to the dilemma, 'Therefore, she was all in white'. In line 8, attention turns to the groom. Alliteration, internal rhyme and a rhyming couplet sum up his appearance, 'He was most elegant too/All dickied up in dignified blue'. The syntax is as carefully arranged as the groom is scrupulously turned out. But the colloquial expression 'dickied up' strikes an almost **comical note**, particularly when linked through assonance with 'dignified'. It would seem as though the groom is not accustomed to being so formally dressed.

The official marriage ceremony is presented as a **connecting experience**, 'They came together'. The bride and groom have embraced tradition, 'as is habitual/In that part of the world,/Through a grave ritual'. The adjective

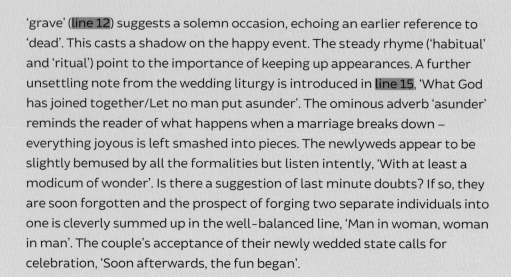

'grave' (line 12) suggests a solemn occasion, echoing an earlier reference to 'dead'. This casts a shadow on the happy event. The steady rhyme ('habitual' and 'ritual') point to the importance of keeping up appearances. A further unsettling note from the wedding liturgy is introduced in line 15, 'What God has joined together/Let no man put asunder'. The ominous adverb 'asunder' reminds the reader of what happens when a marriage breaks down – everything joyous is left smashed into pieces. The newlyweds appear to be slightly bemused by all the formalities but listen intently, 'With at least a modicum of wonder'. Is there a suggestion of last minute doubts? If so, they are soon forgotten and the prospect of forging two separate individuals into one is cleverly summed up in the well-balanced line, 'Man in woman, woman in man'. The couple's acceptance of their newly wedded state calls for celebration, 'Soon afterwards, the fun began'.

Everyone **rejoices in the marriage ceremony** because it ensures the continuation of society, so it truly is 'a great day' (line 19). Broad vowelled assonance, 'Long hours', echo the lengthy celebrations, so full of over-indulgence and lack of inhibition that the poet describes the festivities as 'Dionysiac', referring to the Greek god of wine and fertility. The lavishness and excess is conveyed in the simile, 'Songs poured out like wine' and in the assonance, 'Praises flowed as they had never done'. All the wedding guests reach new levels of perception, 'The people there/Seemed to see each other in a new way'. Attention is drawn to the extraordinary significance of the reception through the alliterative phrase, 'distinction of the day'. For Kennelly, love is the impetus that demands and enables the self to express and receive. The bride's beautiful appearance, 'And all the time she was all in white', appears to be the catalyst for the outpouring of joy. Repetition and alliteration in the run-on lines draw attention to her willing participation, 'Enjoying every song and speech/Enjoying every sip and every bite' (line 27).

The groom's thoughts are also recorded – and he is enchanted by his lovely bride, 'Such whiteness seems both beautiful and true'. In turn, she is delighted with her new husband, 'He looks so good in blue'. The couple sit together and 'Things seemed to fit'. Yet the **reader is left feeling increasingly uneasy**. Short lines contain glib comments ('Blue suits him'). The couplet in lines 35-36 obviously does not rhyme, ('sat', 'fit'). But once again, the reader is distracted by the noise of the party, 'And the loud crowd sang and danced/ The whole day long, the whole night long'. Caught up in the excitement, they lose all touch with reality: 'There could never be anything but dance and song' (line 39).

The **mood alters dramatically** when the bride changes her dress. In a simple stand-alone line, the groom states: 'He never saw the white dress again.' Did the magic also go out of the relationship? Was the fairytale over so soon? Pathetic fallacy accentuates the strangely subdued mood, 'the trees wore their rainy veils/ With a reticent air' (line 43). An atmosphere of diffidence, secrecy and reserve replaces the boisterous wedding party. The bride's personality also changes, no longer delighted to enjoy 'every sip and every bite', but instead becoming more self-obsessed, 'It's good to get away, she whispered,/Touching her beautiful hair'.

In line 47, she retreats even more, 'She closed her eyes'. There is an underlying sense that the couple have been actors who have just played their parts in a **public performance**. But at least the noisy party-goers are now replaced by the contrasting trees as 'silent guests'. The newly-weds retreat into their own private worlds, 'A tide of thoughts'. She appears to reach out to her new husband in the concluding line, '"Darling, it was a great day," she said'. Is the tone enthusiastic or half-hearted? Is the new bride simply saying what she is expected to say? Might there be an ironic acceptance that the future will not be quite so wonderful?

The poet has succeeded in challenging readers to consider the difficulty facing two people, two separate entities actually becoming one. As always, **Kennelly's poetry examines and questions the world we live in**, confronting personal weaknesses in human behaviour. He feels 'almost everyone needs a cover', but when masks and costumes are left aside, is there only emptiness and a sense of disconnectedness? Is happiness only momentarily attainable on 'a great day', but impossible to sustain in ordinary life? Kennelly has presented a familiar event and made it strangely disquieting.

✒ Writing About the Poem

'Kennelly's poetry stimulates and intensifies the reader's sense of wonder.' Discuss this statement, supporting your answer with particular reference to the poem 'A Great Day'.

Sample Paragraph

'A Great Day' opens with the traditional image of the bride, 'She was all in white'. Kennelly succeeds in making us look at the familiar wedding ritual again through his use of suggestion. The emphasis is on appearance, both bride and groom are 'most elegant'. All, on the surface, is as it should have been, the wedding was indeed a 'great day', full of 'dance and song'. However, through the poem is the feeling that 'something is not quite right'. The repetition of 'Seemed' and 'seems' strikes an uneasy note. 'Things seemed to fit', but when the bride changes her clothes, the mood suddenly changes too. The connection between the couple is already coming 'asunder': the bride breaks off communication, 'She closed her eyes', and they each become locked in their own thoughts, 'A tide of thoughts flowed in her head,/In his head'. Although a note of affection concludes the poem, the reader is left with 'a modicum of wonder' that the joining together of two individuals, 'Man in woman, woman in man', is not so easy. Kennelly raises the question and leaves it to us to search for the answer or to ask another question.

EXAMINER'S COMMENT

An impressive high-grade response that includes several good discussion points, such as the poet's use of suggestion. Good sense of engagement with the text and effective use of apt reference. Accurate quotations are well integrated into critical commentary. Clarity of expression throughout (e.g. 'threaded', 'dynamic pulse falters').

✍ Class/Homework Exercises

1. 'Kennelly has remarked that poetry remains a bewildering and enlightening adventure in language.' Discuss this view, with particular reference to the poem 'A Great Day'.
2. 'Brendan Kennelly's evocative use of language displays resilience and hope in a troubling world.' To what extent is this true of 'A Great Day'? Support your argument with reference to the text.

⊙ Points to Consider

- Stream of consciousness format allows readers to share intimately Kennelly's reflections on the 'great day'.

- Subtle suggestion and repetition create an unsettling atmosphere.

- Colloquial language lends an air of informality.

- Rhyme and assonance used to link and contrast ideas and moods.

- Ambivalent, thought-provoking ending.

10  Fragments

BRENDAN KENNELLY

What had he to say to her now?
Where was the woman he believed he had known
In a street, out walking, by the sea,
In bed, working, dancing, loving the sun

And saying so, always for the first time?   5
Who was this stranger with the graven face?
What led to the dreaming-up of a home?
And what was he, at sixty? Who was

That man lifting the blackthorn stick
With the knobbed top from its place   10
At the side of the fire, quietly dying?

He listened to his own steps in the walk
Past the reedy mud where plover rose
And scattered, black fragments, crying.

graven: death-like, etched.

blackthorn stick: shillelagh, knotty Irish stick.

reedy: marshy, rush-filled.
plover: short-legged wading birds.
fragments: remnants, scraps.

'where plover rose'

199

👤 Personal Response

1. Identify and briefly comment on the changing tones through the poem, supporting your answer with close reference to the text.
2. What is your impression of the woman referred to in line 2? Support your answer with reference to the poem.
3. Write your own personal response to the poem, highlighting the impact it made on you.

👁 Critical Literacy

Throughout much of his poetry, Brendan Kennelly emphasises that the world cannot be understood easily. Knowledge (and particularly self-knowledge) is an ongoing process of questioning and reformulations of the same questions, in order to find a more appreciative angle of what they seek to clarify. 'Fragments' is a poignant, reflective poem that can be interpreted in several ways, exploring the individual's attempts to understand the past while at the same time facing an uncertain future. Kennelly's method has been to combine apparently disparate perspectives in service to universal themes – often addressing the essential meaning of life itself.

From the outset of this sonnet, questions dominate. The speaker's deep sense of disillusionment and separation is signalled in the **half-hearted tone** of voice in line 1: 'What had he to say to her now?' Still struggling to come to terms with the unnamed 'woman he believed he had known', the narrator wonders where she might be at present and imagines her 'out walking, by the sea' or 'working'. The glimpses of these once familiar scenes appear pitiful now, suggesting the bittersweet nature of a failed relationship. Perhaps the true response to the opening question is that there really is nothing left to say – even if she were to return. Has the couple's initial closeness and spontaneity ('always for the first time') been irreparably lost?

The mood darkens further in stanza two with the startling description of 'this stranger with the graven face'. The speaker's tone is detached and he seems **alienated** from others – as well as from himself. Mention of the woman's 'graven' expression counters the happier memories of their lives together ('dancing, loving the sun'). The feelings of incredulity increase as he challenges the romantic notion of earlier times when they were planning a future together: 'What led to the dreaming-up of a home?' Both the dismissive tone and underlying irony reflect a deeply felt cynicism about the possibility of enduring love. It's the cue for the narrator to reflect on the fleeting nature of human experiences, relationships and his own achievements: 'And what was he, at sixty?'

The question is pursued through stanza three as the poem **moves from the here-and-now to the mystical** with deceptive ease.

In imagining – or remembering – 'That man lifting the blackthorn stick', he transcends ordinary time and place. The speaker's thoughts become fixated on a traditional Irish image – the elderly man sitting close to the fire, 'quietly dying'. In describing 'That man', the narrator associates his own life with the persona of his father and forefathers. Were their lives as uncertain as his? And were they a constant source of wonder to themselves?

Detailed imagery from the Irish countryside creates the subdued setting and elegiac mood in stanza four. Acutely aware of his place among the generations, the speaker 'listened to his own steps' as he passed 'the reedy mud where the plover rose'. Despite the pervading feeling of isolation and despondency, there is a recognition of the **timeless natural beauty** that marks Kennelly's sense of place. The run-through lines, broad assonant effects and sibilant 's' sounds add a delicate, musical quality. Above all, the final image of the plover – 'black fragments, crying' – is particularly evocative, symbolising the remnant memories of a forsaken life.

The conclusion is undoubtedly bleak, but not entirely tragic. Even though the speaker is still unable to realise the full extent of his regret, the **eloquent linguistic expression** of the poet's narrative has somehow humanised him. There is an acknowledgment that people find short-lived moments of happiness where they can while enduring the attrition of ordinary day-to-day living.

Kennelly has written elsewhere about the betrayal that underlines human relationships: 'I wonder if many people feel as I do – that in the society we have created it is very difficult to give your full, sustained attention to anything or anybody for long, that we are compelled to half-do a lot of things, to half-live our lives, half-dream our dreams, half-love our loves'.

✒ Writing About the Poem

'By confronting life's uncertainties in his poetry, Kennelly finds a way out of that pain.' Discuss this view, with particular reference to 'Fragments'.

Sample Paragraph

In 'Fragments', Kennelly tackles the subject of how to deal with the past. He does not refer directly to himself, but the breakdown of his marriage has been well documented. By distancing himself, he makes the theme universal so that others can relate to it. I found the phrase 'the woman he believed he had known' very revealing because it is impossible to know another person completely. The poet admits to still being unsure about his ex, 'What had he to say to her now?' and these questions are never really resolved as he remembers, 'this stranger'. He is even more confused about himself, 'what was he at sixty?' Kennelly pictures himself as an old man beside an open coal fire 'quietly dying'. In the last stanza, he finds comfort in nature, watching the plover rising like 'scattered black fragments, crying'. I believe Kennelly is saying that it is perfectly natural to feel sorrow and to be unsure about life. The poem might not cancel out his pain, but in the end, he seems to come to terms with it.

EXAMINER'S COMMENT

A good, personal high-grade response that shows close engagement with the poem. The paragraph includes some very incisive discussion, effectively supported by apt quotation – sometimes well integrated into the commentary. Overall expression is lively and varied.

✒ Class/Homework Exercises

1. 'A disturbing sense of underlying sadness is frequently found in Brendan Kennelly's poems.' In your opinion, how true is this of 'Fragments'? Support your answer with reference to the poem.
2. 'Kennelly's poetry often has a universal significance that raises interesting questions about the human condition.' To what extent is this true of 'Fragments'? Support your answer with reference to the poem.

⊙ Points to Consider

- Central themes include relationships, memory and the passing of time.
- Characteristic use of simple language, imagery and natural speech rhythms.
- Poem's structure based around a series of rhetorical questions.
- Varied moods and tones: introspective, nostalgic, cynical, despondent, realistic, etc.

11 The Soul's Loneliness

BRENDAN KENNELLY

it's nothing to go on about
but when I hear it
in the ticking of the clock

beside the books and photographs
or see it in the shine   5
of an Eason's plastic bag at midnight

Eason's: popular book store.

or touch it in the tree I call
Christ there outside my window
swaying in the day's afterglow

I shiver a little at the strangeness   10
of my flesh, the swell of sweat,
the child's poem I'll never forget

and find my eyes searching the floor
for a definition of grace
or a trace of yourself I've never noticed before.   15

'touch it in the tree'

👤 Personal Response

1. Based on your reading of the poem, what is your impression of the speaker? Support your answer with reference to the text.
2. Choose one aural image from the poem that appeals to you and comment briefly on its effectiveness.
3. Write your own personal response to the poem, highlighting the impact it made on you.

👁 Critical Literacy

Brendan Kennelly believes that poetry is a constant search for an answer never found: 'There is objectivity and there is the voices. I think they are connected. You are objective as well as being open to absorbing another identity; the identity of the floor or the roof or the light.' This poem considers what goes on in the 'shadowlands' of the poet's mind when he is in a state of loneliness, of mesmerised emptiness. The mystery of creation finds dramatic expression in its simple structure and awestruck lyricism.

Kennelly begins his exploration of his own spiritual awareness with a dismissive line, 'it's nothing to go on about'. At one level, soul-searching might seems unnecessary. The deliberate use of the lowercase 'i' in line 1 highlights the brushing aside of the issue. Yet through 10 run-on lines and three run-through stanzas, the poem records the rush of the poet's **mystical imagination** in full flow. The reader shares in this heightened sense of consciousness as the wonder of ordinary things is revealed.

The poet experiences awakening, purification, illumination and transformation. An everyday domestic sound, 'the ticking of the clock' (**stanza one**) and a common sight, 'an Eason's plastic bag' (stanza two) are reimagined through repetition ('it'), careful patterning of the slender vowel 'i' ('ticking', 'beside', 'midnight') and soft alliteration ('see', shine'). Both poet and reader encounter **the sensation of being alive** with greater intensity and sensitivity.

In stanza three, Kennelly moves from experience of sound and sight to touch. The repeated letter 't' emphasises the tactile sensation, 'touch it in the tree'. Again, the poet is enjoying a **fleeting glimpse of the miraculous quality of nature** – his senses are leading him to the divine spark that ignites only in the loneliness of the soul. Illumination occurs when the mind is no longer clouded by familiarity, and becomes lucid, awake, able to 'see into the life of things' when sensitised. The mystic poet searches for beauty, goodness and truth – all of which he finds 'in the tree I call/Christ there outside my window'. The gentle movement of the tree in the evening sunset, 'swaying in the day's afterglow', is beautifully suggested through resonant broad-vowel assonance.

The fourth stanza details another stage of the mystical experience, purification, **the letting go of one's ego**, 'I shiver a little at the strangeness/of my flesh'. Sibilance accentuates this inexplicable feeling. The alliterative phrase, 'swell of sweat', captures the physicality of the self while the distant memory of 'the child's poem' evokes Kennelly's enduring emotional life. All are left aside for a moment as he suddenly becomes alert to the sacredness of matter: 'my eyes searching the floor/for a definition of grace'. He is willing to open up, to look beyond himself and discover 'a trace of yourself I've never noticed before'.

The eager anticipation of transcendence becomes tangible. Kennelly has spoken of his belief in otherness, other ways of being at one with the world. Throughout the poem, **he has sought spiritual fulfilment** by battling against cosy familiarities and inviting new presences ('Christ', 'grace') into the abject loneliness of his own inner consciousness.

As in so many of Kennelly's poems, his dreamlike world is infused with animistic presence. This underlying sense of being **part of a universal spirit** is pervasive and the 'yourself' he addresses in line 15 could refer to anyone and everyone – including himself, of course. Such a surging, hopeful conclusion is both redemptive and reassuring. The price for loving life's miracles is isolation.

Kennelly has observed: 'Poetry is a singing art of natural and magical connection because, though it is born out of one person's solitude, it has the ability to reach out and touch in a humane and warmly illuminating way the solitude, even the loneliness of others ... Poetry is one of the most vital treasures that humanity possesses; it is a bridge between separated souls'.

✒ Writing About the Poem

'By confronting loneliness in his poetry, Kennelly gains a new level of awareness in his life.' Discuss this view, with particular reference to 'The soul's loneliness'.

Sample Paragraph

Kennelly both hates and delights in solitude. The actual title, 'The soul's loneliness' and the touching image of 'the ticking of the clock' acknowledge this awareness from the start. Every single thing excites his imagination, even 'the shine/of an Eason's plastic bag at midnight'. His eyes become unsealed as he begins to recognise the extraordinary in the ordinary. The poet begins to see the divine 'in the tree I call/Christ there'. He also brings us on this journey leading to an intense realisation of his own place in God's creation. Through the skilful use of sound effects –

both emphatic alliteration ('see it in the shine') and assonance ('Eason's plastic bag'), he enables readers to look again and to become aware. The soothing movement of the tree ('swaying in the day's afterglow') is re-enacted through the slow progress of broad vowels. As readers, we also experience Kennelly's vision of the world when he gains a deeper understanding of the loneliness of the soul.

✒ Class/Homework Exercises

1. 'Through his distinctive use of language, Brendan Kennelly is able to shape and articulate both joyous and troubling moments.' In your opinion, how true is this of 'The soul's loneliness'? Support your answer with reference to the poem.
2. 'Kennelly's poetry discovers, protects and celebrates the deepest values of the heart.' To what extent is this true of 'The soul's loneliness'? Support your answer with reference to the poem.

⊙ Points to Consider

- Central themes include loneliness, spiritual awareness and connection.
- Aural effects – alliteration, assonance and run-on lines – all capture the mystic experience.
- Poem's dreamlike, serene mood embodies the delight to be found in solitude.
- Effective use of structure, simple diction, rhythm, etc.

12 🔊 Saint Brigid's Prayer
(from the Irish)

BRENDAN KENNELLY

I'd like to give a lake of beer to God.
    I'd love the Heavenly
Host to be tippling there
    for all eternity.

Host: multitude of angels.
tippling: imbibing, drinking.

I'd love the men of Heaven to live with me,   5
    to dance and sing.
If they wanted, I'd put at their disposal
    vats of suffering.

vats: casks, tanks.

White cups of love I'd give them
    with a heart and a half;   10
sweet pitchers of mercy I'd offer
    to every man.

pitchers: jugs, containers.

I'd make Heaven a cheerful spot
    because the happy heart is true.
I'd make the men contented for their own sake.   15
    I'd like Jesus to love me too.

I'd like the people of Heaven to gather
    from all the parishes around.
I'd give a special welcome to the women,
    the three Marys of great renown.   20

the three Marys: pious women mentioned in the Bible.

I'd sit with the men, the women and God
    there by the lake of beer.
We'd be drinking good health forever
    and every drop would be a prayer.

'Brigid's Prayer'

👤 Personal Response

1. In your opinion, is this a serious or comic poem? Refer to the text in your answer.
2. Kennelly's use of language throughout this poem is vibrant and energetic. Do you agree? Support your answer with reference to the text.
3. Write your own personal response to the poem, referring closely to the text in your answer.

👁 Critical Literacy

Saint Brigid is the patron saint of poetry in Ireland. Down through the centuries, old pagan rituals and new Christian celebrations became associated with her feast day, 1 February. Her fabled love of beer is perfectly summed up in this 10th-century poem which is attributed to her, but adapted by Kennelly and narrated in her voice.

Saint Brigid's reputation for hospitality is evident in the celebratory tone of the opening lines. Her mischievous dream to join the 'tippling' angels in Heaven clearly suggests that she would like to see more joy in the world. Her personal enthusiasm – 'I'd like', 'I'd love' – is equally evident. The whimsical image of 'a lake of beer' typifies Irish people's fondness for exaggeration – and sometimes for glorifying alcohol. From the outset, Kennelly establishes a relaxed, **good-humoured atmosphere**. Neither the saint's unusual sentiments nor the colloquial language are characteristic of a formal conventional 'prayer'.

Brigid turns her attention to 'the men of Heaven' in lines 5-12, inviting them to 'live with me'. The request is a reminder of Ireland's conservative, male-dominated society. As a nun working with impoverished families, she would have seen the effects of patriarchal behaviour and drunkenness. The mood of the poem changes significantly when she offers to provide 'vats of suffering', suggesting that it's time for men to understand the harsh reality so many women have experienced. The critical voice grows **increasingly moralistic**, proposing that Irishmen should swap their self-indulgent 'vats' of beer for kinder 'cups of love'. As a sign of forgiveness to 'every man', Brigid will whole-heartedly give them 'sweet pitchers of mercy' – to encourage them to act more compassionately.

The assertive feminist perspective continues in lines 13-16, but within a positive Christian context. Looking forward to the prospect of Heaven as 'a cheerful spot', Brigid's self-confidence is emphasised through repetition ('I'd make') and by the **mischievous tone** of her promise to keep the men happy 'for their own sake'. The casual expression and jaunty rhythm of everyday speech reveal her good-natured personality which is based primarily on her unreserved religious faith: 'I'd like Jesus to love me too'.

Lines 17–20 focus on Ireland's traditional rural communities – often defined by shared religious links. While Brigid is keen to re-unite 'all the parishes around', once again she singles out the countless women she admires for 'special welcome'. In her eyes, they are all unsung heroines like 'the three Marys of great renown'. The poem's **last lines** present an **idyllic picture** of Heaven where men and women are equally treated alongside God. The emphasis is firmly placed on enjoyment and 'drinking good health' for all eternity, reflecting Brigid's theology. This final image – which grows out of the central comparison between drinking and glorifying God in prayer – leaves readers in no doubt about the poet's own enthusiasm for life.

Like so many of the personae in Kennelly's poems, Saint Brigid represents the search for unity and meaning in a world of division and suffering. In her femininity, she inclusively embodies several kinds of cross currents, some of them apparently contradictory – male and female, pagan and Christian, ancient and modern. Brigid was also a woman who believed in celebrating **the wonder of being alive** – something that made her particularly appealing to the poet – so that her life itself inspired unity and reconciliation.

✒ Writing About the Poem

'Brendan Kennelly creates living poetry without ever resorting to overly convoluted or pretentious language.' To what extent is this true of the poem 'Saint Brigid's Prayer'? Support your answer with reference to the text.

Sample Paragraph

The language used throughout 'Saint Brigid's Prayer' is simple and even childlike at times. The chanting of 'I'd like' or 'I'd make' is more nursery rhyme than formal prayer. This gives vitality to what she says. Lines are short and the images Kennelly creates, such as 'the lake of beer', are vivid. The poem reads easily, with a singalong beat. The poet avoids complex or long drawn-out descriptions. Instead, he uses common expressions, 'a heart and a half', 'the happy heart is true'. This is how ordinary Irish people speak, especially older people in some country areas. The themes in this poem are clearly expressed with the minimum of fuss. Kennelly gets to the point that St Brigid was a woman well ahead of her time. She doesn't take men too seriously and believes everyone should make the most of life. The poem ends on an upbeat note that shows Paradise as a happy place with 'everyone drinking good health' equally, just as Brigid imagined that 'cheerful spot'.

EXAMINER'S COMMENT

This succinct top-grade paragraph manages to cover a wide range of aspects very successfully. Effective points are made regarding the poet's themes, diction and rhythm. Accurate quotations provide good support and the expression throughout is confident and controlled.

✒ Class/Homework Exercises

1. 'Brendan Kennelly's poetic style can be strikingly spirited and playful.' To what extent is this true of 'Saint Brigid's Prayer'? Support your answer with reference to the text.
2. In your opinion, does the poem 'Saint Brigid's Prayer' have relevance to our modern world? Support the points you make with close reference to the text.

⊙ Points to Consider

- Brigid envisions Heaven as being a place of infinite hospitality.
- Realistic views about Irish society, gender and Christianity.
- Advocates the positive aspects of religion to bring love and joy.
- Addresses issues about abusing alcohol and its detrimental effects.
- Use of colloquial language and natural rhythms of ordinary speech.
- Variety of tones: animated, comic, critical feminist, positive, etc.

Sample Leaving Cert Questions on Kennelly's Poetry

1. **'Intense feelings of innocence and joy sometimes give way to yearning and loneliness in Kennelly's intricately crafted poems.'** Discuss this statement, developing your answer with reference to both the themes and poetic language of the poetry of Brendan Kennelly on your course.

2. **'Kennelly often makes effective use of various narrative voices to celebrate the beauty and mystery of life.'** Discuss this statement, developing the points you make with reference to the poetry of Brendan Kennelly on your course.

3. **'Kennelly's reflective poems frequently explore the complexity of Irish life with curiosity, creativity and insight.'** To what extent do you agree or disagree with this statement? Develop your answer with reference to the poetry of Brendan Kennelly on your course.

Understanding the Prescribed Poetry Question

Marks are awarded using the PCLM Marking Scheme:
P = 15; C = 15; L = 15; M = 5
Total = 50

- **P** (Purpose = 15 marks) refers to the set question and is the launch pad for the answer. This involves engaging with all aspects of the question. Both theme and language must be addressed, although not necessarily equally.

- **C** (Coherence = 15 marks) refers to the organisation of the developed response and the use of accurate, relevant quotation. Paragraphing is essential.

- **L** (Language = 15 marks) refers to the student's skill in controlling language throughout the answer.

- **M** (Mechanics = 5 marks) refers to spelling and grammar.

- Although no specific number of poems is required, students usually discuss at least 3 or 4 in their written responses.

- Aim for at least 800 words, to be completed within 45–50 minutes.

How do I organise my answer?

(Sample question 1)

'Intense feelings of innocence and joy sometimes give way to yearning and loneliness in Kennelly's intricately crafted poems.' Discuss this statement, developing your answer with reference to both the themes and poetic language of the poetry of Brendan Kennelly on your course.

Sample Plan 1

Intro: (*Stance: agree with viewpoint in the question*) Kennelly's poetry ranges from delight and inspiration to longing and isolation. Complex wordplay, startling imagery, inventive use of narrative voices and varied tones create memorable poems where he sees 'into the life of things'.

Point 1: (*Longing – compound words, poetic form*) '"Dear Autumn Girl"' tenderly addresses poet's desire to connect with his poetic muse. Innovative blending of varied sonnet forms, unique rhyme scheme, original compound words ('leaf-argosies') display poet's creative powers.

Point 2: (*Loneliness/resilience – vivid imagery, repetition, rhythm*) 'Begin' presents striking images of isolation ('arrogant loneliness of swans') and loss ('old friends passing') contrasted with the dynamic struggle for life ('seagulls foraging for bread') and love ('couples sharing a sunny secret').

NOTE

In keeping with the PCLM approach, the student has to take a stance by agreeing, disagreeing or partially agreeing with the statement that:

– **Kennelly's intense feelings of innocence and joy** (goodness, honesty, innocence, delight, wonder, merriment, triumph) **sometimes give way to yearning and loneliness** (desire, longing, craving, abandonment, grief, isolation)

... in:

– **intricately crafted poems** (startling imagery, complex sound effects, distinctive rhythms and rhymes, original use of poetic forms, narrative voices, contrast, variety of tones, etc.)

Point 3: (*Innocence/loneliness – imagery, alliteration, compound words*) 'Things I Might Do' uses contrast to heighten the sense of innocence ('small white church') when compared with an empty seedy scene ('backroom of a brothel'). Insistent alliteration reinforces the crude anonymous encounter.

Point 4: (*Merriment – extended metaphor, colloquial language*) 'Saint Brigid's Prayer' examines social drinking ('lake of beer', 'cups of love') as a symbol for glorifying God ('every drop would be a prayer') using the persona of the mischievous Saint Brigid. Colloquial expressions ('a heart and a half') and childlike phrases ('I'd like', 'I'd make') capture the saint's innocence and jollity.

Conclusion: Kennelly crafts poetry to make a 'kind of singing sense out of confusing experience'. Evocative scenes of longing and loneliness are placed beside vigorous images of resilience, innocence and celebration, all part of the great tapestry of life captured in Kennelly's intricate language.

Sample Paragraph: Point 1

In '"Dear Autumn Girl"', Kennelly's feelings about the beauty of the autumnal season are vividly expressed. The poet's use of fresh compound phrases, such as 'helter-skelter days' and 'mad leaf-argosies' reflect his initial sense of delight. However, Kennelly's desire for creative inspiration is expressed in a self-critical tone, 'I try but fail'. The ironic alliterative phrase, 'poverty of praise', acknowledges that he has failed to give his muse 'proper praise'. His dream-girl embodies Irish cultural identity and he emphasises this through the octet/sestet structure, mixing subtle rhymes ('days'/'praise') with wistful half-rhymes ('head'/'created'). Kennelly also adds his own intricate rhyme scheme in the sestet. The vivid imagery of the girl's 'flung golden hair' in 'September's homage rays' excites the poet's creativity so that he exclaims, 'I see what is, I wonder what's to come'. This carefully crafted poem moves smoothly from longing to joy.

EXAMINER'S COMMENT

A confidently written top-grade paragraph, showing close engagement with Kennelly's poem. Insightful analysis of the poet's innovative language – particularly his use of rhyme. Accurate supportive references and suitable quotations are effectively integrated into the critical commentary. Excellent expression (e.g. 'ironic alliterative phrase', 'embodies Irish cultural identity') throughout this impressive response.

(Sample question 2)

'Kennelly often makes effective use of various narrative voices to celebrate the beauty and mystery of life.' Discuss this statement, developing the points you make with reference to the poetry of Brendan Kennelly on your course.

NOTE

In keeping with the PCLM approach, the student has to take a stance by agreeing and/or disagreeing that Kennelly:

- **makes effective use of various narrative voices** (stories told in his own voice and by named and unnamed characters (or objects) that offer surprising, nuanced and dramatic perspectives, engaging reflections, enthusiastic pleas, compelling commentaries, poignant confessions, etc.)

... to celebrate:

- **the beauty and mystery of life** (the appeal, glory, wonder and mystery of the natural cycle of life, creativity, newness, mortality, love/ hate, sympathy, destruction, etc.)

Sample Plan 2

Intro: (*Stance: agree with viewpoint in the question*) Kennelly frequently assumes another identity in his desire to understand the wonder and loveliness of life. These include figures from history and the Bible. He becomes an inquisitive child, a grieving widow. Such narrative approaches pose questions about life, creativity, mortality, guilt and forgiveness, love and loss through Kennelly's fresh, musical poetry.

Point 1: (*Bread – natural cycle of life/creativity*) 'Bread' acknowledges the cruelty of life ('cut off my head') and the violence of the creative impulse ('slits', 'stabs') in a description of his grandmother's bread-making. The dough resigns itself to suffer ('go through fire') to achieve the transformation into 'perfection', just as people endure suffering through the natural, yet harsh transitions of life's cycle.

Point 2: (*Young child – mortality/purpose*) 'Poem from a Three Year Old' captures the incessant curiosity of a questioning child. The secret and wonder of living are explored in this dreamlike monologue. Fractured syntax and diction convey the little girl's random thoughts ('flowers and people all the same/ together lying there').

Point 3: (*Reflective voice – contrasting emotions*) 'Things I Might Do' offers little celebration, but explores the variety of emotions that all humans are capable of – betrayal of trust ('treacherous head') / forgiveness ('come home to me'). Consequences and truth have to be faced. The reader is left to consider the possibility of salvation.

Point 4: (*Saints – glorifying God and humanity*) 'Saint Brigid's Prayer' expresses the saint's enthusiasm for living and is likely to represent the poet's own philosophy. Use of the extended drinking metaphor, repetition of positive verbs ('like', 'love'), lively rhythms and exuberant tones all revel in Irish communal life and the Christian faith.

Conclusion: Kennelly's many personas offer subtle perspectives on life. Their varied tones all address readers directly, so that we can hear the boisterous infant 'I want to play' or the stoic bread's 'I am fine'. The poet sees things in a new way through these narrative voices.

Sample Paragraph: Point 2

In 'Poem from a Three Year Old', Kennelly takes on the persona of a young girl fascinated by the wonder of the world. She is full of questions about life. Broken syntax and ceaseless questions convey her confused thinking, 'How you know a flower that's old?' Kennelly lets the reader observe the world through the child's eyes, 'What happens all the dirt you sweep from flowers and people?' Unlike adults, the innocent child takes nothing for granted. She is also fascinated by good and evil. Life's cyclical regeneration is emphasised in repetition of the adjective 'new'. However, after all the hectic run-on lines, the three final lines stand alone. In the end, we must all consider the reality of mortality, 'And will the new young people die?' as well as the point of human existence – 'And why?' Kennelly has demonstrated his desire to understand this beautiful yet puzzling world by becoming someone else and letting us hear their views.

> **EXAMINER'S COMMENT**
>
> *A solid high-grade standard, with excellent expression throughout and good engagement with the poem. Main points were well-supported by suitable quotations. Some of the discussion veered towards general criticism and a little more focus on the extent of celebration (a key element of the question) – perhaps through a more thorough examination of tone – would have been welcome.*

Leaving Cert Sample Essay

'Kennelly's reflective poems explore the complexity of Irish life with curiosity, creativity and insight.' To what extent do you agree or disagree with this statement? Support your answer with reference to the poetry of Brendan Kennelly on your course.

Sample Essay

1. Kennelly's poems address many subtle aspects of Irish life in imaginative and innovative ways. This poet adopts the persona of a saint, a young widow and a reviled invader to examine difficult issues of Ireland's past and present. He uses a range of writing forms, various tones and vivid language to reveal profound truths for himself and his readers.

2. Kennelly assumes the personality of the mischievous saint in his translation of 'Saint Brigid's Prayer'. In this prayer to the saint of Irish poetry, the poet lets us hear the lilting voice of the ordinary Irish person, 'With a heart and a half'. But this sing-along poem contains an awareness about Irish life. Our history is scarred by many divisions, but this saint proposes a common thread of joy, a focus on a celebration of being alive to heal the differences. Saint Brigid paints a very happy picture of all Irish people, men, women and God sitting by 'the lake of beer' wishing one another well, 'drinking good health forever'. In this unusual prayer, the extended metaphor of drinking is used to show the possibility of a 'contented' human race.

3. In a translation of an Irish lament, 'A Cry for Art O' Leary', Kennelly takes the persona of the widow, Eibhlín Dubh Ní Chonaill. The poet contrasts tender images of love with violent outbursts of hatred. The young wife's love is depicted a dynamic image composed of slender vowels, 'Your pin glinting silver/ Glittered in your shirt'. The contentment of their married life is conveyed in the soft repetitive 'm' sound in the line 'Till milking-time hummed for me'. However, Irish literature is one of loss, in part due to its troubled history. The Catholic rebel O'Leary dared to break the strict Penal Laws. We learn that he refused to sell his thoroughbred horse to the Protestant Morris who subsequently ordered Art's murder. The haunting image of a rider-less horse, 'blood on your saddle' is the first indication to Eibhlín that her husband has been killed.

4. Vigorous verbs show her reaction, 'leaped', 'clapped'. The depth of loss is highlighted in the traumatic line, 'You swept my man from me'. A poignant description evokes the tragic consequences of this man's brutal murder, 'Two children play in the house/ A third lives in me'. Kennelly reflects the widow's sorrow in the simple metaphor, 'My heart is a lump of grief'. The poem concludes with the insight into the young woman's ability to endure. Kennelly's version of Art O'Leary offers a perceptive insight into Ireland's violent history – and particularly the human cost experienced by victims and their families.

5. 'Oliver to His Brother' is Kennelly's adaptation of a letter written by Oliver Cromwell. Although a hated figure in Ireland due to many massacres of the Irish population, Cromwell now emerges in a different light. Kennelly, once again, becomes another character. An affectionate opening, 'Loving brother' challenges us to regard this monster as a human being. Run-on lines convey the warm-hearted father: 'our children have so much leisure/They can travel far to eat cherries' He indulges his daughter and longs to hear from her, wanting her to write 'often to me'.

6. But this loving tone is soon replaced by the blunt voice of the realist politician and confident leader, 'I have things to, all in my own way'. Cromwell, the ruthless agent of destruction offers this cold explanation, 'Men die their different ways'. A hard alliterative 'd' sound suggests the collapse of his victims to the ground. The religious Cromwell is oblivious to the havoc he has caused. Kennelly uses an original compound word to portray this new reality that Cromwell has imposed – the country is now 'Christblessed fields'. The poem concludes with Cromwell's ominous promise, 'I have work to do in Ireland'. Kennelly has challenged us to accept that Cromwell is more than a one-dimensional villain. Cromwell also loves his family, is religious, believes in order and is coldly pragmatic.

BRENDAN KENNELLY

INDICATIVE MATERIAL

Curiosity, creativity and insight are elements of Kennelly's reflective poems:

- contrasting moods/tones – introspective, nostalgic, celebratory, questioning, angry, etc.
- elaborate sound effects and varied images – nature, romance, religion, mysticism, violence, etc.
- inventive use of personas and different poetic forms, etc.

... that explore:

- the complexity of Irish life (beauty and mystery of being, unity in creation, innocence, love and idealism versus hatred, division and hopelessness, etc.)

7. In 'A Great Day', the poet portrays an Irish wedding, a time of celebration and happiness. Yet Kennelly challenges this joyful vision by inserting the line, 'Something about snow is not quite right'. He also describes the groom with a comical verb, 'All dickied up in dignified blue'. Kennelly casts a shadow on the happy occasion with references to 'dead' and 'a grave ritual'. A stand-alone line, 'He never saw the white dress again' suggests how quickly the sparkle can leave a relationship. The bride's comment is in the past tense, 'Darling, it was a great day'. The poet has described a traditional happy event and introduced an unsettling note, 'Things seemed to fit'. But do they? Will the couple ever experience such happiness again?

8. Kennelly is always curious about the world. His poems address intriguing aspects of Irish life, often raising questions about our unhappy history. His poems are highly perceptive and thought-provoking and his inventive style presents us with a lively sense of wonder.

(821 words)

EXAMINER'S COMMENT

The opening paragraph provides a clear overview that addresses the question and introduces some of the main discussion points that are developed within the essay. Paragraph 2 could benefit with more thorough treatment. The 'insight' in 'A Great Day' also deserved greater exploration. Critical commentary on both 'A Cry for Art O' Leary' and 'Oliver to His Brother' is much more detailed, with most aspects of the question being tackled successfully. Overall, some good close engagement with both Kennelly's poetry and the question – although the 'curiosity' element could have been given more attention throughout. Assured expression and supportive quotes throughout contribute greatly to this high-grade essay.

GRADE: H2
P = 13/15
C = 12/15
L = 13/15
M = 5/5
Total = 43/50

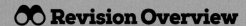 Revision Overview

'Begin'
This affirmative, lyrical poem urges readers to celebrate life despite its disappointments. The emphatic opening urges readers to appreciate every ordinary experience to the full.

'Bread'
Kennelly frequently wrote in a persona. This beautifully conceived poem considers the chaotic nature of existence. The image of wheat becoming bread illustrates life's interconnectedness.

'"Dear Autumn Girl"'
In expressing the beauty and excitement of the changing seasons, Kennelly gains insight into poetic inspiration from the close relationship between people and nature.

'Poem from a Three Year Old'
Through the wonder-filled narrative voice of a young child, Kennelly presents a compelling poetic vision of human innocence and uncertainty.

'Oliver to His Brother'
Kennelly adopts the personality of one of Ireland's most reviled figures, presenting an unlikely view of Oliver Cromwell as a family man.

'I See You Dancing, Father'
Nostalgic poem about the lasting power of family love. Kennelly reflects on how people can celebrate the natural pleasures of being alive in simple, spontaneous ways.

'A Cry for Art O'Leary'
Set in the late 18th century and written in the style of a traditional Irish lament, this poem dramatises the intense experience of one young woman's love and loss.

'Things I Might Do'
Identifying to an extent with Judas Iscariot, the speaker in this poem explores some of the feelings that human beings experience – and the consequences of their individual choices.

'A Great Day'
In this subtle and closely-observed portrait of an Irish wedding, the poet raises unsettling questions about aspects of romantic love and modern-day marriage.

'Fragments'
Reflective sonnet about a failed relationship in which Kennelly addresses familiarly poignant themes, including love, betrayal, sadness and regret.

'The soul's loneliness'
Multi-layered poem exploring the mystery of life's spiritual meaning. Kennelly is fascinated by the individual's awareness of being part of a greater universal spirit.

'Saint Brigid's Prayer'
In this lively offbeat poem, Kennelly adopts the Irish saint's 'voice' to express his personal enthusiasm for the natural celebration of life, a recurring theme in his writing.

BRENDAN KENNELLY

Last Words

'With considerable honesty and bravery, Kennelly enters and becomes others in order to perceive, understand and suffer.'
Aidan Murphy

'What emerges from Kennelly's entire body of work is a relationship with his subjects that is based on curiosity and mischievous respect.'
Katleyn Ferguson

'A writer is not interested in explaining reality, he's only interested in capturing it.'
Brendan Kennelly

| JOY/HOPE | MEANING OF LIFE | CREATIVITY | IDENTITY | LOSS | DEATH | LOVE | HISTORY/ MEMORY | WONDER | NATURE |

D. H. Lawrence
1855–1930

'Ours is an excessively conscious age. We know so much, we feel so little.'

David Herbert Lawrence was born in Nottinghamshire, England, on 11 September 1885. A miner's son, he was to become a rebellious and polemical writer with radical views. Though better known as a novelist (*The Rainbow, Women in Love, Lady Chatterley's Lover*), Lawrence was also a prolific poet.

His collected writings represent an extended reflection on the dehumanising effects of modernity and industrialisation. In them, Lawrence confronts issues relating to emotional health and happiness, spontaneity, human sexuality and instinct.

Some of his best-loved poems address the physical and inner life of plants and animals; others are bitterly satirical and express outrage at the hypocrisy of conventional society. In much of his later poetry, he attempted to capture emotion through free verse. D. H. Lawrence travelled extensively and spent many years in Italy. A lifelong sufferer from tuberculosis, he died on 2 March 1930 in the South of France. He is now widely regarded as one of the most influential writers of the 20th century.

Investigate Further

To find out more about D. H. Lawrence, or to hear readings of his poems, you could search some useful websites such as YouTube, BBC Poetry, poetryfoundation.org and poetryarchive.org, or access additional material on this page of your eBook.

Prescribed Poems

○ **1 'Call into Death'**
Written the year his mother died of cancer, Lawrence's poem addresses one of the great taboos of society – the reality that death comes to all. **Page 220**

○ **2 'Piano'**
One of D. H. Lawrence's best-known lyrics in which the poet reminisces about an idyllic moment from childhood and his conflicted desire to return to its warmth and security. **Page 224**

○ **3 'The Mosquito'**
This dramatic poem is presented in the form of an imagined one-sided dialogue during a confrontation between man and insect. **Page 228**

○ **4 'Snake'**
In this famous poem, Lawrence examines the conflict between education (and accepted social attitudes) and the desires people often hold. **Page 235**

○ **5 'Humming-Bird' (OL)**
Lawrence re-interprets the geological past and restores it to its own special sense of excitement. **Page 242**

○ **6 'Intimates'**
This short, witty poem dramatises the negative aspects of love and challenges appearances in relationships. **Page 246**

○ **7 'Delight of Being Alone'**
One of D. H. Lawrence's most conventional and beautiful poems, it expresses the poet's romantic attitudes about the pleasures of being alone and reflects his closeness to nature. **Page 250**

○ **8 'Absolute Reverence'**
Although Lawrence insists that he feels 'absolute reverence to nobody and to nothing human', this short poem expresses his pantheistic, mystical reverence towards a universal life force. **Page 251**

○ **9 'What Have They Done to You?'**
This fiercely persuasive condemnation of modernity describes Lawrence's aversion to machines and the industrial age. **Page 252**

○ **10 'Baby-Movements II: "Trailing Clouds"' (OL)**
This early Lawrence poem is part of a two-poem sequence ('Baby-Movements'), apparently based on a description of his landlady's baby daughter. **Page 257**

○ **11 'Bavarian Gentians'**
Lawrence explores his own journey towards death as portrayed through a variety of moods, including awareness, anger, terror and eventual acceptance. **Page 260**

(OL) indicates poems that are also prescribed for the Ordinary Level course.

1 Call into Death

Since I lost you, my darling, the sky has come near,
And I am of it, the small sharp stars are quite near,
The white moon going among them like a white bird among snow-berries,
And the sound of her gently rustling in heaven like a bird I hear.

And I am willing to come to you now, my dear,   5
As a pigeon lets itself off from a cathedral dome
To be lost in the haze of the sky; I would like to come
And be lost out of sight with you, like a melting foam.

For I am tired, my dear, and if I could lift my feet,
My tenacious feet, from off the dome of the earth   10
To fall like a breath within the breathing wind
Where you are lost, what rest, my love, what rest!

snow-berries: round white berries eaten by birds, but poisonous to humans.

dome: round roof.

haze: mist, cloud.

tenacious: clinging, firmly held.

'among snow-berries'

👤 Personal Response

1. Lawrence's poems often explore difficult subject matter. In your opinion, what is the main theme or message of 'Call into Death'? Support your answer with reference to the text.
2. Lawrence uses several similes in this poem. Choose one that appeals to you and comment briefly on its effectiveness.
3. Write your own personal response to the poem, highlighting the impact it made on you.

👁 Critical Literacy

'Call into Death' is part of D. H. Lawrence's two-volume *Collected Poems* (1928). He divided the collection into 'Rhyming Poems' and 'UnRhyming Poems' (to which this particular poem belongs). Lawrence wrote this poem in 1910, the year his mother died of cancer, confessing 'in that year, for me, everything collapsed, save the mystery of death, and the haunting of death in life. I was twenty-five and from the death of my mother, the world began to dissolve around me, beautiful, iridescent, but passing away substanceless. Till I almost dissolved away myself and was very ill ...'

This tender 12-line elegy has the poet crying out in the direction of death like a mystic in the desert, attempting to get attention. Lawrence's relationship with his mother was close, 'so sensitive to each other that we never needed words'. The poet had also suffered several relationship break-ups in the year prior to his mother's death. Genuine emotion is caught in the plain, honest conversational expression: 'Since I lost you, my darling' (line 1). Lawrence turns his back on traditional poetry that elaborated and decorated poetic verse for effect, not feeling. He believes that the experiences of loss have given him a **new insight into life**, the oneness of the ordered universe, 'the sky has come near'. He feels part of it now: 'I am of it.' The sibilant alliteration, 'small, sharp stars', accentuates the pinpoint light radiating from these planets.

Lawrence's vivid **observational skill** is displayed in the beautiful simile of the moon moving like 'a white bird among snow-berries' (line 3). A haunting sense of the unity of all creation is conveyed in the imagery pattern. The long irregular line length mirrors the moon's majestic journey through the heavens, while insistent rhyme ('near', 'hear') adapts to the idea of the oneness of the universe and man. Onomatopoeia ('rustling') conveys the soft sound of the mother bird searching for food. Lawrence fully acknowledges the natural inclusion of death in life, just as the 'white moon' shines in the dark sky – though it is not always visible to the human eye – and the 'white bird' is camouflaged among the white berries.

The second verse opens with a warm term of endearment, 'my dear', as the poet wishes to immediately and voluntarily join his loved one, 'I am willing to come to you now'. Using another simile, Lawrence expresses his wish to launch himself into oblivion, 'As a pigeon lets itself off from a cathedral dome/To be lost in the haze of the sky' (lines 6–7). The bird disappears from view of the human world, lost in the mist and clouds, yet it still lives. **Death and life are not separate events**, but part of the whole human experience. Like the bird, Lawrence needs to become invisible to the human eye and join his beloved, 'like a melting foam'. Irregular rhyme ('dome', 'come', 'foam') adds a subtle quality to the harmonious mood. The repetition of the suffix 'ing' in the first and last lines of the two verses knits them closely together ('darling'/'rustling', 'willing'/'melting').

The **lethargic mood** in the third verse is in contrast to the previous two. Lawrence admits the reason for his wish to leave this world, 'For I am tired'. But his feet cling stubbornly to the earth, 'tenacious'. The repetition of 'feet' suggests the sheer physical effort the poet is making in his attempt to escape, not like the bird from the dome of a cathedral, but from the 'dome of the earth' (line 10). However, there is a final sense of resurgence as he imagines the effortless flight into the realm of his loved one. Lawrence sees himself easing into death with the grace of a breath joining the wind. The gentle repetition and affectionate tone of 'what rest, my love, what rest' brings the poem to a serene conclusion.

The poet has succeeded in **confronting one of the great taboos** of society, the terrifying reality that death comes to all. He has even emphasised its advantages. Characteristically, his honest poetry confronts one of life's bitterest experiences, death and loss. In the final poignant verse, Lawrence changes his linking mechanism, joining the verb 'lift' in line 9 with 'lost' in its concluding line, and unlike the previous two verses, there is no rhyme. His wish is not granted. He cannot yet escape the earth.

✒ Writing About the Poem

'D. H. Lawrence's poetry addresses complex ideas in fresh, vivid yet controlled language.' Discuss this statement in relation to 'Call into Death'.

Sample Paragraph

The complex concept of death in the midst of life is explored successfully by Lawrence in 'Call into Death'. One of his beliefs was that death is not an end, but is part of the cycle of life. Using precisely observed details from the natural world, Lawrence puts forward his intricate view of life and death. Repetition and the comparison of 'a white bird among snow-berries' illustrates the difficulty of seeing what is actually there. The ease of the descent into oblivion is captured by another simile, 'a pigeon lifts itself off from a cathedral dome'. Bodily substance disappears into another simile, 'melting foam'. But the wish and the reality conflict. Hard 't' sounds show the strong pull of the earth on the living, 'tired', 'lift', 'feet'. Yet the poem ends with the wish of entering another level of consciousness, falling into easeful death, as naturally as 'a breath' joins 'the breathing wind'. Life is not final any more than the dead are disconnected from the living; they exist in our memory.

> **EXAMINER'S COMMENT**
>
> *Shows close engagement with the poem. Overall, a high-grade standard that focuses well on the two elements of the question – ideas and style. Despite slight awkwardness of expression, there are some supported discussion points that effectively explore Lawrence's beliefs in the natural life cycle and his innovative use of sound effects.*

✒ Class/Homework Exercises

1. 'Lawrence's poems are spontaneous and fresh, but they often investigate dark and disturbing subjects.' Discuss this view with reference to the poem 'Call into Death'.
2. 'Lawrence's personal poetry engages readers through carefully composed language and imagery.' To what extent is this true of 'Call into Death'? Support your answer with reference to the poem.

⊙ Points to Consider

- **Central themes include death, loss, longing, grief, escape, peace.**

- **Poetic techniques – irregular line length, rhyme and linking devices, sound effects.**

- **Effective use of imagery drawn from the natural world.**

- **Varied tones – affection, sorrow, longing, tiredness, sense of achievement, etc.**

Handwritten notes (top):
More conventional poem = end rhyme use
People personal = a lot of personal pronoun
Conflict between his adult and child self

2 Piano

Handwritten: Begins in the presents go to the past then back to present

Handwritten (right): End rhyme = creates a sense of warmth comfort

Handwritten (left): onomatopoeia / sibilance / gives appealing / hazy feeling

Softly, in the dusk, a woman is singing to me; _[handwritten: He arrives at an idyllic version of his childhood]_
Taking me back down the vista of years, till I see
A child sitting under the piano, in the boom of the tingling strings
And pressing the small, poised feet of a mother who smiles as she sings.

vista: scenic view, panorama.

poised: perched, composed.

Handwritten (left): enjambment = run on line / Reaction on atmosphere / of that he cant control it

Handwritten: alliteration sibilance

In spite of myself, the insidious mastery of song
Betrays me back, till the heart of me weeps to belong
To the old Sunday evenings at home, with winter outside
And hymns in the cosy parlour, the tinkling piano our guide.

Handwritten: 5 / longs for his past

Handwritten: image that outside / personification is unsafe

insidious: subtle, deceptive.
Betrays: tricks, compels.

Handwritten (left): warm imagery inside / The music hurt too much that he cant enjoy the music now

So now it is vain for the singer to burst into clamour
With the great black piano appassionato. The glamour
Of childish days is upon me, my manhood is cast
Down in the flood of remembrance, I weep like a child for the past.

Handwritten: different piano / 10

clamour: loud noise, racket.
appassionato: impassionate performance.
glamour: charm, mystique.

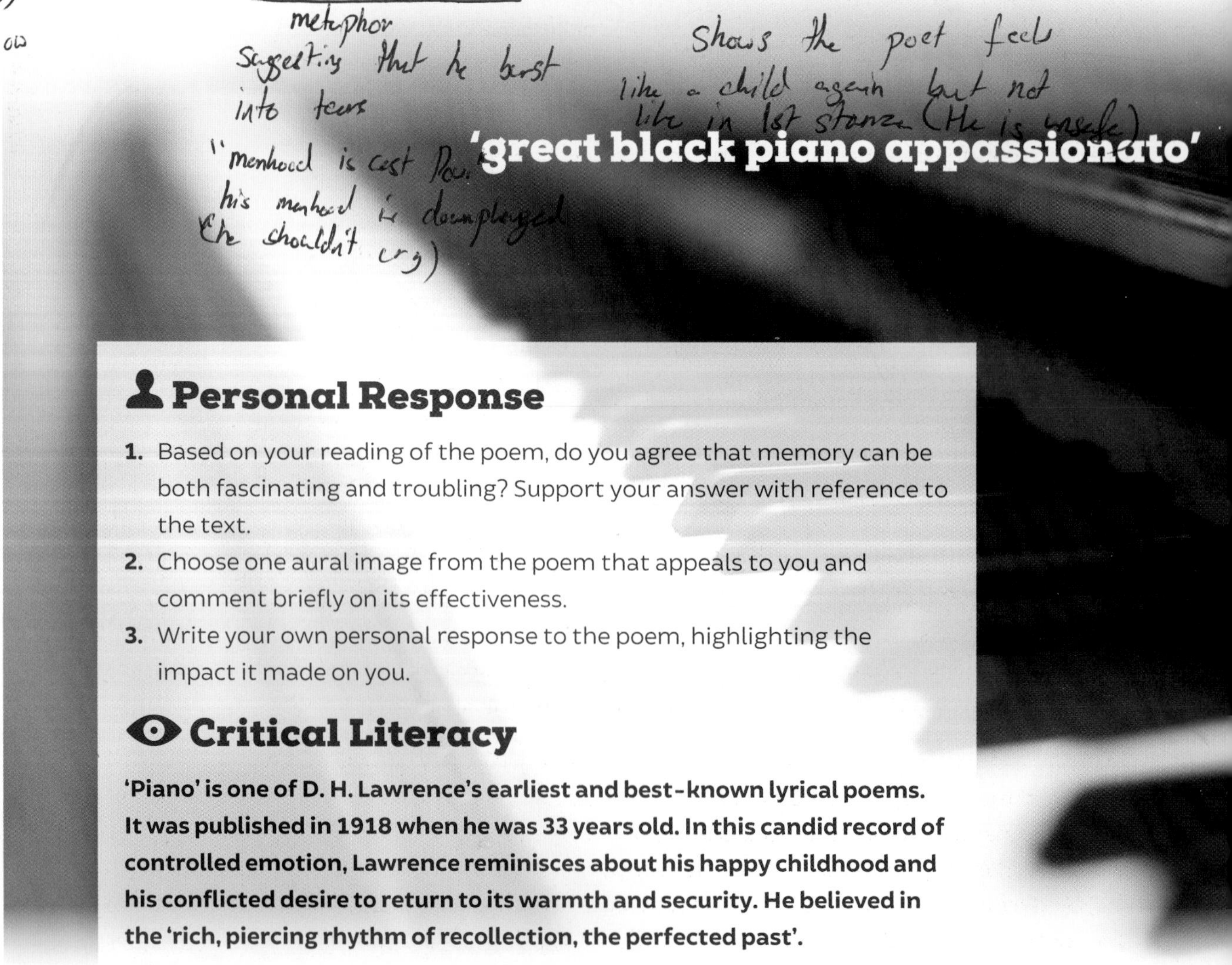

Handwritten: metaphor / Suggesting that he burst into tears
Handwritten: "manhood is cast Down" his manhood is downplayed (he shouldn't cry)
Handwritten: Shows the poet feels like a child again but not like in 1st stanza (He is unsafe)

'great black piano appassionato'

👤 Personal Response

1. Based on your reading of the poem, do you agree that memory can be both fascinating and troubling? Support your answer with reference to the text.
2. Choose one aural image from the poem that appeals to you and comment briefly on its effectiveness.
3. Write your own personal response to the poem, highlighting the impact it made on you.

👁 Critical Literacy

'Piano' is one of D. H. Lawrence's earliest and best-known lyrical poems. It was published in 1918 when he was 33 years old. In this candid record of controlled emotion, Lawrence reminisces about his happy childhood and his conflicted desire to return to its warmth and security. He believed in the 'rich, piercing rhythm of recollection, the perfected past'.

Lyrical poetry expresses strong emotion, typically from a first-person point of view. Lawrence's title has multiple aspects. While 'Piano' refers to the concert that the adult poet is attending in the present, it is also a reference to Lawrence's childhood memory of listening to his mother playing. Interestingly, the word 'piano' itself is the Italian musical direction to play softly.

Aptly, the poem begins with the adverb, 'Softly'. Immediately, a **gentle mood** is being created, 'in the dusk', just between evening and night-time. The atmosphere is entirely appropriate for a poem exploring connections and disconnections between past and present. Lawrence describes a somewhat anonymous event: 'a woman is singing', the atmospheric 's' sounds similar to that of a whisper. The absence of detail initially suggests a lack of engagement on his part but it also releases him to travel down the 'vista of years'. This metaphor of such a panoramic view evokes the wide expanse of the past which poet and reader alike must journey through to reach childhood again. Each has to travel 'back down' from the heights of maturity and adulthood.

The recollections of the past are sharp and detailed, in contrast to the bland opening scene in the present. The **descriptive flashback** reveals a tender image of a young child sitting 'under the piano', pressing his mother's feet while she plays and sings. In line 3, the viewpoint suddenly changes to the third person ('A child') as the poet realises that he is no longer that little boy. The use of tactile imagery and the present tense ('sitting', 'pressing') conjures up a vivid sensual memory. Indeed, the scene is one of familiar comfort and childlike innocence, of intimacy and security.

Lawrence makes full use of **aural techniques**, particularly assonance ('boom', 'tingling strings') to convey the contrasting deep and high piano notes. The mother's grace and skill are highlighted in the detail 'small, poised feet'. Simple language has established a nostalgic, happy serenity throughout the first stanza. Sibilant 's' and slender vowel sounds ('smiles', 'sings') evoke an ideal picture of a relaxed family scene.

In the more sombre second quatrain, the poet indulges in self-analysis. The focus on how the flashback makes him feel brings the outlook back to the first person. Lawrence recalls his childhood days with reluctance ('In spite of myself'). Knowing that he is being sentimentally nostalgic, he is unwilling to return to the past – as many people are – because sometimes it is simply too sad to remember happy times and to realise that they are gone for good. A run-on line features the subtle, **treacherous allure of earlier times**, 'the insidious mastery of song/Betrays me back'. The explosive 'b' in the alliterative phrase delivers the message that he feels he has been cheated. As an adult, Lawrence is now aware of the gap between his idealised childhood perceptions and the reality of loss.

Yet he has been inveigled into the past by the singing and he is overwhelmed ('the heart of me weeps'). The disjointed syntax reflects his obvious distress. Lawrence desperately **longs for his old identity** back in the comforting family home. His romantic feelings flow, unstoppable for 'the old Sunday evenings at home', 'And hymns in the cosy parlour'. The cold 'winter outside' provides a fitting contrast to this warm sanctuary. Ironically, the 'tinkling piano' still acts as a moral compass. In childhood, it represented the close connection ('our guide') between mother and child. Now it counsels the poet about the gulf between childhood and adulthood.

The third stanza opens with the conjunction, 'So', indicating the effects of revisiting the past. Lawrence is now no longer interested in the present. He feels it is both useless and arrogant ('vain') of the musician at the concert to display vocal artistry. His wry dismissal is expressed in the negative phrase, 'burst into clamour'. The heavily stressed 'great black piano appassionato' contrasts starkly with the appealing 'tinkling piano' and its broad vowels mimic the melodramatic artistic display of emotion. The **poet admits that he has been seduced** by 'The glamour/Of childish days'. Even the unusual juxtaposition of the more adult noun 'glamour' alongside 'childish' suggests the superficial deception of memory. Lawrence accepts that he is looking at the past through rose-tinted glasses.

In the end, the **power of remembrance breaks him**, 'my manhood is cast/Down'. He has been led from the beginning ('Taking me back', 'Betrays me back') although he is fighting what he sees as a sentimental response. Placing the adverb 'Down' at the beginning of the line emphasises the conflict Lawrence is experiencing by being lured back in time. He reverts to behaving in the frank, open manner of a child, publicly displaying his feelings, 'I weep like a child'. The gentle sounds of his mother on a Sunday evening have surpassed the sophisticated dramatic performance of the singer in the present. More than anything, he now wants 'the past'.

Although the poem explores the floodgates unleashed by random memories, its **form is tightly controlled**. Three quatrains (four-line stanzas) trace the progress of thought in the poem, alternating present and past with inner and outer feelings. The couplet rhyme scheme *(aa-bb-cc-dd-ee-ff)* is reminiscent of a simple hymn or nursery rhyme. The sprung rhythm (irregular metrical stress on key words) reflects ordinary speech ('Softly', 'Taking', 'Betrays', 'Down'). However, the long, irregular line lengths at the conclusion of each stanza and the frequent use of enjambment suggest the uncontrolled 'flood of remembrance' that can sweep away restraint.

Throughout this beautiful and haunting poem, Lawrence is writing from the perspective of a middle-aged man. But in his subconscious mind, his childhood and adulthood are almost one, as he weeps 'like a child for the past'. In this there is a duality and a contrast. As in so much of his poetry, he portrays the complex workings and dealings of the human heart in a characteristically refined and elegant manner.

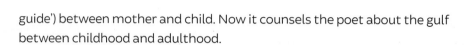

✒ Writing About the Poem

'D. H. Lawrence's poems often explore the devastating consequences of memory in carefully composed lines.' Discuss this view, with particular reference to 'Piano'.

Sample Paragraph

Lawrence carefully crafts his lyric poem, 'Piano', into three quatrains which move seamlessly from present to past and back again. Using rhyming couplets ('me'/'see', 'song'/'belong'), the poet seeks to control the 'flood of remembrance' activated by the spark, 'in the dusk, a woman is singing to me'. The adult Lawrence is weeping for what can never be, a return to the happy security of childhood. The poem itself works just as 'insidiously' on the readers, pulling them back through rhythms and rhymes reminiscent of simple childhood songs. Lawrence's memories will not be contained neatly into the three quatrains, but break through in frequent enjambment ('The glamour/Of childish days') and irregular line lengths, particularly in the first stanza when he describes his memory of sitting as a child under the piano. The poet's juxtaposition of the appealing 'glamour' of childhood with the discordant 'clamour' of the singer clearly shows how memory has conquered him. The poem concludes with the realisation of his paradoxical position, openly expressing his nostalgia for the past while still feeling guilty at his disappointment with the present.

EXAMINER'S COMMENT

A well-written response that focuses effectively on the poet's use of language techniques in treating the theme of memory. Informed discussion points on structure, rhyme, enjambment and contrast are aptly illustrated. Assured expression (using varied sentence length and impressive vocabulary) throughout contributes greatly to the top-grade standard.

✒ Class/Homework Exercises

1. 'Lawrence's poetry often struggles to record immature experience faithfully and yet at the same time escape from it.' In your opinion, how true is this of 'Piano'? Support your answer with reference to the poem.
2. 'D. H. Lawrence explores the country of the heart in intricate, sensual poetry.' To what extent is this evident in 'Piano'? Support your answer with reference to the poem.

◉ Points to Consider

- **Central themes include recollection, loneliness, self-awareness.**

- **The opening stanza juxtaposes the present with childhood recollections.**

- **Aural effects – repetition, assonance and onomatopoeia – vividly recreate the past.**

- **The poem's structure reflects the poet's struggle with memory.**

- **Conflicting moods of nostalgia, regret, longing and pragmatism vie in this lyric.**

Humor to the poem
mosquito is personified throughout the whole poem
— Free verse poem but question gives coherence

6 question within poem

3

The Mosquito

Mosquito: Spanish word meaning 'little fly'. This small midge-like insect feeds on blood and is a transmitter of harmful diseases.

Personification —

When did you start your tricks,
Monsieur?

tricks: mischievous, deceitful actions.
Monsieur: formal address to a Frenchman ('sir').

Sarcastically suggest that the mosquito can think for itself

What do you stand on such high legs for?
Why this length of shredded shank,
You exaltation?   5

raised high of the ground

shredded shank: ragged lower legs.
exaltation: joy.

The poet is struck by the mosquito extreme tininess and somethin

Is it so that you shall lift your centre of gravity upwards
And weigh no more than air as you alight upon me,
Stand upon me weightless, you phantom?

I heard a woman call you the Winged Victory   10
In sluggish Venice.
You turn your head towards your tail, and smile.

a Greek statue

Winged Victory: statue of Nike, Greek Goddess of Victory.
sluggish: listless, slow-moving.

How can you put so much devilry
Into that translucent phantom shred
Of a frail corpus?

description of mosquito

translucent: glowing, radiant.
phantom: ghost, spirit.
corpus: body, mass.

something effortless or graceful of its flight

Simile —

Queer, with your thin wings and your streaming legs,   15
How you sail like a heron, or a dull clot of air,
A nothingness.

suggesting that the mosquito is so light that it can be compared to air

heron: long-legged fish-eating bird.
clot: lump.

Sense of vulnerability is shown in the poet as he fears its speed and stealth

Yet what an aura surrounds you; —admiration
Your evil little aura, prowling, and casting a numbness on my mind.

aura: force, glow.

Pugnacious tone = the poet is eager or quick to argue

That is your trick, your bit of filthy magic: 20
Invisibility, and the anaesthetic power
To deaden my attention in your direction.

Highlights the disgust he has for the mosquito

anaesthetic: deadening, numbing.

metaphor

But I know your game now, streaky sorcerer.
Queer, how you stalk and prowl the air
In circles and evasions, enveloping me,   25
Ghoul on wings
Winged Victory.

There's a level of malevolence

negative connotations, hyping the mood for the impending battle

sorcerer: magician, wizard.

evasions: avoidances, equivocations.
Ghoul: ghost, spirit.

The poet is amazed by the level of devillery by something so small

Settle, and stand on long thin shanks
Eyeing me sideways, and cunningly conscious that I am aware,
You speck.   30

speck: spot, scrap.

"trick", "filthy magic", "deaden my attention" gives a hypnotic effect by its sound buzzing

malevolence = evil

I hate the way you lurch off sideways into air
Having read my thoughts against you.

lurch: stagger, sway.

Come then, let us play at unawares,
And see who wins in this sly game of bluff.
Man or mosquito.

The poet claims he knows the mosquitos trick
Compete a game of bluff
By pretending to play this game he imagines the mosquito knows
whats going on and this is giving human qualities to the mosquito

game of bluff: contest, scam.

You don't know that I exist, and I don't know that you exist.
Now then!

It is your trump,
It is your hateful little trump,

repetition shows his annoyance

trump: winner, decider.

You pointed fiend,   40
Which shakes my sudden blood to hatred of you:
It is your small, high, hateful bugle in my ear.

fiend: villain, devil.

Shape of — noise produce by the mosquito
trumpet / mosquito face — fills the poet with hate

Why do you do it?
Surely it is bad policy.

— acknowledges that it cant help from making this noise / not doing this
to annoy him

They say you can't help it.   45

If that is so, then I believe a little in Providence protecting the innocent.
But it sounds so amazingly like a slogan
A yell of triumph as you snatch my scalp.

Providence: destiny, wisdom.

image of pompous politician
gives importance

Blood, red blood
Super-magical
Forbidden liquor.

The mosquito has taken the iniative and bites the poet
complete ecstesy
body of the mosquito from transparent to red with blood
intoxicated by blood   50

I behold you stand
For a second enspasmed in oblivion,
Obscenely ecstasied
Sucking live blood,   55
My blood.

enspasmed: suddenly caught.
oblivion: unconsciousness, nothingness.

Such silence, such suspended transport,
Such gorging,
Such obscenity of trespass.

greedy
awful / inappropiate

obscenity: indecency.
trespass: invasion.

You stagger   60
As well as you may.
Only your accursed hairy frailty,
Your own imponderable weightlessness
Saves you, wafts you away on the very draught my anger makes in its snatching.

imponderable: unknown.
wafts: blows.
draught: breeze.

This draught made by the poet own blows
the mosquito to safety

Song of Triumph

Away with a <u>paean</u> of derision,
You winged blood-drop. — *body turned red*

Can I not overtake you? — *clashing himself to beat the mosquito*
Are you one too many for me,
Winged Victory?
Am I not mosquito enough to out-mosquito you? — *act like mosquito* 70
become stealthy like mosquito

Queer, what a big stain my sucked blood makes — *His blood makes big smear*
Beside the <u>infinitesimal</u> faint smear of you! — *small smear*
Queer, what a dim dark smudge you have disappeared into!

tiny

Siracusa   *I killed the mosquito*

abrupt ending in the stanza, Alliteration, repetition, exclamation
melee   a strong blow like the
blow that killed the mosquito

65

paean: rapturous expression.
derision: contempt, mockery.

infinitesimal: tiny, insignificant.
smear: mark, splodge.
smudge: spot, scrap.

'I know your game now, streaky sorcerer'

👤 Personal Response

1. Based on your reading of the poem, describe the encounter between man and creature. In your opinion, is it fascinating or disturbing, or both? Support your answer with reference to the text.
2. Choose one example of repetition used in the poem that appeals to you and comment briefly on its effectiveness.
3. Write your own personal response to the poem, highlighting the impact it made on you.

👁 Critical Literacy

D. H. Lawrence's 1923 poetry collection, *Birds, Beasts and Flowers*, was named after a Victorian hymn and included 'The Mosquito'. Lawrence reflects on the 'otherness' of the non-human world in this visualisation of the animal kingdom. He wrote 'The Mosquito' on 17 May 1920 while staying at the Grand Hotel in Syracuse, Sicily. In his memoirs, Lawrence recalls it as 'a rather dreary hotel – and many bloodstains of squashed mosquitos on the bedroom walls'. He exclaimed, 'Ah, vile mosquitos!' This inspired his confident, witty poem.

'The Mosquito' is an odd, contradictory poem in the form of an imagined **one-sided dialogue** on the occasion when man confronts insect. The narrative voice is presented in verse paragraphs and the spaces between are occupied by the presence of the mosquito whose internal responses are interpreted by the poet.

The mosquito is a small midge-like fly that lives by piercing human skin and sucking blood. This can cause a nasty rash. The insect, while not dangerous itself, can be the carrier of diseases, such as malaria and the Zika virus.

At first, the speaker is slightly condescending, **adopting a superior attitude to the little mosquito** by addressing it sarcastically with extravagant titles ('Monsieur', 'You exaltation') and wondering about its deceptive 'tricks' (line 1). The poet poses a series of questions: 'What do you stand on such high legs for?' Alliteration suggests the insect's threadlike thinness, 'shredded shank' (line 4). Yet, while physically insignificant, the creature has the ability to defy the forces of nature – and is able to 'lift your centre of gravity upwards' – unlike human beings. Its flimsy buoyancy fools the poet who can barely feel it, 'Stand upon me weightless'. Lawrence remains focused on the insect's insubstantiality – like a spirit or 'phantom' (line 8). It reminds him of how a woman he once knew described the mosquito as 'the Winged Victory', a famous statue in the Louvre Museum honouring Nike, the Greek goddess of Victory. Both insect and statue inhabit moments where action and stillness meet. The ominous irony is that the malaria-transmitting mosquito, winged itself, can boast its own past conquests of mankind. The poet notes that the creature's flowing movement and action of alighting contrasts sharply with the stagnant canals of Venice.

In line 11, Lawrence describes the mosquito's threatening action in the alliterative phrase, 'You turn your head towards your tail'. It is almost as if **the creature is aware of its own power**. He even imagines it beginning to 'smile', turning the tables on him and gaining control. In response, Lawrence's own attitude also changes. He no longer regards the insect with patronising amusement, but becomes puzzled and afraid. The poet recognises the insect's slightness ('translucent phantom shred/Of a frail corpus') as bizarre, 'Queer' (line 15). He attempts to rationalise the flimsiness of what he sees, 'thin wings and streaming legs' by using the simile, 'like a heron', the long-legged wading bird. Yet the mosquito still has a forceful quality. Lawrence becomes fascinated by its 'evil little aura'. He sees it as a 'prowling' predator stalking its prey. It has assumed the position of authority and the poet is reduced to the paralysis of a victim, 'casting a numbness on my mind'. The extended line winds slowly – just like the encircling insect.

By line 20, Lawrence finally has the answer to the question he initially posed regarding the mosquito's 'tricks'. He accepts that it can cast a spell ('filthy magic') – the undetected creature has the power to sedate or freeze its prey. He even suggests the hypnotic effect of the insect through internal half-rhymes ('attention', 'direction'). However, in line 23 the poet suddenly becomes hyper-aware, 'I know your game now'. **The battle between nature and human nature is on**. The striated insect's mesmerising quality is conveyed in the soft sibilant description, 'streaky sorcerer'. Lawrence regards its ability to inhabit the air as unsettling and eerie. Broad vowels capture the lazy circling of the hunter-insect ('stalk', 'prowl') while the poet continues to feel increasingly trapped. In frustration, he resorts to name-calling, 'Ghoul on wings', but then he remembers the statue to Victory. Is the insect about to get its victory by alighting on the poet? The tension rises.

Once again, **the insect out-manoeuvres the man**. Not only does the mosquito use its ace card, but it also sounds its 'high, hateful bugle' in the poet's ear. He analyses the mosquito's behaviour, using formal business language to criticise its tactics, 'Surely it is bad policy'. But the creature does not operate in this way, surviving instead on instinct. A single, stand-alone line announces, 'They say you can't help it'. For a moment, Lawrence relaxes because he believes that 'Providence' is protecting the blameless, 'the innocent'. But he becomes aware of the insect's mantra ('slogan') and the climax of the poem is reached in line 48 when the mosquito finally strikes ('snatch my scalp'). Sinister sibilance underlines the the insect's deceit.

A striking incantatory passage draws attention to **the goal of the mosquito**, 'Blood, red blood'. Its sole quest was always for something 'Super-magical/ Forbidden liquor'. The creature is consumed into total ecstasy as it gorges on the poet's blood, 'enspasmed in oblivion'. Lawrence is outraged because it has invaded his body, ('My blood') and has grossly violated their separateness by crossing a forbidden frontier, 'Such obscenity of trespass' (line 59). The exaggerated effect of the mosquito's action on the poet is conveyed in the repetition of 'Such'.

Lawrence is satisfied at witnessing the insect 'stagger', commenting wryly, 'As well as you may'. He now treats it as one who has become intoxicated. But once more, it is the mosquito's weightlessness that lifts it out of harm and past the poet's exhaling breath. The **insect's escape is caricatured** by the very long line, 'Saves you, wafts you away on the very draught my anger makes in its snatching'. We can sense Lawrence's extreme frustration in his futile attempts to catch the annoying creature.

Not for the first time, the **mosquito reigns supreme**, emitting a 'paean of derision', a joyful expression of disdain. And once again, Lawrence is reduced to impotent abuse: 'You winged blood-drop' (line 66). Three rapid quick-fire questions simulate the poet's breathless dash as he rushes around the room attempting to catch the tiny creature, culminating in the pathetic, convoluted 'Am I not mosquito enough to out-mosquito you?' The poet is now less important than his enemy. He has fallen very far from his opening position of the condescending man patronising the little insect. The mosquito is 'Winged Victory'. Yet, while Lawrence reluctantly admits to some admiration for its cleverness and strategy, it is not enough to prevent him from swatting it, reducing the creature to a 'dim dark smudge'.

So **the man eventually kills**. Is this how humans react when confronted by something beyond their understanding? Lawrence comments on how remarkably big the 'stain' of his own blood is in contrast to the tiny 'infinitesimal faint smear' (line 72) of the insect. Is he attempting to reassert his earlier dominance? We are left to consider whether man has really won by this act of annihilation. Or has the insect actually reduced man to the animal status, persuading him to follow the law of the jungle, kill or be killed?

As in so much of his narrative poetry, Lawrence writes in **free verse**. Certain repeated words ('Queer', 'Such', 'Winged Victory'), spacing between the verse paragraphs, and the internal pattern of sounds ('shredded shank', 'attention', 'direction') all create rhythm and structure. The carefully chosen vocabulary ('devil', 'evil', 'filthy', 'evasions', 'sideways', 'cunningly', 'fiend', 'obscenity of trespass', 'accursed') adds to the association of the insect with wickedness in the poet's mind.

Lawrence believed that free verse was appropriate for poetry of the 'immediate present'. Through this form, he involves the reader in his account of a random clash between man and nature. The poem follows the rhythm of **a hostile exchange**, tracing the outraged thoughts and almost manic tussle of wills between human and creature from the opening threat and ensuing contest to bloodshed and closing death.

🖋 Writing About the Poem

'D. H. Lawrence's poems capture the raw physical world with intensity and vigour.' Discuss this view, with particular reference to 'The Mosquito'.

Sample Paragraph

'The Mosquito' opens with a direct address from the speaker who is quick to mock the insect – 'When did you start your tricks, Monsieur?' Lawrence creates the vividly individualised presence of the insect with its 'shredded shanks' as it confronts the human. Through the poet's skill, we follow the angry human as he observes the insect. His growing irritation is conveyed in vindictive references to the insect's personality, 'pointed fiend'. The mosquito never stops moving, it will 'stalk and prowl the air'; and manoeuvre in 'circles and evasions'. The creature is challenging the human's supremacy by its 'anaesthetic power'. The man's helplessness is graphically conveyed through forceful language, 'deaden my attention in your direction'. The predator succeeds in 'enveloping' the man. But it is the act of sucking blood from the victim that is most vigorously highlighted. Short, abrupt lines conjure up the power of the mosquito as it gorges on 'Blood, red blood'. Reading the poem, I get a strong sense of how the insect is only following the rules of the natural world, obeying its instinct for survival.

EXAMINER'S COMMENT

Good, confident response that focuses on the raw physicality of nature. Discussion points are very well supported with suitable references. Expression is impressive, with a strong, varied vocabulary ('individualised presence', 'perceived personality', 'manoeuvre', 'mystical transcedence'). Overall, a top-grade paragraph, well-rounded off with the concluding sentence.

✒ Class/Homework Exercises

1. 'D. H. Lawrence strips away sentimentality and consolation through his free verse poems.' In your opinion, how true is this of 'The Mosquito'? Support your answer with reference to the poem.
2. 'Conflict and drama are recurring features in Lawrence's poems.' Discuss this statement, with particular reference to 'The Mosquito'.

⊙ Points to Consider

- **Man's relationship with nature and the animal world is a central theme.**

- **Powerful aural effects – repetition, alliteration, sibilant 's'.**

- **Satanic and magical terms, unusual similes and metaphors.**

- **Long sweeping lines interspersed with short one-/two-word lines.**

- **Range of attitudes, e.g. arrogance, uneasiness, derision, frustration, fulfilment, aggression, etc.**

4 Snake

D. H. LAWRENCE

A snake came to my water-trough
On a hot, hot day, and I in pyjamas for the heat,
To drink there.

Repetition = creates a mood of anticipation

In the deep, strange-scented shade of the great dark carob-tree
I came down the steps with my pitcher   5
And must wait, must stand and wait, for there he was at the trough
   before me.

— Repetition = anticipation

He reached down from a fissure in the earth-wall in the gloom
And trailed his yellow-brown slackness soft-bellied down, over the edge
   of the stone trough *Run on line = captures the snake movement*
And rested his throat upon the stone bottom,
And where the water had dripped from the tap, in a small clearness,   10
He sipped with his straight mouth, *Rhyme = to show that the snake is captivating! hypnotic effect*
Softly drank through his straight gums, into his slack long body,
Silently. *atmosphere of reverence = shows admiration for the snake*
in voices

Someone was before me at my water-trough,
And I, like a second-comer, waiting.   15
un rhymed couplet! showing his growing frustration with the snake as its acting indifferent/ nonchalante

He lifted his head from his drinking, as cattle do, *I snake is humorous*
And looked at me vaguely, as drinking cattle do, *Protrayed in a non harmful way*
And flickered his two-forked tongue from his lips, and mused a moment,
And stooped and drank a little more, *alliteration*
Being earth-brown, earth-golden from the burning bowels of the earth   20
On the day of Sicilian July, with Etna smoking.
Volcanoe   ominous mood

The voice of my education said to me
He must be killed, *society has conditioned him to think a certain*
For in Sicily the black, black snakes are innocent, the gold are venomous.
similarity between the volcanoe and snakes dangeros potential both is calm but has

And voices in me said, If you were a man
You would take a stick and break him now, and finish him off.   25
Plasure by manliness and what a man should do

But must I confess how I liked him,
How glad I was he had come like a guest in quiet, to drink at my
   water-trough
And depart peaceful, pacified, and thankless, *— personifieing the snake*
Into the burning bowels of this earth?
uncomfethle with the manly hood the narrow view of manly hood

Glossary

snake: limbless reptile; some are poisonous.
trough: container.
carob-tree: Mediterranean red-flowered tree.
pitcher: container, small bucket.
fissure: crevice, opening.
slackness: looseness, sagging.
second-comer: late arrival.
mused: reflected, wondered.
bowels: depths, underground.
Etna: Mount Etna, an active volcano in Sicily.
venomous: poisonous, deadly.

Was it cowardice, that I dared not kill him?
Was it perversity, that I longed to talk to him?
Was it humility, to feel so honoured?
I felt so honoured.

Shows his uncertain view through rhetorical question

perversity: obstinacy, contrariness.

And yet those voices: 35
If you were not afraid, you would kill him!

And truly I was afraid, I was most afraid,
But even so, honoured still more
That he should seek my hospitality
From out the dark door of the secret earth.
alliteration

The rest of the poem is the poet trying to decide which feeling is stronger – the sense of admiration for the snake or the insecurity he feels at letting the snake take priority over him in his own home

The snake is completely oblivious to the agonizing to poet

He drank enough
And lifted his head, dreamily, as one who has drunken,
And flickered his tongue like a forked night on the air, so black,
Seeming to lick his lips,   *simile*
And looked around like a god, unseeing, into the air,   45
And slowly turned his head,   *sibilence = captures the sensuality of the snakes movement*
And slowly, very slowly, as if thrice adream,
Proceeded to draw his slow length curving round
And climb again the broken bank of my wall-face.

suggest poise

long vowel sounds enhance the sense of the snakes languorous movement and lack of threat.

thrice adream: in deep unconsciousness.

atmosphere ripe with tension

And as he put his head into that dreadful hole,
And as he slowly drew up, snake-easing his shoulders, and entered
    farther,
A sort of horror, a sort of protest against his withdrawing into that
    horrid black hole,
Deliberately going into the blackness, and slowly drawing himself after,
Overcame me now his back was turned.

Contrast with the snake poised movement and the poets rash clumsy attack

the tone of the Poem changed from one of admiration to panic and fear

I looked round, I put down my pitcher,   55
I picked up a clumsy log
And threw it at the water-trough with a clatter.

clatter: crashing sound.

simile : conveys the speed the snakes can go

I think it did not hit him,
But suddenly that part of him that was left behind convulsed in
    undignified haste.
Writhed like lightning, and was gone   60
Into the black hole, the earth-lipped fissure in the wall-front,
At which, in the intense still noon, I stared with fascination.
Repetition of "I" shows his accountability

convulsed: shuddered, collapsed.

Writhed: thrashed, struggled.

The poet seems to be frank and reflective

And immediately I regretted it.
I thought how paltry, how vulgar, what a mean act!
I despised myself and the voices of my accursed human education.   65

paltry: low, contemptible.

Acted upon impulses that came not from the poet but instead from the accursed human education

And I thought of the albatross,
And I wished he would come back, my snake.

For he seemed to me again like a king,
Like a king in exile, uncrowned in the underworld,
Now due to be crowned again.

70

And so, I missed my chance with one of the lords
Of life.
And I have something to expiate;
A pettiness.

Taormina

albatross: white ocean bird; a metaphor for worry or guilt. In Coleridge's poem, 'The Rime of the Ancient Mariner', an albatross was the bird that a sailor repented killing.

expiate: correct, redress.

pettiness: spitefulness, small-mindedness.

D. H. LAWRENCE

Handwritten annotations:
The Rime of the Ancient Marine
Reference to an old ballad
albatross = regret

Simile

— He realize that he had done something wrong and needs to atone

expiate = to make amends

'like a guest in quiet'

👤 Personal Response

1. In your own words, describe the mood and atmosphere that Lawrence creates in lines 1–13.
2. Choose two vivid images from the poem and comment briefly on the effectiveness of each.
3. In your view, what is the central theme or message of 'Snake'? Support your answer with reference to the poem.

⊙ Critical Literacy

'Snake' was written when D. H. Lawrence was living in Taormina, a hilltop town on the east coast of Sicily, in 1920–21, and is probably his best-known poem. It dramatises a confrontation between the refined human mind and the native forces of the earth, embodied by a snake that appears one morning at the narrator's water-trough. The experience is transformed by Lawrence and invested with mythical grandeur. The poem can be examined not only as a prime example of Lawrence's free verse technique, but as one in which the 'immediate present' comes to life on the page and in the mind of the reader.

The poem's opening lines establish the sweltering Mediterranean setting. 'On a hot, hot day', Lawrence's narrator takes his pitcher to the water-trough. Repetition – a prominent feature of this free verse poem – initiates the **hypnotic rhythm**. Lawrence's style is simple, the diction colloquial, and the word order that of common speech. But the effect is reserved and dignified. Domestic and exotic images are combined as the pyjama-clad human observes the snake 'In the deep, strange-scented shade of the great dark carob-tree'. At first, the presumptuous narrator views the snake as an intruder forcing him to 'stand and wait'.

Light and dark are contrasted in the snake's vivid golden colour and the surrounding gloom. Lawrence conveys the creature's physicality with emphasis on his 'straight mouth', 'slack long body' and flickering 'two-forked tongue'. Run-through lines and emphatic sibilant sounds suggest the snake's **slow, subtle movement**. The poet stretches his sentences, using multiple adjectives in lines such as 'yellow-brown slackness' and 'soft-bellied down' (line 8). Many phrases such as these use hyphenation, so that several words are elongated. Lawrence also hooks his sentence-long stanzas together by beginning lines with conjunctions: 'And must wait', 'And trailed'. When we trace the visual structure of the lines on the page, it seems almost as if the snake has swallowed the poem's form.

Lines 7–13 provide a **sensual description** of the animal's precise behaviour. Unlike the human observer, it acts entirely on instinct. Yet Lawrence personifies the reptile: 'He reached down', 'sipped with his straight mouth'.

The snake's natural ease within this timeless primal setting creates a strong sense of harmony. It is completely unaware of the human intruder, clearly out of place in this wilderness. There is something slightly ridiculous about the speaker's immediate reaction. Coming from the civilised world, he accepts that he is now the 'second-comer' in an orderly queue – but with begrudging resentment.

The tense stand-off between the human and natural worlds continues through lines 16-26. Compelled by an inherent reverence, the narrator watches closely as the snake drinks. He focuses on its graceful movements, comparing it to domesticated farm animals, 'drinking cattle'. Slow, deliberate rhythms suggest the intense heat and languor of the **sultry Mediterranean atmosphere**. But this is where the snake is in its true element: 'earth-golden from the burning bowels of the earth.' Meanwhile, distant volcanic smoke from Mount Etna testifies to the inner earth's hidden powers.

Both fear and fascination are evident in the speaker's **internal struggle** between rational and natural feelings. His 'education' has always warned him that the snake is dangerous: 'in Sicily the black, black snakes are innocent, the gold are venomous.'

Although he has been taught to destroy these creatures, he cannot bring himself to harm the snake because he 'liked him' and was glad 'he had come like a guest in quiet' (line 28). This tense scene can also be interpreted on a symbolic level. Associated with evil, the snake assumes a more ominous meaning. Emerging from the 'burning bowels of this earth', it is particularly suggestive of the biblical serpent.

The narrator continues to struggle with the two conflicting 'voices' he hears: one insists that the snake should be killed while the other maintains that it deserves respect and must therefore be spared. In his **conflicted, deepening consciousness**, the speaker moves from casual description to insightful confession. An urgent series of rhetorical questions reflects this intense inner debate: 'Was it cowardice, that I dared not kill him?' Increasingly conscious that he does not belong in the underworld of the snake, he wavers between an uncomfortable sense of 'perversity' and feeling 'honoured' (line 32). But the expectations of his masculine conditioning persist: 'If you were a man', *If you were not afraid, you would kill him!'*

The powerfully crafted syntax and unbroken rhythm of lines 41-49 work together to produce a **mesmerising effect**. Repeated references to the snake's dreamlike and unhurried presence add to the wistful tone. The narrator envisions this majestic creature as a mythical lord of the underworld ('like a god, unseeing'), an embodiment of all those mysterious forces of nature that man fears and neglects. Lawrence's detailed imagery is characteristically compelling. The snake's black tongue flickers 'like a forked night on the air', the dramatic simile suggesting a lightning flash plunging the noon-day scene into momentary night. It seems as though dark powers inhabit the 'door of the secret earth': Mount Etna might erupt, the deadly snake might strike. Suddenly the tone becomes harsh and ugly as the speaker reverts to the conditioned reflex of a rationalistic culture.

Faced with the snake's withdrawal into a fissure ('the blackness'), the narrator's **fearful imagination takes over** and he almost becomes incoherent. His disgust expresses itself in hysterical terms – 'dreadful', 'horrid'. He is overcome by 'a sort of protest' that causes him to act: 'I picked up a clumsy log/And threw it at the water-trough' (line 56). This cowardly action has an instant effect; the snake loses its former dignity and becomes 'convulsed', an obscene writhing thing, a reptile of the mind.

It's interesting that the narrator expresses neither triumph nor relief, but **deep revulsion** and self-disgust at causing such pointless violence: 'immediately I regretted it' (line 63). He regards his behaviour as 'mean' and 'vulgar', likening himself to the fictional Ancient Mariner who killed the albatross and was then compelled to acknowledge his offence. The speaker's 'paltry' action leads him to reverse the usual hierarchy. It is his 'human education' that is 'accursed', while in its majestic naturalness, the snake remains 'one of the lords /Of life' (line 71). The snake has recoiled into the underground and now appears to be like 'a king in exile', whereas in the open air it was a powerful sovereign. The ending fades away on a note of self-loathing as the narrator comes to terms with the 'pettiness' of what he has done.

Lawrence's 'Snake' is a typically resonant discourse between the teachings of reason and natural intuition. The poet presents us with a triumph of style and idiom, a highly memorable example of free verse where perception is embodied in rhythms that are an essential part of the poem's meaning. Religious terminology – of atoning for sin – would indicate that Lawrence is using the snake as a symbol of the battle between good and evil. Perhaps its real significance lies in the wider questions it raises about how human beings face up to the moral challenges of the natural world.

✒ Writing About the Poem

'Drama and tension are recurring features of Lawrence's poems.'
Discuss this statement, with particular reference to 'Snake'.

Sample Paragraph

Lawrence's poem 'Snake' has many dramatic elements, particularly conflict. The poet sets the scene on a 'hot day' in Sicily. The atmosphere is edgy with intense heat. He is challenged by the 'yellow-brown' snake seeking water and a stalemate occurs. In the background, a volcanic mountain adds to the tension – 'Etna smoking'. I thought that the real conflict was taking place within the man's mind, saying 'take a stick and break him now'. This internal debate is agonising. Several rhetorical questions show how conflicted the man is – 'Was it cowardice?' His 'education' tells him to kill but he feels 'so honoured' that the snake is seeking 'hospitality'. Lawrence uses striking images of darkness and light to illustrate the conflict between good and evil. The snake has come from 'the dark door of the secret earth'. When the drama reaches a climax and the man throws the stick at the snake, it retreats back into the 'horrid black hole'. In a way, the conflict has been resolved and the man is left with his guilt – an anti-climax.

EXAMINER'S COMMENT

Informed discussion focusing well on aspects of drama (setting, conflict, tension, climax, contrasting images). Ranges over a variety of points, e.g. 'internal debate is agonising'. Supporting quotations are integrated successfully into the commentary. Expression is clear, but slightly pedestrian, e.g. the second-last sentence. Overall, a good, solid response that just falls short of the top grade.

✒ Class/Homework Exercises

1. 'D. H. Lawrence makes effective use of rhythm and repetition to convey meaning in his poems.' To what extent is this true of 'Snake'? Support your answer with reference to the poem.
2. 'Lawrence's poetry often addresses themes that have a universal significance.' To what extent do you agree with this view? Support your answer with reference to 'Snake'.

⊙ Points to Consider

- **Key themes include the natural world, human culture, nature, sin and guilt.**

- **Conflicting 'voices' within him represent natural instinct and cultural conditioning.**

- **Dramatic tension created by the confrontation between man and nature.**

- **Effective use of precise description, vivid imagery, contrasting tones and moods.**

- **The rhythm of the loose verse often suggests the snake's movement.**

Handwritten annotations at top:

Theme = nature
beauty of nature / complexity of evolution

5 Humming-Bird

Form = free verse; mixture of stanza length
- couplets
- tercets
- quatrain

imagery = optimistic vibrance of nature

Title: There are over 300 species of humming-birds. All are small and brilliantly coloured. They get their name from the humming sound created by their rapidly beating wings. They are the only group of birds able to fly backwards.

I can imagine, in some otherworld
Primeval-dumb, far back
In that most awful stillness, that only gasped and hummed,
Humming-birds raced down the avenues.

Annotation: internal rhyme

Primeval-dumb: pre-historic, elemental, primordial.

Annotation: image is optimistic / adds electric effect

Before anything had a soul,
While life was a heave of Matter, half inanimate,
This little bit chipped off in brilliance
And went whizzing through the slow, vast, succulent stems. 5

Annotation: dull, boring until the humming bird came
Annotation: end rhyme

Matter: substance.
inanimate: lifeless.
succulent stems: luscious stalks.

Annotation: alliteration show the vitality of the bird
Annotation: The poet is becoming more assertive

I believe there were no flowers then,
In the world where the humming-bird flashed ahead of creation. 10
I believe he pierced the slow vegetable veins with his long beak.

Annotation: The humming bird lived in its time that its ahead of its time

Probably he was big
As mosses, and little lizards, they say, were once big.
Probably he was a jabbing, terrifying monster.

Annotation: colloquial
Annotation: If the lizards were once big it could be the same with the humming bird
Annotation: earlier on life it was big but it is now small after evolution

We look at him through the wrong end of the long telescope of Time, 15
Luckily for us.

Annotation: lines alternate in length mixture of length makes a more playful, imaginative effect

Españ ola

'ahead of creation'

👤 Personal Response

1. From your reading of lines 1–4, what image do you get of the prehistoric world? Support your answer with reference to the text.
2. Choose two aural images from the poem that appeal to you and comment briefly on their effectiveness.
3. In your opinion, what point is Lawrence making in line 15: 'We look at him through the wrong end of the long telescope of Time'?

👁 Critical Literacy

Like so many of the poems in Lawrence's *Birds, Beasts and Flowers* collection (published in 1923), 'Humming-Bird' has a fresh, modern feel and spontaneity. It is thought that Lawrence wrote this short poem after reading several vivid descriptions of humming-birds, so it is probably not a record of immediate experience. Instead, the poet reinterprets the geological past and restores it to its own special sense of excitement. Through his poetic imagination, he creates a timeless image of the humming-bird whose life force evokes the hidden power of its evolution.

The poem travels 'far back' in geological time to the origin and predominance of the humming-bird. Lawrence sets the chilling scene: 'some otherworld/Primeval-dumb.' He imagines the 'most awful stillness' of a strange pre-historic setting. When the humming-bird appears, it flashes through the poem: 'raced down the avenues.' The ecstatic opening four lines include playful internal rhyme ('dumb', 'some') and sibilant effects ('stillness', 'gasped') that suggest the **unexpected presence** of these primal creatures.

Dynamic verbs ('chipped off', 'whizzing') capture the life force and energy of the humming-bird, highlighting the 'awful stillness' of the surrounding 'half inanimate' natural environment where sprawling plants leave only 'avenues' between them. **Lawrence controls the pace of the poem** beautifully – contrasting the lumbering 'heave of Matter' with the agility and darting pace of the humming-bird, which is 'a little bit chipped off in brilliance' (line 7). In this unfamilar primeval location, these small birds provide an unexpected striking flash of colour.

The poet is filled with enthusiasm and a childlike sense of wonder about pre-human times, 'Before anything had a soul'. He sees the humming-bird as the first independent entity to evolve from undifferentiated matter – the original isolated soul. Lawrence is also **a master of free verse and informal language**. Throughout 'Humming-Bird', the pace alternates between the shorter curt lines and the longer free-winging descriptions associated with the bird in flight: 'And went whizzing through the slow, vast, succulent stems' (line 8). Throughout the poem, this jaunty lilt to the rhythm mirrors the bird's swift movement.

In imagining the long distant past, Lawrence considers how the earliest birds would have survived in a flowerless environment by living off the sap of plants ('pierced the slow vegetable veins'). A range of song-like **auditory techniques** – the onomatopoeic verb, slender vowels and the alliterative 'v' effect – echoes the determined efforts to survive within the prehistoric habitat.

Reiteration and recapitulation are features of Lawrence's train of thought, which is propelled forward and held together by such repeated phrasing as 'in some otherworld', 'In that most awful stillness' and 'I believe', 'I believe'. Such repetition continues into the poem's final lines where the poet speculates on the likely size of the first humming-bird: 'Probably he was big' and 'Probably he was a jabbing, terrifying monster' (line 14). The emphasis on the humming-bird's antecedents is disturbingly realistic. But although this is a somewhat bizarre vision, Lawrence clearly rejoices at the nightmare image he has created.

He concludes on **an ironic note**, personifying the bird and showing it appropriate respect. The thought that the prehistoric creature was 'once big' – and indeed monstrous – should make us revise our attitude to his smaller, contemporary counterpart 'through the long telescope of Time'. The poet might well be reminding readers that humans were not always masters of creation. Is he warning us against complacency and that there will also be something new to displace the old?

The 'long telescope of Time' – the image magnified by the capitalised 'T' – occupies an extended line, whereas the succinct line 16 startles us with the implication of **human limitation**. Today's humming-birds are small and – as the telescope metaphor indicates – we see them in inappropriate scale. The colloquial final line, 'Luckily for us', half-humorously leaves the reader to decide how a proper perspective might challenge our own human status and exaggerated sense of self-importance.

Lawrence's **witty poem quivers with energy**, mirroring the alternating order and chaos inherent in creation. It typifies many of the poet's hallmarks – the lightness of touch, the immediacy of the voice and quicksilver language – all of which are the perfect embodiment of the wondrous humming-bird.

🖋 Writing About the Poem

'D. H. Lawrence's most memorable poems have a spontaneity and sense of drama that make an immediate impact on readers.'

Sample Paragraph

'Humming-Bird' is an exotic, imaginative poem in which the poet imagines the bird in a primeval-dumb world, in an 'awful stillness' before 'anything had a soul. Lawrence begins with 'I imagine' and then takes us on a dreamlike journey to when life was starting on earth. It's a very dramatic scene. Then suddenly out of the great void, the humming-bird is seen as flashing 'ahead of creation', piercing 'the slow vegetable veins with his long beak'. The images of nature are cinematic. The sense of immediacy is evident in the conversational language and everyday speech rhythms – 'This little bit chipped off in brilliance' for example, referring to how the colourful bird accidentally evolved into life. Some of the expressions are colloquial – 'Probably he was big' and 'Luckily for us'. The tone is always one of excitement and wonder. I liked Lawrence's fascination with these tiny birds. The poem was both thoughtful and playful – almost like a song in its lively rhythm – the kind of poetry I enjoy.

EXAMINER'S COMMENT

A good personal response to the question. The focus on spontaneity is sustained throughout and includes interesting points on Lawrence's dreamlike poetic vision and informal language use. There is also some impressive discussion on key aspects of dramatic style (imagery, rhythm and tone). Overall, a confident high-grade standard.

✒ Class/Homework Exercises

1. 'Lawrence often makes imaginative use of evocative sound effects to convey meaning in his poetry.' Discuss this statement with particular reference to 'Humming-Bird'.
2. 'Throughout much of his poetry, D. H. Lawrence is primarily interested in making discoveries.' Discuss this view, with particular reference to 'Humming-Bird'.

⊙ Points to Consider

- Free verse achieves greater emotional intensity than simple fragmented prose.

- Lawrence articulates the essence of the humming-bird.

- He also challenges us to re-evaluate our views on evolution.

- Effective use of varying line lengths and informal tone.

- Wide-ranging aural effects – repetition, sibilance, assonance and alliteration.

6 Intimates

Title: close friends (n.), implies (v.).

Don't you care for my love? she said bitterly.

I handed her the mirror, and said:
Please address these questions to the proper person!
Please make all requests to head-quarters!
In all matters of emotional importance   5
please approach the supreme authority direct!
So I handed her the mirror.

And she would have broken it over my head,
but she caught sight of her own reflection
and that held her spellbound for two seconds   10
while I fled.

'spellbound'

👤 Personal Response

1. Based on your reading of the poem, describe the relationship between the speaker and his female companion. Support your answer with reference to the text.
2. Lawrence uses several poetic techniques in the poem, including direct speech, repetition, alliteration and run-on lines. Choose one technique that particularly appeals to you and comment briefly on its effectiveness.
3. Write your own personal response to the poem, outlining the impact it made on you.

D. H. LAWRENCE

⊙ Critical Literacy

'Intimates' is a short, witty poem from Lawrence's collection, *More Pansies*, published in 1932 after his death from tuberculosis. In his introduction, the poet wrote: 'This little bunch of fragments is offered as a bunch of pensées ... handful of thoughts.' They were based on 'Pensées' by the French philosopher Blaise Pascal, fragments of thoughts and theology, such as, 'Do you believe people to wish good of you? Don't speak'. Lawrence also refers to the French word 'panser', to dress or bandage a wound. He regarded these verses as medicinal, administering them to the emotional wounds we suffer in modern civilisation. He regarded 'Each little piece' as a thought which comes from the heart, 'with its own blood and instinct running in it ... if you hold my pansies properly to the light, they may show a running vein of fire'.

The title, 'Intimates', if used as a noun suggests a loving relationship, but if as a verb, it can mean 'insinuates' or 'hints'. Lawrence sets up the expectation that this couple really understand each other. However, the poem begins with jolting directness and readers are placed, without warning, in the middle of a **spiteful argument** between the couple. A woman's acerbic question plaintively intones, 'Don't you care for my love?' (**line 1**). She is complaining about a lack of concern for her happiness and the welfare of their relationship. The use of the verb 'said' indicates that this is more a statement than a plea. Her tone is harsh: 'bitterly.' The implication is clearly that the man is not particularly interested.

But he is stung into action and hands her 'the mirror'. The definite article suggests that she used this mirror frequently. In a clipped detached tone, he issues a list of formal requests. The repeated use of the word 'Please', usually found in polite conversation, seems not only absurd but sardonic and cold. The alliteration of the hard 'p' sound ('Please', 'proper person') conveys an anger barely concealed. The adjective 'proper' (**line 3**) not only refers to the correct person to whom the questions should be addressed, but also indicates a prudish one. Meanwhile, he continues to reprimand her, 'Please make all requests to head-quarters'. The **sarcastic inference** of this odd remark suggests that the fraught relationship is being controlled by a third party or some other outside influence.

The speaker feels increasingly **frustrated**, as it appears that the woman is not even listening to him. Paradoxically, in stilted language that is anything but sensitive, he directs that 'all matters of emotional importance', should be with the person who has the unnamed official power that can enforce obedience, 'please approach the supreme authority direct' (**line 6**). He then concludes his terse argument with the conjunction 'So'. It is left to the reader to decide whether the section concludes as 'and then' he handed her the mirror or 'therefore' he handed her the mirror. If the latter is the case, it would signify that he thinks he has won the argument. Lawrence places a creative pause at this stage to allow us to imagine the woman's feelings of anger rising.

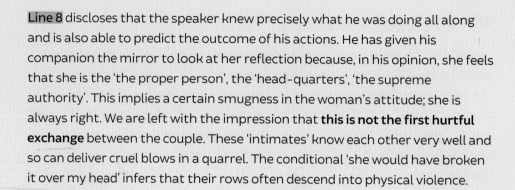

Line 8 discloses that the speaker knew precisely what he was doing all along and is also able to predict the outcome of his actions. He has given his companion the mirror to look at her reflection because, in his opinion, she feels that she is the 'the proper person', the 'head-quarters', 'the supreme authority'. This implies a certain smugness in the woman's attitude; she is always right. We are left with the impression that **this is not the first hurtful exchange** between the couple. These 'intimates' know each other very well and so can deliver cruel blows in a quarrel. The conditional 'she would have broken it over my head' infers that their rows often descend into physical violence.

However, the mood changes on the conjunction 'but'. Wryly, the speaker recounts how the woman sees herself in the mirror and becomes mesmerised by 'her own reflection'. The use of the pronoun 'own' and the emphatic verb 'spellbound' paint a picture of an extremely **self-interested person**. Run-on lines capture the 'two seconds' she spends gazing at herself. They hint at the vanity of the fairy tale Wicked Queen who asks 'Mirror, mirror on the wall, who is the fairest of them all?' **Line 11** heralds the man's last evasive action, 'while I fled'. Fearing the worst, he makes a hasty escape while his companion is preoccupied. The monosyllabic verb 'fled' has a finality that suggests a victory of sorts in this particular skirmish. The man has escaped the stifling constraints of the woman's demands – for the moment.

While the female character in this poem has been exposed as domineering and self-obsessed, the man's behaviour throughout has not exactly been admirable. Is the poet suggesting that while the couple know each other well, they are by no means 'Intimates'? The only victim of their feud is the relationship itself. This unsettling poem challenges readers. The poet has **presented this small domestic drama through quoted conversation and actions**, but has refrained from commenting directly. Is the poem simply holding up a reflective surface allowing the reader to look at personal relationships and the lack of successful communication? Lawrence believed that poetry makes us more aware of ourselves. 'Intimates' provides an opportunity to examine the conflict between frustration and fulfilment in relationships and in ourselves.

✒ Writing About the Poem

'D. H. Lawrence believed that all poems should be personal sentiments with a sense of spontaneity.' Discuss this statement in relation to the poem 'Intimates'.

Sample Paragraph

'Intimates' opens on the jarring note of a complaining woman, 'Don't you care for my love?' The frustration is conveyed through reported conversations and the behaviour of the woman and her partner. The man's spontaneous action in handing the mirror to the self-obsessed woman and his list of deeply wounding orders suggests a dysfunctional couple. Genuine personal sentiments are disclosed – the woman does not feel appreciated while he feels harangued by 'the supreme authority'. At the same time, the reader's sympathy sways towards the woman who is subjected to such derision. She also has to contend with a man who runs away – another unexpected development. He, however, feels stifled by her superiority, 'the proper person'. An insistent rhyme adds to the man's growing feeling of claustrophobia, 'said', 'head', 'fled'. Through capturing the spontaneity of the fight, Lawrence reveals the truth that an argument is not genuine contact and only succeeds in destroying the relationship.

EXAMINER'S COMMENT

Good, intelligent high-grade response that engages closely with the poem. The idea of spontaneity is addressed effectively through specific expressions (such as 'spontaneous', 'unexpected' and 'growing'). Apt quotations are successfully integrated into the discussion and assured vocabulary ('derision', 'harangued by', 'contend with', 'feeling of claustrophobia', etc.) is impressive.

✒ Class/Homework Exercises

1. 'Lawrence's poetry often uses particular everyday scenes to explore issues that have much wider universal significance.' Discuss this view with reference to the poem 'Intimates'.

2. 'D. H. Lawrence's carefully crafted poetry frequently challenges social constraints.' To what extent is this true of 'Intimates'? Support your answer with reference to the poem.

⊙ Points to Consider

- **Central themes include conflict, lack of communication, vanity, deception.**

- **Poetic techniques – direct speech, contrast between personal and formal language, alliteration, repetition, run-on lines, creative pause, paradox.**

- **Varied tones – disappointment, hurt, anger, sarcasm, mockery, etc.**

7 Delight of Being Alone

[handwritten top: Free verse / theme = solitude]

[handwritten: repetition of delight adds a note of melodic confidence]

[handwritten left margin: opening line is unambiguous bold statement]

[handwritten left margin: personification]

[handwritten left margin: enjambment allows him to begin the final line with the central image of the poem "alone"]

I know no greater <u>delight</u> than the sheer delight of being alone.
It makes me realise the delicious pleasure of the <u>moon</u> *[handwritten: he is identifying with the moon]*
<u>that she has in travelling</u> by herself: throughout time,
or the splendid growing of an <u>ash-tree</u> *[handwritten: identifying with the ash-tree]*
alone, on a hill-side in the north, humming in the wind.   5

[handwritten: contrast in imagery — the moon is always travelling the tree is always rooted — yet both are alone]

◉ Critical Literacy

**This is one of Lawrence's most conventional and beautiful poems. It was
published after his death in *Last Poems* (1932).**

[handwritten left margin: He is possibly suggesting that his "delight" at being alone was something he felt whether he was mobile or stationary]

The simple directness and sincerity of the opening line shows Lawrence's
enthusiasm for 'the sheer delight of being alone'. His emphasis on 'delight'
establishes the mood of deep satisfaction. The poet's acknowledgment of
the 'delicious pleasure of the moon' is enhanced by the use of **richly sibilant
sounds**. As always, Lawrence's appreciation of nature is beyond doubt. The
moon has long been a traditional symbol of solitude and self-sufficiency
– and the poet now senses its mysterious power 'throughout time'.

[handwritten right margin: the poet was dying when he wrote this poem – this suggests he was willing to embrace the end of his life]

To some extent, line 2 reads like an excerpt from the diary of a man who is
seriously ill. This would explain Lawrence's desire to take up a form outside
of his human body, that of the night-wandering moon. He is drawn to the
'splendid growing of an ash-tree … humming in the wind', described with
precise eloquence. The poem takes on a **mystical quality** with the
suggestion that Lawrence's soul may become part of the spirit of the
timeless natural world. His attraction to the moon and the lonely tree on
a hillside is the refuge of his poetic imagination – the last refuge.

[handwritten right margin: Sibilance – makes me realise the delicious pleasure]

[handwritten right margin: effect adds melody to the poem – euphonic/euphony (pleasant sounds) and contributes to an upbeat mood]

'humming'

8 Absolute Reverence

I feel absolute reverence to nobody and to nothing human,
neither to persons nor things nor ideas, ideals nor religions nor institutions,
to these things I feel only respect, and a tinge of reverence
when I see the fluttering of pure life in them.

But to something unseen, unknown, creative   5
from which I feel I am a derivative
I feel absolute reverence. Say no more!

reverence: devotion, worship.
ideals: dreams, principles.
institutions: organisations, establishments.
tinge: touch, hint.

derivative: product, result.

 Critical Literacy

D. H. Lawrence always maintained that he was 'a profoundly religious man'. His religion was certainly real enough, but unorthodox and informal. For Lawrence, it was essentially mystical, similar to other visionary poets, such as Shelley and Yeats.

The poem's emphatic opening establishes Lawrence's belief that all of reality is identical with divinity. His passionate tone can be understood positively as the view that nothing exists outside of God. He goes on to clarify his deeply felt opposition to conventional doctrines and organised religions.

The poet's sympathies lie entirely with what he calls 'the fluttering of pure life', an image that immediately evokes the vitality and beauty of nature. His God is the transcendent reality of which the material universe and human beings are mere manifestations.

D. H. Lawrence's poetry is a long and rich exploration of reverence towards the mystery of life: 'something unseen unknown, creative/from which I feel I am derivative.' There is no logic in such lines, but they sum up Lawrence's pantheistic, mystical, and wholly sincere worship and the life force that lies at the root of all his thinking.

'fluttering
of pure life'

[Handwritten top:] Political Poem. Central ideas = exploitation

9 What Have They Done to You?

[Handwritten:] Provides backbone. Title [repeated] of the poem repeated so much it becomes a chant

What have they done to you, men of the masses, creeping back
and forth to work?

[Annotations:] the masses: the working classes. Suggesting shame / Has a steady rhythm, mimi represents the routine of their daily lives. Balance

What have they done to you, the saviours of the people, oh what have
they saved you from while they pocketed the money?

[Annotations:] saviours: redeemers, protectors. Sarcasm — Employers is seen as the enemy of the people

Alas, they have saved you from yourself, from your own frail dangers
and devoured you from the machine, the vast maw of iron.

[Annotations:] referencing how the poor cant be left idle or the cause trouble. tone = angry. metaphor — working men being chewed up by industry will

They saved you from your squalid cottages and poverty of <u>hand to</u>
<u>mouth</u>   5

and embedded you in workmen's dwellings, where your wage is the
dole of work, and the dole is your wage of nullity.

[Annotations:] colloquial phrase. Paid a bit more than the dole, contribute to the sense of worthlessness

They took away, oh they took away your man's native instincts and
intuitions

and gave you a board-school education, newspapers, and the cinema.

[Annotations:] your natural instincts are taken away. the real danger. turning point striking

They stole your body from you, and left you an <u>animated carcass</u>
to work with, and nothing else: 10
unless <u>goggling</u> eyes, to <u>goggle</u> at the film
and a board-school brain, stuffed up with the ha'penny press.

[Annotations:] thus gone is exploitation. metaphor. Repetition used to show frustration. Machine cwg sensitivity. slamming the education system and unsympathetic to the workless

Your instincts gone, your intuitions gone, your passions dead
Oh carcass with a board-school mind and a ha'penny newspaper
intelligence,
what have they done to you, what have they done to you, Oh what
have they done to you?   15

[Annotations:] anger reaches its peak. Coherence through the use of repetition. Repetition. sees them as part participant

Oh look at my fellow-men, oh look at them
the masses! Oh, what has been done to them?

[Annotations:] overcome with emotion

[Handwritten bottom left:] mix of enjambe. Free verse poem. couplet (2 line stanzas) tercet (3 line stanza) Quatrain (4 line stanza) allows us to pay attention to the anger instead of structure of the piece

[Handwritten bottom right:] tone is angry & passionate. repetition is used a lot throughout the poem to show his disgust "You" "Your" repetition. Metaphor used to highlight his anger and shows how people are being exploited

👤 Personal Response

1. In your opinion, what is the dominant tone of this poem? Is it angry, powerful, ironic, sentimental, uncontrolled, etc.? Support your answer with reference to the text.
2. Choose one memorable image (visual or aural) from the poem and comment on its effectiveness.
3. Based on your reading of the poem, what impression do you get of the poet, D. H. Lawrence? Support your answer with reference to the text.

👁 Critical Literacy

D. H. Lawrence did not profess to be a socialist, but there can be no doubt that he possessed strong ideas about what he believed was wrong with the money-wages-profit system and what sort of society would be best for humans to live in. Lawrence describes his aversion to modernity in 'What Have They Done To You?'. The poem is thought to have been written during the poet's visits to Majorca and Tuscany in 1929.

'the vast maw of iron'

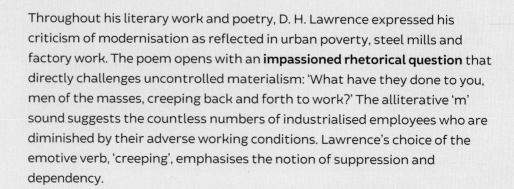

Throughout his literary work and poetry, D. H. Lawrence expressed his criticism of modernisation as reflected in urban poverty, steel mills and factory work. The poem opens with an **impassioned rhetorical question** that directly challenges uncontrolled materialism: 'What have they done to you, men of the masses, creeping back and forth to work?' The alliterative 'm' sound suggests the countless numbers of industrialised employees who are diminished by their adverse working conditions. Lawrence's choice of the emotive verb, 'creeping', emphasises the notion of suppression and dependency.

The impassioned rhetorical tone and emotive language, which will dominate the entire poem, continues in line 2 as the poet mocks the so-called 'saviours of the people'. In accusing the wealthy employers of exploitation ('they pocketed the money'), Lawrence points out the obvious irony that this was the only saving involved. But the poet's anger is moderated with expressions of **regretful frustration** ('Alas'). However, his compassion for the poor and their 'frail dangers' is quickly replaced by fury at what he sees as their victimisation. The new industrial age has: 'devoured you with the machine, the vast maw of iron.' Lawrence's choice of violent metaphorical language symbolises the monstrous dehumanising effect of mass mechanisation.

Lines 5–6 focus on the wretched 'hand to mouth' living conditions of working-class people who are expected to be grateful for any kind of employment. Repulsive imagery ('squalid cottages') and broad vowel assonance ('mouth', 'dole', 'nullity') add to our understanding of the pathos Lawrence associates with such widespread hardship. The extended line lengths and turgid rhythms also suggest their relentless struggle for survival.

A significant change of emphasis occurs in line 7, however, when **the poet broadens his scathing criticism**. Up until this point, the 'they' targeted by Lawrence referred to the powerful factory owners and captains of industry. Now he turns his attention to the **wider establishment forces** in politics and education: 'board-school education, newspapers, and the cinema.' From his point of view, ordinary people are not just oppressed by poverty, but are also controlled through the conservative school system. In addition, their lives are further diminished by cheap journalism and popular entertainment.

The tone becomes increasingly melodramatic as Lawrence rages against the ruling class – those who misuse power to stifle creativity and reduce the common worker to a passive 'animated carcass' (line 9). In a series of exasperated outbursts, he again attacks the country's press and media, and castigates the film industry – presumably for producing undemanding escapism designed for 'goggling eyes'. The 'ha'penny press' is further accused of keeping readers' minds 'stuffed up' with useless information.

The poet's central argument that most ordinary citizens are systematically diverted from improving their lives builds to a climax in the final lines. Questions now begin with the exclamatory 'Oh', highlighting the anguish he feels. The plaintive repetition of 'what have they done to you?' is all but an **admission of utter despair**. In contrast to the protracted oratorical style throughout the poem, the ending is terse and to the point. Lawrence's reference to his 'fellow-men' (line 16) has particular significance both with and without irony. While he is aiming a final cynical blow at those who have no respect for humanity, there is no denying the poet's own tender feeling for other people. Indeed, the entire poem is primarily a persuasive expression of Lawrence's aversion to modernity – articulated through repetitive language describing the monotonous, menial tasks of factories and the enslavement of his fellow Britons. In strongly denouncing the dehumanising effects of industrialisation, the poet raises interesting questions about modern society and community, about freedom and constraint. It is left to readers to decide whether Lawrence's use of hyperbole and excessive rhetoric enriches or devalues his sentiments.

🖋 Writing About the Poem

'D. H. Lawrence writes dramatic poems that often combine critical commentary with heartfelt compassion.' Discuss this view, with particular reference to 'What Have They Done to You?'.

Sample Paragraph

When we first studied 'What Have They Done to You?', it actually seemed more like a political speech than a poem. Lawrence held strong views and believed that the traditional English way of life had changed for the worst. In his opinion, factory towns had turned workers into slaves. The poem is filled with persuasive techniques, especially repetition. Lawrence uses negative images of 'squalid' houses and assembly-line workers being 'devoured' by the 'vast maw of iron'. He views modern-day life as unnatural. Although the language suggests savagery, there is always a sense that the poet's main concern is with the vulnerable workers and their poverty-stricken families. Expressive verbs such as 'took away' and 'stole' emphasise his concern for these people. The 'animated carcass' comparison combines Lawrence's anger at their mistreatment with sympathy. He ends with 'Oh look at my fellow-men' – which, for me, sums up his attitude.

EXAMINER'S COMMENT

A good high-grade response. The introductory comments showed engagement with Lawrence's strongly held views. Points were developed and aptly illustrated with accurate quotation. Some impressive discussion regarding the poet's persuasive style and use of negative language was balanced by illustrations of his sympathetic tone.

🖋 Class/Homework Exercises

1. 'Lawrence is severely critical of what he views as "a state of suppression" in which individuals are tormented and made inhuman by the processes of industrialisation.' Discuss this statement with reference to 'What Have They Done to You?'.

2. In your opinion, how relevant is 'What Have They Done to You?' to modern times? Support your answer with reference to the poem.

⊙ Points to Consider

- **Key themes: the suppression of natural human individuality by industrialisation.**

- **Contrasting tones: anger, frustration, sympathy, irony, anguish, dejection.**

- **Effective use of metaphorical language, onomatopoeia and vivid imagery.**

- **Rhetorical style – repetition, questions, speech rhythms, emotive language, etc.**

10 Baby-Movements II: 'Trailing Clouds'

As a drenched, drowned bee
Hangs numb and heavy from the bending flower,
    So clings to me,
My baby, her brown hair brushed with wet tears
    And laid laughterless on her cheek,   5
Her soft white legs hanging heavily over my arm
    Swinging to my lullaby.
My sleeping baby hangs upon my life
    As a silent bee at the end of a shower
    Draws down the burdened flower.   10
She who has always seemed so light
    Sways on my arm like sorrowful, storm-heavy boughs,
Even her floating hair sinks like storm-bruised young leaves
Reaching downwards:
    As the wings of a drenched, drowned bee   15
    Are a heaviness, and a weariness.

numb: dazed, deadened.

clings: attaches.

burdened: laden, weighed down.

boughs: small branches.

'the burdened flower'

👤 Personal Response

1. Why, in your opinion, does Lawrence compare the sleeping child to 'a drenched, drowned bee'? Support your answer with reference to the text.
2. Lawrence makes use of sound throughout the poem. Choose one aural image from the poem and briefly comment on its effectiveness.
3. Write your own personal response to the poem, highlighting the impact it made on you.

👁 Critical Literacy

'Trailing Clouds' is part of a two-poem sequence called 'Baby-Movements', one of D. H. Lawrence's earliest works. It was first published in 1909, apparently based on a description of his landlady's baby daughter. The poem was later renamed 'A Baby Asleep After Pain'. Lawrence's original title had been taken from a poem by William Wordsworth ('trailing clouds of glory do we come/From God, who is our home'). Wordsworth believed in the eternal spiritual nature of life.

Lawrence's opening lines are dominated by the striking image of a 'drenched, drowned bee'. The speaker – most likely the voice of the baby's mother – compares the clinging infant to the dying insect on the 'bending flower'. The poet is fond of images drawn from the natural world, such as the **bee and flower motif**. His rhythms are apparently casual, yet carefully controlled. The alliterative 'd' sound suggests a laden inertia. Broad vowel assonance ('Hangs numb and heavy') adds to the pain the bee feels.

Lines 4–7 focus closely on the mother's natural sense of connection with her child ('My baby') and their close physical interaction. There is a hypnotic, dreamlike quality to the description. The combined force of **multiple sound effects** – alliteration, assonance and sibilance – is remarkable for the lucidity, lightness and vivid precision that Lawrence achieves. The infant's hair is 'brushed with wet tears/And laid laughterless on her cheek'. The poet does not treat his images as abstract or merely visual. They are dynamic and changeable – 'legs hanging heavily', 'Swinging'. Tactile images suggest the contact between bodies. The baby appears to be almost an extension of her mother's body ('over my arm'). Such clarity of diction and use of luminous details are characteristic of Lawrence. The mother's attentive rocking movement is matched by instinctive tenderness echoed in the gentle sound of the 'lullaby'.

The poem's central simile is repeated in lines 8–10. This fragile, helpless child is utterly reliant on her mother: 'My sleeping baby hangs upon my life.' Is there a hint that the strain is nearly too much to bear? The **lethargic mood** continues, expressed mostly through onomatopoeic effects: 'Draws down the burdened flower.' While Lawrence cannot resist the impulse to rhyme ('shower', 'flower'), the restraint in the ebb and flow of the language is mesmerising.

Imagistic in its loosened rhythms, the poem repeatedly focuses on the similarity between the dazed, heavy bee and the infant in her mother's arms. But the **tone changes** towards the end as the reality of the baby's dependency becomes evident. The child is no longer 'so light'; indeed, her mother's arms now seem 'like sorrowful, storm-heavy boughs' (line 12). Once again, the powerful assonance adds to the poignancy. There is a disquieting awareness of being weighed down – both physically and emotionally. Is this a natural reaction to parental responsibility? Or a deeper realisation about the cycle of life and death?

Over the course of this short poem, Lawrence has interwoven a lyrical scene with a disturbing dramatic situation. The final lines are infused with a deep sense of despondency. In a nightmarish sequence, the child's 'floating hair' is now sinking 'like storm-bruised young leaves'. We are left with a distressing image of a person struggling helplessly, being **overwhelmed by a greater natural power** just like the 'drenched, drowned bee'. D. H. Lawrence's poetry often shows a concern with the pressures of life and culture. His oblique approach is open to various interpretations about the experience of motherhood, but there is no denying the concluding mood of complete surrender to an inevitable 'weariness'.

✒ Writing About the Poem

'D. H. Lawrence's poems can offer revealing insights into disturbing themes.' Discuss this view, with reference to "Trailing Clouds".

Sample Paragraph

'Trailing Clouds' seemed ambiguous. Nature is beautiful, but can quickly become stormy. In comparing the tiny baby to a drowned bee, the poet appeared to be already mourning the child's life. The baby 'clings' to its parent for dear life. To me, the verb suggested desperation – as though life is a struggle that ends in death. The child has been crying and its wet hair lies 'laughterless'. The mood is negative throughout. There are so many downbeat references to the baby, 'legs hanging heavily'. Nature grows even more ominous with the mention of 'storm-heavy boughs' and a truly stark image of the baby drowning like the bee. The ending is surreal, a feeling of being out of control, 'Reaching downwards'. Lawrence seems to be exploring the idea of human life being determined by fate. As in the natural world, humans are subject to unknown forces outside their power. The final lines comparing the bee's wings to 'a weariness' are the most disturbing of all and emphasise Lawrence's pessimistic outlook on life.

EXAMINER'S COMMENT

A solid high-grade response that explored interesting aspects of the poem and included some well-focused discussion about Lawrence's 'negative outlook'. Incisive points on imagery and mood were effectively illustrated. Expression was impressive throughout, with some good use of vocabulary ('ambiguous', 'ominous', 'surreal'). Overall, a good personal answer.

✎ Class/Homework Exercises

1. Identify and comment on Lawrence's portrait of the sleeping child in the poem '"Trailing Clouds"'. In your opinion, is it realistic or sentimental? Support your answer with reference to the text.
2. 'Lawrence often makes use of carefully organised imagery to create thought-provoking moments of drama and tension.' To what extent is this true of '"Trailing Clouds"'? Support your answer with reference to the poem.

⊙ Points to Consider

- **Imagistic style – effective use of repetition, rhyme, visual and aural imagery.**
- **Poem is structured around the extended bee and flower simile.**
- **Lawrence explores aspects of life's transience and touches on spiritual themes.**
- **Contrasting moods and atmospheres – tender, reflective, oppressive, fearful, etc.**

11 Bavarian Gentians

Title: small trumpet-shaped blue flower.

Not every man has gentians in his house
In soft September, at slow, sad Michaelmas.
Bavarian gentians, tall and dark, but dark
darkening the daytime torch-like with the smoking blueness of Pluto's gloom,
ribbed hellish flowers erect, with their blaze of darkness spread blue,   5
blown flat into points, by the heavy white draught of the day.

Torch-flower of the blue-smoking darkness, Pluto's dark-blue blaze
black lamps from the halls of Dis, smoking dark blue
giving off darkness, blue darkness, upon Demeter's yellow-pale day
whom have you come for, here in the white-cast day?   10

Reach me a gentian, give me a torch!
let me guide myself with the blue, forked torch of a flower
down the darker and darker stairs, where blue is darkened on blueness
down the way Persephone goes, just now, in first-frosted September,
to the sightless realm where darkness is married to dark   15
and Persephone herself is but a voice, as a bride,
a gloom invisible enfolded in the deeper dark
of the arms of Pluto as he ravishes her once again
and pierces her once more with his passion of the utter dark
among the splendour of black-blue torches, shedding fathomless darkness 20
        on the nuptials.

Give me a flower on a tall stem, and three dark flames,
for I will go to the wedding, and be wedding-guest
at the marriage of the living dark.

Michaelmas: feast of St Michael the Archangel, 29 September, protector against the dark of night.
Pluto: ruler of the underworld (Hades), god of death and earth's fertility.

Dis: Roman god of the underworld where souls go after death.
Demeter: goddess of the harvest and agriculture; mother of Persephone.

Persephone: abducted bride of Pluto.

nuptials: wedding ceremony.

'blaze of darkness spread blue'

👤 Personal Response

1. Based on your reading of the poem, outline Lawrence's attitude to death. Support your answer with reference to the text.
2. Choose one aural image from the poem that appeals to you and comment briefly on its effectiveness.
3. Write your own personal response to the poem, highlighting the impact it made on you.

👁 Critical Literacy

'Bavarian Gentians' is one of D. H. Lawrence's final poems, published posthumously in 1932. He wrote the poem in September 1929 when he was suffering from tuberculosis, a disease of the lungs, from which he would soon die. Lawrence's early life had been spent in the English coal mining town of Eastwood. Later on, he wrote of remembering 'a sort of inner darkness, like the gloss of coal in which we moved and had our being'.

The first stanza opens with a modest, off-hand observation: 'Not every man has gentians in his house/In soft September, at slow, sad Michaelmas.' The sensual evocation of autumn is conveyed in the slow, reflective pace of the two run-on lines where sibilant 's' sounds establish a soporific (sleep-inducing) mood. The September setting is significant – the month facing into winter, the season of decay. Michaelmas (line 2) is the Christian feast of St Michael, known as the 'protector against the devil, especially at the time of death'. For Lawrence, the gentians signify the shadow of death. The depressive person often obsesses over a particular object or event and Lawrence is fascinated by the intense blue of the flowers. The colour blue has long been associated with sadness; people in a downbeat mood are said to be suffering from 'the blues'. The tone is **dejected and dreamy**, seducing the reader with its slow rhythm. However, the momentum builds through slightly modified repetition, 'tall and dark', 'dark/darkening'.

The flowers seem to throw no light at all on the day. Then, suddenly, they change into magical tokens, becoming 'torch-like' (line 4). In the poet's imagination, their deep colour reminds him of the blue–black of the fires of Hell, 'smoking blueness of Pluto's gloom'. The reader is persuaded by Lawrence's **obsessive preoccupation** to closely observe every detail of the 'ribbed hellish flowers erect'. Their majestic 'blaze of darkness' (line 5) is again linked to the flash of fire. Their posture ('blown flat into points' by 'the heavy white draught' of wind) is carefully noted. The bright white of the day is a stark contrast to the darkness of both the flowers and Pluto's wretched underworld. All through this section, the languor is similar to falling into a trance brought on by the contemplation of these beautiful blue flowers.

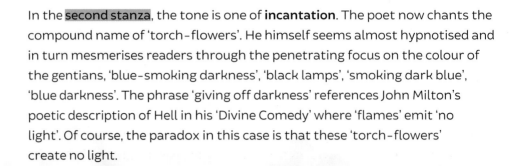

In the second stanza, the tone is one of **incantation**. The poet now chants the compound name of 'torch-flowers'. He himself seems almost hypnotised and in turn mesmerises readers through the penetrating focus on the colour of the gentians, 'blue-smoking darkness', 'black lamps', 'smoking dark blue', 'blue darkness'. The phrase 'giving off darkness' references John Milton's poetic description of Hell in his 'Divine Comedy' where 'flames' emit 'no light'. Of course, the paradox in this case is that these 'torch-flowers' create no light.

The infernal darkness of the gentians not only alludes to Lawrence's gloomy mood, but also to the darkness of the underworld where Pluto reigns supreme 'in the halls of Dis'. Image after image of darkness permeate these lines just as Lawrence's infected lungs became flooded with tuberculosis when he was faced imminent death. The poet is all too aware of the answer to his question (line 10), 'whom have you come for here in the white-cast day?' The combined force of irregular metre and sonorous sound effects add to the **unsettling atmosphere**.

Throughout the poem, Lawrence alludes to **Greek myth**. Pluto, the ruler of the underworld, abducts Persephone, the daughter of the goddess of fertility, Demeter. Although Pluto makes Persephone his queen, Demeter secures a compromise: Persephone can return every April to her mother for six months, after which (in 'first-frosted September') she must go back to her husband and the underworld. During the time Persephone is away from her mother,

Demeter mourns her absence and the countryside becomes barren. When Persephone returns in springtime, the earth becomes fertile once again. In the third stanza, the mood changes dramatically. The tone turns imperative, electrified into action through energetic verbs, 'Reach me', give me'. Lawrence now intends to use the gentians as a torch to lead him into death. **No longer a helpless victim** (in stark contrast to the abducted Persephone), he is determined to act independently: 'let me guide myself.' Long run-on lines spiral into a vortex while the poet descends 'down the darker and darker stairs'. Emphatic use of the heavy alliterative 'd' sound suggests the dismal atmosphere of the underworld where 'blue is darkened on blueness'. The colour of the flowers is becoming extinguished by the enveloping desolation.

It is a vision of unrelenting gloom: 'the sightless realm where darkness is married to dark.' The cadence of the line falls on the last monosyllabic word, imitating Persephone's (and the poet's) descent into Hades. She now loses her body – becoming 'but a voice' – and is cloaked in 'the arms of Pluto' who claims his bride in a macabre fantasy 'among the splendour of black-blue torches'. Pluto's desire for Persephone ('his passion of the utter dark;') is reflected in the strong sexual imagery. Throughout this **surreal Gothic scene**, the gentians shine in the incomprehensible atmosphere of an extraordinary wedding, not with light but 'shedding fathomless darkness on the nuptials'.

In the concluding three lines, the tone changes once more. There is a sense of **dignified acceptance** in the poet's formal request, 'Give me a flower', contrasting with the earlier desperate grasp ('Reach'). Calmly and courageously, Lawrence accepts the inevitable invitation of death: 'I will go to the wedding.' Paradoxically, he describes the place where Pluto and Persephone have their marriage ceremony as 'the living dark'. This refers to the ability of the dark earth to receive the dead flower's seed in autumn and to bring it back to life the following spring. Nature buries and regenerates. The compelling drama concludes with the poet preparing to enter this dark realm forever. Does he hope for an afterlife in death?

'Bavarian Gentians' is sustained by a combination of repetitive rhythm, monotonous melody and the obsessive litanies expressing the poet's deepest thoughts and fears. In the end, Lawrence succeeds in uniting the natural beauty of the blue flowers with an overflowing description of their colour, leading to an erotically and morbidly charged descent into the mythical underworld. He is a poet without a mask.

✒ **Writing About the Poem**

'D. H. Lawrence's last poems study death with precise, reverential fascination.' Discuss this view, with particular reference to 'Bavarian Gentians'.

263 |

Sample Paragraph

'Bavarian Gentians' explores the fall towards oblivion through a keen description of its seductive powers. Hypnotically, the poet weaves the 'blue-smoking darkness' of the flowers through the poem so that they become both the guide to death as well as a symbol of it. Strict observation not only of the flower's colour but also its texture ('ribbed') and shape ('blown flat into points') causes this beautiful flower to become a focal point. The terror of the descent into nothingness is conveyed in the alliterative phrase 'down the darker and darker stairs'. Soft syllables emphasise the story of Pluto and Persephone's nuptials ('shedding fathomless darkness'). The poet presents us with the threshold between life and death as the earth buries and nurtures. The poem ends on a dignified note. Respectfully, Lawrence accepts the invitation in the slow-moving line, 'for I will go to the wedding, and be wedding guest'. The struggle with death now loses importance as the poet quietly approaches 'the living dark'.

EXAMINER'S COMMENT

A mature and thoughtful response to the question. Informed discussion points focus throughout on the poet's precise style and reverential tone. Excellent use of accurate quotations and support reference. Expression is also impressive: varied sentence length, wide-ranging vocabulary and good control of syntax. Top-grade standard.

✒ Class/Homework Exercises

1. 'Lawrence's sensual language and vivid imagination convey his intense vision of life.' In your opinion, how true is this of 'Bavarian Gentians'? Support your answer with reference to the poem.
2. 'D. H. Lawrence's dark themes are explored through honest free verse.' To what extent is this evident in 'Bavarian Gentians'? Support your answer with reference to the poem.

⊙ Points to Consider

- **Direct, immediate exploration of death, oblivion, self-awareness.**

- **Rolling, dreamlike style, irregular line length and metre.**

- **Repetition and other aural effects create spell-binding fantasy.**

- **Use of Greek mythology enriches the poem's universal appeal.**

- **Dramatic impact of colour imagery patterns.**

- **Poet's own journey towards death portrayed through moods of awareness, anger, terror and acceptance.**

Sample Leaving Cert Questions on Lawrence's Poetry

1. 'D. H. Lawrence's stark, innovative poetry celebrates sensuality in an over-intellectualised world.' Discuss this view, supporting your answer with reference to the poems by Lawrence on your course.

2. 'D. H. Lawrence, the rebel poet, is passionately in love with language.' To what extent do you agree with this view? Support the points you make with reference to the poems by Lawrence on your course.

3. 'Lawrence's intensely confessional poetry contains a richness of wide-ranging imagery.' Discuss this statement, supporting your answer with reference to the poetry of Lawrence on your course.

How do I organise my answer?

(Sample question 1)

'D. H. Lawrence's stark, innovative poetry celebrates sensuality in an over-intellectualised world.' Discuss this view, supporting your answer with reference to the poems by Lawrence on your course.

Sample Plan 1

Intro: *(Stance: agree with viewpoint in the question)* Lawrence – master craftsman, profound thinker – creator of raw, honest poetry glorying in nature's creative beauty, critical of modern society. Unique and intense poetic voice – free verse, precise description, experimental structures, startling imagery patterns.

Point 1: *(Celebration of the joys of nature – sensual imagery)* 'Delight of Being Alone' and 'Absolute Reverence' champion Lawrence's belief in living through the senses – 'It makes me realise the delicious pleasure of the moon/that she has in travelling by herself' (emphatic sibilance and line length). Worships divine in nature – 'But to something unseen, unknown … I feel absolute reverence'.

Point 2: *(Rhetorical language used to challenge the effects of modernism)* 'What Have They Done to You?' – extended reflection on dehumanising effects of industrialisation. Use of contrasting verbs to showcase the difference between oppressed work force, joyless and passive ('creeping') and capitalist employers.

Understanding the Prescribed Poetry Question

Marks are awarded using the PCLM Marking Scheme: P = 15; C = 15; L = 15; M = 5 Total = 50

- **P** (Purpose = 15 marks) refers to the set question and is the launch pad for the answer. This involves engaging with all aspects of the question. Both theme and language must be addressed, although not necessarily equally.
- **C** (Coherence = 15 marks) refers to the organisation of the developed response and the use of accurate, relevant quotation. Paragraphing is essential.
- **L** (Language = 15 marks) refers to the student's skill in controlling language throughout the answer.
- **M** (Mechanics = 5 marks) refers to spelling and grammar.
- Although no specific number of poems is required, students usually discuss at least 3 or 4 in their written responses.
- Aim for at least 800 words, to be completed within 45–50 minutes.

NOTE

In keeping with the PCLM approach, the student has to take a stance by agreeing and/or disagreeing that:

– **Lawrence's stark innovative poetry** (startling juxtapositions, original use of poetic forms – elegy, ode, lyric, dialogue, reminiscence, free verse etc., irregular line length, clever linking devices, derisory/ celebratory tones, precise description, vivid imagery, contrast, repetition, aural effects, variety of tones – anger, hurt, regret, derision, warmth, searing honesty, etc.)

... celebrates:

– **sensuality in an over-intellectualised world** (delight in physicality and sensory experience of nature, criticism of man's intellectual relationship with nature, condemnation of modern society – oppressive industrialisation, over-intellectualised relationships between people, transience, nostalgia, tense dramatisations, etc.)

Point 3: *(Exuberant view of nature – vibrant poetic style)* 'Humming-Bird' – visualising creature's physicality. Dynamic verbs used to celebrate this beautiful bird ('flashed', 'whizzing', 'pierced'). Similarly, in 'Snake', the conflict focuses on the relationship between nature and human nature.

Point 4: *(Candid portrayal of a couple who argue – sharp bitter tones)* 'Intimates' – honest exploration of deadening effect of modern relationships. In this domestic drama, the couple communicate through words rather than senses. Contrasting language and varying tones throughout.

Conclusion: Poetry defined by two elements: Lawrence's glorification of the natural world and his condemnation of modern civilisation. Recurring tensions between heart and head.

Sample Paragraph: Point 4

The difficulty the modern world has in forming relationships is explored in the ironically titled 'Intimates'. Lawrence focuses on a bitter marital row. The couple's knowledge of each other does not add warmth and intimacy, but is used to bombard each other with hurtful weapons. The opening question, 'Don't you care for my love?' suggests an unhappy woman who craves affection. The man's startling reaction, 'I handed her the mirror', signals his spiteful attack. The poet juxtaposes the polite, request 'please', which is transformed into sarcasm as part of a list of orders aimed at his partner. Their relationship is defined by the words they say. His fury at the woman's superiority is conveyed in the references to 'head-quarters', 'supreme authority'. The relationship is cold, lacking sensuality or feeling. The man's final comment, 'while I fled', imitates his frantic dash for freedom from the stifling verbal arguments. This relationship is doomed because it is based on harsh intellectualising.

EXAMINER'S COMMENT

As part of a full essay, this is an informed response that illustrates Lawrence's interest in the tension between emotion and rationality. Key sentences address the essay wording, e.g. 'Their relationship is defined by the words they say'. The paragraph traces the progress of thought within the poem, using apt references along the way to illustrate discussion points. Syntax is well-controlled and there is no awkwardness in the expression. Vivid adjectives such as 'startling' and 'stifling' maintain the focus on an important element of the question ('innovative'). A confident, top-grade answer.

(Sample question 2)

D.H. Lawrence, the rebel poet, is passionately in love with language.' To what extent do you agree with this view? Support the points you make with reference to the poems by Lawrence on your course.

Sample Plan 2

Intro: *(Stance: agree with viewpoint in the question)* Lawrence – rebellious outsider from working class background. Believed 'man had lost the art of living'. Hard, radical views – dares to address society's taboos (death and men's expression of emotion), also challenges man's exploitative use of power to dominate nature and fellow men.

Point 1: *(Personal challenge of loss and grief – vivid visual and aural imagery)* 'Call into Death' – last of society's taboos, death comes to all. Controlled 12-line elegy contains the raw emotion of a son at his mother's death. Plain, conversational language expresses loss, 'Since I lost you, my darling'. Death is seen as part of natural cycle of life – not seen but still present.

Point 2: *(Nostalgic reflection on childhood – rich sound effects)* 'Piano' – another relationship poem. Again, tightly controlled form (three quatrains, couplet rhyming scheme) contain floodgates of unmanly emotive memories. Vivid flashback to childhood. Aural effects conjure the music – onomatopoeia for the low notes ('boom') and assonance for the high notes ('tingling strings').

Point 3: *(Powerful language underlines this dramatic experience)* 'The Mosquito' – challenges man's destruction of what he does not understand through examination of man's combative relationship with nature's creatures. Startling use of satanic and supernatural imagery shows man's contempt for creature ('evil little aura', 'filthy magic', 'streaky sorcerer', 'Ghoul on wings').

Point 4: *(Emphatic ejection of mass industrial society)* 'What Have They Done to You?' – poet challenges man's exploitative use of power to dominate nature. Intense poetic voice and rhetorical language depict the oppressive industrial age that dehumanised ('devoured') the 'masses'.

Conclusion: Lawrence – we should be 'true' to our 'animal instincts'. Fresh, controlled language and imagery show how to understand that death is part of the cycle of life, how to express emotion, how to respect the harmony of living systems.

NOTE

In keeping with the PCLM approach, the student has to take a stance by agreeing and/ or disagreeing that:
- **Lawrence the rebel poet** (outsider, working class background, radical views, addresses societal taboos, male domination, conflict, sin/guilt, escape/peace, etc.)

... is passionately in love with:
- **language** (satanic, supernatural, natural imagery, variety of tones and attitudes, juxtaposition/ contrast, differing line lengths, direct speech, colloquialisms, rhetorical style, repetition, detailed description, colour, etc.)

Sample Paragraph: Point 4

'What Have They Done to You?' attacks man's inhumanity to his fellow man. This scathing assault on industrialisation is contained in a list of rhetorical questions. The human being's individuality has been suppressed to the state of a drone insect. The workers are 'creeping', thoughtlessly going 'back and forth' to monotonous jobs, their motion similar to the mindless movement of the great machines in their factories. Lawrence's love of vibrant imagery is evident in personifying the factory as a mechanical monster which 'devoured' the working man in its 'vast maw'. Broad assonance underlines the horrific dehumanisation. The poet's aversion to what is happening is vividly shown in the alliterative 'men of the masses'. The poem is filled with energetic language. Man is demeaned to its physical essence, 'carcass'. All through the poem, long, irregular run-on lines express anger. A curt ending sharply contrasts with a heartfelt expression of pity, 'Oh, what has been done to them?'

EXAMINER'S COMMENT

As part of a full essay answer to question 2, this is a confident top-grade response that remains focused on Lawrence's love of language. Well-supported discussion points highlight a range of the poet's stylistic features – including rhetorical questions, graphic imagery and sound effects. Impressive expression (e.g. 'scathing assault', 'demeaned to its physical essence') and assured language control throughout.

Leaving Cert Sample Essay

'Much of the power and humanity in Lawrence's provocative poetry is derived from the poet's distinctive writing style'. To what extent do you agree or disagree with this view? Support your answer with reference to the poetry of D.H. Lawrence on your course.

Sample Essay

1. D.H. Lawrence's poetry is modern and accessible. Many of his poems show a great awareness of nature. Others express his outrage at the hypocrisy of society and he is often critical of our industrialised way of life. Compelling poems, such as 'Piano', 'The Mosquito', 'Snake', 'Call into Death' and 'Bavarian Gentians' explore disturbing themes, e.g. identity, man's relationship with nature, loss and death. His tone can vary greatly, from tender to savage, depending on his point of view.

2. 'Piano' describes the consequences of bittersweet memories. Gentle sibilant language, 'Softly, in the dusk, a woman is singing to me', brings Lawrence back in time. A tender memory is brought to life using the present tense, a little child 'sitting under the piano'. He imagines the scene, 'pressing the small, poised feet of a mother'. Skilful use of onomatopoeia allows us to share this heart-breaking reminiscence, 'the boom of the tingling strings'. Lawrence is a thought-provoking poet who makes us face the uncomfortable truth that none of us can really go

back to the happiness of youth, so the adult poet weeps 'like a child for the past'. His distinctive poetic style uses long run-on lines to suggest the flow of memories. I think this poem provokes readers with painful realities. People can only imagine their past – it can never be re-lived.

3. Overwhelming emotion also runs through 'Call into Death'. A conversational remark opens the poem, 'Since I lost you, my darling'. The tender tone suggests the close relationship between the poet and his mother who had just passed away. Lawrence uses a childlike simile, 'The white moon going among them like a white bird among snow-berries' to suggest that loss is a natural part of life. Soft assonant sounds and colour detail add to the beauty of this image by which he suggests that everything and every human dies. The long line mimics the moon's journey across the sky. Lawrence is hoping the dead are still present in nature. However, he has to confront harsh reality once more. His mother is 'lost, in death. The truth is he cannot reach her. The poet confronts us with a bitter truth of life – everything changes.

4. In 'Snake', Lawrence examines the vigorous power struggle between man and nature. This reflective poem begins with the arrival of the snake beside the poet's water trough on a very hot Mediterranean day. The free verse narrative style makes the conflict between human and animal very accessible. Short, simple phrases convey the intuitive nature of the snake, 'flickered his two-forked tongue from his lips, and mused a moment'. In contrast, formal language describes the poet's logical thinking, 'The voice of my education said to me/He must be killed.' Immediately Lawrence regrets attacking 'my snake'. His arrogance is clearly evident, he does not own the creature. Just as in 'Piano', the poet wants to change the past, 'I wished he would come back'. But no amount of wishing will change what has been done, 'I missed my chance'. This is another of Lawrence's thought-provoking poems. We are left thinking about human savagery and the abuse of power.

5. The conflict between people and nature is also found in 'The Mosquito'. The one-sided debate poem shows the poet's fury that the little insect has dared to cross civilised boundaries when it attacked him. Unlike the viewpoint in 'Snake', the mosquito feels no guilt, but it glories in attacking the human, 'enspasmed in oblivion'. Repetition highlights the sense of triumph following the attack, 'Such silence', 'Such gorging'. The mosquito has followed its natural instinct in which it satisfied its basic need for survival. Unlike in 'The Snake' where he, Lawrence, felt guilty about his attitude to nature, in this case, his ego tells him to kill the insect in order to prove his power. It's ironic that Lawrence first viewed the mosquito as powerful and a threat to humans. But at the end, it is reduced to nothing.

INDICATIVE MATERIAL

- **Power and humanity in Lawrence's provocative poetry** (challenging/ confrontational treatment of love, memory, death, nature, modernity, cosmic harmony, etc.)

... is derived from:

- **the poet's distinctive style** (dramatic narratives, free verse, striking description, engaging tones, startling visual/ aural imagery, contrasting moods, irregular rhyme, rhythm, line length, etc.)

6. 'Not every man has gentians in his house' is the conversational opening to 'Bavarian Gentians' – another poem addressing the subject of death. Modern man prefers not to think of death at all. Lawrence was interested in such taboo subjects. He wanted his poems to make people face up to reality. He himself goes to death voluntarily, 'let me guide myself', surrounded by the 'blue-smoking darkness' of the gentian flowers. He sees himself as a 'wedding guest' attending a ceremony lit by the 'splendour of black-blue torches'. The poem's hypnotic rhythm encourages readers to join him. Once more, Lawrence confronts the truth about dying. Its lack of certainty and fearfulness are emphasised through the use of powerful alliteration, 'darkness is married to dark'. Like 'Call into Death', the poem suggests that life continues after people die. The poet has revolted against the 'normal approach' to death.

7. Lawrence has created challenging poems through his skilful poetic language. His vigorous poetry addresses some of life's basic questions, such as love, nature, loss and death.

(830 words)

EXAMINER'S COMMENT

A reasonably strong – but uneven – response that attempts to engage with all key elements of the question ('power', 'humanity', 'provocative' and 'distinctive style') with varying degrees of success. Excellent use of accurate quotations throughout. Good engagement with the poems, generally, and the supported analysis of Lawrence's stylistic features is impressive – particularly the critical discussion about sound effects, tone, rhythm and line length. However, some of the commentary is general – and higher marks would have been awarded for more focused points on the power and humanity in the poet's writing. Expression is also note-like in places and slightly awkward (e.g. paragraph 3). A solid H2 standard, overall.

GRADE: H2
P = 12/15
C = 11/15
L = 12/15
M = 5/5
Total = 40/50

Revision Overview

'Call into Death'
Plaintive elegy addresses complex subjects, including themes of loss and death.

'Piano'
First-person reminiscence of past domestic scene, juxtaposed with present. Themes of childhood, memory and identity.

'The Mosquito'
Detailed exploration of one of the poet's recurring themes, man versus nature, dramatised through his encounter with the mosquito.

'Snake'
Addresses man's position in the natural world. Simple narrative account with snake, using internal conversation.

'Humming-Bird'
Dramatic and challenging imaginary account of evolution of bird. Free verse structure reflects random aspect of nature.

'Intimates'
Witty account of problems of communication. Dialogue and actions of bitter row between two lovers.

'Delight of Being Alone'
Beautiful autobiographical poem addresses positive and adverse aspects of isolation.

'Absolute Reverence'
Reveals the poet's mystical view of life. Reverence only for creative force in contrast to all that he does not revere.

'What Have They Done to You?'
Scathing critique of contemporary British society.

'Baby-Movements II: "Trailing Clouds"'
Formal imagistic ode addresses transience and loss of innocence.

'Bavarian Gentians'
Personal study of poet's journey towards self-awareness and death.

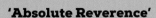 Last Words

'Lawrence was in a direct line of descent from such earlier poets as Blake, Coleridge and Whitman, for whom imagination was everything.'
Keith Sagar

'The accuracy of Lawrence's observations haunts the mind permanently.'
Kenneth Roxroth

'These are my tender administrations to the mental and emotional wounds we suffer from.'
D. H. Lawrence

 DEATH   CHILDHOOD   HISTORY/ MEMORY   NATURE   CONFICT   TIME   RELATIONSHIPS   RELIGION/ SPIRITUALITY

Adrienne Rich
(1929–2012)

'Poetry can break open locked chambers of possibility, restore numbed zones to feeling, recharge desire.'

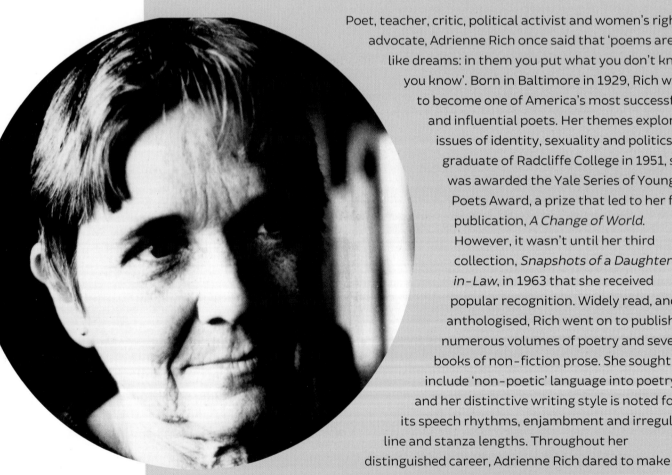

Poet, teacher, critic, political activist and women's rights advocate, Adrienne Rich once said that 'poems are like dreams: in them you put what you don't know you know'. Born in Baltimore in 1929, Rich was to become one of America's most successful and influential poets. Her themes explore issues of identity, sexuality and politics. A graduate of Radcliffe College in 1951, she was awarded the Yale Series of Younger Poets Award, a prize that led to her first publication, *A Change of World*. However, it wasn't until her third collection, *Snapshots of a Daughter-in-Law*, in 1963 that she received popular recognition. Widely read, and anthologised, Rich went on to publish numerous volumes of poetry and several books of non-fiction prose. She sought to include 'non-poetic' language into poetry and her distinctive writing style is noted for its speech rhythms, enjambment and irregular line and stanza lengths. Throughout her distinguished career, Adrienne Rich dared to make poetry out of the prosaic, humdrum, and sometimes secret events of women's lives. Years after her death at the age of 82, her poems still retain their extraordinary power.

Investigate Further

To find out more about Adrienne Rich, or to hear readings of her poems, you could search some useful websites such as YouTube, BBC Poetry, poetryfoundation.org and poetryarchive.org, or access additional material on this page of your eBook.

Prescribed Poems

○ **1 'Aunt Jennifer's Tigers' (OL)**
The poet explores the theme
of power by contrasting the
imaginary tigers with the
oppressed life of their creator,
Aunt Jennifer, who was trapped
in an unfulfilled marriage.
Page 274

○ **2 'The Uncle Speaks in the Drawing Room' (OL)**
This poem considers aspects of
social unrest while addressing the
nature of patriarchal power and
its effects. **Page 277**

○ **3 'Power'**
Celebrating the life of Marie Curie,
the poem contrasts the different
ways in which power can be used.
Page 281

○ **4 'Storm Warnings'**
Powerlessness and change are
central themes in the poem.
Just as people are at risk from
approaching storms, they are also
vulnerable to their own changing
emotions. **Page 284**

○ **5 'Living in Sin'**
The poem contrasts ideal
romantic relationships with the
more mundane experiences of
everyday reality. **Page 288**

○ **6 'The Roofwalker'**
Using the extended metaphor
of a builder at work, the poet
raises interesting questions about
alienation and personal decision-
making. **Page 292**

○ **7 'Our Whole Life'**
The poem is an exploration of the
failure of language to adequately
communicate human experiences.
Page 296

○ **8 'Trying to Talk with a Man'**
Set in a remote desert location
where nuclear tests are
taking place, the poem traces
the breakdown of a couple's
relationship. **Page 299**

○ **9 'Diving into the Wreck'**
This thought-provoking poem
combines the description of an
amateur dive to investigate a
shipwreck with an exploration
of social/political history and
change. **Page 303**

○ **10 'From a Survivor'**
The poem focuses on a failed
marriage and on the broader
issue of changing male-female
relationships. **Page 309**

(OL) indicates poems that are also
prescribed for the Ordinary Level course.

1 Aunt Jennifer's Tigers

Aunt Jennifer's tigers prance across a screen,
Bright topaz denizens of a world of green.
They do not fear the men beneath the tree;
They pace in sleek chivalric certainty.

Aunt Jennifer's fingers fluttering through her wool   5
Find even the ivory needle hard to pull.
The massive weight of Uncle's wedding band
Sits heavily upon Aunt Jennifer's hand.

When Aunt is dead, her terrified hands will lie
Still ringed with ordeals she was mastered by.   10
The tigers in the panel that she made
Will go on prancing, proud and unafraid.

prance: walk with exaggerated, bouncing steps.

screen: surface on which an image is formed.

topaz: semi-precious stone, yellow or light blue.

denizens: inhabitants, occupants.

sleek: glossy, smooth, shiny.

chivalric: behaving in a formal, courteous way.

ivory: hard, white bony substance that forms elephant tusks.

ordeals: painful or difficult experiences.

'The massive weight of Uncle's wedding band'

👤 Personal Response

1. This poem illustrates the power of a symbol. Comment on Rich's choice of symbols.
2. 'Rich challenges us with her ideas on relationships.' To what extent is this true in 'Aunt Jennifer's Tigers'?
3. Would you regard the ending of the poem as positive or negative? Explain your answer with reference to the text.

⊙ Critical Literacy

'Aunt Jennifer's Tigers' was published when Adrienne Rich was just 21. It appeared in her first volume of poetry, *A Change of World*. Rich wrote: 'It was important to me that Aunt Jennifer was a person as distinct from myself as possible, distanced by the formalism of the poem, by its objective observant tone.' The tigers represent an aspect of Aunt Jennifer's personality that she herself is not at liberty to display.

This formal lyric with its rigorous three-quatrain structure and rigid rhyme (*aabb, ccdd, eeff*) depicts the aunt in a **confined and restricted situation. She is forced to create an alternative world in order to express her innermost thoughts. The fierce noble tigers of the** first quatrain are a symbol of the aunt's imagination and creative force. Her embroidery speaks volumes in an oppressive world that forces her to remain silent. The tigers are shown as being energetic and playful, signifying great vigour, assertion and fearlessness. Strong verbs, 'prance' and 'pace', vividly sketch these proud dynamic creatures: 'They do not fear the men beneath the tree.' Ironically, they have been hunted by humans almost to the point of extinction. Their bright colours are exotic and unrealistic. The term 'chivalric' is interesting as it has its origins in Medieval history when powerful knights had a reputation for honourable behaviour and for the respect they showed to women. Is this what is missing from the aunt's relationship with her husband?

Throughout the **second quatrain**, Aunt Jennifer is portrayed in sharp contrast to the beautiful jungle animals. Exhausted and insecure, **she seems to be overwhelmed** with life. The poet's use of alliteration ('fingers fluttering') suggests a fragile, sensitive person who struggles with simple tasks, finding 'even the ivory needle hard to pull'. As a dominated wife, she suffers acute emotional pressure, highlighted by 'The massive weight' that 'Sits heavily'. Yet her fear is never fully articulated. Is she afraid of her husband, society, the Church? A ring usually symbolises union; here it stands for confinement and domination. Does she – unlike the tigers – fear men? All through the stanza, there is a palpable sense of the absent 'Uncle'. His presence is particularly underlined by the forceful tone and strict iambic pentameter in the line: 'The massive weight of Uncle's wedding band.'

While the first quatrain described the tigers and the second gives us a picture of Aunt Jennifer and the missing uncle, the **third quatrain** moves to **the future**, to a time when 'Aunt is dead'. But even here she is still experiencing distress and every part of her is fearful, 'terrified hands'. The striking description, 'ringed with ordeals she was mastered by', highlight the poet's resentment of the subjugation of women. Although Rich's poetic voice is trenchant, the poem ends on a positive note as the tigers, symbols of the aunt's imaginative powers – her inner life – achieve a kind of artistic immortality. These stunning creatures will go on, 'prancing, proud and unafraid'. The timid aunt's gesture of defiance through her needlework

creations (a craft usually associated with women) will live on forever. Is this her victorious rebellion against patriarchal culture?

☙ Writing About the Poem

'Some critics claim that Adrienne Rich's poems are gloomy and downbeat.' Discuss this view with particular reference to 'Aunt Jennifer's Tigers'.

Sample Paragraph

My reaction to Rich's poems is positive not negative. I don't think her poems are gloomy. How can critics say that about 'Aunt Jennifer's Tigers'? Especially when the tigers are described using exotic colours of 'topaz' shining from the screen in silent, yet powerful protest against the confinement she finds herself in, 'The massive weight of Uncle's wedding band'? All of us are bound in by forces beyond our control, but Rich shows us how it is possible to 'speak' even though we are like the Aunt, 'terrified'. Is this not upbeat? In the final lines, in defiance of all her suppression, 'terrified hands', it is the tigers, symbolising Aunt Jennifer's repressed desires, which will go on 'prancing, proud and unafraid'. Sometimes we speak most powerfully when we are silent. With such a strong uplifting ending, how could anyone suggest that Rich's poems are gloomy?

EXAMINER'S COMMENT

This lively middle-grade response is generally well-focused and aptly supported. The paragraph shows a good sense of engagement with the poem. Expression is reasonably fluent, though over-reliant on questions. More thorough analysis of the poet's attitude and subtle tone would have raised the standard.

✍ Class/Homework Exercises

1. 'Adrienne Rich challenges us with her ideas on marriage.' To what extent do you agree with this statement? Discuss with reference to 'Aunt Jennifer's Tigers'.
2. Comment on the effectiveness of Rich's choice of verbs throughout this poem.

⊙ Points to Consider

- **Central themes include marriage and male–female relationships.**
- **Effective use of vivid imagery and symbolism.**
- **Contrast between the powerful and the oppressed.**
- **Varied tones (objective, ironic, didactic) convey the poet's view.**
- **Ambiguous ending – art endures but inequality also continues.**

ADRIENNE RICH

2

The Uncle Speaks in the Drawing Room

I have seen the mob of late
Standing sullen in the square,
Gazing with a sullen stare
At window, balcony, and gate.
Some have talked in bitter tones,   5
Some have held and fingered stones.

These are follies that subside.
Let us consider, none the less,
Certain frailties of glass
Which, it cannot be denied,   10
Lead in times like these to fear
For crystal vase and chandelier.

Not that missiles will be cast;
None as yet dare lift an arm.
But the scene recalls a storm   15
When our grandsire stood aghast
To see his antique ruby bowl
Shivered in a thunder-roll.

Let us only bear in mind
How these treasures handed down   20
From a calmer age passed on
Are in the keeping of our kind.
We stand between the dead glass-blowers
And murmurings of missile-throwers.

Title: Drawing Room: room where visitors are entertained.

mob: disorderly crowd.
sullen: surly, resentful.

follies: foolish actions or ideas.

frailties: physical or moral weaknesses.

crystal: clear and brilliant glass.

missiles: objects or weapons aimed at a target.

grandsire: old-fashioned word for grandfather.
aghast: overcome with amazement or horror.
ruby bowl: red glass bowl.

in the keeping of our kind: in the care and charge of people like us.
glass-blowers: people who make glass objects by shaping molten glass.

'these treasures handed down'

👤 Personal Response

1. The voice in the poem belongs to 'The Uncle'. What type of man do you think he is? Consider what he says and how he speaks.
2. Choose two symbols or metaphors that are used in the poem and briefly explain what you think each represents.
3. In your view, what do you think is the central theme or message in the poem? Refer to the text in your answer.

👁 Critical Literacy

'The Uncle Speaks in the Drawing Room' is part of Rich's poetry collection, *A Change of World* (1951). While these early poems had formal structures and elegant formats, they often addressed disturbing themes, including issues of social class divisions and fears about nuclear war. In this poem, the persona is a man who is the representative of high-class culture.

The **opening stanza** introduces a world of **order, wealth and refinement**. This is established in the title phrase, 'Drawing Room'. The choice of the definite article to describe 'The Uncle' suggests that he is distant and aloof. Who is he addressing in this beautiful, privileged setting? Does the uncle's tone seem condescending, patronising? Look at the use of the word 'mob'. Is it a dismissive term? Notice the alliteration in the line, 'Standing sullen in the square', as it describes the suffocating atmosphere of threat from the people gathered outside.

The uncle is certainly speaking from an advantaged position of authority in his residence with 'balcony and gate'. Would you view him as an image of old-fashioned conservative values? Consider how the regular rhyme scheme (*abbacc*), the controlled seven-syllable line and the strict structure of six-line stanzas all stress the orderly world of the poem's speaker. **This formal style suits the persona** of the conservative uncle. Meanwhile, the crowd 'talked in bitter tones' and 'fingered stones' in an intimidating manner. Are they an obvious symbol of discontent and menace?

In **stanza two**, the uncle's **arrogant tone** is evident as he states that the mob's ill-advised threat will soon 'subside'. He disparages the crowd's grievances as mere 'follies'. However, he is also concerned that his much-prized material possessions, the 'crystal vase and chandelier' might be damaged during these uncertain times of social unrest. To him, they are vulnerable treasures, 'frailties of glass'. Could this also be a reference to the fragility of accepted social values? What does this suggest about the uncle? Does he simply represent the 'haves' and the crowd the 'have-nots'?

The smug reassurances of the uncle continue in the **third stanza**, 'Not that missiles will be cast'. There is a certain bravado in his voice as he again dismisses the notion of danger, 'None as yet dare lift an arm'. But the hint of trouble is still present in the phrase, 'as yet'. He reminisces about a former upheaval when 'our grandsire' lost some valuable possessions, including 'his antique ruby bowl'. Was the ruling order being challenged even then? Is the 'thunder-roll' a foreboding metaphor for an earlier disturbance? The verb 'Shivered' suggests both the shattering of glass and the cold blast of revolution. Rich's onomatopoeic effects vividly convey the **violence of social upheaval and its chilling consequences**.

In the **closing stanza**, the speaker seems to assume that readers will agree with all his assertions. This is indicated by his use of the plural first-person pronoun 'us' in the line, 'Let us only bear in mind'. The uncle is equally confident that he is speaking to people of like class ('our kind'), those who are used to wealth and privilege. He is also proud that he and his class are **maintaining the old order, the status quo**, 'these treasures'. Once more, he resorts to the notion of tradition as a means of protecting power. He clearly sees it as his duty to stand as custodian between those who have created this world of privilege, 'the dead glass-blowers' and the 'missile-throwers' who seek to destroy it.

The uncle's concluding comment is to sneer at the 'murmurings' of the restless crowd, perhaps hoping that their mumbling incoherence (vividly captured in the broad assonant sounds) will inevitably fail. However, **his tone appears to lack conviction**. Is it possible that beneath all the empty rhetoric, he realises that his generation might be the last line of defence between his great ancestors and the unruly mob that will destroy the life of privilege he has known?

✒ Writing About the Poem

Rich once wrote that a reader could be 'fairly encoded in poetry'. What do you think is the code or hidden message of 'The Uncle Speaks in the Drawing Room'? Support your answer with reference to the text.

Sample Paragraph

'The Uncle Speaks in the Drawing Room' is a poem which both by its use of symbols and tone has a subversive message. The uncle symbolises conservative values, 'treasures handed down' which 'are in the keeping of our kind'. His wealth and privilege are conveyed by words such as 'Drawing Room', 'balcony', 'crystal vase'. It's ironic that the uncle is intent on keeping the 'mob' outside, 'We stand between', as he speaks, a room which was designed for receiving visitors. He is under threat. The mob represents those who want the old social order swept away. But to the uncle, their 'murmurings' are unintelligible. This gulf between the classes is the poem's hidden message. The underclass are 'missile-throwers' threatening violence, 'fingered stones'. The uncle's ruling class, represented by possessions, is fragile and likely to be shattered, 'Shivered'. This is a powerfully coded poem about one of the most fundamental conflicts in society.

Class/Homework Exercises

1. 'Rich draws on vivid language to create thought-provoking poems.' Discuss this statement with particular reference to 'The Uncle Speaks in the Drawing Room'.
2. In your view, what does this poem suggest about the personality and views of Adrienne Rich? Support your response with reference to the text.

Points to Consider

- Central themes include unrest and instability in a class-divided society.
- Rich addresses key issues of power – its use and abuse.
- Formal writing style, controlled four-stanza structure.
- Central tone is pompous and arrogant.
- Effective use of symbols, alliteration, assonance and sibilance throughout.

3 Power

ADRIENNE RICH

Living   in the earth-deposits   of our history

Today a backhoe divulged   out of a crumbling flank of earth
one bottle   amber   perfect   a hundred-year-old
cure for fever   or melancholy   a tonic
for living on this earth   in the winters of this climate   5

Today I was reading about Marie Curie:
she must have known she suffered   from radiation sickness
her body bombarded for years   by the element
she had purified
It seems she denied to the end   10
the source of the cataracts on her eyes
the cracked and suppurating skin   of her finger-ends
till she could no longer hold   a test-tube or a pencil

She died a famous woman   denying
her wounds   15
denying
her wounds   came   from the same source as her power

1974

backhoe: mechanical digger.
flank: side.
amber: orange-yellow.
melancholy: deep sadness.

Marie Curie: (1867-1934) pioneering scientist.
radiation sickness: illness caused by damaging radioactive rays.
bombarded: attacked.

cataracts: medical condition causing blurred vision.
suppurating: festering.

👤 Personal Response

1. Briefly explain what you understand by the first line of the poem.
2. From your reading of the poem, what image do you get of Marie Curie?
3. Describe the dominant tone in the final stanza. Refer to the text in your answer.

👁 Critical Literacy

Written in free verse and using a stream of consciousness technique, this wonderful, thought-provoking poem is overtly a portrait of the famous female scientist, Marie Curie. It also invites readers

'she must have known'

to consider the nature, use and abuse of power. When Adrienne Rich wrote 'Power' in 1974, the study of women's historically marginalised contributions to society was still taking shape.

The **opening line** ('Living in the earth-deposits of our history') seems almost like the poem's subtitle in highlighting the importance of understanding the past. **What does history teach us?** In **stanza two**, the speaker connects past and present by focusing on the unearthing of a perfectly-preserved 'hundred-year-old' medicine bottle that might have been sold once as an all-purpose 'cure'. The image of the backhoe excavating 'a crumbling flank of earth' suggests a divided and disharmonious world. We can only imagine the suffering of past generations whose efforts to survive ('living on this earth') made them easy targets for exploitation. The extended spaces separating key words interrupt the rhythm and reflect the idea of time passing in fragmented segments.

Stanza three focuses on the life of Marie Curie. This eminent scientist, who dedicated her life to advancing medical research, embodies the positive use of power. The initial word ('Today') echoes line 2 and sharply contrasts Curie's indisputable contribution with the bogus cure-alls of earlier times. The tone is appreciative and sympathetic: 'she must have known she suffered.' What seems to fascinate the speaker most is **Marie Curie's courage and selflessness** as she continued to take life-threatening risks – 'her body bombarded for years' – while working with dangerous radioactive materials.

The speaker also notes the **tragic irony** of the scientist's life; the radium she struggled to purify eventually killed her. Shocking images of Curie's illness, especially 'the cracked and suppurating skin' highlight her obvious lack of self-pity and her refusal to allow herself to be diverted from her life's work. The **last stanza** repeatedly emphasises how she went to her death 'denying her wounds'. The tone seems to waver between admiration and regret. This final view of Curie as 'a famous woman' refusing to acknowledge that her suffering resulted 'from the same source as her power' makes her an enigmatic figure, a universal symbol of endurance.

Curie gave her whole life to addressing and overpowering the challenges she herself encountered. In committing herself wholeheartedly to what she believed in, she demonstrated her own individual power in improving other people's lives. Is Rich implying that such example should inspire us all to take a principled stand on contemporary issues, such as racism, sexism and other injustices? In the end, this poem revisits history to reconstruct **two contrasting views of power**. The poet leaves readers free to consider the differences between cynical opportunism and genuine devotion to work. The final phrase ('her power') is optimistic, suggesting the potential within people to change the world for the better.

⬛ Writing About the Poem

'Adrienne Rich's poem, "Power", challenges readers to revise traditional attitudes regarding the roles of women in society.' To what extent do you agree with this view? Support your answer with reference to the poem.

Sample Paragraph

Rich's poem 'Power' made interesting points about the subject of power. It told two stories and showed that power can corrupt or help, depending on how it is applied. Marie Curie had the vision necessary to succeed in helping people through her research into radioactivity as a cure for cancer. The poet shows how Curie was ironically killed by the destructive power of her own discovery because she could not accept that 'her wounds came from the same source as her power'. However, she was a motivating figure – for both idealistic women and men alike – who used power for our common good. On the other hand, the amber bottle that the backhoe turns up has sinister implications. However, Rich does not lecture us on the misuse of power, instead she allows us to think about the contribution made by Marie Curie during her lifetime. The poem concludes on a hopeful note with a tribute to Curie as a pioneering chemist who dedicated herself to others. Curie was the first woman to win a Nobel Prize – and this in itself speaks volumes about our patriarchal world. I found her to be inspirational.

EXAMINER'S COMMENT

This high-grade personal response presents a consistent view of how the theme of power is explored in the poem. The point about the amber bottle would have benefitted from some more clarification. Overall, references are used effectively to support discussion points. Expression is clear and assured throughout (e.g. 'sinister implications', 'selflessly dedicated herself').

✎ Class/Homework Exercises

1. What impact did the poem 'Power' have on you? Refer to the text in your response.
2. Comment on Adrienne Rich's use of sensual imagery throughout the poem.

⊙ Points to Consider

- **Central themes focus on aspects of power – personal and public.**

- **Anecdotal style; various tones – detached, reflective, ironic, didactic.**

- **Reference to Marie Curie's research effectively used to illustrate the poet's viewpoint.**

- **Innovative layout; effective use of alliteration and assonance.**

4 Storm Warnings

The glass has been falling all the afternoon,   **glass:** barometer.
And knowing better than the instrument
What winds are walking overhead, what zone
Of gray unrest is moving across the land,
I leave the book upon a pillowed chair   5
And walk from window to closed window, watching
Boughs strain against the sky   **boughs:** branches.

And think again, as often when the air
Moves inward toward a silent core of waiting,   **core:** centre.
How with a single purpose time has traveled   10
By secret currents of the undiscerned   **undiscerned:** unseen.
Into this polar realm. Weather abroad
And weather in the heart alike come on
Regardless of prediction.   **prediction:** forecast.

Between foreseeing and averting change   15   **averting:** avoiding.
Lies all the mastery of elements   **elements:** weather.
Which clocks and weatherglasses cannot alter.
Time in the hand is not control of time,
Nor shattered fragments of an instrument
A proof against the wind; the wind will rise,   20
We can only close the shutters.

I draw the curtains as the sky goes black
And set a match to candles sheathed in glass   **sheathed:** enclosed,
Against the keyhole draught, the insistent whine   protected by.
Of weather through the unsealed aperture.   25   **aperture:** opening.
This is our sole defense against the season;
These are the things that we have learned to do
Who live in troubled regions.

👤 Personal Response

1. With reference to the opening stanza, comment on Adrienne Rich's description of the developing storm.
2. Choose one image from stanza four that you consider particularly interesting and briefly explain your choice.
3. In your opinion, what does the poem suggest about people's attempts to control their lives? Support the points you make by quotation or reference.

👁 Critical Literacy

ADRIENNE RICH

In everyday conversation, we often use the weather as a metaphor for our moods – 'up bright and early', 'feeling fine', 'under the weather', etc. 'Storm Warnings' is one of Adrienne Rich's earliest published works. She described it as 'a poem about powerlessness'. Characteristically, the poet raises interesting questions about attitudes to the world around us and about how much control human beings actually have over how they live.

The poem opens dramatically as unsettled weather closes in. The speaker senses the approaching storm 'better than the instrument'. The ominous atmosphere in **stanza one** is illustrated by the disturbing personification of the winds 'walking overhead' and the image of the gathering clouds ('gray unrest') which are 'moving across the land'. The speaker's **restlessness adds further tension** as she walks 'from window to closed window'. The alliterative 'w' and sibilant 's' sounds suggest growing unease: 'Boughs strain against the sky.'

The gathering storm causes the speaker to 'think again' as she considers the impact of weather and time. The **distinction between nature and human nature becomes increasingly blurred** in **stanza two**. As the winds strengthen, the speaker becomes more passive – 'a silent core of waiting'. **Lines 12–14** draw a direct parallel between weather conditions and human experience ('weather in the heart'). Human beings are fated to endure both, 'Regardless of prediction'. In a symbolic way, the encroaching thunderstorm allows the

'gray unrest'

speaker to recognise all the other unwelcome forces ('secret currents') that can affect our fragile lives in 'this polar realm'. The image of the stranded individual at the mercy of the freezing elements is an unnerving one that foreshadows the reference to 'troubled regions' at the end of the poem.

Stanza three begins with a clear emphatic statement: knowledge and preparation ('foreseeing') are essential for survival. But such 'mastery of elements' is difficult. The speaker acknowledges the limitations of humans to endure storms of any kind. We are reminded of our place in the world: 'Time in the hand is not control of time.' Rich's stark image of the 'shattered fragments of an instrument' emphasises the ironic tone as the speaker acknowledges the reality that 'the wind will rise'. All she can do is retreat and protect herself as best she can. She also knows that her own experience is shared by others: 'We can only close the shutters.' **Powerlessness is a universal experience.** The plural pronoun and measured rhythm highlight our shared need to resist uninvited change and injustice by taking positive action.

This realisation seems to offer some encouragement and the poetic voice is much more purposeful in **stanza four**: 'I draw the curtains as the sky goes black.' Like the delicate candle-flame under glass, the speaker avoids the changing weather for the time being. It is an expedient solution of sorts, based on an understanding of the actual threat she faces. **The poem ends on a quietly resilient note** as the speaker faces up to the reality of damage limitation: 'These are the things that we have learned to do.' The tone is typically dignified and sympathetic to every individual under pressure 'in troubled regions'.

✒ Writing About the Poem

In your view, what is the central theme or message in 'Storm Warnings'? Support your answer with reference to the poem.

Sample Paragraph

I think 'Storm Warnings' simply describes the way people try to protect themselves. Especially when faced with a storm. The atmosphere is edgy. The theme is a wake-up call. People are not all-powerful. The narrator moves nervously about the house checking the temperature and looking out at the clouds. She senses the danger 'better than any instrument'. This makes me think that the storm outside is simply a symbol of her fears. The poem is based around this comparison. Rich is suggesting that people can do little to control their lives. But the message is far from negative. The key sentence for me is 'We can only close the shutters'. This sums up the situation very well. Fate may be powerful, but we have the power to make our own luck. For me, there is some redemption in the upbeat final stanza – 'I draw the curtains as the sky goes black'. The main message appears to be a realistic one – we do whatever we can to survive life's bad times.

EXAMINER'S COMMENT

This high-grade paragraph includes some incisive discussion and personal engagement with the poem. Relevant quotations are used effectively. Although the opening section is note-like, the writing is lively and coherent throughout. A more developed analysis of the point about redemption would have improved the grade.

✎ Class/Homework Exercises

1. Identify the dramatic elements in 'Storm Warnings' and comment briefly on their effectiveness.
2. Write your own personal response to the poem, referring closely to the text in your answer.

⊙ Points to Consider

- The idea of human vulnerability under pressure is central to the poem.

- Effective use of the extended storm metaphor.

- Impact of vivid visual imagery and dynamic sound effects.

- Personification of the wind adds a dramatic quality to the scene.

5 Living in Sin

She had thought the studio would keep itself;
no dust upon the furniture of love.
Half heresy, to wish the taps less vocal,
the panes relieved of grime. A plate of pears,
a piano with a Persian shawl, a cat   5
stalking the picturesque amusing mouse
had risen at his urging.
Not that at five each separate stair would writhe
under the milkman's tramp; that morning light
so coldly would delineate the scraps   10
of last night's cheese and three sepulchral bottles;
that on the kitchen shelf among the saucers
a pair of beetle-eyes would fix her own—
envoy from some village in the moldings ...
Meanwhile, he, with a yawn,   15
sounded a dozen notes upon the keyboard,
declared it out of tune, shrugged at the mirror,
rubbed at his beard, went out for cigarettes;
while she, jeered by the minor demons,
pulled back the sheets and made the bed and found   20
a towel to dust the table-top
and let the coffee-pot boil over on the stove.
By evening she was back in love again,
though not so wholly but throughout the night
she woke sometimes to feel the daylight coming   25
like a relentless milkman up the stairs.

studio: one-room studio flat with small kitchen and bathroom.

heresy: deviation from what is socially acceptable.
vocal: noisy.

picturesque: pleasant to look at, forming a picture.

writhe: twisting, painful movement.

delineate: show by outlining or drawing.
sepulchral: gloomy, melancholy.

envoy: messenger.
moldings: skirting boards.

demons: voices, evil spirits.

relentless: persistent, uncompromising.

'the scraps of last night's cheese'

👤 Personal Response

1. 'Living in Sin' is not an expression that is often used today. What did this phrase originally mean? Has society's views on this matter changed? How?
2. Comment on Adrienne Rich's use of imagery and language throughout the poem. Support your answer with reference to the text.
3. In your view, is this an optimistic or pessimistic poem? Give a reason for your answer, supporting your response with reference to the text.

👁 Critical Literacy

'Living in Sin' was published in 1955 when the view of society at that time was to disapprove of unmarried couples living together. This 26-line single-stanza poem captures the contrast between a young woman's romantic notions and the disenchantment she feels towards her partner and her domestic arrangements.

The poem's title prompts the reader to question why any person is judged to be 'living in sin'. Beginning with a flashback, the female speaker recalls how she once imagined living with the man she loved. The **opening lines** effectively convey her naivety, 'She had thought the studio would keep itself'. Dreaming of a fairy tale relationship, she had convinced herself that they would share an ideal life together, 'no dust upon the furniture of love'. Might this also apply to the couple's relationship? This perfect domestic scenario is deftly sketched, like a photographic display in a glossy home magazine, 'A plate of pears,/a piano with a Persian shawl'. Almost inevitably, such **idealised views** seem too good to be true.

Indeed, the reality proves to be very different. The **contrasting picture of everyday life** is seen through the poet's clever selection of details: the heavy sound of the 'milkman's tramp', the cold 'morning light', the leftovers of a late meal, 'scraps/of last night's cheese and three sepulchral bottles' (**line 11**). Rich's disenchanted tone matches the sad truth that the couple's day-to-day routine has become tedious. The situation gets even worse as the woman is faced with an infestation of insects, wryly described as 'a pair of beetle-eyes would fix her own'. Their hidden world is captured in the phrase 'envoy from some village in the moldings'. Despite her disappointment, however, she does not feel that she can complain. It would be a form of betrayal, 'Half heresy'.

The woman's partner emerges, seemingly oblivious to the unsatisfactory domestic situation. His indifference is sharply contrasted with the speaker's keen awareness. He yawns while attempting a few notes at the piano – and quickly 'declared it out of tune' (**line 17**). Making no attempt to conceal his apathy, he simply shrugs his shoulders and goes off to buy cigarettes.

Everything about him suggests that he is entirely self-absorbed and lacking in commitment. **He does not engage with the woman.** Is this why 'living in sin' has lost its allure? Is the woman, 'jeered by the minor demons', now being forced to act as a dutiful housewife? Ironically, she sets about making the studio a more appealing place, but the coffee-pot boils over. Is this indicative of the minor frustrations of life which take the gloss from a relationship?

Despite all this, the woman is not prepared to give up on her dream, 'By evening she was back in love again' (**line 23**). Yet there is a subtle difference, 'though not so wholly'. Does the final image suggest a relationship growing cold? The speaker has revived only some of her feelings – but these are far from certain: 'throughout the night/she woke sometimes to feel the daylight coming/like a relentless milkman up the stairs.' The cover of night seems to temporarily hide the reality of her relationship, allowing the woman to **relive her fantasy** – for the moment.

Written in **free verse** (without regular stanzas, line length or rhyme), the poem relies on sustained steady rhythm to convey its central tone of disillusionment. Does the measured pace suggest the disappointing monotony of real life? Look at the repetition of the 'milkman'. What does this suggest? Does this free verse underline the free living of the young couple? Or does it hint at the disorder of their apartment?

The poem is also in the tradition of an **aubade**. Such poetry often describes young lovers at dawn, parting after a night of passion with expressions of undying love. A famous aubade occurs in Shakespeare's play, 'Romeo and Juliet'. Is this the type of daring romance the young woman was expecting?

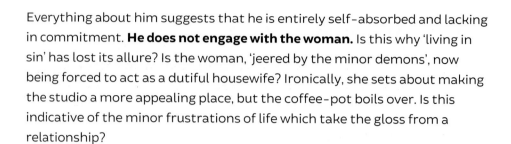

✒ Writing About the Poem

Comment on Adrienne Rich's use of contrast throughout the poem. Support your answer with reference to the text.

Sample Paragraph

Rich uses contrast to highlight modern dilemmas and to raise interesting questions. Having read 'Living in Sin', I felt I could really sense the woman's growing dissatisfaction with her lover and her living situation. This is eloquently expressed in the contrast between 'a plate of pears' and 'the scraps of last night's cheese and three sepulchral bottles'. The exciting life she had hoped to lead is echoed in the alliteration of the repeated letter 'p'. Everything was supposed to be perfect, glossy, exotic. Instead, 'that morning light so coldly' reveals the reality. The leftover food, graphically described as 'scraps' – even the sound of the word is repulsive – and the three sad bottles spoke volumes to me. The image of the young girl's boyfriend is the direct opposite to her fantasy figure. What a contrast as her lover appears, unshaven, yawning, dying not for her but for a cigarette! These contrasts vividly speak of the gap between the idealised version of life the young woman expected, and the mundane reality.

> **EXAMINER'S COMMENT**
>
> *This perceptive top-grade response sensitively explores key contrasts in the poem, and successfully shows how they illuminate the poem's central theme. Apt quotations and references reflect a close understanding of both the subject matter and the poet's language use (e.g. alliterative effects). Expression is lively and confident.*

✑ Class/Homework Exercises

1. Comment on the significance of the line, 'By evening she was back in love again'. In your opinion, what point is the poet making?
2. Write a personal response to 'Living in Sin', referring to both its central theme and the poet's language use. Support your answer with reference to the text.

⊙ Points to Consider

- **Key themes explore romantic love and the contrasting expectations of the sexes.**
- **Informal structure (free verse) adds immediacy and makes the poem accessible.**
- **Effective use of narrative style, metaphor, vivid imagery.**
- **Variety of tones – frustration, rejection, disillusionment, etc.**

6

The Roofwalker

– For Denise Levertov

Over the half-finished houses
night comes. The builders
stand on the roof. It is
quiet after the hammers,
the pulleys hang slack.   5
Giants, the roofwalkers,
on a listing deck, the wave
of darkness about to break
on their heads. The sky
is a torn sail where figures   10
pass magnified, shadows
on a burning deck.

I feel like them up there:
exposed, larger than life,
and due to break my neck.   15

Was it worth while to lay—
with infinite exertion—
a roof I can't live under?
—All those blueprints,
closing of gaps,   20
measurings, calculations?
A life I didn't choose
chose me: even
my tools are the wrong ones
for what I have to do.   25
I'm naked, ignorant,
a naked man fleeing
across the roofs
who could with a shade of difference
be sitting in the lamplight   30
against the cream wallpaper
reading—not with indifference—
about a naked man
fleeing across the roofs.

Dedication: Denise
Levertov, post-war Anglo-
American poet and activist.

pulleys: wheel and rope
device for lifting weights.

listing: leaning.
deck: floor of ship.

infinite exertion: non-stop
effort.

blueprints: plans, models.

👤 Personal Response

1. Comment on the choice of adjectives in the first stanza. What do they suggest about the poet's state of mind?

2. Choose one interesting visual image from the poem and comment on its effectiveness.

3. In your opinion, is there a definite conclusion reached at the end? Would you regard the poem as optimistic or pessimistic? Support your answer with reference to the text.

👁 Critical Literacy

'The Roofwalker' was published in Adrienne Rich's collection, *Snapshots of a Daughter-in-Law* (1963). The poem focuses on Rich's struggle to live her life the way she chooses. It also shows that our personal lives have public consequences – and that people can sometimes waste a great deal of time and energy creating lives for which they are not suited. When the poem was written in 1962, Rich was reassessing her personal life and political views.

The poem **opens** as darkness is beginning to descend on a building-site. A group of roofers are finishing up their work, 'the pulleys hang slack', after all the ferocious effort and strain of the day. Rich describes the roofwalkers as 'Giants'. Do they see themselves as important? **Does society regard them as impressive?** They are working on an unstable rooftop, 'a listing deck'. Is this an effective metaphor for trying new and hazardous things? A building site is traditionally associated with men. But the site is 'half-finished'.

'on a listing deck'

Does this incompleteness suggest that new skills are needed? What else was a male preserve during the early 1960s?

From ground-level, the roofwalkers look as though they are on a tilting ship. The metaphor is extended to suggest that nightfall is about to descend on them like waves. The sky is a 'torn sail' **(line 10)**. We can imagine the workers silhouetted against the ragged dusky clouds. The men are seen as insubstantial ('shadows'). They are also described as being in an increasingly risky position ('a burning deck'). But while there is **a disturbing sense of imminent danger**, the men seem unconcerned about the precarious position they are in and that they might be in danger of a fall.

Lines 13–15 introduce the personal pronoun 'I', the interior world that the speaker is experiencing. **She now identifies directly with the roofwalkers**: 'I feel like them up there.' All of them are vulnerable to sudden change, they are all 'exposed'. Each is trying to do an impossible job against the odds ('larger than life'). Notice how the three lines stand on their own, apart from the rest of the poem, mirroring the silhouetted roofwalkers. The speaker also feels apart. Like the roofers who are risking physical injury, she is beginning to make radical changes in her personal life. For her, the roof is dangerous, but it is also a vantage point, providing a larger vision.

From **line 16** onwards, the **building metaphor is developed** further. The speaker reflects on the enormous amount of sustained energy used to create something which she is preparing to leave behind, 'with infinite exertion'. She wonders if it was of any benefit to construct a roof that she can no longer live under. We are left to wonder about what the roof is actually sheltering. What exactly is she challenging that was so carefully crafted, 'blueprints … measurings, calculations'? The speaker is adamant about one thing, however. She feels that she was forced into the role she now occupies: 'A life I didn't choose/chose me.' Does she need to escape from the constraints of marriage, motherhood and patriarchal culture?

While the speaker equates the building of the roof with the reconstruction of her own life, she admits that she is not equipped to deal with this: 'my tools are the wrong ones.' In the **nightmare scene** that follows, she envisions herself as 'a naked man fleeing/across the roofs' **(line 27)**. The frantic tone reflects her sense of isolation, of feeling 'ignorant'. In particular, the repetition of 'naked' emphasises the speaker's defencelessness. If things were slightly different, she could be secure 'in the lamplight/against the cream wallpaper', reading sympathetically about someone else attempting change and in danger, instead of experiencing these things herself.

Although she associates herself with men in this deeply personal poem, it is obvious that the speaker **no longer views maleness as power**. However, the turmoil of the roofwalker is the motivation that leads her to define herself on her own terms and in alliance with other women.

✒ Writing About the Poem

Comment on Adrienne Rich's use of metaphors throughout 'The Roofwalker'. Support your answer with reference to the text.

Sample Paragraph

Rich's metaphors are central to this poem. The building site, traditionally a man's world, becomes a metaphor for patriarchal traditions. The site had 'blueprints' and 'calculations'. Nothing new was getting in. I think this could refer to any institution which was historically male-dominated. But it is now an endangered place, 'the wave of darkness' is about to be unleashed. Rich's feminist views are evident throughout. The roofers are now in an unsafe place, 'a burning deck', facing uncharted waters. They are seen as insubstantial, 'shadows'. The 1960s was a time of radical social progress when women dared to demand equal rights. The macho male 'roof' society would no longer survive in its present form. Rich's poem not only refers to the breaking down of oppressive male influence, but it can also refer to any change in society, as new ideas arise. Those who are involved in social change can feel 'naked', 'ignorant'. They often wish they were not leading the charge, but 'sitting in the lamplight' – a symbol of comfort – rather than trying to activate change.

> **EXAMINER'S COMMENT**
>
> *A clear and insightful response to a challenging question, offering a wide-ranging interpretation of the poem's metaphors and explaining how they convey the poem's central themes. Excellent expression throughout and discussion points are backed up with judicious use of suitable quotation. A top-grade standard.*

✎ Class/Homework Exercises

1. Would you regard Rich's poem 'The Roofwalker' as optimistic or pessimistic, overall? Support your answer with reference to the text.
2. In your opinion, what image of Adrienne Rich herself emerges from this poem? Support your response with suitable reference to the text.

⊙ Points to Consider

- **Central themes include human personal responsibility, vulnerability and alienation.**

- **Effective use of the sustained builder image.**

- **Variety of tones – personal reflection, confusion, determination, etc.**

- **Impact of repetition, detailed description, metaphorical language.**

7 Our Whole Life

Our whole life a translation
the permissible fibs

and now a knot of lies
eating at itself to get undone

Words bitten thru words   5

meanings burnt-off like paint
under the blowtorch

All those dead letters
rendered into the oppressor's language

Trying to tell the doctor where it hurts   10
like the Algerian
who walked from his village, burning

his whole body a cloud of pain
and there are no words for this

except himself   15

translation: interpretation.
permissible fibs: acceptable untruths.

blowtorch: fuel-burning tool for removing paint.

dead letters: useless words; undelivered mail.
rendered: turned into.
oppressor's language: words used by tyrants.

'Trying to tell the doctor where it hurts'

👤 Personal Response

1. The poet mentions 'fibs' and 'lies' in the opening lines of the poem. What do you think she really means by this?
2. How would you describe the poet's tone in lines 3–7? Give reasons to explain your response.
3. Write your own personal response to this poem, highlighting the impact it made on you.

👁 Critical Literacy

Communication breakdown is often the cause of conflict and suffering in the world. The abuse of language has been part of propaganda and oppression throughout history. It is still used to disempower minorities, racial groups, women in society and entire nations. From a feminist viewpoint, Rich's poetry combines an impassioned poetic imagination and an engagement with political issues. In 'Our Whole Life', she addresses important aspects of language and communication.

The poem begins with a series of dramatic claims, all of which reflect Rich's dissatisfaction with the **limitations of language**. Life is reduced to 'a translation'. Her frustration is evident in the derisive phrase, 'permissible fibs', suggesting a certain compliance by those who are victims of everyday language. The opening statement ('Our whole life') is unclear. Is the poet referring to people in general or to any marginalised group whose voice is ignored?

In **lines 3–7**, the tone becomes more urgent as the speaker uses a number of violent images to highlight the distortion of language. It is 'a knot of lies/ eating at itself'. Its chaotic effects are reflected in the aggressive phrase, 'Words bitten thru words'. The sense of harshness associated with the abuse of language is heightened in the vivid comparison, 'meanings burnt-off like paint/under the blowtorch'. **Searing onomatopoeic effects** emphasise the intensity of the painful lies that cause untold pain within relationships.

The poem's central viewpoint is found in **lines 9–11**: 'All those dead letters/ rendered into the oppressor's language.' Traditionally, men have controlled language in patriarchal societies. As a result, language is worthless for those adversely affected and subjugated by misinformation. The hopelessness of the oppressed to find ways of articulating the truth about their lives is similar to a child 'Trying to tell the doctor where it hurts'. This **simple comparison** manages to combine angry frustration with agonising sympathy for the victim.

The poem's most **startling image** occurs in the **final lines** where the failure of language is likened to an Algerian war victim 'who walked from his village, burning'. For Rich, the horror of his experience is almost beyond description – 'there are no words for this'. Nothing can adequately communicate the man's tragedy 'except himself'. The language used throughout this short poem has itself been stripped largely of punctuation and precise grammar. This produces a much more forceful and dramatic impact that reflects Rich's passionate feelings.

✒ Writing About the Poem

Comment on Adrienne Rich's use of imagery throughout 'Our Whole Life'. Support the points you make with reference to the poem.

Sample Paragraph

Rich uses powerful imagery in 'Our Whole Life'. One of the poem's themes is the way language fails to communicate the truth when people talk to each other. She suggests the way people tie themselves in knots by comparing everyday language to 'the knot of lies'. She suggests how we keep trying to explain what we really mean to say. But the 'knot of lies' ends up 'eating into itself'. Many images are to do with burning. Such as when Rich describes the words we use as damaging, 'under the blowtorch' burning off old paint. There is something very violent here. This suggests the destructive power of language. Mainly by those who want to oppress other people. The most memorable image is of the Algerian victim – 'his whole body in a cloud of pain'. I've seen some disturbing photographs of war victims and they are also beyond words. This is the most effective image. To me, it suggests the horror of inhumanity to man.

EXAMINER'S COMMENT

A reasonably good personal response that engages with the text and generally focuses well on the effectiveness of imagery. The discussion ranges over the whole poem. Language control is uneven – too note-like in places – and the verb 'suggests' is overused. There are also minor errors in some of the quotations. Overall, a solid middle-grade standard.

✎ Class/Homework Exercises

1. In your opinion, what is the central theme or message in 'Our Whole Life'? Refer closely to the text in your response.
2. Comment on Rich's use of emotive and disturbing language in this poem.

◉ Points to Consider

- **Poet focuses on the ways that language has been used to control people.**
- **The female experience has been largely lost in translation.**
- **Effective use of vivid symbols and dramatic imagery.**
- **Variety of tones – didactic, frustrated, angry, etc.**

8 Trying to Talk with a Man

ADRIENNE RICH

Out in this desert we are testing bombs,

that's why we came here.

Sometimes I feel an underground river
forcing its way between deformed cliffs
an acute angle of understanding   5
moving itself like a locus of the sun
into this condemned scenery.

What we've had to give up to get here—
whole LP collections, films we starred in
playing in the neighborhoods, bakery windows   10
full of dry, chocolate-filled Jewish cookies,
the language of love-letters, of suicide notes,
afternoons on the riverbank
pretending to be children

Coming out to this desert   15
we meant to change the face of
driving among dull green succulents
walking at noon in the ghost town
surrounded by a silence

that sounds like the silence of the place   20
except that it came with us
and is familiar
and everything we were saying until now
was an effort to blot it out—
coming out here we are up against it   25

Out here I feel more helpless
with you than without you
You mention the danger
and list the equipment
we talk of people caring for each other   30
in emergencies—laceration, thirst—
but you look at me like an emergency

desert: the Nevada Desert where nuclear weapons were tested during the 1950s.

deformed: misshapen.

acute angle: angle less than 90°.
locus: position.

condemned scenery: poisoned landscape.

LP collections: long-playing music discs.

succulents: desert plants, cacti.

laceration: flesh wound, gash.

Your dry heat feels like power
your eyes are stars of a different magnitude
they reflect lights that spell out: EXIT   35
when you get up and pace the floor

talking of the danger
as if it were not ourselves
as if we were testing anything else.

magnitude: size, measure.

👤 Personal Response

1. Based on your reading of lines 8–14, what was the couple's relationship like in the past?
2. Choose one image or symbol from the poem that you found particularly effective. Briefly explain your choice.
3. Write a short personal response to the poem, explaining its impact on you.

👁 Critical Literacy

Adrienne Rich wrote 'Trying to Talk with a Man' in 1971. The poem focuses on a woman and man who try to salvage their relationship by isolating themselves in the desert. Its title clearly indicates that lack of communication is threatening to end the couple's relationship. The poem also reflects people's anxiety over the testing of nuclear weapons. Characteristically, Rich questions traditional thinking about issues of gender and power.

'we are testing bombs'

The **opening lines** seem dismissively factual: 'Out in this desert we are testing bombs,/that's why we came here.' From the outset, **political and personal themes are interwoven**. The desert setting is under threat: 'condemned scenery' and military tests are destroying the landscape. But is Rich's relationship with her husband also condemned? The tension that is present is suggested by the powerful image of the underground river 'forcing its way between deformed cliffs'. Does the metaphor reflect the conflict between growth and decay? Between progress and failure? Is the poet coming close to 'an acute angle of understanding' her marriage for what it really is?

Imagery from the couple's domestic life is juxtaposed with the arid location. **Lines 8–14** offer an insight into their early years together: 'What we've had to give up to get here.' The **tone is ambiguous, both nostalgic and resentful**. Most of the memories listed refer to the conventional moments of a romantic relationship: 'whole LP collections, films we starred in.' But the romance is abruptly undermined by the disturbing reference to 'the language of love-letters, of suicide notes'. The poet faces up to the tragic reality of the past. Were all the written expressions of love a dreadful mistake? Did the couple deceive themselves all along?

In **lines 15–25**, the desert wasteland ('surrounded by a silence') becomes a more evocative metaphor for their misguided relationship. The desolate setting is highlighted by the repetition of 'silence' and the haunting image: 'walking at noon in the ghost town.' Rich recognises the **symbolism** for herself: the silent desert 'is familiar', signifying the emptiness of a doomed marriage. She is compelled to accept the truth ('we are up against it') that all meaningful communication has ended. The frank admission that she feels 'more helpless/with you than without you' marks a crucial turning point – a daring admission of failure.

On the edge of nuclear destruction, the poet recognises that military and interpersonal violence echo each other as the couple become distant figures, 'talking of the danger/as if it were not ourselves'. The tone becomes increasingly frustrated as she voices her deepest fears: 'Your dry heat feels like power' **(line 33)**. **Dramatic tension builds** as her husband – now seen as a destructive force – remains in denial: 'you get up and pace the floor.' Nevertheless, the end of the relationship is also clearly reflected in his eyes as 'lights that spell out: EXIT'.

The **last three lines** sum up the poet's feelings of relief. The journey into the desert has clarified her view of the disintegrating marriage. To a great extent, the focus has moved away from the danger of nuclear experiments, 'as if we were testing anything else'. The ending is poignant and moving. Once again, the tone seems to reflect **feelings of loss and sadness** with a bittersweet understanding of what might have been. As in so much of her

work, Rich exposes power imbalances between the sexes. In this case, she succeeds in connecting the risk of 'testing bombs' with the personal danger of one couple's miscommunication.

✒ Writing About the Poem

In your view, what is the dominant atmosphere in 'Trying to Talk with a Man'? Support your answer with reference to the poem.

Sample Paragraph

I found this to be a disturbing poem. The atmosphere is tense. The title implies dissatisfaction. The narrator is frustrated – 'Trying to talk'. The mood is also intimidating. The narrator and her lover have gone into the desert to view the US Army bomb sites. However, it becomes clear that this uneasy background is really a context for their own danger-filled relationship. Deserts are lonely places where nothing grows. This makes the whole poem disturbing and intimidating. The narrator sees 'deformed cliffs' all around – symbols of her own feelings about a hopeless love affair that is about to fall apart. The poem is written using nervous rhythms, in broken fragments, using little punctuation – 'Your dry heat feels like power' is typical of the disappointed tone. This adds further tension The poem concludes on a reflective note when the narrator faces up to the tragic fact that she can no longer communicate with her lover. This is symbolised by the 'EXIT' sign she imagines. The final atmosphere is pessimistic. The couple have no future together.

EXAMINER'S COMMENT

This paragraph focuses effectively on the tension within the poem. Discussion points are coherent and quotes are integrated effectively into the critical commentary – with interesting reference to stylistic features, such as rhythm and symbolism. Apart from some repetition and a tendency towards short sentences, the expression is varied and lively. A good high-grade standard.

✐ Class/Homework Exercises

1. 'Adrienne Rich's poems are often concerned with tensions.' To what extent is this the case in 'Trying to Talk with a Man'? Refer to the poem in your answer.
2. In your opinion, what points does this poem make about modern-day society? Support your response with reference to the text.

⊙ Points to Consider

- **Lack of communication and the failure of relationships are key themes.**
- **Vivid images and symbols illustrate the couple's fraught relationship.**
- **Varying tones – frustrated, regretful, realistic, pessimistic, etc.**
- **Effective use of everyday conversational language.**

9 Diving into the Wreck

ADRIENNE RICH

First having read the book of myths,
and loaded the camera,
and checked the edge of the knife-blade,
I put on
the body-armor of black rubber   5
the absurd flippers
the grave and awkward mask.
I am having to do this
not like Cousteau with his
assiduous team   10
aboard the sun-flooded schooner
but here alone.

There is a ladder.
The ladder is always there
hanging innocently   15
close to the side of the schooner.
We know what it is for,
we who have used it.
Otherwise
it's a piece of maritime floss   20
some sundry equipment.

I go down.
Rung after rung and still
the oxygen immerses me
the blue light   25
the clear atoms
of our human air.
I go down.
My flippers cripple me,
I crawl like an insect down the ladder   30
and there is no one
to tell me when the ocean
will begin.

First the air is blue and then
it is bluer and then green and then   35
black I am blacking out and yet
my mask is powerful

myths: ancient tales, folklore.

body-armor: wet-suit.

Cousteau: Jacques Cousteau, French underwater explorer and filmmaker.
assiduous: methodical, professional.

schooner: sailing ship.

maritime: naval, seafaring.
floss: thread.
sundry: varied, miscellaneous.

immerses: surrounds, overwhelms.

atoms: basic elements, particles.

it pumps my blood with power
the sea is another story
the sea is not a question of power   40
I have to learn alone
to turn my body without force
in the deep element.

And now: it is easy to forget
what I came for   45
among so many who have always
lived here
swaying their crenellated fans
between the reefs
and besides   50
you breathe differently down here.

I came to explore the wreck.
The words are purposes.
The words are maps.
I came to see the damage that was done   55
and the treasures that prevail.
I stroke the beam of my lamp
slowly along the flank
of something more permanent
than fish or weed   60

the thing I came for:
the wreck and not the story of the wreck
the thing itself and not the myth
the drowned face always staring
toward the sun   65
the evidence of damage
worn by salt and sway into this threadbare beauty
the ribs of the disaster
curving their assertion
among the tentative haunters.   70

This is the place.
And I am here, the mermaid whose dark hair
streams black, the merman in his armored body
We circle silently
about the wreck   75
we dive into the hold.
I am she: I am he

crenellated: having ridges or notches.
reefs: outcrops of jagged rocks.

prevail: survive.

flank: side.

threadbare: worn, shabby.

tentative: unsure, timid.
haunters: divers who repeatedly explore wrecks.

mermaid: mythical sea creature (part-woman and part-fish).
merman: male version of a mermaid.

ADRIENNE RICH

whose drowned face sleeps with open eyes
whose breasts still bear the stress
whose silver, copper, vermeil cargo lies   80   **vermeil:** precious metal,
obscurely inside barrels   gilded silver or gold.
half-wedged and left to rot
we are the half-destroyed instruments
that once held to a course
the water-eaten log   85   **log:** day-to-day ship's
the fouled compass   record.
                                                                        compass: instrument
                                                                        showing direction.

We are, I am, you are
by cowardice or courage
the one who find our way
back to the scene   90
carrying a knife, a camera
a book of myths
in which
our names do not appear.

'bluer and then green'

👤 Personal Response

1. Describe the atmosphere in the opening stanza. Support your view with reference to the text.
2. Choose two striking images from the poem that you find particularly effective. Briefly explain your choice in each case.
3. At one level, this poem is about a shipwreck. In your view, what else is the speaker exploring? Refer closely to the text in your answer.

👁 Critical Literacy

The poem (written in the first person) narrates the speaker's quest as she explores a sunken ship. She dives deep to investigate the cause of the disaster and to salvage whatever treasures remain. The sea is a traditional literary symbol of the unconscious – and to dive is to probe beneath the surface for hidden meanings, to discover submerged desires and emotions. The poem's title raises several questions. What is the history of the wreck? What is the speaker's connection with it? Like the diver, readers will be rewarded by repeated explorations of this provocative poem.

In the opening lines of **stanza one**, the speaker addresses the reader directly, as if recalling her initial interest ('having read the book of myths') in this forgotten shipwreck. (Is this also a likely reference to the historic view of women in patriarchal societies?) The tone is observational and detached. There is a sense of nervous anticipation as the speaker makes military-style preparations (she sees her wet-suit as 'body-armor') before her adventure. At times, she can almost laugh at her own amateurish appearance in 'absurd flippers' and 'awkward mask'.

Stanzas two to four focus on the underwater experience. As in many of Rich's poems, **the setting acts as an extended metaphor** for exploring other issues, such as gender roles. Armed with stories of what might have happened to the wreck, the speaker uses the ladder on the side of the schooner to begin her descent. On a metaphorical level, of course, the dive represents a journey of self-discovery. The ladder (or opportunity for finding truth) 'is always there' – but only for those who choose to use it.

Moving steadily downwards, the diver experiences a variety of sensations: helplessness ('the oxygen immerses me'), exhilaration ('the clear atoms') and pain ('My flippers cripple me'). The uncontrollable descent is suggested by the short lines, rapid rhythm and hypnotic repetition of the phrase, 'I go down'. The **sense of alienation and insignificance** increases: 'there is no one/to tell me when the ocean/will begin.' Fear of the unknown is also emphasised in the stark admission: 'I crawl like an insect down the ladder.' However, deep down in this startling deep-sea world, the speaker manages to reach an understanding of how she can survive and triumph in this anonymous environment 'I have to learn alone/to turn my body without force'.

This is both reassuring and challenging. The ladder now takes on a greater significance, becoming a symbol of what is possible in a person's life. In **stanzas five to six**, the speaker reminds herself not to forget the reason for her journey – 'to explore the wreck'. Her interest in discovery has made her more determined than ever ('words are purposes') and she is increasingly fascinated by the wonder of the undersea world. As she uses a flashlight to examine what remains of the sunken ship ('the treasures that prevail') there is a suggestion that she is slowly coming to terms with the past ('the damage that was done').

Throughout **stanza seven**, **the mood is more resigned and faintly beautiful**. Gentle assonant sounds ('the drowned face always staring/toward the sun') add a note of poignancy. Whether applied to a tragic shipwreck, an individual's life, or social and political history over the centuries, nothing can alter the 'disaster' of past generations. Yet, even within the wreck of history, there exists a 'threadbare beauty' that can still be appreciated.

The poem becomes increasingly dreamlike in **stanzas eight to nine**. The diver imagines herself as a fabled mermaid or merman. Does this androgynous (genderless) creature emphasise the common experiences of all human beings who search for meaning in their lives? But the persona quickly turns into a more compelling figure 'whose drowned face sleeps with open eyes'. **Roles become blurred** as the speaker is identified closely with the shipwreck: 'we are the half-destroyed instruments/that once held to a course.' Ironically, the damage done to the drowned ship has corroded equipment that might once have guided the way. Nevertheless, the fact that lost treasure ('silver, copper, vermeil cargo') still lies hidden in the wreck offers the possibility of future rewards.

In **stanza ten**, the sunken ship is depicted as a **symbol of the traditional female role in society**: 'our names do not appear.' The challenge to 'find our way' and discover the truth about established social structures involves everyone. Although the wreck demonstrates disaster, much can still be salvaged. This is characteristic of Rich's feminist perspective that social structures need to improve – particularly regarding issues concerning human rights and gender equality. The final lines are realistic, forecasting that people will come 'back to this scene' and explore the wreck of history. The poem ends as it began, with a flashback to the earlier preparation for the dive, another reminder that planning and organisation are essential elements of any journey or movement.

🖋 Writing About the Poem

Comment on the poet's description of the underwater world in 'Diving into the Wreck'. Support your answer with reference to the poem.

Sample Paragraph

In 'Diving into the Wreck', Rich uses colour images to make the water vivid. She seems overwhelmed by the beauty of 'the blue light' and 'the clear atoms'. The deeper she dives, the more the colours change – 'it is bluer'. As the waters get darker, she almost blacks out. From the contrasting colour images, I can sense this eerie world. Rich also gives us a clear idea of the freedom underwater. Everything is different close to the ocean floor – including the fish who have their natural habitat there. The poet describes them swaying 'between the reefs'. Throughout the poem, the imagery and rhythm succeed in suggesting the fluid movement of this world – 'the sea is another story'. The absence of punctuation combined with run-on lines add to our understanding of the free movement in this world.

EXAMINER'S COMMENT

This is a reasonably well-controlled response that attempts to directly address the question. The extended discussion on the use of colour imagery is supported by apt reference. The final point about rhythm is very good, but deserves further development and illustration. Overall, a good mid-grade standard that shows engagement with the poem.

🖊 Class/Homework Exercises

1. 'Diving into the Wreck' is typical of Adrienne Rich's poetry in that it is layered with hidden meaning. Discuss this view, supporting your answer with reference to the poem.
2. In your opinion, is this ultimately an optimistic or pessimistic poem? Explain your response, supporting the points you make by suitable quotation or reference.

⊙ Points to Consider

- Poet explores aspects of society, particularly male–female roles.
- Extended metaphor of the exploratory sea dive sustained throughout.
- Stunningly vivid imagery, symbolism and personification reinforce themes.
- Effective use of assonance, alliteration and sibilance.

10 From a Survivor

ADRIENNE RICH

Survivor: someone who exists after a difficult experience or who lives after the death of another.

The pact that we made was the ordinary pact
of men & women in those days

pact: formal agreement.

I don't know who we thought we were
that our personalities
could resist the failures of the race   5

Lucky or unlucky, we didn't know
the race had failures of that order
and that we were going to share them

Like everybody else, we thought of ourselves as special

Your body is as vivid to me   10
as it ever was: even more

since my feeling for it is clearer:
I know what it could and could not do

it is no longer
the body of a god   15
or anything with power over my life

Next year it would have been 20 years
and you are wastefully dead
who might have made the leap
we talked, too late, of making   20

Next year it would have been 20 years: reference to the 19 years the poet and her husband spent together.
wastefully: without achieving.

which I live now
not as a leap
but a succession of brief amazing moments

each one making possible the next

'we thought of ourselves as special'

👤 Personal Response

1. Why do you think the poet uses '&' between 'men' and 'women' in line 2? What does this suggest to you?
2. Do you think the poem's ending is optimistic or pessimistic? Give a reason for your response.
3. Write your own personal response to the poem, supporting the points you make with reference to the text.

👁 Critical Literacy

'From a Survivor' was written in 1972. Rich had begun dating her poems from 1956 so that her readers could see 'my sense of being engaged in a long continuing process'. This intensely personal poem is a considered reflection on the beginning and the aftermath of Rich's own failed marriage. The tone varies from reminiscence to sorrow, wistfulness, acceptance and quiet optimism.

The title suggests that this is a message from someone who has lived through a difficult experience. In **line 1**, the word 'pact' is an unusual way of referring to marriage vows. The term is more usually applied to a formal agreement between warring factions. What might this indicate about relations between men and women? The adjective 'ordinary' implies that getting married was the conventional thing to do at that time. While the use of the ampersand symbol '&' joining 'men & women' might reinforce the idea that heterosexual marriage was taken for granted, the abbreviation could also suggest that such a general presumption should have been much more carefully considered.

The poem's **fragmented appearance** on the page gives the impression of Rich's tentative stream of thought as she seeks to come to terms with her feelings. The tone is almost derogatory: 'I don't know who we thought we were' **(line 3)**, linking the poet and the reader in an intimate way. She now realises that she and her young husband were naïve, that they assumed they would have a happy married life together where others had been unsuccessful. Conversational language gives the poem a wonderful sense of immediacy, 'our personalities/could resist the failures of the race'.

Looking back on the marriage, Rich is still not sure whether it was good or bad luck that they were unaware of the pitfalls that lay ahead, 'failures of that order', or that they were going to be part of them. She reminds us of the intense feelings that exist in the early stages of romantic relationships, 'Like everybody else, we thought of ourselves as special' **(line 9)**. The ongoing momentum of the line stretching across the page highlights the couple's **youthful optimism**. Unfortunately, they were not to find lasting happiness together.

Despite the tensions of their marriage, the poet's affection for her late husband endures. Rich's tone is affectionate as she remembers his physical presence, 'Your body is as vivid to me/as it ever was' **(line 11)**. Time has passed and her 'feeling' has become 'clearer', free from doubt and confusion. She now knows that the man she married was an ordinary human being who had abilities and limitations. Significantly, the poet no longer views him as a 'god', who has 'power' over her life. Social and cultural changes (brought about largely by the feminist movement) give Rich a more informed perspective on how her marriage disempowered her.

In **lines 16–20**, the poet reflects on the passing years and on what might have been. Her former husband is 'wastefully dead'. The description underlines Rich's deep sense of compassion over the tragic loss of someone who had so much to offer. As in all relationships, of course, there is **an element of mystery**. What did he not achieve? What was the 'leap' he could have made? Was this a challenge he could have taken on? Why was it 'too late' when they 'talked' about it?

The tone through **lines 21–24** is much **more positive**. Rich feels that her success in life has been a sequence of small steps ('brief amazing moments'). But these have a charged momentum of their own, 'each one making possible the next'. The poem ends without a full stop, suggesting that this movement will continue. The survivor is progressing onward.

✒ Writing About the Poem

How has the order and structure of 'From a Survivor' helped you to understand the poem? Support your answer with reference to the text.

Sample Paragraph

I was very struck by the disjointed appearance of the shape of the poem, 'From a Survivor'. It was very like everyday life itself, uneven and unpredictable. As I read the poem, structured with flowing run-on lines and little punctuation, I felt as if Rich was speaking to me in a stream of consciousness as she reflected on the innocence of the young couple before marriage. I liked the longest line, 'Like everybody else, we thought of ourselves as special'. It summed up the ambition of young lovers as it extended right across the page. But the tone becomes more regretful as the poet faces the realisation that the couple will have no wedding anniversary. This was suggested by short lines, such as 'and you are wastefully dead'. I also liked the way the poet structured the ending, as it concludes with gentle optimism. Life is good, there is no need for the 'leap'. The lack of a full stop at the very end emphasises the idea that life goes on, particularly for a survivor.

✒ Class/Homework Exercises

1. Relationships are an important theme in Rich's poetry. Discuss this statement with particular reference to the poem 'From a Survivor'.
2. In your opinion, what is the central or dominant tone in this poem? Briefly explain your response.

⊙ Points to Consider

- **Female–male power structures and failed relationships are central themes.**

- **Absence of punctuation creates an uninterrupted fluent rhythm.**

- **Simple conversational language makes the poem accessible.**

- **Various moods – personal, reflective, regretful, optimistic, etc.**

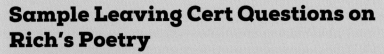

Sample Leaving Cert Questions on Rich's Poetry

1. 'Adrienne Rich's poetry is interesting both for its universal themes and its effective language use.' Discuss this statement with reference to the poems on your course.

2. 'Rich makes effective use of symbols and metaphors to explore personal experiences and offer perceptive insights about history and society.' To what extent do you agree or disagree with this statement? Support your answer with reference to the poetry of Adrienne Rich on your course.

3. 'The poems of Adrienne Rich are carefully crafted to expose dark themes of disappointment and resilience.' To what extent do you agree or disagree with this view? Support your answer with reference to the poetry of Adrienne Rich on your course.

How do I organise my answer?

(Sample question 1)

'Adrienne Rich's poetry is interesting both for its universal themes and its effective language use.' Discuss this statement with reference to the poems on your course.

Sample Plan 1

Intro: *(Stance: agree with viewpoint in the question)* Rich – personal anger/frustration expressed through interesting images, traditional portrayal of women in a patriarchal society, compassionate philosophical insights portrayed through striking symbols and innovative language use.

Point 1: *(Frustration – form/style)* 'Living in Sin' – aubade with a difference, common experience of unfulfilled young women in modern relationships ('She had thought'), use of symbolism of light ('morning light/so coldly would delineate'), inventive verbs ('stalking', 'writhe', 'fix'), realistic, resigned conclusion ('back in love again,/though not so wholly').

Point 2: *(Role of women – striking imagery)* 'The Roofwalker' – addresses the role of a woman worldwide, effective use of extended building metaphor ('my tools are the wrong ones'), common dread of exposing oneself to ridicule ('I'm naked, ignorant,/a naked man fleeing').

Understanding the Prescribed Poetry Question

Marks are awarded using the PCLM Marking Scheme:
P = 15; C = 15; L = 15; M = 5
Total = 50

- **P** (Purpose = 15 marks) refers to the set question and is the launch pad for the answer. This involves engaging with all aspects of the question. Both theme and language must be addressed, although not necessarily equally.

- **C** (Coherence = 15 marks) refers to the organisation of the developed response and the use of accurate, relevant quotation. Paragraphing is essential.

- **L** (Language = 15 marks) refers to the student's skill in controlling language throughout the answer.

- **M** (Mechanics = 5 marks) refers to spelling and grammar.

- Although no specific number of poems is required, students usually discuss at least 3 or 4 in their written responses.

- Aim for at least 800 words, to be completed within 45–50 minutes.

NOTE

In keeping with the PCLM approach, the student has to take a stance by agreeing and/or disagreeing that Rich's poetry is interesting for its:

- **universal themes** (power/ powerlessness, control, women's role in patriarchal society, vulnerability, nature, etc.)

... and its:

- **effective language use** (vivid symbolism, extended metaphor, imagery, compelling tones, strong verbs, dramatic settings, etc.)

Point 3: (*Power – symbols, structure*) 'Power' – interesting exploration of the nature of power in the world, conversational tone accessible to the reader ('Today I was reading about'), Marie Curie is a paradoxical symbol of the good and bad aspects of power throughout history ('suffered', 'denied').

Point 4: (*Challenges – metaphor, structure*) 'Storm Warnings' – shared experience of individuals through troubled times ('These are the things that we have learned to do/who live in troubled regions'), use of extended storm metaphor ('weather abroad/And weather in the heart'), structure of poem mirrors movement of the storm.

Conclusion: Rich rewards readers by expressing engaging universal themes in a fresh way, using vibrant imagery and rich symbolism to explore life's difficulties.

Sample Paragraph: Point 2

In 'The Roofwalker', Rich deals with the role of women in a patriarchal society. 'Over the half-finished houses/night comes. The builders/ stand on the roof.' A building site, 'a man's world', becomes a metaphor for tradition renewing itself. However, Rich pictures an imminent revolt, transforming the image of the construction site into that of a 'burning deck'. This changing imagery pattern suggests a rushed voyage into a liberated society and the destruction of the old carefully built values, 'closing of gaps,/ measurings, calculations'. There is a sharp change in the short three-line stanza as she envisages herself in the precarious position of a roofwalker, 'I feel like them up there:/exposed'. The act of walking on an unstable roof is a very interesting metaphor for Rich's experience of being a female writer. She is operating in a male-dominated world of literature where there has not been an equal place traditionally for the female voice.

EXAMINER'S COMMENT

As part of a full essay answer, this clear response uses 'The Roofwalker' effectively to illustrate Rich's distinctive writing style in exploring her themes. Carefully chosen quotations show close engagement with the development of thought within the poem. Impressive expression (e.g. 'she envisages herself in the precarious position') and assured personal interaction with the poem contributes to the top-grade standard.

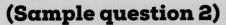

(Sample question 2)

'Rich makes effective use of symbols and metaphors to explore personal experiences and offer perceptive insights about history and society.' To what extent do you agree or disagree with this statement? Support your answer with reference to the poetry of Adrienne Rich on your course.

NOTE

In keeping with the PCLM approach, the student has to take a stance by agreeing and/or disagreeing that Rich's poetry:

– **explores personal experiences and offers perceptive insights about history and society** (political and personal issues, marriage, relationships, communication, power, society's victims, etc.)

... through the effective use of:

– **symbols and metaphors** (powerful similes, vivid symbolism, metaphors, contrasting tones, dramatic incidents, etc.)

ADRIENNE RICH

Sample Plan 2

Intro: *(Stance: agree with viewpoint in the question)* Rich – struggled to find a voice for herself and those who were disenfranchised. Experimental language, vivid images, striking symbols offer insightful views of key themes – particularly relating to social structures.

Point 1: *(Victim – tone, personification, imagery)* 'Our Whole Life' – limitations and distortion of language, mocking tone ('permissible fibs'), unnerving personification of cannibalism ('knot of ties/eating at itself'), violent similes ('meanings burnt off like paint'), revealing concluding image of Algerian victim.

Point 2: *(Lack of communication – symbols)* 'Trying to Talk with a Man' – interwoven political and personal themes addressed in this tense, disturbing poem about lack of communication. Desert nuclear test site becomes powerful metaphor for couple's failing relationship.

Point 3: *(Vulnerability – metaphor)* 'Storm Warnings' – incisive exploration of human vulnerability and the harsh realities of everyday life ('in troubled regions'), poet's developed storm metaphor ('weather in the heart') suggests that people must endure emotional turmoil and learn to deal with tragic situations.

Point 4: *(Relationship difficulties – poetic structure, perspective)* 'From a Survivor' – perceptively personal and reflective poem examining different stages of a relationship. Fragmented appearance of poem mirrors style of stream of thought. Defiant attitude – poet continuing on with life, in small 'steps'.

Conclusion: Rich is unafraid to confront the difficulties of modern life through unusual images and symbols, innovative use of structure, drawing on deeply personal experiences. She gives a voice to those who don't have one in this unforgiving world.

Sample Paragraph: Point 3

'Storm Warnings' uses form to emphasise its central message. Using the metaphor of a developing storm, the poem is concerned with facing up to change. Rich's long opening sentence runs through twelve lines, with all the energy of the rainstorm. This symbolises an interior emotional state, 'Weather abroad/And weather in the heart', and neither can be controlled. The candles reminds me of a power failure caused by a storm. When a storm breaks, all the comforts of modern civilisation seem helpless against the elements, 'shattered fragments'. We have all felt powerless in situations beyond our control, whether facing an exam, or waiting on the results of hospital tests. Rich captures the unease as she moves restlessly about, 'I leave the book'. She calmly states how people have learned to deal with tragedies, 'These are the things we have learned to do/Who live in troubled regions'. Weather has been effectively used as a metaphor for our everyday human moods.

EXAMINER'S COMMENT

As part of a full essay answer to question 2, this is a good high-grade response that focuses well on the poem's central metaphor of the storm. The personal engagement is slightly overdone, but there is general engagement with the text and accurate quotations support discussion points. Expression is clear and controlled throughout.

INDICATIVE MATERIAL

- **Rich often examines aspect of power and powerlessness** (patriarchy, feminism, power politics, male/female relationships, control, freedom, etc.)

... in compelling poems:

- **layered with rich imagery and meaning** (striking symbols, interesting imagery, dramatic illustrations, sound effects, subtle and varied tones – provocative, confessional, persuasive, didactic, etc.)

Leaving Cert Sample Essay

'Rich often examines aspects of power and powerlessness in compelling poems that are layered with rich imagery and meaning.' To what extent do you agree or disagree with this statement? Support your answer with reference to the poetry of Adrienne Rich on your course.

Sample Essay

1. Adrienne Rich was born in Baltimore, USA, in 1929. As a child, her father encouraged her to read and she spent much of her free time in her family's library where she grew to love literature. By the time she was 22, she published her first poetry collection. Rich was writing in the 1960s and 1970s, during the feminist and civil rights protests and the war in Vietnam, so her themes became focused mainly on people who held power or were powerless. Her poems became more confrontational, dealing with political issues, such as women's role in society, class and racism. During her lifetime, Rich published numerous collections and became America's best-known woman poet. She died in March 2012 at the age of 82.

2. As a socially conscious poet, Rich often examines issues that explore aspects of control and submissiveness. 'Aunt Jennifer's Tigers' deals with a private, personal relationship through vivid imagery and contrast. 'The Uncle Speaks in the Drawing Room' addresses public authority and people's weakness using imagery, tone and sound effects. Her poem 'Living in Sin' studies male selfishness and the illusion women can have as a result of their naïve romantic expectations. Many of Rich's poems are filled with frustration and anger. She wished to break down barriers and does not feel at ease in today's patriarchal world.

3. In 'Aunt Jennifer's Tigers', Rich places the aunt in a harshly controlled situation under the 'massive weight of Uncle's wedding band'. The strict structure of the poem and rigid rhyme scheme ('screen'/'green', 'tree'/'certainty') emphasise the tough limitations placed on this unfortunate woman. But Rich also shows the aunt's hidden strengths – as displayed in her colourful tapestry. Her powerful imagination erupts through the embroidery where fierce 'tigers prance across a screen'. An exotic world is seen here, 'Bright topaz denizens of a world of green'. Vivid dynamic verbs associated with the tigers are forceful, 'pace', 'prancing'. Yet those associated with the aunt are feeble, 'fluttering'. Rich is making the key point about the inequality in the relationship between a dominant male and a subservient woman.

4. 'The Uncle Speaks in the Drawing Room' also examines dominance. The tone used by the uncle is extremely arrogant. Even the title suggests his self-importance. This man also uses 'us', the plural first-person pronoun, 'Let us only bear in mind'. Such an arrogant figure assumes everyone will agree with his opinion. The people he addresses are sneeringly dismissed as 'the mob'. Rich uses detailed description to convey this wealthy arrogant character's world of sheer privilege, 'crystal vase and chandelier'. Her use of sound effects suggests the opposition of the crowd, e.g. hissing sibilant sounds show their sense of rebellion, 'Standing sullen in the square'. This is also found in the final line – 'murmurings of missile-throwers' where the alliteration suggests the threat of the discontented underclass of people who are being controlled by an arrogant man.

5. 'Power' is a tribute to the world-famous scientist Marie Curie, a woman Rich clearly admires. Fearlessly, Curie worked with dangerous materials, 'her body bombarded for years' – a disturbing military image. The poet tells a short anecdote about finding an old cure-all medicine bottle and this reminds her of the brave endurance of Marie Curie. Horrific images of her suffering, 'the cracked and suppurating skin' are listed. To a large extent, Rich is protesting about the exclusion of women from positions of research. Curie was the exception who proved the rule about such inequality. The 'amber' bottle is a symbol of the male-dominated medical world while Marie Curie still stands as a lone figure against the patriarchy of the scientific establishment, the first woman to win a Noble Prize.

6. 'Living in Sin' returns to the male/female power struggle in a couple's relationship. The power of the male is seen in his lack of sensitivity and complete indifference to his partner's romantic dreams. Alliteration and vivid imagery represent the ideal appearance of romantic happiness and elegance, 'A plate of pears, a piano with a Persian shawl'. Yet the young woman's arrogant partner dismisses the piano as 'out of tune'. He is only interested in his own needs, such as going out to buy cigarettes. The monotony of normal life is highlighted through the steady rhythm and the repetition of 'milkman'. Here, the woman is not enjoying feelings of love. and feels as if she is being taken for granted. She is putting up with frustration while she struggles to organise the couple's untidy home, 'let the coffee-pot boil over'. Yet another obedient woman is disillusioned. Male oppression dominates.

7. Rich explores male dominance and privilege in poems which frequently address inequality. Through her use of vivid imagery, sound effects and tone, she repeatedly challenges us to examine the wide gap between power and powerlessness.

(790 words)

EXAMINER'S COMMENT

While some brief biographical context can be useful at times, the general details about Rich's background are over-written here in the introduction and take away from the expected emphasis on the prescribed poems. Otherwise, the main essay included some impressive critical analysis of Rich's central themes and style – particularly in paragraphs 3, 5, and 6. Good use was also made of suitable reference and quotation. More consideration could have been given to 'layered with meaning' and further focus on effective imagery would also be expected for the top grade. General expression is reasonably good although there is some repetition and 'arrogant' is over-used in Paragraph 4.

GRADE: H2
P = 13/15
C = 12/15
L = 12/15
M = 5/5
Total = 42/50

◯◯ Revision Overview

'Aunt Jennifer's Tigers'
Themes of power, oppression and revolution, female/male relationship and contrasting roles in society.

'The Uncle Speaks in the Drawing Room'
Addresses key themes of power, powerlessness between rich and poor.

'Power'
Exploration of use and abuse of power between men and women.

'Storm Warnings'
Themes of the power balance between humans and nature.

'Living in Sin'
Aubade, love poem examines romantic love and disenchantment, woman's position in life.

'The Roofwalker'
Central themes of personal responsibility and public consequences, woman's place in a patriarchal world.

'Our Whole Life'
Theme of broken communication leads to disenfranchisement. Harsh visual and aural imagery depicts limitations and distortion of language.

'Trying to Talk with a Man'
Presents themes of communication difficulties, the breakdown of relationship between man and woman.

'Diving into the Wreck'
Revealing focus on theme of male/female roles in society. Traditional female role represented by metaphor of shipwreck.

'From a Survivor'
Presents recurring themes of male/female roles in society, broken relationships.

💬 Last Words

'All her life she has been in love with the hope of telling utter truth, and her command of language from the first has been startlingly powerful.'
W. S. Merwin

'Adrienne Rich's poems speak quietly but do not mumble ... do not tell fibs.'
W. H. Auden

'What is possible in this life? What does love mean, this thing that is so important? What is this other thing called "freedom" or "liberty" – is it like love, a feeling?'
Adrienne Rich

POWER

RELATIONSHIPS

CONFICT

NATURE

LOVE

SUFFERING

HISTORY/ MEMORY

William Wordsworth
1770–1850

'The world is too much with us.'

William Wordsworth was one of the most influential of England's Romantic poets. Like his friend, the poet Samuel Taylor Coleridge, he explored the inner self and looked for knowledge through the imagination. As a young man, Wordsworth developed a profound love of nature, a theme reflected in many of his poems. He believed that poetry was created from 'emotion recollected in tranquillity'. In 1799, he and his sister, Dorothy, settled in Grasmere in the Lake District, and it was there that he wrote his most famous poem, 'I Wandered Lonely as a Cloud', in 1804. His masterpiece is generally considered to be *The Prelude*, a lengthy semi-autobiographical poem of his early years which the poet revised many times. Wordsworth was England's Poet Laureate from 1843 until his death in 1850.

Investigate Further

To find out more about William Wordsworth, or to hear readings of his poems, you could search some useful websites such as YouTube, BBC Poetry, poetryfoundation.org and poetryarchive.org, or access additional material on this page of your eBook.

Prescribed Poems

○ 1 'To My Sister'

Wordsworth's simple invitation to his sister, Dorothy, to join him on a day of 'idleness' illustrates his deep sense of discovering divine creation in nature. **Page 322**

○ 2 'A slumber did my spirit seal'

This short, thought-provoking poem (one of the 'Lucy poems') explores the mystery of life, time, death and eternity. **Page 326**

○ 3 'She dwelt among the untrodden ways' (OL)

Another of the 'Lucy poems'. Although we learn little about the life and death of this child of nature, she had a profound effect on Wordsworth. **Page 329**

○ 4 'Composed Upon Westminister Bridge'

This well-known sonnet captures and celebrates the calm early morning view from Wordsworth's vantage point of Westminster Bridge in the centre of London.**Page 332**

○ 5 'It is a beauteous evening, calm and free' (OL)

The poem was written after Wordsworth met with his estranged daughter in France. He associates the beauty of the evening with the child's innate closeness to God. **Page 336**

○ 6 'The Solitary Reaper'

Because the words of the reaper's song are incomprehensible, the speaker in the poem is free to focus on its expressive beauty and the blissful mood it creates in him. **Page 339**

○ 7 from *The Prelude*: 'The Stolen Boat'

A seemingly harmless childhood adventure returns to haunt Wordsworth and teaches him that human behaviour is subject to nature's moral laws. **Page 343**

○ 8 from *The Prelude*: 'Skating' (OL)

This memory of skating with his friends on a frozen lake is much more positive. However, the poet is still drawn towards the greater beauty and mystery of his natural surroundings. **Page 347**

○ 9 'Tintern Abbey'

After five years' absence, Wordsworth revisits the abbey ruins in the beautiful Welsh valley of the River Wye. This lengthy, reflective monologue celebrates the abbey's pastoral setting and highlights the poet's intimate relationship with nature. **Page 350**

(OL) indicates poems that are also prescribed for the Ordinary Level course.

1 To My Sister

It is the first mild day of March:
Each minute sweeter than before,
The redbreast sings from the tall larch
That stands beside our door.

There is a blessing in the air,   5
Which seems a sense of joy to yield
To the bare trees, and mountains bare,
And grass in the green field.

My sister! ('tis a wish of mine)
Now that our morning meal is done,   10
Make haste, your morning task resign;
Come forth and feel the sun.

Edward will come with you; and, pray,
Put on with speed your woodland dress;
And bring no book: for this one day   15
We'll give to idleness.

No joyless forms shall regulate
Our living calendar:
We from today, my Friend, will date
The opening of the year.   20

Love, now a universal birth,
From heart to heart is stealing,
From earth to man, from man to earth:
– It is the hour of feeling –

One moment now may give us more   25
Than years of toiling reason:
Our minds shall drink at every pore
The spirit of the season.

Some silent laws our hearts will make,
Which they shall long obey: 30
We for the year to come may take
Our temper from today.

redbreast: common name for the robin.

Edward: Wordsworth and his sister were taking care of a friend's son whose real name was Basil Montague.

And from the blessed power that rolls
About, below, above,
We'll frame the measure of our souls: 35
They shall be tuned to love.

Then come, my Sister! come, I pray,
With speed put on your woodland dress;
And bring no book: for this one day
We'll give to idleness.   40

**And from the blessed …
above:** a similar idea is
found in lines 100–102 of
'Tintern Abbey'.

'The redbreast sings'

👤 Personal Response

1. Describe the dominant mood in this poem. Support your answer with reference to the text.

2. What does the poem reveal to you about Wordsworth's own personality? Use reference to the text in your response.

3. In your opinion, do the views expressed by Wordsworth in 'To My Sister' have any relevance to our modern world? Give reasons to support your response.

👁 Critical Literacy

A bright spring morning will almost certainly lift our spirits and make us feel glad to be alive. 'To My Sister' was written in 1798, when Wordsworth was living near the beautiful Quantock Hills in Somerset. The scene is a March morning at the start of a mild English spring. All the poet does is ask his sister to wear her warm outdoor clothes, bring the young boy they were caring for and join him in taking the day off. The poem is made up of 10 four-line stanzas, each with a regular abab rhyme scheme.

POETRY FOCUS

In the first two stanzas, Wordsworth uses simple and direct description to convey a vibrant sense of the new spring season – 'the first mild day of March'. Vivid images of the 'redbreast' and the 'green field' are evidence of his closeness to nature. The poet's **conversational language** is engaging and his enthusiastic tone ('Each minute sweeter than before') increases as he acknowledges 'a blessing in the air'. It seems as though nature itself, in all its god-given wonder and beauty, is inviting him to embrace this great 'sense of joy'.

Wordsworth is obviously **keen to share his feelings** with his sister, Dorothy, to whom he seems devoted. In stanzas three and four, he urges her to forget about work and hurry outside to 'feel the sun'. The emphatic tone of the exclamation ('My sister!') echoes his sense of urgency. She should also dress for the outdoors ('your woodland dress') and 'bring no book'. The run-on line ('for this one day/We'll give to idleness') adds to the energetic rhythm and emphasises Wordsworth's eagerness that they should seize the moment while they can. It's clear that the poet feels there is a great deal more to be learned out of doors than from any book. For him, life's sensual pleasures (the sights and sounds of the great outdoors) are what matter most.

From stanza five onwards, the poet reflects on the intimate relationship between people and nature. He dismisses the restrictive routines of daily life as 'joyless forms' and looks forward to a new 'living calendar'. For Wordsworth, the mysteries and delights of nature will be both **an emotional and spiritual experience**. Springtime is a new birth, an astonishing stirring of 'universal' love. This 'hour of feeling' will bring him into harmony with a greater love, a cosmic force that enriches the whole of creation – nature and human nature – 'From earth to man, from man to earth'.

The poet develops this idealistic theme of **nature's positive influence** in stanzas seven to nine by contrasting the limitations of people's 'toiling reason' with the limitless delights on offer in our natural surroundings, which 'Our minds shall drink at every pore'. Wordsworth is equally convinced of nature's beneficial effects, not just in allowing us to get in touch with our feelings, but in humanising society's 'laws' and transforming all our lives so that 'They shall be tuned to love'.

In the final stanza (almost identical to stanza four), the poet again asks his sister to join him in enjoying the pleasures of nature. The relaxed tone, brisk rhythm and regular end-rhymes leave us in no doubt about Wordsworth's increasingly cheerful mood. Throughout the poem, he has used simple, everyday language to **celebrate the beauty of creation**. It is ironic that planning a whole day of 'idleness' could produce such worthwhile lessons for the poet – especially the belief in the way our senses can recognise the 'blessed power' of creation.

| 324

🖋 Writing About the Poem

It has been said that there is a vitality to Wordsworth's language. Do you agree that this quality is evident in 'To My Sister'? Give reasons for your answer, illustrating your points with reference or quotation.

Sample Paragraph

'To My Sister' is typical of Wordsworth's poetry. The writing is colloquial, especially the opening where he sets the scene – 'It is the first mild day of March'. But immediately he fills in the scene with lively images of the robin singing and the 'tall larch' outside his door. The tone becomes more enthusiastic and imperative in stanza three, where Wordsworth persuades Dorothy to accompany him on a day of idleness. 'My sister!' and 'Make haste' reflect his excitement at the thought of exploring the great outdoors. The dynamic rhythm also gives the poem energy and vigorous balance in some of the lines – 'From earth to man, from man to earth'. There are also a number of upbeat images, such as when he describes nature as 'Our living calendar'. There is energetic repetition – for example, when he mentions the 'blessed power' that exists 'About, below, above'. To a large extent, the strength of Wordsworth's writing is its simplicity. His use of language keeps the poem moving along at a strident pace, making his enthusiasm for nature infectious.

EXAMINER'S COMMENT

A well-focused top-grade response that addresses the question directly. Selected key quotations are handled with assurance to illustrate the energy and originality of Wordsworth's writing. Expression is impressive throughout, with varied sentence lengths and controlled expression (e.g. 'more enthusiastic and imperative', 'dynamic rhythm', 'strident pace').

🖋 Class/Homework Exercises

1. Wordsworth set out to use 'language actually spoken' by ordinary people. In your view, did he succeed in doing this in 'To My Sister'? Support your answer with reference to the text of the poem.

2. Trace the pattern of varying tones used by Wordsworth over the course of this poem, commenting on the impact they make. Support your answer with reference to the text.

⊙ Points to Consider

- **Wordsworth's close relationship with his sister is a central theme.**

- **Emphasis on the strong spiritual benefits of the natural world.**

- **The personal beliefs of the poet are in keeping with those of the Romantic Movement.**

- **Effective use of repetition, blend of nature imagery, variety of tones.**

2 A slumber did my spirit seal

A slumber did my spirit seal;
  I had no human fears:
She seemed a thing that could not feel
  The touch of earthly years.

No motion has she now, no force;   5
  She neither hears nor sees;
Rolled round in earth's diurnal course,
  With rocks, and stones, and trees.

slumber: sleep.
spirit: soul, consciousness.
seal: close up.

motion: movement.

diurnal: daily.

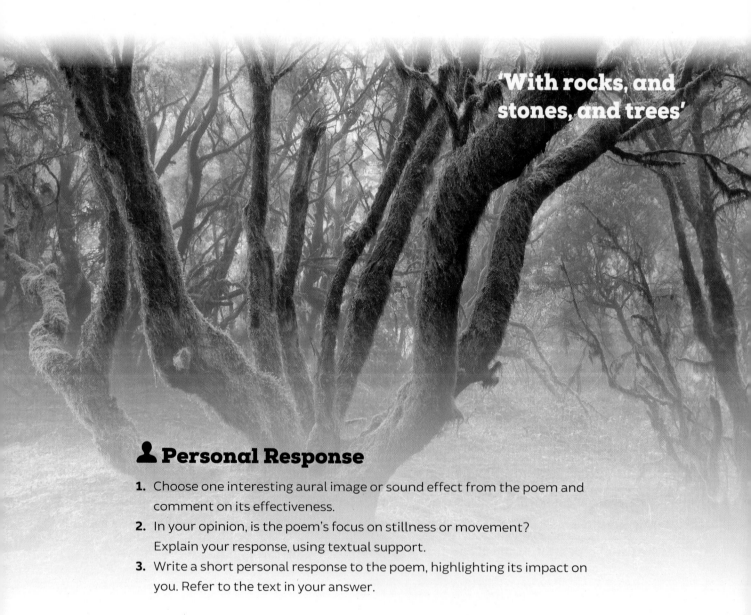

'With rocks, and stones, and trees'

👤 Personal Response

1. Choose one interesting aural image or sound effect from the poem and comment on its effectiveness.

2. In your opinion, is the poem's focus on stillness or movement? Explain your response, using textual support.

3. Write a short personal response to the poem, highlighting its impact on you. Refer to the text in your answer.

◉ Critical Literacy

This poem is part of the collection known as the 'Lucy poems' and was regarded by Coleridge, a close friend of Wordsworth's and fellow Romantic poet, as a 'most sublime epitaph'. An elegy is usually written for someone famous who has achieved great things in his/her life. This elegy is written for the unknown Lucy, whose importance was her effect on the poet. The poem suggests Lucy's qualities and how Wordsworth was affected by her death.

The 'Lucy poems' cannot be related to one specific person, although it is often thought that Wordsworth's sister Dorothy, with whom he had a very close relationship, may be the inspiration for these poems. But it is not clear if they actually refer to a real person or someone imagined. The opening image in the first stanza is one of the poet falling into a pleasant sleep. The alliteration of the soft 's' sound induces a relaxed feeling. The poet is now in another state, one of **suspended animation**, where there are no 'human fears'. He is beyond considerations of passing time, loss and death. The use of the past tense shows that this is a recollected incident. 'She' suggests a mystery. We are given no details except that she is beyond the reach of time: 'could not feel/The touch of earthly years'. It appeared ('seemed') as if she did not grow old. We are left wondering if this is a delusion.

In stanza two, the change of tense unsettles: 'No motion has she now.' Time has touched her. There has been a radical change in her condition. Lucy is incapable of action or strength. But now we are left with another enigmatic mystery: although she herself is incapable of ordinary physical movement, she is 'Rolled round'. **Now she is part of the great force of nature.** She is no longer an individual. The alliteration of 'r' and the word 'diurnal' (the only word in the poem that has more than two syllables) add to this feeling of continuous movement of the earth as it spins on its axis. Lucy has been able to connect with nature in a way that the poet cannot.

Wordsworth believed that if a poet's 'works be good, they contain within themselves all that is necessary, to their being comprehended and relished'. In that case, the identity of 'She' is irrelevant. The poet ends with an **acceptance that transience is inevitable and natural**, yet also mysterious and ambiguous. The punctuation of the final line causes the reader to pause and reflect on life and death. This little lyric is deceptive, as contained within its eight lines is a complex exploration of life, transience, mortality and eternity. As the earth revolves on its axis, so the poem revolves on two musical words, 'slumber' and 'diurnal'. This short lyric poem is haunting in its simplicity. By narrating the story of Lucy's immortality, Wordsworth seems to desire the same peace Lucy has found after becoming part of nature.

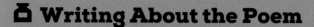 Writing About the Poem

'Wordsworth's carefully crafted poems move from personal relevance to universal relevance.' Based on your reading of 'A slumber did my spirit seal', would you consider this statement to be true? Support your response with references from the text.

Sample Paragraph

'A slumber did my spirit seal' explores the poet's response to loss and his acceptance of change. This simple poem, with its regular lines and even rhythm, deals with huge themes, transience and death. In the first stanza, 'She' is above the march of time, 'could not feel/The touch of earthly years'. She is not real, a 'thing' which does not age. She is no longer aware, 'neither hears nor sees'. She is not a conscious individual, but part of the bigger picture of the world of nature as she is 'Rolled round'. The alliteration emphasises the fact that as the earth goes through its daily course she is moved, as are the 'rocks, and stones, and trees'. The interconnectedness of all things is stressed, as all move around according to the laws of nature. The use of the present tense encourages the reader to view her as part of nature's grand plan of continuity. The highly personal feeling of loss felt by everyone at some point in their lives is translated into a universal acceptance of transience.

EXAMINER'S COMMENT

A mature top-grade answer to a challenging question. Good engagement with both theme (the personal leading to universal significance) and style (sound effects, present tense, etc.). Points are clearly stated and aptly supported. The accomplished final sentence rounds off the discussion effectively.

✎ Class/Homework Exercises

1. 'A slumber did my spirit seal' is an example of a poem that is both sad and uplifting at the same time. Discuss with reference to the text.
2. Comment on the poet's use of language throughout the poem. Support your answer with reference to the text.

⊙ Points to Consider

- One of several 'Lucy poems' recording Lucy's life and death.

- Wordsworth uses characteristically simple language.

- Some effective imagery and metaphors.

- Range of tones – emotive, reflective, gloomy, etc.

3

She dwelt among the untrodden ways

WILLIAM WORDSWORTH

She dwelt among the untrodden ways
   Beside the springs of Dove,
A Maid whom there were none to praise
   And very few to love:

A violet by a mossy stone   5
   Half hidden from the eye!
– Fair as a star, when only one
   Is shining in the sky.

She lived unknown, and few could know
   When Lucy ceased to be;   10
But she is in her grave, and, oh,
   The difference to me!

untrodden: remote; unspoiled.
Dove: an English river.

Maid: young girl.

'But she is in her grave'

👤 Personal Response

1. Choose one image from the poem that you find particularly effective. Briefly explain your choice.
2. From your own reading of the poem, what is your impression of Lucy?
3. Comment on the tone of the last two lines. Is it optimistic or pessimistic? Give reasons for your answer.

◉ Critical Literacy

'She dwelt among the untrodden ways' is the best-known of Wordsworth's short series of 'Lucy poems'. These were probably written during the winter of 1799 when he was living in Germany. This short poem combines the beauty and simplicity that is the hallmark of Wordsworth's work. It is written with a sparseness that captures Lucy's plain character and natural way of life. While Lucy remains an enigmatic figure, it seems clear that the poet is deeply affected by her death.

In the opening stanza, Wordsworth chooses very **simple language** (mainly one-syllable words) to describe the isolated area where Lucy lived. Her anonymity is emphasised from the start – she is 'A Maid whom there were none to praise'. No details are given. Instead, her sincerity and gentleness are suggested. Although she is a solitary figure and somewhat unappreciated, she is one of nature's children. The poet also highlights her loneliness – she had 'very few to love'. He himself admires her rustic simplicity and seems to believe that more sophisticated people can learn a lot from her.

The second stanza explores Lucy's innocence and beauty through **contrasting images**. Wordsworth sees her as a 'violet by a mossy stone' in harmony with her rustic world. However, he balances this view of a simple country girl with a more forceful simile. She is also 'Fair as a star, when only one/Is shining in the sky'. These vivid comparisons are both drawn from nature to highlight Lucy's modest charm and striking individuality. They might also reflect Wordsworth's own deep sense of the mystery in all of creation.

This idea is developed further in the third stanza with a renewed **focus on Lucy's 'unknown' life**. While Wordsworth is clearly affected by Lucy's life and death, we are left to guess about his own thoughts and feelings. The final lines are emphatic, perhaps suggesting pain and loss at her death. However, the poet does not clarify the 'difference' Lucy's passing has made. Is the tone mournful or celebratory – or both? Is he simply reminding us that we can never fully know another person?

'She dwelt among the untrodden ways' contains several features associated with traditional folk ballads and fairy tales, which often told unhappy stories of young girls in a dramatic style. Tragic tales of such young lives were also a common feature of the Romantic poets. Wordsworth's account of Lucy is much more restrained (she simply 'ceased to be') and concentrates on his own reaction to her death. The use of regular rhyme along with a quietly dignified rhythm contributes much to the poem's **attractive musical qualities** – and to the mysterious appeal of Lucy herself.

🖋 Writing About the Poem

'"She dwelt among the untrodden ways" closely identifies human beings with the natural world.' Discuss this statement, supporting your answer with reference to the poem.

Sample Paragraph

I would agree with this view. Lucy is the central figure and she is portrayed as a personification of nature. She is described as living in the wilderness 'among the untrodden ways'. Wordsworth celebrates her closeness to the earth – she grows up alongside the riverbank – 'the springs of Dove'. There is a childlike quality to Wordsworth's writing which links the simplicity of his language to the humble life Lucy led. But Lucy is also compared to a single star 'shining in the sky'. The word 'shining' suggests the beauty of her life and the impact it has made on the poet. This comparison shows her uniqueness. She is the 'only one' in the sky. This suggests that every life is equally important as part of God's creation. Wordsworth believed in a shared spirit throughout nature. In her grave, Lucy has returned to this universal spirit. In both life and death, she is part of nature.

EXAMINER'S COMMENT

A well-focused high-grade paragraph that makes clear points in response to the question. Quotations are used effectively throughout. The style is a little note-like (with an over-reliance on short sentences) and repetitive in places, but the final point is confidently expressed.

✒ Class/Homework Exercises

1. In your opinion, is 'She dwelt among the untrodden ways' still relevant today? Give a reason for your answer.
2. How effective is Wordsworth's use of monosyllabic language, regular rhyme and the features of fairy tales in capturing Lucy's character in this poem? Refer closely to the text in your response.

⊙ Points to Consider

- **Emphasis on harmonious, universal world of nature.**

- **Simple language captures Lucy's innocence.**

- **Contrasting natural imagery.**

- **Regular rhyme, rhythm, gentle musical effects.**

4 Composed Upon Westminster Bridge

3 September 1802

Earth has not anything to show more fair:
Dull would he be of soul who could pass by
A sight so touching in its majesty:
This City now doth, like a garment, wear
The beauty of the morning; silent, bare,   5
Ships, towers, domes, theatres, and temples lie
Open unto the fields, and to the sky;
All bright and glittering in the smokeless air.
Never did sun more beautifully steep
In his first splendour, valley, rock, or hill;   10
Ne'er saw I, never felt, a calm so deep!
The river glideth at his own sweet will:
Dear God! the very houses seem asleep;
And all that mighty heart is lying still!

fair: beautiful; fine.

doth: does.

towers, domes, theatres, temples: the panoramic view of London, including the Houses of Parliament, Westminster Abbey and the dome of St Paul's Cathedral.
steep: soak; saturate.

'The beauty of the morning'

👤 Personal Response

1. Which one of these words best describes the poet's tone in the opening line: emphatic, reflective, sentimental, persuasive? Briefly explain your response.
2. Choose one image from the poem that you find particularly interesting. Give a reason for your choice.
3. Does the ending of the poem suggest uneasiness or calm? Does the poet feel that this moment will soon be gone or that it will always remain?

👁 Critical Literacy

Written, according to Wordsworth, 'on the roof of a coach' as he set out for France to visit his daughter Caroline and her mother, the poet succeeds in capturing the freshness and beauty of a city before the day's rush begins. His sister Dorothy accompanied him and wrote of the scene in her journal: 'The City, St Paul's, with the River and a multitude of little boats, made a most beautiful sight as we crossed Westminster Bridge.' Wordsworth uses the strict form of the Petrarchan sonnet as he meditates on the scene, which Dorothy describes as having 'the purity of one of nature's own grand spectacles'.

The poem opens with the confident assertion that the world has no sight more beautiful than this early morning scene of London: 'Earth has not anything to show more fair.' The strong **monosyllables underline the statement** and create a note of expectancy in the reader. The poet goes on to claim that only a person who was lacking in spirit would not find this scene emotionally moving. Although the poem is set in a particular place and time – London on 3 September 1802 – the scope of the poem, like the city, moves beyond its boundaries to celebrate the beauty of nature.

The word 'majesty' suggests that the scene has the grandeur of both king and God. In line 4, the focus of the poem moves from the general to the particular, signalled by the word 'This'. The city is given a capital letter, as if it were a person, and further **personification** is used to show how London assumes this beauty: 'This City now doth, like a garment, wear/The beauty of the morning.' People wear magnificent clothes to create an impression, but clothes are changed frequently and this suggests that the beauty of the city is only temporary, as it can be cast aside like an item of clothing.

Wordsworth did not like cities; he regarded them as dehumanising places full of noise. Notice how the adjectives used reinforce this idea: 'silent, bare.' The panoramic sweep of the cityscape from Westminster Bridge is impressive: 'Ships, towers, domes, theatres, and temples.' These 'lie/Open' – the city has the capacity to expand, bringing in its surroundings, the 'fields' and the 'sky'. The poet shows us the interconnectedness of city and nature.

Even the buildings appear 'bright and glittering'. The air is 'smokeless'. Why? The capital is quiet before the morning rush of people, factories and transport turn it into the ugly, chaotic place Wordsworth disliked. He regarded the 'hum of cities torture'. This is why the image of the 'garment' is so apt. **Unlike the beauty of nature, which is permanent, the beauty of the city is transient.** This concludes the octet of this 14-line Petrarchan sonnet.

In the sestet, the poet compares the perfection and attraction of early morning London to a country scene, where the sun saturates 'valley, rock, or hill' with its bright light, as if it were the first day of the world: 'In his first splendour.' He is **reacting positively** to his surroundings, and the use of the present tense throughout adds to the sense of immediacy. As a Romantic, he delights in the world around him. The exclamation marks show Wordsworth's surprise at this experience. Here he uses the first-person personal pronoun 'I' as he emphatically states 'Ne'er saw I, never felt, a calm so deep!' The river echoes the peaceful state, as it is undisturbed by its busy traffic at this early hour in the morning.

The gentle rhythm and the assonance of the slender vowel sound 'i' allow the reader to experience this serenity: 'The river glideth at his own sweet will.' The emotional intensity of the phrase 'Dear God!' is at odds with the calm. Is Wordsworth realising how temporary this beauty is? The personification continues as he describes the silence of the houses that 'seem asleep'. Again, appearance is stressed by the use of the word 'seem'. The final image encompasses both the buildings and the inhabitants: 'all that mighty heart is lying still!' **This is how Wordsworth prefers the city, when it most closely resembles nature.** He does not passively observe – the sight raises questions within him which he shares with us.

✒ Writing About the Poem

'Wordsworth's choice of the sonnet form enriches the subject matter of his poem "Composed Upon Westminster Bridge".' Discuss this statement, supporting the points you make with close reference to the text.

Sample Paragraph

'Westminster Bridge' celebrates the city of London before its everyday frenzy. The poem's sonnet structure (14 lines consisting of an octet and sestet and including a strict rhyming scheme) creates a soothing effect. For Wordsworth, a city is an alien place, but here the regular rhythm and assonance contribute to the 'deep calm' experienced by the poet. His response is enthusiastic, 'Dull would he be of soul who could pass by/A sight so touching in its majesty'. This creates a fresh immediacy in the poem. The rhyme scheme reinforces the subject matter as Wordsworth states that the city of London is 'fair' because it is deserted and 'bare', without the presence of people. All the sights around him 'lie/Open ... to the sky'. So the great city is able to operate at its 'own sweet will' because it is 'lying still'. The formal sonnet structure is ideally suited to the serene, orderly city at dawn.

EXAMINER'S COMMENT

This well-informed response shows a depth of analysis of the poem's structure which is combined with a real sense of personal engagement. Clear understanding of the sonnet form throughout. An interesting and developed examination of the rhyme scheme is effectively supported with apt quotations. Expression is also impressive. An assured high-grade standard.

✒ Class/Homework Exercises

1. 'Wordsworth is often described as a poet of intense emotion.' Discuss this view with particular reference to 'Composed Upon Westminster Bridge'.
2. Wordsworth's subject matter comes from 'incidents and situations from common life'. Having studied this poem, would you agree or disagree with this statement? Refer closely to the text in your answer.

⊙ Points to Consider

- **Petrarchan sonnet celebrating the city of London.**

- **Emphatic tone reflects poet's enthusiasm.**

- **Effective use of personification and onomatopoeia.**

- **Colloquial expression, detailed description, use of comparison, etc.**

5 It is a beauteous evening, calm and free

It is a beauteous evening, calm and free,
The holy time is quiet as a Nun
Breathless with adoration; the broad sun
Is sinking down in its tranquillity;
The gentleness of heaven broods o'er the Sea:　　　　　5
Listen! the mighty Being is awake,
And doth with his eternal motion make
A sound like thunder – everlastingly.
Dear Child! dear Girl! that walkest with me here,
If thou appear untouched by solemn thought,　　　　10
Thy nature is not therefore less divine:
Thou liest in Abraham's bosom all the year;
And worshipp'st at the Temple's inner shrine,
God being with thee when we know it not.

Dear Child: Caroline, the daughter of Wordsworth and Annette Vallon.

Abraham's bosom: biblical reference for heaven.
Temple's inner shrine: the holiest place.

'The gentleness of heaven broods'

👤 Personal Response

1. Select two images from the poem that effectively show the harmony and perfection of nature. Give reasons for your choice in each case.
2. In your view, what is the poet's attitude towards the 'mighty Being'? Support your answer with reference to the text.
3. From your reading of the poem, what is your impression of the young girl? Support your answer with reference to the text.

◉ Critical Literacy

'It is a beauteous evening, calm and free' is thought to have originated from the reunion between Wordsworth and his estranged nine-year-old daughter. The poem was written after their visit to a beach near Calais in the autumn of 1802. It is a typical Petrarchan sonnet, consisting of an octave (eight lines) and a sestet (six lines). The form was popularly used by Petrarch, a 14th-century Italian writer. Other types of sonnets have less intricate rhyme patterns. The octave (or octet) usually describes a problem, while the sestet offers the resolution to it. The term 'sonnet' itself derives from the Italian 'sonetto', meaning 'little song'.

In the opening lines of 'It is a beauteous evening', Wordsworth is watching the sun set over the ocean. The evening is beautiful and calm, inspiring a mood of religious wonder, like 'a Nun/Breathless with adoration'. The explicit religious simile reflects the **poet's own intimate, spiritual relationship with nature**. There is an obvious emphasis on the reverential silence ('calm', 'quiet', 'gentleness') of the setting. This is further enhanced by the use of assonance, particularly the broad vowel sounds ('holy', 'adoration', 'broods') and by the measured rhythm of the early lines. In the midst of such tranquillity, Wordsworth's attention shifts and he suddenly notices the sound of the waves. The noise, 'like thunder', shows that the ocean is awake and its unceasing motion brings thoughts of eternity to the poet's mind.

In lines 6–8, we see the poet's **mystical view of nature**. The exclamation 'Listen!' signals his recognition of a mystical presence. The 'mighty Being' may refer to God or nature – or to God manifested through nature. At any rate, this indefinable force is in 'eternal motion' and 'everlastingly' omnipotent, making 'A sound like thunder'. Is it paradoxical that such a deafening spiritual insight should occur within the stillness of this sublime setting?

In the final six lines, Wordsworth addresses the young child ('Dear Child! dear Girl!') who walks with him by the sea. The repetition of 'dear' clearly suggests his great affection for her. Although she seems untouched by the 'solemn thought' that he is gripped by, this does not make her 'less divine'. He recognises the natural sanctity of childhood as a time when she 'worshipp'st at the Temple's inner shrine'. In other words, **she is always in the presence of God**. Is Wordsworth simply celebrating the child's instinctive spirituality? Or might he also be envious of her innate closeness to God?

The poem's conventionally Christian message is similar to the central theme of 'Composed Upon Westminster Bridge'. The religious references and biblical language ('beauteous', 'doth', 'thy') are in keeping with the **dignified tone** throughout the sonnet. In the reverential final lines, Wordsworth seems to link the young girl's spiritual beauty with the evening itself, 'calm and free'. It is as though he senses that Heaven is touching the earth and the child is as sacred as the beautiful sunset.

✒ Writing About the Poem

What is the poet's attitude to nature in 'It is a beauteous evening, calm and free'?

Sample Paragraph

Wordsworth is extremely positive about nature. The picture he paints is of a hushed evening scene along the seashore. It is 'calm and free'. He associates nature with religion all through the poem. This is seen where he says the evening is a 'holy time'. Wordsworth finds comfort in the tranquillity of nature. The beautiful image of the 'gentleness of heaven' over the sea creates a reassuring atmosphere. I can imagine the beauty of this peaceful moment when he gets a chance to think about life. Wordsworth seems to believe that nature and childhood are both divine. There is a common energy or power in nature and in the young child who is accompanying him on his walk. He refers to this natural force as a 'mighty Being'. The same power is present in the child – 'God being with thee'. Although the poem is quite short, it is clear that Wordsworth finds intense spiritual significance in the natural world.

EXAMINER'S COMMENT

A solid high-grade response, supported by suitable reference and quotation. Some further comment on how the poet's style (especially tone and rhythm) reflects his appreciation of nature would have enhanced the answer. However, the final succinct sentence rounds off the paragraph effectively.

✒ Class/Homework Exercises

1. How would you describe the dominant mood of this sonnet? Support your answer with reference to the text of the poem.
2. Comment on the impact of Wordsworth's use of sensuous language throughout this poem.

⊙ Points to Consider

• Petrarchan sonnet expressing the poet's feelings for his daughter.

• Descriptive octave followed by meditative sestet.

• Vivid imagery ranges from nature to religion.

• Effective use of varying tones – heartfelt, reflective, emphatic, etc.

6 The Solitary Reaper

WILLIAM WORDSWORTH

Behold her, single in the field,
Yon solitary Highland Lass!
Reaping and singing by herself;
Stop here, or gently pass!
Alone she cuts and binds the grain,   5
And sings a melancholy strain;
O listen! For the Vale profound
Is overflowing with the sound.

No Nightingale did ever chaunt
More welcome notes to weary bands   10
Of travellers in some shady haunt,
Among Arabian sands:
A voice so thrilling ne'er was heard
In springtime from the Cuckoo-bird,
Breaking the silence of the seas   15
Among the farthest Hebrides.

Will no one tell me what she sings? –
Perhaps the plaintive numbers flow
For old, unhappy, far-off things,
And battles long ago: 20
Or is it some more humble lay,
Familiar matter of today?
Some natural sorrow, loss, or pain,
That has been, and may be again?

Whate'er the theme, the Maiden sang   25
As if her song could have no ending;
I saw her singing at her work,
And o'er the sickle bending; –
I listened, motionless and still;
And, as I mounted up the hill,   30
The music in my heart I bore,
Long after it was heard no more.

Behold her: look at her.

Yon: that.

melancholy strain: sorrowful melody.
Vale profound: deep valley.

chaunt: sing.

Hebrides: islands off the west coast of Scotland.

plaintive numbers: sad verses.

lay: song.

theme: meaning, type of song.

sickle: curved blade used for cutting grass or grain.

'singing at her work'

👤 Personal Response

1. Comment on Wordsworth's use of tone in the first stanza. In your response, consider his choice of verbs and use of punctuation.

2. The poem is rich in imagery. Choose one image (visual or aural) and comment on its effectiveness.

3. In your opinion, why did the song have such a lasting impact on the poet? Refer to the text in your answer.

👁 Critical Literacy

On a tour of Scotland with his friend, the Romantic poet Coleridge, and his own sister Dorothy, Wordsworth came upon a lone girl reaping and singing a sad song in Erse, a type of Gaelic dialect. Although he could not understand what she was singing about, the sound of the song made such an impact on the poet that he composed this poem about it two years later, as part of his collection *Lyrical Ballads.* The girl sings of events long ago, the poet remembers the girl's song and now we remember the song also. This is 'emotion recollected in tranquillity'.

Wordsworth **addresses the reader directly**, 'Behold her ... O listen!' in the opening. This creates a sense of immediacy and intimacy between the poet and the reader. The use of the present tense adds to the freshness of the scene: 'she cuts and binds … And sings.' This freshness challenged the poets of the time, the Augustans. The Romantic poets believed in using the 'language of conversation' in their work, unlike the poetic diction that was the fashion. They were also obsessed with solitude – here, the girl is described as 'solitary', 'single', 'Alone'. The reaper is alone with nature. These poets focused on individual experience. The liberal use of exclamation marks adds energy to the scene. When he offers the choice of stopping to listen or of 'gently' passing, the poet is suggesting that to move on would show a lack of spirit, as the music is so enticing.

The second stanza, which **deals with Wordsworth's reaction to the scene**, uses the imagery of birdsong. The nightingale singing in the heat of the desert ('Arabian sands') conjures up an exotic, magical place. The Romantics revelled in the allure of foreign places. The cuckoo is then described singing in a completely different scenario – the cold, hostile, windswept North Atlantic, 'the farthest Hebrides'. The singing causes a reaction in the listeners; the nightingale's song is full of 'welcome notes to weary bands'. The cuckoo breaks the 'silence of the seas' as it signals the return of spring. In hostile settings, the birds bring relief, comfort and hope. Does the 'Highland Lass' do the same? And for whom – the reader, Wordsworth or both?

In the third stanza, we are brought back to the actual scene. Wordsworth's conversational tone invites us to **ponder what she is really singing about**: 'Will no one tell me what she sings?' Again, the focus is on the listener rather than the song, which is sung in traditional Erse. Perhaps she sings of 'old, unhappy, far-off things'. Others might hear a haunting song, telling of secrets hidden in the mists of time, a favourite topic of the Romantics. Although the song's subject matter is imperfectly understood, the mood is sensed: 'sorrow, loss, or pain.' The use of rhetorical questions invites us to join Wordsworth in wondering about the meaning of the song.

Finally, in the fourth stanza, the poet concludes that it doesn't matter what the young girl is singing about ('Whate'er the theme'), it is how she sang that stays with him. She sings in a free-flowing manner, 'As if her song could have no ending'. This might refer to the unfamiliar Gaelic tunes which give a haunting and inconclusive sound. The lack of an ending also symbolises that this song will reverberate down the generations, both passed on through the oral traditions of the area and also because **it remains in Wordsworth's memory** and is then made into a poem that is passed onto the us: 'The music in my heart I bore,/Long after it was heard no more.' The poem concludes in the past tense. The beauty and mystery of the scene surpasses time.

📇 Writing About the Poem

Wordsworth stated that poetry should 'treat of things not as they are, but as they appear; not as they exist in themselves, but as they seem to exist to the senses'. Discuss this view with reference to 'The Solitary Reaper'.

Sample Paragraph

In my opinion, it is not the actual event of hearing the girl in the fields singing which is the focus of this poem, but Wordsworth's reaction, and subsequently our response to his reaction. The impact this girl's song had on his senses is all-important, 'I listened motionless and still'. Wordsworth uses the imagery of birdsong to explain the lasting impact of this young woman's voice. His imagination takes him from the 'Vale profound' to a song in the heat of the 'Arabian sands', and then to the 'farthest Hebrides', as he explains how comfort and hope is brought to listeners. But nothing is 'so thrilling' as the 'Maiden's song'. He prefers the human voice. So the emphasis in this poem is on the impact the music had ('The music in my heart I bore'). Although Wordsworth describes the girl vividly in stanza one, 'Alone she cut and binds the grain,/ And sings a melancholy refrain', it is when he is reflecting and speculating on the song that really remains with the reader.

✒ Class/Homework Exercises

1. Comment on Wordsworth's attitude to nature in 'The Solitary Reaper'. Support your answer with reference to the text.
2. In your own words, describe the impact of the girl's song on Wordsworth. Support your answer with reference to the poem.

⊙ Points to Consider

- Memory and nature are central themes.
- The poem blends detailed description with personal reflection.
- Effective use of vivid comparisons and contrasts.
- Sibilant and alliterative effects add a musical quality to the poem.

7 from *The Prelude:* The Stolen Boat

The Prelude is Wordsworth's longest poem. It is largely autobiographical and contains much of the poet's own ideas on poetry and on life.

One summer evening (led by her) I found
A little boat tied to a willow tree
Within a rocky cave, its usual home.
Straight I unloosed her chain, and stepping in
Pushed from the shore. It was an act of stealth   5
And troubled pleasure, nor without the voice
Of mountain-echoes did my boat move on;
Leaving behind her still, on either side,
Small circles glittering idly in the moon,
Until they melted all into one track   10
Of sparkling light. But now, like one who rows,
Proud of his skill, to reach a chosen point
With an unswerving line, I fixed my view
Upon the summit of a craggy ridge,
The horizon's utmost boundary; for above   15
Was nothing but the stars and the grey sky.
She was an elfin pinnace; lustily
I dipped my oars into the silent lake,
And, as I rose upon the stroke, my boat
Went heaving through the water like a swan;   20
When, from behind that craggy steep till then
The horizon's bound, a huge peak, black and huge,
As if with voluntary power instinct
Upreared its head. I struck and struck again,
And growing still in stature the grim shape   25
Towered up between me and the stars, and still,
For so it seemed, with purpose of its own
And measured motion like a living thing,
Strode after me. With trembling oars I turned,
And through the silent water stole my way   30
Back to the covert of the willow tree;
There in her mooring-place I left my bark, –
And through the meadows homeward went, in grave
And serious mood; but after I had seen
That spectacle, for many days, my brain   35
Worked with a dim and undetermined sense
Of unknown modes of being; o'er my thoughts
There hung a darkness, call it solitude
Or blank desertion. No familiar shapes
Remained, no pleasant images of trees,   40

her: nature.

unswerving: straight.

elfin pinnace: small boat.

bound: boundary.
As if ... instinct: as though it had special powers.

covert: shelter.

bark: boat.

undetermined: uncertain.

unknown modes: mysteries.
solitude: alienation.

343 |

Of sea or sky, no colours of green fields;
But huge and mighty forms, that do not live
Like living men, moved slowly through the mind
By day, and were a trouble to my dreams.

mighty forms: terrifying
dreams.

'an elfin pinnace'

👤 Personal Response

1. What impression of nature is given in lines 1–11 of the poem?
2. A significant change of tone occurs after line 21. Briefly explain the change. How does Wordsworth convey this change through his use of language?
3. Write your own personal response to the poem. Your answer should make close reference to the text.

👁 Critical Literacy

Taken from Wordsworth's long autobiographical poem, *The Prelude*, this extract narrates a childhood experience dominated by fear. Written in blank verse (unrhymed with a regular iambic pentameter rhythm), the poem recalls a memorable occurrence on a tranquil summer evening. In many of his poems, the poet seemed to be happiest when he had only nature for company. However, in 'The Stolen Boat', Wordsworth projects his own feelings onto a hostile landscape and discovers that nature is enforcing a moral lesson that was to affect him for the rest of his life.

The poem opens with a few well-chosen **narrative details** ('summer evening', 'little boat', 'rocky cave') that recreate this memorable scene from early boyhood. Wordsworth remembers being captivated by the beauty of nature ('led by her') and it first seems that he is casually recalling a nostalgic moment from his past. However, the mood changes in line 5: 'It was an act of stealth.' The underlying sense of wrongdoing is emphasised by the phrase 'troubled pleasure', a further admission of disquiet.

Any guilty feelings are quickly replaced with a vivid description of the exquisite surroundings on that magical evening. The image of the child alone in the boat is powerfully evoked through vivid details, such as 'I dipped my oars into the silent lake' and 'Small circles glittering idly in the moon'. There is an increasing sense of the poet's close **affinity with his natural surroundings** as he grows aware of the 'sparkling light' all around him. By line 12, he imagines himself as a young romantic hero and thinks of the boat as 'an elfin pinnace' being spirited over the water. He is conscious also of his own strength confidently guiding the small craft. The simile ('heaving through the water like a swan') effectively captures all the delicacy and naturalness of the movement.

However, this sublime experience is dramatically interrupted in lines 21–22 with the appearance of 'a huge peak, black and huge' towering before him. The child imagines it as a monstrous figure that 'Upreared its head'. **His terror grows out of his guilt**, which in turn causes him to invest the cliff with awesome, primitive powers. Ironically, the insistent repetition of 'I struck and struck again' underscores the boy's powerlessness. He is compelled to recognise nightmarish forces that he cannot control. Indeed, the more he tries to escape the 'grim shape', the more the mountains seem to shadow him.

The disturbing sequence is relieved with the child's shameful return to 'the covert of the willow tree'. But the menacing experience ('That spectacle') continues to haunt him and he tries to understand its significance 'for many days'. Through the rest of the poem, Wordsworth attempts to clarify his vague understanding ('a dim and undetermined sense') of the moral relationship between human beings and the natural world. He feels as if nature has punished him for his earlier wrongdoing in stealing the boat. An **uneasy mood of guilt and uncertainty** dominates lines 39–44. This is emphasised by a series of negatives ('no pleasant images of trees', 'no colours of green fields'). There is little doubt that the poet still finds difficulty coming to terms with such a traumatic event from his past. Only in composing the poem many years later does Wordsworth recognise the way such episodes have shaped his life. He can finally acknowledge that the experience was sublime.

✒ Writing About the Poem

How does Wordsworth present nature in 'The Stolen Boat'? Does it seem beautiful, benevolent, intimidating or mysterious?

Sample Paragraph

Wordsworth is usually described as a great lover of nature. This is true of many of his poems. But it is not the case with 'The Stolen Boat'. At first, he presents what looks like a harmless childhood memory. He 'found' a little

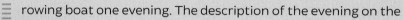

rowing boat one evening. The description of the evening on the 'silent lake' seems relaxed. Nature is a watchful female figure and he is 'led by her'. But this doesn't last. The mountain suddenly seems threatening – a 'craggy steep'. To his innocent mind, it becomes a 'living thing' looming over him. He is terrified. He retreats back to the shoreline where he tries to come to terms with stealing the boat. His own guilt-ridden conscience is now like nature itself – 'a darkness'. The incident has taught him a lesson. Human nature is part of the natural world. Wordsworth believes that there is a definite link between our human moral laws and the harmony of nature. In the end, he seems troubled by all that has happened and more respectful of nature.

✒ Class/Homework Exercises

1. 'The Stolen Boat' has been described as a highly dramatic poem. Do you agree with this view? Give reasons for your answer, supporting the points you make with reference to the text.
2. In your own words, trace Wordsworth's changing emotions over the course of the poem. Support your answer with reference to the text.

⊙ Points to Consider

- Poet's boyhood experience brings him closer to the wonders of nature.

- Detailed language and vivid imagery of the natural world.

- Effective use of personification, repetition, varying moods.

- Wordsworth draws some moral strength from the dramatic incident.

8 from *The Prelude: Skating*

And in the frosty season, when the sun
Was set, and visible for many a mile
The cottage windows blazed through twilight gloom,
I heeded not their summons: happy time
It was indeed for all of us – for me   5
It was a time of rapture! Clear and loud
The village clock tolled six, – I wheeled about,
Proud and exulting like an untired horse
That cares not for his home. All shod with steel,
We hissed along the polished ice in games   10
Confederate, imitative of the chase
And woodland pleasures,– the resounding horn,
The pack loud chiming, and the hunted hare.
So through the darkness and the cold we flew,
And not a voice was idle; with the din   15
Smitten, the precipices rang aloud;
The leafless trees and every icy crag
Tinkled like iron; while far distant hills
Into the tumult sent an alien sound
Of melancholy not unnoticed, while the stars   20
Eastward were sparkling clear, and in the west
The orange sky of evening died away.
Not seldom from the uproar I retired
Into a silent bay, or sportively
Glanced sideway, leaving the tumultuous throng,   25
To cut across the reflex of a star
That fled, and, flying still before me, gleamed
Upon the glassy plain; and oftentimes
When we had given our bodies to the wind,
And all the shadowy banks on either side   30
Came sweeping through the darkness, spinning still
The rapid line of motion, then at once
Have I, reclining back upon my heels,
Stopped short; yet still the solitary cliffs
Wheeled by me – even as if the earth had rolled   35
With visible motion her diurnal round!
Behind me did they stretch in solemn train,
Feebler and feebler, and I stood and watched
Till all was tranquil as a dreamless sleep.

rapture: wonderful excitement; bliss.

exulting: rejoicing.

shod with steel: wearing skates.
games/Confederate: playing in groups.

din: loud noise.

Smitten: struck by.
precipices: steep cliffs.

melancholy: deep sorrow.

Glanced: moved.
tumultuous throng: noisy crowd of skaters.
reflex: reflection.

glassy plain: smooth ice.

diurnal: daily.

train: line.

👤 Personal Response

1. 'It was a time of rapture!' How is the boy's feeling of 'rapture' conveyed throughout the poem?
2. What impression of Wordsworth himself as a young boy do you get from reading 'Skating'?
3. What picture of nature emerges from this poem? Support your answer with reference to the text.

👁 Critical Literacy

This extract from *The Prelude* is a fond memory of Wordsworth's schooldays. The poem describes an evening's ice-skating on the frozen surface of Esthwaite Water in the north-west of England. It was getting dark and the lights in the cottages plus the chiming of the clock reminded him that he should be indoors. However, his desire to continue skating with his friends was so strong that he decided to take no notice of time. For Wordsworth, the centre of this extraordinary experience is the way in which people and landscape are so closely interrelated.

In the opening lines, the poet invites us into the special world of his boyhood with a simple description of a memorable winter scene – 'the frosty season'. His personal narrative has a richly **nostalgic tone and the vivid imagery immediately sets the scene**: 'The cottage windows blazed through twilight gloom.' As the poet begins to relive the moment, his language reflects the intense sense of delight and freedom that he felt during that 'happy time'. The repetition and run-on lines emphasise the tremendous excitement he recalls: 'for all of us – for me/It was a time of rapture!'

Wordsworth goes on to describe the thrilling experience of skating in lines 7–14. What is most noticeable is the **vitality of the language**, particularly the dynamic verbs ('wheeled', 'hissed', 'flew'). Acutely observing the movement, he makes use of both the urgent rhythm and a powerful simile to capture his exhilaration: 'I wheeled about,/Proud and exulting like an untired horse.' The comparison is developed further when he describes the skaters as seemingly 'shod with steel'. Musical sibilance reinforces the importance of the memory: 'We hissed along the polished ice.' Caught up in the moment, the children imagine themselves as wild hounds pursuing a hare: 'The pack loud chiming.' Onomatopoeia ('We hissed along') conveys the fast movement. Speed is more obviously shown by the use of the verb 'flew'.

Indeed, **sound effects are used successfully throughout**, including lines 15–22, where the poet continues to bring the noisy scene to life: 'with the din/Smitten, the precipices rang aloud.' The activity ('uproar') is in contrast with the 'silent' landscape surrounding the skaters. Wordsworth remembers leaving 'the tumultuous throng' to seek out a quieter area where he skates round and round. When he stops, he feels the earth is still spinning on 'her diurnal round' and for a brief moment he feels connected to the wider universe surrounding him. Fascinated as always by the vast solitude, he takes time to reflect on the

'It was a time of rapture!'

mysterious relationships between people and nature. The underlying sense of sadness is never explained. Perhaps the assonant phrase 'alien sound/Of melancholy' reflects the reality of time passing and that even echoes die.

After all the dramatic exuberance, the mood becomes subdued and reverential in the eloquent final lines. Overcome by the beauty and majesty of 'the shadowy banks on either side', Wordsworth tells us that he simply 'stood and watched'. Although the boy does not realise that he is learning about the transience of life, the adult poet does. 'All was tranquil as a dreamless sleep' might refer to the dying of day, just as other images (the sun setting and the child spinning in circles on his skates) signified the harmonious movement of the universe. To a large extent, the poem is about the passage of time, which is in itself a difficult concept. In the skating episode, the child Wordsworth is simply playing on a lake with his friends. However, such life-shaping memories (he later called them 'spots of time') made him see **nature as a formative force that enriches our understanding of life**.

🖋 Writing About the Poem

From your reading of 'Skating', would you say that Wordsworth is a writer of great descriptive power? Support your answer with reference to the text of the poem.

Sample Paragraph

I think 'Skating' is remarkably descriptive. Wordsworth uses contrast to describe the cottage windows, which 'blazed through twilight gloom' and skilfully weaves these with revelations about his own exited emotions – 'It was a time of rapture!' He really gives me a sense of what it was like to be skating on ice. The feeling of moving at speed and yet being close to danger is suggested through lively phrases like 'I wheeled about' and 'sweeping through the darkness'. Wordsworth builds up a vivid picture of the landscape at dusk. There are 'leafless trees', an 'orange sky' and 'solitary cliffs'. He also uses comparisons to show the recklessness of the children playing. They are like a pack of wild dogs chasing 'the hunted hare'. Such descriptive details really bring out the excitement of the scene.

EXAMINER'S COMMENT

A focused high-grade response, very well-supported by useful reference and quotations. The expression is varied and controlled. While some mention of sound effects would have been welcome, there is a convincing sense of engagement with how Wordsworth's descriptive power creates a pervasive mood of exhilaration within the poem.

✒ Class/Homework Exercises

1. Comment on the effectiveness of rhythm and movement in 'Skating', supporting your answer with reference to the text.
2. In your opinion, is this a realistic childhood memory? Or is it nostalgic and sentimental? Support your answer with reference to the poem.

Tintern Abbey

Five years have past; five summers, with the length
Of five long winters! and again I hear
These waters, rolling from their mountain-springs
With a soft inland murmur. – Once again
Do I behold these steep and lofty cliffs,   5
That on a wild secluded scene impress
Thoughts of more deep seclusion; and connect
The landscape with the quiet of the sky.
The day is come when I again repose
Here, under this dark sycamore, and view   10
These plots of cottage-ground, these orchard tufts,
Which at this season, with their unripe fruits,
Are clad in one green hue, and lose themselves
'Mid groves and copses. Once again I see
These hedge-rows, hardly hedge-rows, little lines   15
Of sportive wood run wild: these pastoral farms,
Green to the very door; and wreaths of smoke
Sent up, in silence, from among the trees!
With some uncertain notice, as might seem
Of vagrant dwellers in the houseless woods,   20
Or of some Hermit's cave, where by his fire
The Hermit sits alone.
                          These beauteous forms,
Through a long absence, have not been to me
As is a landscape to a blind man's eye:
But oft, in lonely rooms, and 'mid the din   25
Of towns and cities, I have owed to them,
In hours of weariness, sensations sweet,
Felt in the blood, and felt along the heart;
And passing even into my purer mind,
With tranquil restoration: – feelings too   30
Of unremembered pleasure: such, perhaps,
As have no slight or trivial influence
On that best portion of a good man's life,
His little, nameless, unremembered, acts
Of kindness and of love. Nor less, I trust,   35
To them I may have owed another gift,
Of aspect more sublime; that blessed mood
In which the burthen of the mystery,
In which the heavy and the weary weight

Five years have past: Wordsworth is now revisiting the ruins of Tintern Abbey and the River Wye, which he had first seen five years earlier on a walking tour.

sycamore: large shady tree.

orchard tufts: small groups of fruit trees.

hue: colour.

groves and copses: wooded areas.

vagrant dwellers: wandering gypsies.
Hermit: loner, recluse.

sublime: exquisite, awe-inspiring.

burthen of the mystery: the weight of the wonder of life.

| 350

Of all this unintelligible world,   40
Is lightened: – that serene and blessed mood,
In which the affections gently lead us on, –
Until, the breath of this corporeal frame
And even the motion of our human blood
Almost suspended, we are laid asleep   45
In body, and become a living soul:
While with an eye made quiet by the power
Of harmony, and the deep power of joy,
We see into the life of things.
                              If this
Be but a vain belief, yet, oh! how oft –   50
In darkness and amid the many shapes
Of joyless day light; when the fretful stir
Unprofitable, and the fever of the world,
Have hung upon the beatings of my heart –
How oft, in spirit, have I turned to thee,   55
O sylvan Wye! thou wanderer thro' the woods,
How often has my spirit turned to thee!

        And now, with gleams of half-extinguished thought,
With many recognitions dim and faint,
And somewhat of a sad perplexity,   60
The picture of the mind revives again:
While here I stand, not only with the sense
Of present pleasure, but with pleasing thoughts
That in this moment there is life and food
For future years. And so I dare to hope,   65
Though changed, no doubt, from what I was when first
I came among these hills; when like a roe
I bounded o'er the mountains, by the sides
Of the deep rivers, and the lonely streams,
Wherever nature led: more like a man   70
Flying from something that he dreads than one
Who sought the thing he loved. For nature then
(The coarser pleasures of my boyish days,
And their glad animal movements all gone by)
To me was all in all. – I cannot paint   75
What then I was. The sounding cataract
Haunted me like a passion: the tall rock,
The mountain, and the deep and gloomy wood,
Their colours and their forms, were then to me
An appetite; a feeling and a love,   80
That had no need of a remoter charm,
By thought supplied, nor any interest
Unborrowed from the eye. – That time is past,

affections: feelings;
sensations.
corporeal frame: body.

fretful: uneasy, distressed.

sylvan: tree-lined banks of
the River Wye.

half-extinguished thought:
memories that are half-
forgotten.

roe: deer.

cataract: waterfall.

351 |

And all its aching joys are now no more,
And all its dizzy raptures. Not for this   85
Faint I, nor mourn nor murmur; other gifts
Have followed; for such loss, I would believe,
Abundant recompense. For I have learned
To look on nature, not as in the hour
Of thoughtless youth; but hearing often-times   90
The still, sad music of humanity,
Nor harsh nor grating, though of ample power
To chasten and subdue. And I have felt
A presence that disturbs me with the joy
Of elevated thoughts; a sense sublime   95
Of something far more deeply interfused,
Whose dwelling is the light of setting suns,
And the round ocean and the living air,
And the blue sky, and in the mind of man:
A motion and a spirit, that impels   100
All thinking things, all objects of all thought,
And rolls though all things. Therefore am I still
A lover of the meadows and the woods,
And mountains; and of all that we behold
From this green earth; of all the mighty world   105
Of eye, and ear, – both what they half create,
And what perceive; well pleased to recognise
In nature and the language of the sense
The anchor of my purest thoughts, the nurse,
The guide, the guardian of my heart, and soul   110
Of all my moral being.
                            Nor perchance,
If I were not thus taught, should I the more
Suffer my genial spirits to decay:
For thou art with me here upon the banks
Of this fair river; thou my dearest Friend,   115
My dear, dear Friend; and in thy voice I catch
The language of my former heart, and read
My former pleasures in the shooting lights
Of thy wild eyes. Oh! yet a little while
May I behold in thee what I was once,   120
My dear, dear Sister! and this prayer I make,
Knowing that Nature never did betray
The heart that loved her; 'tis her privilege,
Through all the years of this our life, to lead
From joy to joy: for she can so inform   125
The mind that is within us, so impress
With quietness and beauty, and so feed
With lofty thoughts, that neither evil tongues,

murmur: complain in a quiet, continuous way.

recompence: compensation.

A presence: an unseen being or influence.

interfused: filled with.

both what … perceive: both what is taken in by the senses and transformed by the imagination.

my dearest Friend: Dorothy, the poet's sister. She accompanied him on this walk when the poem was composed.

Rash judgements, nor the sneers of selfish men,
Nor greetings where no kindness is, nor all   130
The dreary intercourse of daily life,   **intercourse:** social activities.
Shall e'er prevail against us, or disturb
Our cheerful faith, that all which we behold
Is full of blessings. Therefore let the moon
Shine on thee in thy solitary walk;   135
And let the misty mountain-winds be free
To blow against thee: and, in after years,
When these wild ecstasies shall be matured
Into a sober pleasure; when thy mind
Shall be a mansion for all lovely forms,   140
Thy memory be as a dwelling-place
For all sweet sounds and harmonies; oh! then,
If solitude, or fear, or pain, or grief,
Should be thy portion, with what healing thoughts
Of tender joy wilt thou remember me,   145
And these my exhortations! Nor, perchance –   **exhortations:** entreaties,
If I should be where I no more can hear   urgent appeals.
Thy voice, nor catch from thy wild eyes these gleams
Of past existence – wilt thou then forget
That on the banks of this delightful stream   150
We stood together; and that I, so long
A worshipper of Nature, hither came
Unwearied in that service: rather say
With warmer love – oh! with far deeper zeal
Of holier love. Nor wilt thou then forget,   155
That after many wanderings, many years
Of absence, these steep woods and lofty cliffs,
And this green pastoral landscape, were to me   **pastoral:** rolling rural.
More dear, both for themselves and for thy sake!

'on the banks of this delightful stream'

👤 Personal Response

1. What is the dominant mood of the poem's opening section (lines 1–22)? What words and images are used to create this mood?
2. Which of these words would you use to describe the tone of the second section (lines 22–49): quiet, intense, contemplative, nostalgic, reverent? Choose two and explain your choice.
3. Write a short personal response to the poem, highlighting the impact it made on you. Support your answer with reference to the text.

👁 Critical Literacy

'Tintern Abbey' comes at the end of Wordsworth's collection, *Lyrical Ballads*. It is an intensely personal poem and shows a new preoccupation with the poet's inner life, as it is explicitly autobiographical and contains Wordsworth's ideas about nature, perception and spiritual growth. It is a reflection on the importance of the natural world to the poet and the way in which his relationship with nature has changed since boyhood. The urge to explain his own life gave rise to his greatest poetry. Wordsworth wrote this poem at the age of 28 in one day as he left Tintern Abbey: 'Not a line of it was altered ... and not any part of it written down till I reached Bristol.'

The opening (lines 1–22) describes the present moment when **the scene at the River Wye was revisited**. At first this seems to be a pictorial account of a landscape in the conventional 18th-century manner. However, on looking closer we realise that this description of the rural scene is **a projection of the poet's own mood of tranquillity**. The repetition of 'I' reminds us of his presence: 'I hear', 'I behold', 'I again repose'. The landscape is a symbol of the unity Wordsworth perceives in nature, as everything merges seamlessly: 'clad in one green hue, and lose themselves.' The tranquil mood is emphasised by the 'quiet of the sky', the 'soft inland murmur' of the river and the wreaths of smoke 'Sent up, in silence'. The **simple language** used records experience in a vivid, clear manner rather than embroidering it, as was the fashion of the times. Wordsworth uses language in ebbs and flows as speech moves in natural conversation: 'These hedge-rows, hardly hedge-rows.' This was a dramatic move away from the formal poetic diction of contemporary poets.

The second section (lines 22–49) shows us **what the place meant to him** in the intervening years between his two visits. The memory of this landscape has been a 'tranquil restoration', as it has had a therapeutic effect on the poet in 'hours of weariness' in city life. It also had a moral influence on him as it encouraged acts of 'kindness and of love'. It gave him the 'gift' of 'that serene and blessed mood' which enabled him to 'see into the life of things'. In this state of heightened perception, he becomes aware of an inner force which permeates the natural world and also himself. Wordsworth becomes less aware of his bodily self, 'our human blood/Almost suspended'. The world then stops being oppressive and problematic: 'the weary weight .../Is lightened'. This 'blessed mood' is a state of suspension where insight occurs in a period of tranquillity. Wordsworth discovers a feeling of the unity of the universe and of being part of that unity: 'become a living soul.'

In **lines 50–57**, **the poet expresses doubts**: 'If this/Be but a vain belief.' The use of natural language speaks to us from the heart as moments of certainty give way to hesitation, pauses to reflect or doubt. He is not sure whether he has really seen into the 'life of things'. There is a desperate need to believe so that he can grasp the meaning of a world that is otherwise 'unintelligible' to him. The repetitions and movement between past and present allow us to feel that we are following Wordsworth's thoughts as he tries to clarify and evaluate what nature has meant to him.

The phrase 'And now' returns the reader to the present, in **lines 58–111**, to stand alongside the poet as he remembers how this place sustained him in the past, how he is enjoying it now and how he realises that this view will sustain him in the future: 'there is life and food/For future years.' Thus past, present and future are fused together in this great harmony. He **recreates his 'boyish days' and traces his relationship with nature**, recalling his unthinking, physical enjoyment ('glad animal movements') and reliving the intense emotional and sensory delights ('aching joys' and 'dizzy raptures'). That is gone: 'That time is past.' Now he is aware of **an invisible force that unifies and drives nature**, a 'motion', a 'spirit' that 'rolls through all things'. The phrase 'I would believe' hints again at his uncertainty. Is he almost forcing himself to believe? Is his adult response to nature (the 'sense sublime') sufficient? Is it really an 'Abundant recompense' for losing 'thoughtless youth'?

In the final section, **lines 111–159**, **he examines his sister's relationship with nature** and dedicates his prayer for her. Dorothy is like a reincarnation of Wordsworth's former self – her 'wild eyes' and 'wild ecstasies' remind him of the 'aching joys' and 'dizzy raptures' of his youth: 'May I behold in thee what I was once.' He prays that nature will be a restorative force for her, helping her to deal with what life is: 'the dreary intercourse of daily life.' His sister's relationship with nature will change as his has done into a 'sober pleasure'. He now anticipates his own death as he looks into the future and hopes that he will live on in Dorothy's memory, 'on the banks of this delightful stream/ We stood together'.

The poem ends on a **religious note**. Wordsworth describes himself as 'A worshipper of Nature' and one capable of 'holier love', as he declares how 'this green pastoral landscape' meant so much to him for its own sake and also for Dorothy's sake. The reader is left with the landscape of the River Wye bound up with its impact on the poet and his responses to it. We view this place through Wordsworth's eyes forever.

🖋 Writing About the Poem

'Growth and development are central preoccupations for Wordsworth.' Discuss how Wordsworth explores the growth of his relationship with nature in the poem 'Tintern Abbey'.

Sample Paragraph

Wordsworth was very interested in his changing relationship with nature. After describing the scenery of the Wye valley, the poet remembers his younger self, 'when like a roe/I bounded o'er the mountains'. Here Wordsworth distinguishes between two phases in his relationship with nature. He describes 'the coarser pleasures' of his boyhood when enjoyment came from physical activity. He traces the intensity of his love of nature at this time, 'To me was all in all'. He responds to the 'colours' of the landscape, but his intellect was not engaged. In the second phase, he includes people in his adult response, 'the still sad music of humanity' and now he realises the unity in all things. He becomes aware of a dynamic, living force which 'rolls' through everything. He wonders if it is sufficient reward for losing the 'dizzy raptures' of youth. But he is not certain. Although he is saying that this more 'sober' response to nature is superior to his 'former pleasures', yet it is the 'sounding cataract' which has 'haunted' him 'like a passion'.

EXAMINER'S COMMENT

A commendable top-rate response to a challenging question. Clear engagement with the poem and some informed commentary on the various phases in Wordsworth's changing relationship with nature. Supportive quotations and references are interwoven throughout the answer. Expression is assured and very well-managed.

🖊 Class/Homework Exercises

1. Seamus Heaney wrote that Wordsworth established how truly 'the child is father to the man'. Discuss how Wordsworth shows that our early life determines our adulthood. Support the points you make with reference to 'Tintern Abbey'.

2. Based on your reading of 'Tintern Abbey', outline briefly what nature means to Wordsworth. Support your answer with reference to the text.

⊙ Points to Consider

- **Key theme is the central significance of nature in Wordsworth's life.**
- **Sensuous appeal of youthful experience contrasted with a deeper mature understanding.**
- **Poet openly expresses his high regard for his sister Dorothy.**
- **Recurring religious imagery reflects the spiritual importance of nature.**
- **Characteristic use of simple language, colloquial speech, varying tones.**

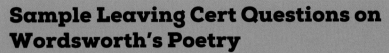

Sample Leaving Cert Questions on Wordsworth's Poetry

1. 'While aspects of transience and death are addressed in Wordsworth's heartfelt poems, these are generally balanced by the poet's own exuberant sense of life.' Discuss this view, supporting your answer with reference to both subject matter and style of the poems by William Wordsworth on your course.

2. 'Wordsworth uses striking imagery and accessible language to show that nature is central to his poetic world.' Discuss this statement, supporting your answer with reference to the poems by William Wordsworth on your course.

3. 'Wordsworth's distinctive poetic voice brings personal memories to life.' Discuss this statement, supporting your answer with reference to the poems by Wordsworth on your course.

How do I organise my answer?

(Sample question 1)

'While aspects of transience and death are addressed in Wordsworth's heartfelt poems, these are generally balanced by the poet's own exuberant sense of life.' Discuss this view, supporting your answer with reference to both subject matter and style of the poems by William Wordsworth on your course.

Sample Plan 1

Intro: *(Stance: agree with viewpoint in the question)* Wordsworth – provocative poet, idolised and dismissed. Believed poetry to be 'the spontaneous overflow of powerful feelings' which pursued the truth of man's knowledge of himself and the worlds around him. Passionate exploration of the beauty and tragedy of life.

Point 1: *(Natural beauty/order – imagery, tone, rhythm)* 'To My Sister' – the poet urges his sister to celebrate the natural beauty of a new day ('Put on with speed your woodland dress'). Underlying sense of transience and mortality. Vivid imagery, vigorous tone and rhythm reflect his intense feelings. Nature's divine quality treated similarly to 'Tintern Abbey'.

Understanding the Prescribed Poetry Question

Marks are awarded using the PCLM Marking Scheme: P = 15; C = 15; L = 15; M = 5 Total = 50

- **P** (Purpose = 15 marks) refers to the set question and is the launch pad for the answer. This involves engaging with all aspects of the question. Both theme and language must be addressed, although not necessarily equally.

- **C** (Coherence = 15 marks) refers to the organisation of the developed response and the use of accurate, relevant quotation. Paragraphing is essential.

- **L** (Language = 15 marks) refers to the student's skill in controlling language throughout the answer.

- **M** (Mechanics = 5 marks) refers to spelling and grammar.

- Although no specific number of poems is required, students usually discuss at least 3 or 4 in their written responses.

- Aim for at least 800 words, to be completed within 45–50 minutes.

Point 2: (*Transience/death – form, repetition, sibilance*) 'A slumber did my spirit seal' – lyrical elegy examines transience and death. Soft sibilance creates the impression of gently falling asleep ('A slumber did my spirit seal'). Repetition ('No motion', 'no force') reflects poet's acceptance of Lucy's changed state of lifelessness, now part of nature.

Point 3: (*Beauty of nature – simple diction, metaphor, regular rhyme*) 'She dwelt among the untrodden ways' – childish monosyllabic words describe Lucy's environment ('the spring of Dove'). Beautiful metaphor ('A violet by a mossy stone/Half hidden') describes Lucy as a personification of nature.

Conclusion: Wordsworth – delight in nature, yet realistic awareness of passing time and mortality addressed through engaging imagery and simple diction. Fills it with the great force for good – nature to be a powerful moral guide for humanity.

Sample Paragraph: Point 1

It is probably a cliché to say that Wordsworth found God in Nature, but his poems illustrate his deep spiritual relationship with the natural world. In 'To My Sister', he invites Dorothy to enjoy a day in the countryside ('Put on with speed your woodland dress'). His excited tone ('make haste') reminds us that there is not a moment to be wasted. For Wordsworth, being absorbed in nature has spiritual significance – 'There is a blessing in the air'. The run-through lines and energetic rhythms suggest the joy he feels – and there is an optimistic feeling right through the poem –'for this one day/We'll give to idleness'. The urgency to enjoy life clearly suggests that Wordsworth is deeply aware of time and the inevitability of death. Nature brings him in touch with a universal consciousness. In simple terms, he believes it will lift the spirits of his sister and himself: 'We'll frame the measure of our souls.'

EXAMINER'S COMMENT

As part of a full essay answer, this is an assured top-grade response that displays a close understanding of the poem. Insightful discussion focuses on Wordsworth's spiritual bond with the natural world. The exploration of the poet's style is impressive. Expression is varied and fluent. Suitable references and quotations support key points throughout.

NOTE

In keeping with the PCLM approach, the student has to take a stance by agreeing and/or disagreeing that Wordsworth uses:

- **striking imagery and accessible language** (sensuous imagery, detailed description, personification, variety of tones, lyricism, accessible language and references, etc.)

... to show:

- **the central place of nature in his poetic world** (developing personal response to nature – physical, emotional, contemplative, nature as a moral guide, consoler, unity in the natural world, etc.)

(Sample question 2)

'Wordsworth uses striking imagery and accessible language to show that nature is central to his poetic world.' Discuss this statement, supporting your answer with reference to the poems by William Wordsworth on your course.

Sample Plan 2

Intro: *(Stance: agree with viewpoint in this question)* Readers coming to Wordsworth's poems expecting a simple visual representation of nature's sights and sounds will be surprised. He is much more interested in the fundamental workings of nature and the relationship between man and nature.

Point 1: *(Meditation on nature – religious imagery, simple diction)* 'Tintern Abbey' – poet uses simple, accessible language and vivid religious imagery in this meditation on the growth of his personal relationship with nature, detailing physical, emotional and contemplative response.

Point 2: *(Moral guide – personification, vivid description)* 'The Stolen Boat' and 'Tintern Abbey' – Nature as a powerful moral guide, effective personification, detailed description.

Point 3: *(Healer and consoler – sensuous imagery)* 'A slumber did my spirit seal'/'Tintern Abbey' – awareness of ultimate unity of all living things. Sensuous natural imagery. Nature seen as healer and consoler.

Point 4: *(Inclusion – blank verse, variety of tone)* Engaging poetic style – 'speaking from the heart', 'a man speaking to men'; blank verse, varied tones, etc.

Conclusion: We enjoy Wordsworth's poetry for its original treatment of nature. He makes our 'eye quiet by the power of harmony' so that 'We see into the life of things'.

Sample Paragraph: Point 3

In the second stanza of 'A slumber', Lucy is dead, unable to hear, move or see. Wordsworth is acutely aware of the forces of nature which control the universe. Death is part of the natural cycle of things. Nothing escapes, not even Lucy, although he deludes himself that she is a 'thing that could not feel/The touch of earthly years'. Lucy is now at one with the universe, 'Rolled round'. As in 'Tintern Abbey', Wordsworth is conscious of an inner life that is part of the natural world. He gains an understanding of the ultimate unity of the mysterious universe – and of being part of that great natural unity. Wordsworth clearly believes that nature teaches us the 'power of harmony', the interconnectedness of everything, 'connect/The landscape with the quiet of the sky'. The poet is exploring nature and its relationship to man, rather than simply describing pretty images.

EXAMINER'S COMMENT

As part of a full essay, this informed response shows a genuine understanding of Wordsworth's preoccupations. The paragraph is clearly written and focuses on the insight to be gained from a mature perception of the significance of nature to the poet. Good use of cross-referencing, demonstrating close engagement with two poems. Accurate and well-integrated quotations support discussion points, further enhancing the top-grade standard.

Leaving Cert Sample Essay

'Wordsworth's intense vision of human experience is characterised by quiet reflection and richly sensuous language.' Discuss this statement, supporting your answer with reference to the poetry of William Wordsworth on your course.

Sample Essay

INDICATIVE MATERIAL

- **Wordsworth's intense vision of human experience** (mystery and harmony of creation, nature's beauty, transience, death, human emotion, interconnectedness, morality, God, etc.)

... is characterised by:

- **quiet reflection and richly sensuous language** (self-examination, recollection, philosophical ideas, vivid imagery/sounds, personification, varied tones and poetic forms, simple language, etc.)

1. Wordsworth was born in 1770 in Cumbria. Both his parents died when he was young and he was brought up by relatives. As a young man, he loved nature. This was an important theme in his poems. 'Westminster Bridge' remembers a carriage journey Wordsworth and his sister Dorothy took to visit his daughter Caroline and her mother. 'It is a beauteous evening' is about a meeting the poet had with his nine-year-old daughter after they visited a beach near Calais in France. 'The Solitary Reaper' was written after Wordsworth went on a walking tour of Scotland with his friend Samuel Coleridge, another poet. He saw a local girl singing in a field, but couldn't understand her language. 'Skating' is about when he himself was a child, skating on a lake in the north of England and even though it was dark and he was frightened, he kept skating. Wordsworth grew up in the Lake District. He spent much of his youth enjoying nature, exploring the mountains and valleys.

2. 'Westminster Bridge' is one of Wordsworth's sonnets on which he uses the first eight lines to describe the beautiful sight of early morning London. He also uses personification, 'This city now like a garment wears the beauty of morning'. This shows how lovely the city is looking as if dressed in the soft morning light. He makes lists, 'Ships, towers, theatres, domes and temples' to prove the greatness of this capital city and busy port as he admires its famous buildings. The list adds great emphasis and gives the impression that Wordsworth has intense admiration for London. In the final six lines, he thinks about the difference between the city and the countryside. He uses a hushed tone, 'Dear God, the very houses are asleep'. This shows how he is deeply affected by the intense feelings he experiences just before the city comes to life. Wordsworth really likes the city when it is 'asleep'. This is when he can reflect on its beauty, 'brightly glittering in the smokeless air'.

3. Another sonnet 'It is a beauteous evening, calm and free' uses the first eight lines to describe the beauty of a scene from nature. A rich sensuous simile, 'The holy time is quiet as a nun breathless with adoration' shows the spiritual side of nature. Wordsworth believed that nature could be seen as proof of God's existence. He also uses assonance of vowels to show an intense feeling of wonder, 'heaven broods over the sea'. In the last six lines, he talks to his daughter, 'Dear Child'. The he starts thinking about how this little girl, although she doesn't know it because she is too young, she is every bit as blessed as the beautiful sunset, 'God being with thee'. Wordsworth tells us his vision of the world that innocent children are special. For Wordsworth, both the beauty of nature and the girl's goodness are holy – signs of God's creation.

4. Another poem dealing with a memory about a country walk is 'The Solitary Reaper'. The poet uses assonance to create the sound a Scottish farm worker is making as she sing a traditional folk song, 'the vale profound overflows with the sound'. This is a poem where a deep feeling is remembered. The poet is telling us of the long lasting effect the mystery song had on him. He remembered it years later as 'music in my heart'. His own experience of life was intense at this time and he always reflected on his experiences. Wordsworth actually creates a new poem from this vivid memory so that we can all share this deep experience. The poem has many examples of sensuous language. He uses broad vowels to show how lonely the girl is, e.g. 'solitary', 'alone'. He also uses soft sibilant sounds like 'sang' and sickle' to suggest the sadness of the girl's song.

5. 'Skating' is also about an event from when Wordsworth was a boy, describing a winter scene. He remembers ice skating with his friends. They enjoyed the experience and were 'bellowing' like a pack of hounds. Suddenly the young boy leaves his noisy friends and becomes aware of how happy he is. Wordsworth loved skating and felt part of his beautiful surroundings when he was young. He feels very excited, 'a time of rapture'. The adult poet is reflecting on what the boy is beginning to learn

about the harmony of the world. He begins to think about the passage of time, 'all was tranquil as a dreamless sleep'. Everything comes to a natural end.

6. Wordsworth had great respect for nature. He could find a sense of a spirit in it. He creates intense pictures of nature's beauty and he reflects on the effect this had on him. He shows how nature teaches people lessons about life and time.

(800 words)

EXAMINER'S COMMENT

Touches on all the main aspects of the question (intense vision, reflection and poetic language). While there is some note-like general commentary, the main body of the essay makes several relevant and focused points. These are focused and a good attempt is made to develop them with suitable reference and quotations (although there are slight misquotes). Unnecessary biographical details are included in the introductory paragraph. Expression varies greatly, but is functional at best and often lapses into awkwardness (with repetitive reliance on 'uses' and 'shows'). Overall, a solid mid-grade response.

GRADE: H3
P = 11/15
C = 11/15
L = 9/15
M = 5/5
Total = 36/50

Improving the introduction

- **Provides a clear and focused introduction.**
- **Does not include irrelevant general biographical details.**
- **Sets out the stance that will be taken in the essay.**
- **Gives an overview of Wordsworth's vision.**
- **Refers to the poet's sensuous language.**
- **Expression is clear, fluent and varied.**
- **No misquotes or mechanical errors.**

Wordsworth defined poetry as 'emotion recollected in tranquillity'. His own poems are powerful portrayals of key themes, such as nature's beauty, transience, memory and links between human beings and God. He often used the sonnet form not only to describe beauty in its octet, but to reflect on its meaning in the sestet. Vivid imagery, aural effects, rich contrasts and personification are used to examine his themes and powerful personal feelings in his poems, 'Westminster Bridge', 'It is a beauteous evening, calm and free', 'The Solitary Reaper' and 'Skating'. Wordsworth is a 'worshipper of Nature'. He felt passionately that nature had a spirit or soul of its own, and his poems are written in a sensual style to reflect his belief that people should experience nature with all the five senses.

👓 Revision Overview

'To My Sister'
Explores themes of close relationship with people and nature, and nature as a force for good.

'A slumber did my spirit seal'
Elegy for unknown Lucy. Themes of loss/death and the effect on poet.

'She dwelt among the untrodden ways'
Addresses themes of loss and death and impact on poet.

'Composed Upon Westminster Bridge'
Exploration of themes of transient beauty and its impact on poet.

'It is a beauteous evening, calm and free'
Addresses nature's beauty and contrasting responses.

'The Solitary Reaper'
Lyric ballad examines theme of recollection through girl's song and remembered event.

from *The Prelude*: 'The Stolen Boat'
Theme of nature as a moral guide for good. Recollection of important moment – trip taken in small boat.

from *The Prelude*: 'Skating'
Themes of transience and interconnectedness of people and place.

'Tintern Abbey'
Lyrical monologue. Theme of importance of nature and its relationship with the narrator.

💬 Last Words

'Wordsworth's poetry still has the ability to engage, provoke, even entertain.'
John L. Mahoney

'Wordsworth's poetry is inevitable ... Nature not only gave him the matter for his poem, but wrote his poem for him.
Matthew Arnold

'Poetry ... takes its origin from emotion recollected in tranquillity.'
William Wordsworth

 RELATIONSHIPS

 NATURE

 DEATH

 TIME

 BEAUTY

 CHILDHOOD

 RELIGION/SPIRITUALITY

W. B. Yeats
1865–1939

'I have spread my dreams under your feet'

William Butler Yeats was born in Dublin in 1865. The son of a well-known Irish painter, John Butler Yeats, he spent much of his childhood in Co. Sligo. As a young writer, Yeats became involved with the Celtic Revival, a movement against the cultural influences of English rule in Ireland that sought to promote the spirit of our native heritage. His writing drew extensively from Irish mythology and folklore. Another great influence was the Irish revolutionary Maud Gonne, a woman as famous for her passionate nationalist politics as for her beauty. She rejected Yeats, who eventually married another woman, Georgie Hyde Lees. However, Maud Gonne remained a powerful figure in Yeats's writing. Over the years, Yeats became deeply involved in Irish politics and despite independence from England, his work reflected a pessimism about the political situation here. He also had a lifelong interest in mysticism and the occult. Appointed a senator of the Irish Free State in 1922, he is remembered as an important cultural leader, as a major playwright (he was one of the founders of Dublin's Abbey Theatre) and as one of the greatest 20th-century poets. Yeats was awarded the Nobel Prize in 1923 and died in 1939 at the age of 73.

Investigate Further

To find out more about W. B. Yeats, or to hear readings of his poems, you could do a search of some of the useful websites available such as YouTube, BBC Poetry, poetryfoundation.org and poetryarchive.org, or access additional material on this page of your eBook.

Prescribed Poems

○ **1 'The Lake Isle of Innisfree' (OL)**
Written when Yeats lived in London and was homesick for Ireland, the poem celebrates the simple joys of nature and the search for peace. **Page 366**

○ **2 'September 1913'**
In this nostalgic poem, Yeats contrasts the disillusionment he feels about the Ireland of his own day with the romanticised past. **Page 369**

○ **3 'The Wild Swans at Coole' (OL)**
Based on the symbolism of the swans, Yeats reviews his own emotional state. He reflects on deep personal concerns: love, ageing and the loss of poetic inspiration. **Page 373**

○ **4 'An Irish Airman Foresees his Death' (OL)**
This war poem is written as a monologue in the 'voice' of Yeats's friend, Major Robert Gregory. Its themes include heroism, nationalism and the youthful desire for excitement. **Page 377**

○ **5 'Easter 1916'**
Yeats explores a variety of questions and issues provoked by the 1916 Rising. In re-evaluating his personal views, he struggles to balance heroic achievement with the tragic loss of life. **Page 381**

○ **6 'The Second Coming'**
The poem addresses the chaos brought about by violence and political change. Having witnessed war in Europe, Yeats feared that civilisation would break down completely. **Page 386**

○ **7 'Sailing to Byzantium'**
Yeats's wide-ranging themes (including old age, transience, death, immortality and art) are all associated with the importance of finding spiritual fulfilment. **Page 390**

○ **8 *from* 'Meditations in Time of Civil War': 'The Stare's Nest By My Window'**
Written in response to the Irish Civil War, the poem tries to balance the destruction caused by conflict with the regenerative power of nature. **Page 395**

○ **9 'In Memory of Eva Gore-Booth and Con Markiewicz'**
Yeats's tribute to the Gore-Booth sisters is a lament for lost youth and beauty. He also reflects on the decline of the Anglo-Irish Ascendancy. **Page 399**

○ **10 'Swift's Epitaph'**
In this short translation from the original Latin inscription commemorating Jonathan Swift, Yeats honours a courageous writer who also came from the Anglo-Irish tradition. **Page 403**

○ **11 'An Acre of Grass'**
Yeats refuses to grow old quietly. Instead, he takes inspiration from William Blake and Michelangelo to continue using his creative talents in search of truth. **Page 406**

○ **12 *from* 'Under Ben Bulben'**
Written shortly before his death, the poem is often seen as Yeats's last will and testament. It includes a summary of his beliefs and ends with the poet's own epitaph. **Page 409**

○ **13 'Politics'**
A short satirical poem in which Yeats rejects political activity, preferring romantic love. **Page 413**

(OL) indicates poems that are also prescribed for the Ordinary Level course.

1

The Lake Isle of Innisfree

I will arise and go now, and go to Innisfree,
And a small cabin build there, of clay and wattles made:
Nine bean-rows will I have there, a hive for the honey-bee,
And live alone in the bee-loud glade.

And I shall have some peace there, for peace comes dropping slow,   5
Dropping from the veils of the morning to where the cricket sings;
There midnight's all a glimmer, and noon a purple glow,
And evening full of the linnet's wings.

I will arise and go now, for always night and day
I hear lake water lapping with low sounds by the shore;   10
While I stand on the roadway, or on the pavements grey,
I hear it in the deep heart's core.

Innisfree: island of heather.
clay and wattles: rods and mud were used to build small houses.

midnight's all a glimmer: stars are shining very brightly in the countryside.
linnet: songbird.

lapping: gentle sounds made by water at the edge of a shore.
heart's core: essential part; the centre of the poet's being.

'I hear lake water lapping with low sounds by the shore'

👤 Personal Response

1. This poem was voted number one in an *Irish Times* poll of the top 100 poems. Why do you think it appeals to so many readers?

2. What does the poem reveal to you about Yeats's own state of mind? Use reference to the text in your response.

3. How does the second stanza describe the rhythm of the passing day? Use quotations to illustrate your response.

👁 Critical Literacy

'The Lake Isle of Innisfree' was written in 1890. Yeats was in London, looking in a shop window at a little toy fountain. He was feeling very homesick. He said the sound of the 'tinkle of water' reminded him of 'lake water'. He was longing to escape from the grind of everyday life and he wrote an 'old daydream of mine'.

This timeless poem has long been a favourite with exiles everywhere, as it **expresses a longing for a place of deep peace**. The tone in stanza one is deliberate, not casual, as the poet announces his decision to go. There are biblical overtones here: 'I will arise and go now,' the prodigal son announces. This lends the occasion solemnity. Then the poet describes the idyllic life of self-sufficiency: 'Nine bean-rows' and 'a hive for the honey-bee'. These details give the poem a timeless quality as the poet lives 'alone in the bee-loud glade'.

Stanza two describes Innisfree so vividly that the future tense of 'I will arise' gives way to the present: 'There midnight's all a glimmer'. The **repetition** of 'peace' and 'dropping' suits the subject, as it lulls us into this tranquil place to which we all aspire to go at some point in our lives. Beautiful imagery brings us through the day, from the gentle white mists of the morning that lie like carelessly thrown veils over the lake to the blazing purple of the heather under the midday sun. The starry night, which can only be seen in the clear skies of the countryside, is vividly described as 'midnight's all a glimmer', with slender vowel sounds suggesting the sharp light of the stars. The soft 'l', 'm' and 'p' sounds in this stanza create a gentle and magical mood.

The third stanza repeats the opening, giving the air of a solemn ritual taking place. The **verbal music** in this stanza is striking, as the broad vowel sounds slow down the line 'I hear lake water lapping with low sounds by the shore', emphasising peace and tranquility. Notice the alliteration of 'l' and the assonance of 'o' all adding to the serene calm of the scene. The only **contemporary detail** in the poem is 'pavements grey', suggesting the relentless concrete of the city. The exile's awareness of what he loves is eloquently expressed as he declares he hears the sound 'in the deep heart's core'. Notice the monosyllabic ending, which drums home how much he longs for this place. Regular end rhyme (*abab*) and the regular four beats in each fourth line reinforce the harmony of this peaceful place.

🖋 Writing About the Poem

'W. B. Yeats writes dramatic poetry that addresses the human desire for harmony and fulfilment.' Discuss this statement with reference to 'The Lake Isle of Innisfree'.

Sample Paragraph

The poem that is most associated with Yeats's heart's desire, 'The Lake Isle of Innisfree', depicts a tranquil refuge from modern living. A dramatic opening, 'I will arise and go now, and go to Innisfree', declares his intention in a tone heightened by the repetition of the single syllable verb. In this idyllic place, time stands still. The steady end-rhyme ('Innisfree', 'honey-bee') and broad vowel sounds ('alone in the bee-loud glade') conjure up an alluring vision of tranquillity. The intensely hypnotic description suggests quietness and security. The alliteration and assonance ('lake water lapping with low sounds by the shore') enables us to experience this perfectly calm atmosphere, even though Yeats is still stranded on the 'pavements grey'. The poet's dream is a universal one, because we all long for peace. In the end, Yeats succeeds in instilling this vision 'in the deep heart's core'.

EXAMINER'S COMMENT

This is a focused top-grade response that addresses the question effectively and shows good engagement with the poem. Ideas are considered closely, clearly expressed and aptly supported by accurate quotes. The sustained focus on sound effects is particularly impressive. Language use throughout is well-controlled, with phrases such as 'intensely hypnotic' conveying the poet's dramatic style.

✒ Class/Homework Exercises

1. 'Yeats is a perceptive and subtle poet, both in terms of his universal themes and lyrical style'. Discuss this view with reference to 'The Lake Isle of Innisfree'.
2. 'Yeats's poems are often defined by a tension between the real world in which the poet lives and an ideal world that he imagines.' Discuss this view with reference to 'The Lake Isle of Innisfree'.

⊙ Points to Consider

- Poetic vision of longing and desire for utopian escape.
- Formal opening and repetition give the sense of a solemn ritual.
- Romantic details and sensual images place the poem out of time while concrete description produces a realistic experience for.
- Verbal music (assonance, alliteration, onomatopoeia) heighten the reader's involvement.
- Traditional rhyming structure and the steady beats of the concluding line of each quatrain add a sense of stability and security.

2 September 1913

What need you, being come to sense,
But fumble in a greasy till
And add the halfpence to the pence
And prayer to shivering prayer, until
You have dried the marrow from the bone?   5
For men were born to pray and save:
Romantic Ireland's dead and gone,
It's with O'Leary in the grave.

Yet they were of a different kind,
The names that stilled your childish play,   10
They have gone about the world like wind,
But little time had they to pray
For whom the hangman's rope was spun,
And what, God help us, could they save?
Romantic Ireland's dead and gone,   15
It's with O'Leary in the grave.

Was it for this the wild geese spread
The grey wing upon every tide;
For this that all that blood was shed,
For this Edward Fitzgerald died,   20
And Robert Emmet and Wolfe Tone,
All that delirium of the brave?
Romantic Ireland's dead and gone,
It's with O'Leary in the grave.

Yet could we turn the years again,   25
And call those exiles as they were
In all their loneliness and pain,
You'd cry, 'Some woman's yellow hair
Has maddened every mother's son':
They weighed so lightly what they gave.   30
But let them be, they're dead and gone,
They're with O'Leary in the grave.

you: merchants and business people.

O'Leary: John O'Leary, Fenian leader, one of Yeats's heroes.

they: the selfless Irish patriots.

the wild geese: Irish Independence soldiers forced into exile in Europe after 1690.

Edward Fitzgerald: 18th-century Irish aristocrat and revolutionary.
Robert Emmet and Wolfe Tone: Irish rebel leaders. Emmet was hanged in 1803. Tone committed suicide in prison after being sentenced to death in 1798.

'Romantic Ireland's dead and gone'

👤 Personal Response

1. Comment on the effectiveness of the images used in the first five lines of the poem.
2. How would you describe the tone of this poem? Is it bitter, sad, ironic, angry, etc.? Refer closely to the text in your answer.
3. Were the patriots named in the poem heroes or fools? Write a paragraph in response to Yeats's views.

👁 Critical Literacy

'September 1913' is typical of Yeats's hard-hitting political poems. Both the content and tone are harsh as the poet airs his views on public issues, contrasting the idealism of Ireland's heroic past with the uncultured present.

Yeats had been a great supporter of Sir Hugh Lane, who had offered his extensive art collection to the city of Dublin, provided the paintings would be on show in a suitable gallery. When the authorities failed to arrange this, Lane withdrew his offer. The controversy infuriated Yeats, who criticised Dublin Corporation for being miserly and anti-cultural. For him, it represented **a new low in the country's drift into vulgarity and crass commercialism**. The year 1913 was also a year of great hardship, partly because of a general strike and lock-out of workers. Poverty and deprivation were widespread at the time, particularly in Dublin's tenements.

The first stanza begins with a derisive **attack on a materialistic society** that Yeats sees as being both greedy and hypocritical. Ireland's middle classes are preoccupied with making money and slavish religious devotion. The rhetorical opening is sharply sarcastic, as the poet depicts the petty, penny-pinching shopkeepers who 'fumble in a greasy till'. Yeats's tone is as angry as it is ironic: 'For men were born to pray and save'. Images of the dried bone and 'shivering prayer' are equally forceful – the poor are exploited by ruthless employers and a domineering Church. This disturbing picture leads the poet to regret the loss of 'Romantic Ireland' in the concluding refrain.

Stanza two develops the contrast between past and present as Yeats considers the **heroism and generosity of an earlier era**. Ireland's patriots – 'names that stilled' earlier generations of children – could hardly have been more unlike the present middle class. Yeats clearly relates to the self-sacrifice of idealistic Irish freedom fighters: 'And what, God help us, could they save?' These disdainful words echo the fearful prayers referred to at the start of the poem. The heroes of the past were so selfless that they did not even concern themselves with saving their own lives.

The wistful and nostalgic tone of stanza three is obvious in the rhetorical question about all those Irish soldiers who had been exiled in the late 17th century. Yeats's high regard for these men is evoked by comparing them to 'wild geese', a plaintive metaphor reflecting their nobility. Yet the poet's admiration for past idealism is diminished by the fact that **such heroic dedication was all for nothing**. The repetition of 'for this' hammers home Yeats's contempt for the pious materialists of his own imperfect age. In listing a roll of honour, he singles out the most impressive patriots of his own class, the Anglo-Irish Ascendancy. For the poet, Fitzgerald, Emmet and Tone are among the most admirable Irishmen. In using the phrase 'All that delirium of the brave', Yeats suggests that their passionate dedication to Irish freedom bordered on a frenzied or misplaced sense of daring.

This romanticised appreciation continues into the final stanza, where the poet imagines the 'loneliness and pain' of the heroic dead. His empathy towards them is underpinned by an **even more vicious portrayal of the new middle class**. He argues that the establishment figures of his own time would be unable to comprehend anything about the values and dreams of 'Romantic Ireland'. At best, they would be confused by the ludicrous self-sacrifice of the past. At worst, the present generation would accuse the patriots of being insane or of trying to impress friends or lovers. Perhaps Yeats is illustrating the cynical thinking of his time, when many politicians courted national popularity. 'Some woman's yellow hair' might well refer to the traditional symbol of Ireland as a beautiful woman.

The poet's disgust on behalf of the patriots is rounded off in the last two lines: 'But let them be, they're dead and gone'. The refrain has been changed slightly, adding further emphasis and a **sense of finality**. After reading this savage satire, we are left with a deep sense of Yeats's bitter disillusionment towards his contemporaries. The extreme feelings expressed in the poem offer a dispirited vision of an unworthy country. It isn't surprising that some critics have accused Yeats of over-romanticising the heroism of Ireland's past, of being narrow minded and even elitist. At any rate, the poem challenges us to examine the values of the state we are in, our understanding of Irish history and the meaning of heroism.

✒ Writing About the Poem

'W. B. Yeats often makes uses of contrasting images of self-interest and selflessness to communicate powerful feelings.' Discuss this statement in relation to 'September 1913'.

Sample Paragraph

Contrast plays a central role in 'September 1913'. The poem's angry opening lines are aimed at the greedy merchants and landlords who 'fumble in a greasy till'. Their mean-spirited behaviour is reflected by vivid imagery. These individuals exploit ordinary people and could not be more unlike the Irish patriots who were prepared to die for the freedom of others – 'names that stilled your childish play'. Yeats also uses the beautiful image of the wild geese spreading 'the grey wing upon every tide' to describe the dignified flight of Irish soldiers who refused to accept colonial rule. The imagery is taken from the world of nature and has a vibrant quality that makes us aware of Yeats's high opinion of those heroes. The poet's feeling is evident in his violent description of the materialistic society of his own time – and especially those who have 'dried the marrow from the bone'. Stark contrasts carry the argument throughout the poem and leave a deep impression on readers.

EXAMINER'S COMMENT

Well-focused on how the poet's imagery patterns convey deeply felt views. This top-grade response is also effectively supported by suitable reference and accurate quotation. Informed discussion covers a range of contrasting images (such as greed, natural beauty and violence). There is evidence throughout of close interaction with the poem. Expression is controlled, and the paragraph is rounded off with a succinct concluding sentence.

✏️ Class/Homework Exercises

1. 'W. B. Yeats manages to create a series of powerfully compelling moods throughout "September 1913".' Discuss this statement with reference to both the subject matter and style of the poem.
2. 'Yeats frequently addresses political themes in poems that are filled with tension and drama.' Discuss this view with reference to 'September 1913'.

⊙ Points to Consider

- **Central contrast between the materialistic present and the romanticised past.**
- **The heroic patriots were idealistic, unlike the self-serving middle classes of 1913.**
- **Various tones – disillusionment, irony, admiration, resignation.**
- **Effective use of repetition, vivid imagery, colloquial language.**
- **Refrain emphasises Yeats's deep sense of disenchantment with Ireland's cynical establishment.**

3 The Wild Swans at Coole

W. B. YEATS

The trees are in their autumn beauty,
The woodland paths are dry,
Under the October twilight the water
Mirrors a still sky;
Upon the brimming water among the stones   5
Are nine-and-fifty swans.

brimming: filled to the very top or edge.

The nineteenth autumn has come upon me
Since I first made my count;
I saw, before I had well finished,
All suddenly mount   10
And scatter wheeling in great broken rings
Upon their clamorous wings.

clamorous: loud, confused noise.

I have looked upon those brilliant creatures,
And now my heart is sore.
All's changed since I, hearing at twilight,   15
The first time on this shore,
The bell-beat of their wings above my head,
Trod with a lighter tread.

Trod ... tread: walked lightly; carefree.

Unwearied still, lover by lover,
They paddle in the cold   20
Companionable streams or climb the air;
Their hearts have not grown old;
Passion or conquest, wander where they will,
Attend upon them still.

lover by lover: swans mate for life; this highlights Yeats's loneliness.

Companionable: friendly.

Attend upon them still: waits on them yet.

But now they drift on the still water,   25
Mysterious, beautiful;
Among what rushes will they build,
By what lake's edge or pool
Delight men's eyes when I awake some day
To find they have flown away?   30

'The bell-beat of their wings above my head'

👤 Personal Response

1. Why do you think the poet chose the season of autumn as his setting? What changes occur at this time of year? Where are these referred to in the poem?

2. In your opinion, what are the main contrasts between the swans and the poet? Describe two, using close reference to the text.

3. What do you think the final stanza means? Consider the phrase 'I awake'. What does the poet awake from?

👁 Critical Literacy

'The Wild Swans at Coole' was written in 1916. Yeats loved spending time in the West, especially at Coole, the home of Lady Gregory, his friend and patron. He was 51 when he wrote this poem, which contrasts the swans' beauty and apparent seeming immortality with Yeats's ageing, mortal self.

The poem opens with a tranquil, serene scene of **autumnal beauty** in the park of Lady Gregory's home in Galway. This romantic image is described in great detail: the 'woodland paths are dry'. It is evening, 'October twilight'. The water is 'brimming'. The swans are carefully counted, 'nine-and-fifty'. The use of the soft letters 'l', 'm' and 's' emphasise the calm of the scene in stanza one.

In stanza two, the poem moves to the personal as he recalls that it is nineteen years since he first counted the swans. The word 'count' links the two stanzas. The poet's counting is interrupted as these mysterious creatures all suddenly rise into the sky. Run-through lines suggest the flowing movement of the rising swans. Strong verbs ('mount', 'scatter') reinforce this elemental action. The great beating wings of the swans are captured in the onomatopoeic 'clamorous wings'. They are independent and refuse to be restrained. The ring is a symbol of eternity. The swans are making the same patterns as they have always made; they are unchanging. Stanza two is linked to stanza three by the phrases 'I saw' and 'I have looked'. Now the poet tells us his 'heart is sore'. He has taken stock and is **dissatisfied with his emotional situation**. He is fifty-one, alone and unmarried and concerned that his poetic powers are lessening: **'All's changed'**. All humans want things to remain as they are, but life is full of change. He has lost the great love of his life, the beautiful Irish activist, Maud Gonne. He also laments the loss of his youth, when he 'Trod with a lighter tread'. Nineteen years earlier, he was much more carefree. The noise of the beating wings of the swans is effectively captured in the compound word 'bell-beat'. The alliterative 'b' reinforces the steady, flapping sound. The poet is using his intense personal experiences to express universal truths.

The swans in stanza four are **symbols of eternity**, ageless, 'Unwearied still'. They are united, 'lover by lover'. They experience life together ('Companionable streams'), not on their own, like the poet. He envies them their defiance of time: 'Their hearts have not grown old'. They do what they want, when they want. They are full of 'Passion or conquest'. By contrast, he is indirectly telling us, he feels old and worn out. The **spiral imagery** of the 'great broken rings' is reminiscent of the spirals seen in ancient carvings representing eternity. Yeats believed there was a cyclical pattern behind all things. The swans can live in two elements, water and air, thus linking these elements together. They are living, vital, immortal, unlike their surroundings. The trees are yellowing ('autumn beauty') and the dry 'woodland paths' suggest the lack of creative force which the poet is experiencing. Yeats is heartbroken and weary. Only the swans transcend time.

Stanza five explores a **philosophy of life**, linked to the previous stanza by the repetition of 'still'. The swans have returned to the water, 'Mysterious, beautiful'. The poem ends on a speculative note as the poet asks where they will 'Delight men's eyes'. Is he referring to the fact that **they will continue to be a source of pleasure to someone else** long after he is dead? The swans appear immortal, a continuing source of happiness as they practise their patterns, whereas the poet is not able to continue improving his own writing, as he is mortal. The poet is slipping into the cruel season of winter while the swans infinitely 'drift on the still water'.

✒ Writing About the Poem

'W. B. Yeats makes effective use of rich, dramatic symbols to address themes of transience and mortality.' Discuss this view with reference to 'The Wild Swans at Coole'.

Sample Paragraph

Two contrasting symbols are used by Yeats in 'The Wild Swans at Coole'. The swans represent youthful passion while autumn symbolises the sadness of ageing. Through his imaginative symbolism, Yeats is presenting the view that life, in all its wonder, is fragile. The swans epitomise the unchanging world of nature. They are 'Wild', free, as seen in the verbs associated with them, 'mount', 'scatter'. The poet's confession, 'And now my heart is sore', engages the reader in accepting the profound truth that humanity cannot conquer time. Unlike the poet, the swans 'drift on the still water,/Mysterious, beautiful', but they are not subject to time's powers. Yeats is connected to the decay of autumn, 'October twilight' where 'woodland paths are dry', all of which signify advancing age. In considering these symbols,

EXAMINER'S COMMENT

A perceptive top-grade response to the question. Informed discussion based on the poet's awareness of key symbols (the swans and the natural world). Effective supporting reference and accurate quotations throughout. Expression is also very good ('accepting the profound truth', 'penetrating question') and the paragraph is rounded off with an impressive personal comment.

Yeats is led to ask a penetrating question about the transience of beauty and the failing of creative energy, 'when I awake some day/To find they have flown away?'I particularly liked the final rhyme which trails off faintly into the distance – just like the 'brilliant creatures'.

✍ Class/Homework Exercises

1. 'W. B. Yeats frequently uses personal aspects of his own life to evocatively explore universal truths.' Discuss this view with reference to 'The Wild Swans at Coole'.
2. 'Yeats often draws on the beauty and stillness of the natural world to convey a deep sense of loss.' Discuss this statement with reference to 'The Wild Swans at Coole'.

⊙ Points to Consider

- Intense personal meditation on the search for lasting beauty in a transient world.

- Sad tone reflects concerns about ageing, romantic rejection, political upheaval, fading creativity.

- Slow rhythm conveys the poet's meditative mood.

- Vivid visual descriptive details portray places and creatures.

- Dynamic verbs, compound words and onomatopoeia capture the energy of the swans.

- Use of contrast highlights the gap between mortality and eternity.

- Poem ends on an optimistic note.

4 An Irish Airman Forsees His Death

Title: The Irish airman in this poem is Major Robert Gregory (1881–1918), son of Yeats's close friend, Lady Gregory. He was shot down and killed while on service in northern Italy.

W. B. YEATS

I know that I shall meet my fate
Somewhere among the clouds above;
Those that I fight I do not hate,
Those that I guard I do not love;
My country is Kiltartan Cross,   5
My countrymen Kiltartan's poor,
No likely end could bring them loss
Or leave them happier than before.
Nor law, nor duty bade me fight,
Nor public men, nor cheering crowds,   10
A lonely impulse of delight
Drove to this tumult in the clouds;
I balanced all, brought all to mind,
The years to come seemed waste of breath,
A waste of breath the years behind   15
In balance with this life, this death.

Those that I fight: the Germans.
Those that I guard: Allied countries, such as England and France.
Kiltartan: townland near the Gregory estate in Co. Galway.
likely end: outcome.

tumult: turmoil; confusion.

'I balanced all'

👤 Personal Response

1. 'This poem is not just an elegy or lament in memory of the dead airman. It is also an insight into the excitement and exhilaration of warfare.' Write your response to this statement, using close reference to the text.

2. Write a paragraph on Yeats's use of repetition throughout the poem. Refer to the text in your answer.

3. In your opinion, what is the central or dominant mood in the poem? Refer to the text in your answer.

👁 Critical Literacy

Thousands of Irishmen fought and died in the British armed forces during World War I. Robert Gregory was killed in Italy at the age of 37. The airman's death had a lasting effect on Yeats, who wrote several poems about him.

Is it right to assume anything about young men who fight for their countries? Why do they enlist? Do they always know what they are fighting for? In this poem, Yeats expresses what he believes is the airman's viewpoint as he comes face to face with death. This **fatalistic attitude** is prevalent in the emphatic opening line. The poem's title also leads us to believe that the speaker has an intuitive sense that his death is about to happen. But despite this premonition, he seems strangely resigned to risking his life.

In lines 3–4, he makes it clear that he neither hates his German enemies nor loves the British and their allies. His thoughts are with the people he knows best back in Kiltartan, Co. Galway. Major Gregory recognises the irony of their detachment from the war. The ordinary people of his homeland are unlikely to be affected at all by whatever happens on the killing fields of mainland Europe. Does he feel that he is abandoning his fellow countrymen? What is the dominant tone of lines 7–8? Is there an underlying bitterness?

In line 9, the speaker takes time to reflect on why he joined the air force and immediately dismisses the obvious reasons of conscription ('law') or patriotism ('duty'). As a volunteer, Gregory is more openly cynical of the 'public men' and 'cheering crowds' he mentions in line 10. Like many in the military who have experienced the realities of warfare, **he is suspicious of hollow patriotism** and has no time for political leaders and popular adulation. So why did Robert Gregory choose to endanger his life by going to war? The answer lies in the key comments 'A lonely impulse of delight' (line 11) and 'I balanced all' (line 13). The first phrase is paradoxical. The airman experiences not just the excitement, but also the isolation of flying. At the same time, his 'impulse' to enlist as a fighter pilot reflects both his **desire for adventure** as well as his regret.

The last four lines explain the real reason behind his decision. It was neither rash nor emotional, but simply a question of balance. Having examined his life closely, Gregory has chosen the heroism of a self-sacrificing death. It is as though he only feels truly alive during the 'tumult' of battle. Yeats's language is particularly evocative at this point. Awesome air battles are effectively echoed in such dynamic phrasing as 'impulse of delight' and 'tumult in the clouds'. This **sense of freedom and power** is repeatedly contrasted with the dreary and predictable security of life away from the war – dismissed out of hand as a 'waste of breath'. From the airman's perspective, as a man of action, dying in battle is in keeping with 'this life' that he has chosen. Such a death would be his final adventurous exploit.

Some commentators have criticised Yeats's poem for glorifying war and pointless risk-taking. Others have suggested that the poet successfully highlights Anglo-Irish attitudes, neither exclusively Irish nor English. The poet certainly raises interesting questions about national identity and ways of thinking about war. However, in elegising Robert Gregory, he emphasises the **airman's daring solitude**. Perhaps this same thrill lies at the heart of other important choices in life, including the creative activity of artists. Is there a sense that the poet and the pilot are alike, both of them taking calculated risks in what they do?

✒ Writing About the Poem

'Some of Yeats's most poignant poems have a tragic vision, a sense that life is meaningless and has to be endured.' Discuss this view, with particular reference to 'An Irish Airman Foresees his Death'.

Sample Paragraph

The title itself the idea of warfare and death. However, the 'Irish Airman' is courageous in the face of danger. Although the word 'fate' suggests an inevitable destiny, the poem is dominated by a mood of resignation. The calm tone – 'I know that I shall meet my fate' – and slow rhythm is like a chant or a prayer. While the pilot is realistic about his chances in war, he seems to have distanced himself from everything. I believe he simply accepts the reality of war and is prepared for anything. He also admits the truth about his passion for adventure – 'A lonely impulse of delight' – and this might signify that he views life as beyond his control. The poem's ending is pessimistic, and he repeats the phrase 'waste of breath' to emphasise the sheer absurdity of life. Overall, the speaker is caught between realism and pessimism. The subtle concluding line sums this up – 'In balance with this life, this death' – and leaves a sense of his tragic dilemma.

EXAMINER'S COMMENT

An insightful, focused response to the question. Perceptive discussion engages with the airman's fatalistic attitude. Apt, accurate quotations are integrated effectively into the commentary. Expression is well-controlled and vocabulary is also impressive ('inevitable destiny', 'sheer absurdity of life', 'subtle concluding line'). A solid, high-grade standard.

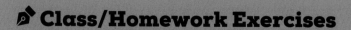 Class/Homework Exercises

1. 'W. B. Yeats's evocative poems can raise interesting questions about national identity.' Discuss this statement with reference to 'An Irish Airman Foresees his Death'.
2. 'Yeats's poetry often explores fatalistic themes with tragic acceptance.' Discuss this view with reference to 'An Irish Airman Foresees his Death'.

⊙ Points to Consider

- Yeats adopts the persona of Major Robert Gregory who died in 1918.
- Dramatic monologue form engages the sympathy of readers.
- Contrasting attitudes and tones: passion, detachment, resignation, courage, joy, loneliness.
- Effective use of repetition, rhyme and contrast.

5 Easter 1916

W. B. YEATS

I have met them at close of day
Coming with vivid faces
From counter or desk among grey
Eighteenth-century houses.
I have passed with a nod of the head   5
Or polite meaningless words,
Or have lingered awhile and said
Polite meaningless words,
And thought before I had done
Of a mocking tale or a gibe   10
To please a companion
Around the fire at the club,
Being certain that they and I
But lived where motley is worn:
All changed, changed utterly: 15
A terrible beauty is born.

That woman's days were spent
In ignorant good-will,
Her nights in argument
Until her voice grew shrill.   20
What voice more sweet than hers
When, young and beautiful,
She rode to harriers?
This man had kept a school
And rode our wingèd horse;   25
This other his helper and friend
Was coming into his force;
He might have won fame in the end,
So sensitive his nature seemed,
So daring and sweet his thought.   30
This other man I had dreamed
A drunken, vainglorious lout.
He had done most bitter wrong
To some who are near my heart,
Yet I number him in the song;   35
He, too, has resigned his part
In the casual comedy;
He, too, has been changed in his turn,
Transformed utterly:
A terrible beauty is born.   40

Title: On 24 April 1916, Easter Monday, about 700 Irish Republicans took over several key buildings in Dublin. These included the Four Courts, Bolands Mills, the Royal College of Surgeons and the General Post Office. The rebellion lasted six days and was followed by the execution of its leaders. The Rising was a pivotal event in modern Irish history.

them: the rebels involved in the Rising.

motley: ridiculous clothing.

That woman: Countess Markiewicz, friend of Yeats and a committed nationalist.

This man: Padraig Pearse, poet and teacher, was shot as a leader of the Rising.

wingèd horse: Pegasus, the mythical white horse that flies across the sky, was a symbol of poetic inspiration.

This other: Thomas MacDonagh, writer and teacher, executed in 1916.

This other man: Major John MacBride was also executed for his part in the rebellion. He was the husband of Maud Gonne.

most bitter wrong: there were recurring rumours that MacBride had mistreated Maud Gonne.

Hearts with one purpose alone
Through summer and winter seem
Enchanted to a stone
To trouble the living stream.
The horse that comes from the road,   45
The rider, the birds that range
From cloud to tumbling cloud,
Minute by minute they change;
A shadow of cloud on the stream
Changes minute by minute;   50
A horse-hoof slides on the brim,
And a horse plashes within it;
The long-legged moor-hens dive,
And hens to moor-cocks call;
Minute by minute they live: 55
The stone's in the midst of all.

Too long a sacrifice
Can make a stone of the heart.
O when may it suffice?
That is Heaven's part, our part   60
To murmur name upon name,
As a mother names her child
When sleep at last has come
On limbs that had run wild.
What is it but nightfall?   65
No, no, not night but death;
Was it needless death after all?
For England may keep faith
For all that is done and said.
We know their dream; enough   70
To know they dreamed and are dead;
And what if excess of love
Bewildered them till they died?
I write it out in a verse –
MacDonagh and MacBride   75
And Connolly and Pearse
Now and in time to be,
Wherever green is worn,
Are changed, changed utterly:
A terrible beauty is born.   80

needless death: Yeats asks
if the Rising was a waste
of life, since the British
were already considering
independence for Ireland.

Connolly: Trade union
leader and revolutionary,
executed in 1916.

👤 Personal Response

1. Describe the atmosphere in the opening stanza of the poem. Refer closely to the text in your answer.
2. 'Easter 1916' has many striking images. Choose two that you find particularly interesting and briefly explain their effectiveness.
3. On balance, does Yeats approve or disapprove of the Easter Rising? Refer to the text in your answer.

👁 Critical Literacy

Yeats, who was in London at the time of the Rising, had mixed feelings about what had happened. He was clearly fascinated but also troubled by this heroic and yet in some ways pointless sacrifice. He did not publish the poem until 1920.

In the opening stanza, Yeats recalls how he used to meet some of the people who were later involved in the Easter Rising. He was unimpressed by their 'vivid faces' and he remembers routinely dismissing them with 'Polite meaningless words'. His admission that he **misjudged these insignificant Republicans** as subjects for 'a mocking tale or a gibe' among his clever friends is a reminder of his derisive attitude in 'September 1913'. Before 1916, Yeats had considered Ireland a ridiculous place, a circus 'where motley is worn'. But the poet confesses that the Rising transformed everything – including his own condescending apathy. In the stanza's final lines, Yeats introduces what becomes an ambivalent refrain ending in 'A terrible beauty is born'.

This sense of shock and the need to completely re-evaluate his views is developed in stanza two. The poet singles out individual martyrs killed or imprisoned for their activities, among them his close friend Countess Markiewicz. He also mentions Major John MacBride, husband of Maud Gonne, who had refused Yeats's proposal of marriage. Although he had always considered MacBride as little more

'All changed, changed utterly'

than a 'drunken, vainglorious lout', Yeats now acknowledges that he too has been distinguished by his bravery and heroism. The poet wonders about the usefulness of all the passion that sparked the rebels to make such a bold move, but his emphasis is on the fact that **the people as well as the whole atmosphere have changed**. Even MacBride, whom he held in utter contempt, has grown in stature.

In stanza three, Yeats takes powerful images from nature and uses them to explore the meaning of Irish heroism. The metaphor of the stubborn stone in the stream might represent the defiance of the revolutionaries towards all the forces around them. **The poet evokes the constant energy and dynamism of the natural world**, focusing on the changes that happen 'minute by minute'. Image after dazzling image conjures up a vivid picture of unpredictable movement and seasonal regeneration (as 'hens to moor-cocks call') and skies change 'From cloud to tumbling cloud'. For the poet, the Rising presented many contradictions, as he weighs the success of the revolt against the shocking costs. In contrasting the inflexibility of the revolutionaries with the 'living stream', he **indicates a reluctant admiration for the rebels' dedication**. Does Yeats suggest that the rebels risked the loss of their own humanity, allowing their hearts to harden to stone? Or is he also thinking of Maud Gonne and blaming her cold-hearted rejection of him on her fanatical political views?

In the final stanza, the poet returns to the metaphor of the unmoving stone in a flowing stream to warn of the dangers of fanaticism. The rhetorical questions about the significance of the rebellion reveal his **continuing struggle to understand** what happened. Then he asks the single most important question about the Rising: 'Was it needless death after all', particularly as 'England may keep faith' and allow Ireland its independence, all of which would prompt a more disturbing conclusion, i.e. that the insurgents died in vain.

Yeats quickly abandons essentially unanswerable questions about the value of the Irish struggle for freedom. Instead, he simply pays tribute to the fallen patriots by naming them tenderly, 'As a mother names her child'. The final assertive lines commemorate the 1916 leaders in dramatic style. Setting aside his earlier ambivalence, Yeats acknowledges that these patriots died for their dreams. The hushed tone is reverential, almost sacred. The rebels have been transformed into martyrs who will be remembered for their selfless heroism 'Wherever green is worn'. The insistent final refrain has a stirring and increasingly disquieting quality. The poem's central paradox, 'A terrible beauty is born', concludes that **all the heroic achievements of the 1916 Rising were at the tragic expense of human life**.

W. B. YEATS

✒ Writing About the Poem

'W. B. Yeats's public poetry responds to particular situations in terms that can often seem unclear and contradictory.' Discuss this view with reference to both the subject matter and style of 'Easter 1916'.

Sample Paragraph

Yeats admired, yet was troubled by the 1916 Rising. He places himself centre stage in the opening anecdote, 'I have met them'. The formal rhyme scheme is dignified and the sound of the resonating refrain, 'All changed, changed utterly', adds a solemn note. Yet Yeats also honestly debates the wisdom of the uprising, asking 'Was it needless death after all?' The image of the heart as a stone reflects the poet's own torn emotions because it not only suggests the fierce determination of those rebels involved, but also underlines the inflexibility of their thinking. The poem concludes with a list of the fallen rebel leaders and the realisation that the implacable stone in the midst of the 'living stream' does change the flow. These famous Irish names had changed history by their deeds. The paradoxical statement, 'A terrible beauty is born', reflects the poet's admiration of the rebels' sacrifice and also his shocked reaction to the bloody events they unleashed.

> **EXAMINER'S COMMENT**
> A focused, top-grade response that addresses the question directly. The commentary throughout shows a very good understanding of Yeats's divided views. Points are aptly supported with accurate quotation. Some perceptive discussion regarding the poet's use of the stone symbol to illustrate his appreciation of how the 1916 Rising had changed Irish history. Expression ('resonating', 'inflexibility', 'implacable') is also impressive.

✒ Class/Homework Exercises

1. 'W. B. Yeats explores complex political themes in richly energetic language.' Discuss this statement with reference to 'Easter 1916'.
2. 'Yeats honestly reflects on change and immortality in his dynamic, lyrical poetry.' Discuss this view with reference to 'Easter 1916'.

⊙ Points to Consider

• Deeply felt elegy commemorating a controversial historical event.

• Effective contrast of formal structure with colloquial language.

• Ambivalent attitudes of admiration and shock.

• Formal rhyme scheme, rhythmic phrases, economy of language.

• Symbolism, repetition, antithesis and paradox all convey the poet's contradictory views.

• Thrilling refrain resonates with the consequence of change.

6 The Second Coming

Turning and turning in the widening gyre
The falcon cannot hear the falconer;
Things fall apart; the centre cannot hold;
Mere anarchy is loosed upon the world,
The blood-dimmed tide is loosed, and everywhere   5
The ceremony of innocence is drowned;
The best lack all conviction, while the worst
Are full of passionate intensity.

Surely some revelation is at hand;
Surely the Second Coming is at hand.   10
The Second Coming! Hardly are those words out
When a vast image out of Spiritus Mundi
Troubles my sight: somewhere in sands of the desert
A shape with lion body and the head of a man,
A gaze blank and pitiless as the sun,   15
Is moving its slow thighs, while all about it
Reel shadows of the indignant desert birds.
The darkness drops again; but now I know
That twenty centuries of stony sleep
Were vexed to nightmare by a rocking cradle,   20
And what rough beast, its hour come round at last,
Slouches towards Bethlehem to be born?

Title: This is a reference to the Bible. It is from Matthew and speaks of Christ's return to reward the good.

in the widening gyre: Yeats regarded a cycle of history as a gyre. He visualised these cycles as interconnecting cones that moved in a circular motion, widening outwards until they could not widen any further, then a new gyre or cone formed from the centre of the circle created. This spun in the opposite direction to the original cone. The Christian era was coming to a close and a new, disturbed time was coming into view. In summary, the gyre is a symbol of constant change.
falcon: a bird of prey, trained to hunt by the aristocracy.
falconer: the trainer of the falcon. If the bird flies too far away, it cannot be directed.
Mere: nothing more than; just; only.
anarchy: lack of government or order. Yeats believed that bloodshed and a worship of bloodshed were the end of an historical era.
blood-dimmed: made dark with blood.
Spiritus Mundi: Spirit of the World, the collective soul of the world.
lion body and the head of a man: famous statue in Egypt; an enigmatic person.
desert birds: birds of prey.
twenty centuries: Yeats believed that two thousand years was the length of a period in history.
vexed: annoyed; distressed.
rocking cradle: coming of the infant Jesus.
rough beast: the Anti-Christ.
Bethlehem: birthplace of Christ. It is usually associated with peace and innocence, and it is terrifying that the beast is going to be born there. The spiral has reversed its spinning. A savage god is coming.

'A shape with lion body and the head of a man'

 Personal Response

1. This poem suggests that politics are not important. Does the poet convince you? Write a paragraph in response, with reference to the text.

2. Yeats uses symbols to express some of his most profound ideas. What symbols in this poem appeal to you? Use reference to the text in your response.

3. 'Yeats is yearning for order, and fearing anarchy.' Discuss two ways in which the poem illustrates this statement. Support your answer with reference to the text.

👁 Critical Literacy

'The Second Coming' is a terrifying, apocalyptic poem written in January 1919 against a background of the disintegration of three great European empires at the end of World War I and against the catastrophic War of Independence in Ireland. These were bloody times. Yeats yearned for order and feared anarchy.

Sparked off by both disgust at what was happening in Europe as well as his interest in the occult, Yeats explores, in stanza one, what he perceives to be the failure at the heart of society: 'Things fall apart'. In his opinion, **the whole world was disintegrating** into a bloody, chaotic mess. This break-up of civilisation is described in metaphorical language. For Yeats, the 'gyre' is a symbol representing an era. He believed contrary expanding and contracting forces influence people and cultures and that the Christian era was nearing its end. Images of hunting show how the old world represented its failing – 'The falcon cannot hear the falconer'. We have lost touch with Christ, just as the falcon loses touch with the falconer as he swings into ever-increasing circles. This bird was trained to fly in circles to catch its prey. The circular imagery, with the repetitive '-ing', describes the continuous, swirling movement. Civilisation is also 'Turning and turning in the widening gyre' as it buckles and fragments.

The **tension** is reflected in a list of contrasts: 'centre' and 'fall apart', 'falcon' and 'falconer', 'lack all conviction' and 'intensity', 'innocence' and 'anarchy'. The strain is too much: 'the centre cannot hold'. The verbs also graphically describe this chaotic world: 'Turning and turning', 'loosed', 'drowned', 'fall apart'. Humans are changing amidst the chaos: 'innocence is drowned'. **Anarchy** is described in terms of a great tidal wave, 'the blood-dimmed tide', which sweeps everything before it. The compound word reinforces the overwhelming nature of the water. Yeats feels that the 'best', the leaders and thinkers, have no energy; they are indifferent and 'lack all conviction'. On the other hand, the 'worst', the cynics and fanatics, are consumed with hatred and violence, 'full of passionate intensity'.

Disillusioned, Yeats thinks **a new order has to be emerging**. He imagines a Second Coming. He repeats the word 'Surely' in a tone of both belief and fear in stanza two. The Second Coming is usually thought of as a time when Christ will return to reward the good, but the image Yeats presents us with is terrifying. **A blank, pitiless creature emerges.** It is straight from the Book of Revelations: 'And I saw a beast rising out of the sea'. This was regarded as a sign that the end of the world was near. Such an unnatural hybrid of human and animal is the Anti-Christ, the opposite force of the gentle infant Jesus who signalled the end of the Greek and Roman Empires. The 'gaze blank' suggests its lack of intelligence. The phrase 'pitiless as the sun' tells us the creature has no empathy or compassion. It 'Slouches'. It is a brutish, graceless monstrosity.

The **hostile environment** is a nightmare scenario of blazing desert sun, shifting sands and circling predatory birds. The verbs suggest everything is out of focus: 'Reel', 'rocking', 'Slouches'. 'The darkness drops again' shows how disorder, disconnectedness and the 'widening gyre' have brought us to nihilism. This seems to be a prophetic statement, as fascism was to sweep the world in the mid-20th century. Then Yeats has a moment of epiphany: 'but now I know'. Other eras have been destroyed before. The baby in the 'rocking cradle' created an upheaval that resulted in the end of 'twenty centuries of stony sleep'.

Yeats believed that a **cycle of history** lasted two thousand years in a single evolution of birth, growth, decline and death. All change causes upheaval. The Christian era, with its qualities of innocence, order, maternal love and goodness, is at an end. The new era of the 'rough beast' is about to start. It is pitiless, destructive, violent and murderous. This new era has already begun: 'its hour come round at last'. It is a savage god who is coming, uninvited. The spiral has reversed its motion and is now spinning in the opposite direction. The lack of end rhyme mirrors a world of chaos. Yeats looks back over thousands of years. We are given a thrilling and terrifying prospect from a vast perspective of millennia.

✒ Writing About the Poem

'Yeats frequently uses powerful and disturbing imagery to express a dark vision of the future.' Discuss this view with reference to 'The Second Coming'.

Sample Paragraph

The themes of stability and chaos are central to 'The Second Coming'. From the opening line, 'Turning and turning in the widening gyre', Yeats presents the disturbing image of the falcon spinning out of control. The sense of disintegration continues and the language becomes more violent – 'The blood-dimmed tide is loosed'. Dramatic details create a dark vision of life – 'anarchy is loosed', 'innocence is drowned'. There is great irony in the poet's prophecy of a new saviour ('The Second Coming'). Unlike the first Christian Messiah, the next one will be a 'rough beast' bringing unknown horrors – 'A shape with lion body'. Yeats believed that Christianity was about to end to be replaced by a world where evil would triumph. The image of the sinister beast, with its 'gaze blank and pitiless as the sun' was particularly chilling.

EXAMINER'S COMMENT

A clear, insightful response to the question. Informed points focused directly on how Yeats's imagery conveyed his pessimistic prophecy. Good choice of accurate quotations provide support throughout. Expression is impressive also: varied sentence length, wide-ranging vocabulary ('sense of disintegration') and good control of syntax. A high-grade standard.

✎ Class/Homework Exercises

1. 'W. B. Yeats's political poems are remarkable for their forceful language and sensuous imagery.' Discuss this statement with reference to 'The Second Coming'.
2. 'Yeats often presents a dramatic tension between order and disorder.' Discuss this view with reference to 'The Second Coming'.

◉ Points to Consider

- **The poem's title has obvious biblical associations.**
- **Scenes of anarchy and disorder lead to an apocalyptical vision of the future.**
- **Variety of tones/moods: foreboding, disillusionment, fear, despair.**
- **Effective use of contrast, dramatic imagery, symbols, striking comparisons.**

7 Sailing to Byzantium

Title: for Yeats, this voyage would be one taken to find perfection. This country only exists in the mind. It is an ideal. The original old city of Byzantium was famous as a centre of religion, art and architecture.

I

That is no country for old men. The young
In one another's arms, birds in the trees
– Those dying generations – at their song,
The salmon-falls, the mackerel-crowded seas,
Fish, flesh, or fowl, commend all summer long   5
Whatever is begotten, born, and dies.
Caught in that sensual music all neglect
Monuments of unageing intellect.

That: Ireland – all who live there are subject to ageing, decay and death.

dying generations: opposites are linked to show that in the midst of life is death.

sensual music: the young are living life to the full through their senses and are neglecting the inner spiritual life of the soul.
paltry thing: worthless, of no importance. Old age is not valued in Ireland.

II

An aged man is but a paltry thing,
A tattered coat upon a stick, unless   10
Soul clap its hands and sing, and louder sing
For every tatter in its mortal dress,
Nor is there singing school but studying
Monuments of its own magnificence;
And therefore I have sailed the seas and come   15
To the holy city of Byzantium.

tattered coat: an old man is as worthless as a scarecrow.
unless/Soul clap its hands and sing: man can only break free if he allows his spirit the freedom to express itself.
Nor is there ... own magnificence: all schools of art should study the discipline they teach, while the soul should study the immortal art of previous generations.

III

O sages standing in God's holy fire
As in the gold mosaic of a wall,
Come from the holy fire, perne in a gyre,
And be the singing-masters of my soul.   20
Consume my heart away; sick with desire
And fastened to a dying animal
It knows not what it is; and gather me
Into the artifice of eternity.

O sages: wise men, cleansed by the holy fire of God.
Come ... artifice of eternity: Yeats asks the sages to teach him the wonders of Byzantium and gather his soul into the perfection of art.
perne in a gyre: spinning; turning very fast.
fastened to a dying animal: the soul trapped in a decaying body.

IV

Once out of nature I shall never take   25
My bodily form from any natural thing,
But such a form as Grecian goldsmiths make
Of hammered gold and gold enamelling
To keep a drowsy Emperor awake;
Or set upon a golden bough to sing   30
To lords and ladies of Byzantium
Of what is past, or passing, or to come.

past, or passing, or to come: in eternity, the golden bird sings of transience (passing time).

'the holy city of Byzantium'

👤 Personal Response

1. This poem tries to offer a form of escape from old age. Does it succeed? Write a paragraph in response, with support from the text.
2. Why are the 'Monuments of unageing intellect' of such importance to the poet? What does this imply about Yeats's Ireland?
3. The poem is defiant in its exploration of eternity. Discuss, using reference or quotation.

⊙ Critical Literacy

'Sailing to Byzantium' confronts the universal issue of old age. There is no easy solution to this problem. Yeats found the idea of advancing age repulsive and longed to escape. Here he imagines an ideal place, Byzantium, which allowed all to enjoy eternal works of art. He celebrates what man can create and he bitterly condemns the mortality to which man is subject.

Yeats wrote, 'When Irishmen were illuminating the Book of Kells … Byzantium was the centre of European civilization … so I symbolise the search for the spiritual life by a journey to that city.'

The poet declares the theme in the first stanza as he confidently declaims that the world of the senses is not for the old – they must seek another way which is timeless, **a life of the spirit and intellect**. The word 'That' tells us he is looking back, as he has already started his journey. But he is looking back wistfully at the world of the lovers ('The young/In one another's arms') and the world of teeming nature ('The salmon-falls, the mackerel-crowded seas'). The compound words emphasise the dynamism and fertility of the life of the senses, even though he admits the flaw in this wonderful life of plenty is mortality ('Those dying generations'). The life of the senses and nature is governed by the harsh cycle of procreation, life and death.

The poet asserts in the second stanza that **what gives meaning to a person is the soul**, 'unless/Soul clap its hands and sing'. Otherwise an elderly man is worthless, 'a paltry thing'. We are given a chilling image of the thin, wasting frame of an old man as a scarecrow in tattered clothes. In contrast, we are shown the wonders of the intellect as the poet tells us that all schools of art study what they compose, what they produce – 'Monuments of unageing intellect'. These works of art are timeless; unlike the body, they are not subject to decay. Thus, music schools study great music and art schools study great paintings. The life of the intellect and spirit must take precedence over the life of the senses. Yeats will no longer listen to the 'sensual music' that is appropriate only for the young, but will study the carefully composed 'music' of classic art.

In Byzantium, the buildings had beautiful mosaics, pictures made with little tiles and inlaid with gold. One of these had a picture of martyrs being burned. Yeats addresses these wise men ('sages') in stanza three. He wants them to whirl through time ('perne in a gyre') and come to **teach his soul how to 'sing'**, how to live the life of the spirit. His soul craves this ('sick with desire'), **but it is trapped in the decaying, mortal body** ('fastened to a dying animal'). This is a horrendous image of old age. The soul has lost its identity: 'It knows not what it is'.

He pleads to be saved from this using two interesting verbs, 'Consume' and 'gather'. Both suggest a desire to be taken away. A fire consumes what is put into it and changes the form of the substance. Yeats wants a new body. He pleads to be embraced like a child coming home: 'gather me'. But where will he go? He will journey into the cold world of art, 'the artifice of eternity'. 'Artifice' refers to the skill of those who have created the greatest works of art, but it also means artificial, not real. Is the poet suggesting that eternity also has a flaw?

The fourth stanza starts confidently as Yeats declares that 'Once out of nature', he will be transformed into the ageless perfect work of art, the **golden bird**. This is the new body for his soul. Now he will sing to the court. But is the court listening? The word 'drowsy' suggests not. Isn't he singing about transience, the passing of time: 'what is past, or passing, or to come'? Has this any relevance in eternity? Is there a perfect solution to the dilemma of old age?

Yeats raises these questions for our consideration. He has explored this problem by contrasting the abundant life of the young with the 'tattered coat' of old age. He has shown us the golden bird of immortality in opposition to the 'dying animal' of the decaying body. The poet has lulled us with end-rhymes and half-rhymes. He has used groups of threes – 'Fish, flesh, or fowl', 'begotten, born, and dies', 'past, or passing, or to come' – to argue his case. At the end of the poem, do we feel that Yeats genuinely longs for the warm, teeming life of the senses with all its imperfections, rather than the cold, disinterested world of the 'artifice of eternity'?

✒ Writing About the Poem

'W. B. Yeats frequently uses vigorous language to denounce transience and old age.' Discuss this view with reference to 'Sailing to Byzantium'.

Sample Paragraph

In 'Sailing to Byzantium', Yeats confronts old age. A grotesque image of an old man as a scarecrow, 'A tattered coat upon a stick', is presented. The figure is unable to move, graphically illustrating old age. The vivid adjective 'tattered' suggests the physical wear and tear elderly people endure. Yeats longed to escape this fate, through a passionate appeal to the 'sages' to 'Consume my heart away'. Thinking of time's decay, he is 'sick with desire' just as in his poem, 'The Wild Swans at Coole' – 'And now my heart is sore'. So Yeats decides to shed the 'dying animal' of his ageing body and change into a golden bird, a precious, immortal work of art, the 'artifice of eternity'. In this way, the poet challenges physical decline. Ironically, the bird's function is reduced o keeping a 'drowsy Emperor awake' while, like the scarecrow, it is 'set upon a golden bough'. I feel that it is the allure of 'The young/In one another's arms' that Yeats really craves. His rich dynamic description of youthful exuberance is achieved through compound words ('salmon-falls'), alliteration ('Fish, flesh, fowl') and rushing enjambment. He longs to be young again.

Class/Homework Exercises

1. 'Yeats's search for truth serves to highlight the intense fury and disillusionment expressed in his poetry.' Discuss this view with reference to 'Sailing to Byzantium'.
2. 'W. B. Yeats makes effective use of imagery and symbolism to communicate thought-provoking insights about life.' Discuss this statement with reference to 'Sailing to Byzantium'.

Points to Consider

- Central themes include transience, old age and the timeless world of art.

- Rich symbols, metaphors, imagery and similes communicate the complexity of man's struggle with transience and decay.

- Balance, contrast and paradox reveal the complexity of the problem of old age.

- Compound words, onomatopoeia, intriguing use of verbs lend energy and passion to the argument.

8 *from* Meditations in Time of Civil War: The Stare's Nest by My Window

The bees build in the crevices
Of loosening masonry, and there
The mother birds bring grubs and flies.
My wall is loosening; honey-bees,
Come build in the empty house of the stare.　　　5

We are closed in, and the key is turned
On our uncertainty; somewhere
A man is killed, or a house burned,
Yet no clear fact to be discerned:
Come build in the empty house of the stare.　　　10

A barricade of stone or of wood;
Some fourteen days of civil war;
Last night they trundled down the road
That dead young soldier in his blood:
Come build in the empty house of the stare.　　　15

We had fed the heart on fantasies,
The heart's grown brutal from the fare;
More substance in our enmities
Than in our love; O honey-bees,
Come build in the empty house of the stare.　　　20

Title: Stare is another name for the starling, a bird with distinctive dark brown or greenish-black feathers.

grubs: larvae of insects.

civil war: the Irish Civil War (1922-23) between Republicans who fought for full independence and supporters of the Anglo-Irish Treaty.
trundled: rolled.

fare: diet (of dreams).

enmities: disputes; hatred.

'days of civil war'

395 |

👤 Personal Response

1. Comment on how Yeats creates an atmosphere of concern and insecurity in stanzas two and three.
2. In your opinion, how effective is the symbol of the bees as a civilising force amid all the destruction of war? Support your answer with close reference to the poem.
3. How would you describe the dominant mood of the poem? Is it positive or negative? Refer closely to the text in your answer.

👁 Critical Literacy

The Irish Civil War prompted Yeats to consider the brutality and insecurity caused by conflict. It also made him reflect on his own identity as part of the Anglo-Irish Ascendancy. The poet wrote elsewhere that he had been shocked and depressed by the fighting during the first months of hostilities, yet he was determined not to grow bitter or to lose sight of the beauty of nature. He wrote this poem after seeing a stare building its nest in a hole beside his window.

Much of the poem is dominated by the images of building and collapse. Stanza one introduces this tension between creativity ('bees build') and disintegration ('loosening'). In responding to the bitter civil war, Yeats finds suitable **symbols in the nurturing natural world** to express his own hopes. Addressing the bees, he asks that they 'build in the empty house of the stare'. He is desperately conscious of the political vacuum being presently filled by bloodshed. His desperate cry for help seems heartfelt in tone. There is also a possibility that the poet is addressing himself – he will have to revise his own attitudes to the changing political realities caused by the war.

In stanza two, Yeats expresses a sense of being **threatened by the conflict** around him: 'We are closed in'. The use of the plural pronoun suggests a community under siege. He is fearful of the future: 'our uncertainty'. Is the poet reflecting on the threat to his own immediate household or to the once powerful Anglo-Irish ruling class? The constant rumours of everyday violence are highlighted in the stark descriptions: 'A man is killed, or a house burned'. Such occurrences almost seem routine in the grim reality of war.

Stanza three opens with a **haunting image**, the 'barricade of stone', an enduring symbol of division and hostility. The vehemence and inhumanity of the times is driven home by the stark report of soldiers who 'trundled down the road' and left one 'dead young soldier in his blood'. Such atrocities add greater depth to the plaintive refrain for regeneration: 'Come build in the empty house of the stare'.

In the final stanza, Yeats faces up to the root causes of war: 'We had fed the heart on fantasies'. Dreams of achieving independence have led to even greater hatred ('enmities') and intransigence than could have been imagined. It is a tragic irony that the Irish nation has become more divided than ever before. The poet seems despairing as he accepts the failure represented by civil conflict: 'The heart's grown brutal'. It is as though he is reprimanding himself for daring to imagine a brave new world. His **final plea for healing** and reconstruction is strengthened by an emphatic 'O' to show Yeats's depth of feeling: 'O honey-bees,/Come build in the empty house of the stare'.

✒ Writing About the Poem

'Yeats's poetic vision is one of darkness and disappointment, balanced by moments of insight and optimism.' Discuss this view with reference to '*from* Meditations In Time Of Civil War: The Stare's Nest By My Window'.

Sample Paragraph

In 'The Stare's Nest By My Window', Yeats reveals his views on the Irish Civil War. Throughout the poem, there are recurring images of decay and destruction. Observing the bees outside his window, he is surprised to see something purposeful going on within the 'loosening masonry'. Although the crumbling building suggests the break-up of the Irish nation, there is also an ironic recognition of something new happening. This is typical of the poet's ambivalent attitude – similar to his view of Easter 1916 as a 'terrible beauty'. The positive image of the bees is symbolic of recovery from the conflict. This is a key theme in the poem and shows that Yeats – who has been shocked by the Civil War – now finds hope in nature. The poet's use of symbolism contrasts the two forces of devastation and regeneration when he urges the bees to 'build in the empty house'. However, there are several dark images that show the poet's realism, e.g. the 'house burned' and the tragic life of the 'young soldier in his blood'. These are stark reminders of human loss – the reality of conflict. But in the end, Yeats seems to argue that we can learn from nature. He hopes that just as the birds take care of their young, Ireland will recover from warfare.

EXAMINER'S COMMENT

A well-written top-grade response. Informed discussion focused throughout on the balance between Yeats's positive and negative attitudes. Accurate quotations provided good support. Cross-referencing shows engagement with the poet's complex views. Expression throughout is very well-controlled ('recurring images', 'ironic recognition', 'stark reminders of human loss').

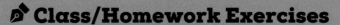

✒ Class/Homework Exercises

1. 'W. B. Yeats often uses startling language and imagery to raise key questions about Irish nationalism.' Discuss this statement referring both to the subject matter and style of 'The Stare's Nest By My Window'.

2. 'Yeats's poems frequently address serious issues in a fresh and accessible style.' Discuss this view with reference to 'The Stare's Nest By My Window'.

◉ Points to Consider

- Another of Yeats's political poems expressing his personal views on Irish history.

- Central themes: Civil War violence and destruction; the natural world.

- Effective use of repetition, varying tones (dismay, hopelessness, acceptance, yearning).

- Contrasting images of destruction ('loosening masonry') and renewal ('bees build').

9 In Memory of Eva Gore-Booth and Con Markiewicz

The light of evening, Lissadell,
Great windows open to the south,
Two girls in silk kimonos, both
Beautiful, one a gazelle.
But a raving autumn shears   5
Blossom from the summer's wreath;
The older is condemned to death,
Pardoned, drags out lonely years
Conspiring among the ignorant.
I know not what the younger dreams –   10
Some vague Utopia – and she seems,
When withered old and skeleton-gaunt,
An image of such politics.
Many a time I think to seek
One or the other out and speak   15
Of that old Georgian mansion, mix
Pictures of the mind, recall
That table and the talk of youth,
Two girls in silk kimonos, both
Beautiful, one a gazelle.   20

Dear shadows, now you know it all,
All the folly of a fight
With a common wrong or right.
The innocent and the beautiful
Have no enemy but time;   25
Arise and bid me strike a match
And strike another till time catch;
Should the conflagration climb,
Run till all the sages know.
We the great gazebo built,   30
They convicted us of guilt;
Bid me strike a match and blow.

Lissadell: the Gore-Booth family home in Co. Sligo.

kimonos: traditional Japanese robes.
gazelle: graceful antelope.

shears: cuts.

Conspiring: plotting; scheming.

Utopia: a perfect world.

folly: foolishness.

conflagration: blazing inferno.
sages: philosophers.

gazebo: ornamental summer house, sometimes seen as a sign of extravagance.

'that old Georgian mansion'

👤 Personal Response

1. What mood does Yeats create in the first four lines of the poem? Explain how he achieves this mood.
2. Would you agree that this is a poem of contrasts? How does Yeats use contrasts to express his thoughts and feelings? Support your points with relevant reference.
3. What picture of Yeats himself emerges from this poem? Use close reference to the text to support the points you make.

◉ Critical Literacy

Yeats wrote this poem about the two Gore-Booth sisters shortly after their deaths. He was 62 at the time. Eva was a noted campaigner for women's rights and Constance was a revolutionary who took part in the 1916 Rising. She later became the first woman elected to the British House of Commons at Westminster. The poet had once been fascinated by their youthful grace and beauty, but he became increasingly opposed to their political activism. Although the poem is a memorial to the two women, it also reveals Yeats's own views about the changes that had occurred in Ireland over his lifetime.

Stanza one begins on a nostalgic note, with Yeats recalling a magical summer's evening in the company of the Gore-Booth sisters. The details he remembers suggest a **world of elegance and privilege** in the girls' family home, Lissadell House, overlooking Sligo Bay. 'Great windows' are a reminder of the grandeur to be found in the Anglo-Irish 'Big House'. Eva and Constance are portrayed as being delicately beautiful, their elusive femininity indicated by the exotic 'silk kimonos' they wear. The poet compares one of the girls to 'a gazelle', stylishly poised and graceful.

The abrupt contrast of mood in line 5 disrupts the tranquil scene. Yeats considers the harsh effects of time and how it changes everything. He describes autumn (personified as an overenthusiastic gardener) as 'raving' and uncontrollable. The metaphor illustrates the way **time destroys** ('shears') the simple perfection of youth ('Blossom'). Typically, Yeats chooses images from the natural world to express his own retrospective outlook.

In lines 7–13, the poet shows his **deep contempt** for the involvement of both the Gore-Booth sisters in revolutionary politics. As far as Yeats is concerned, their activism 'among the ignorant' was a great mistake. These beautiful young women wasted their lives for a 'vague Utopia'. The graphic image of one of the girls growing 'withered old and skeleton-gaunt' is also used to symbolise the unattractive political developments of the era. Repulsed by the idea, Yeats retreats into the more sophisticated world of Lissadell's 'old Georgian mansion'.

The second stanza is in marked contrast to the first. Yeats addresses the spirits ('shadows') of Eva and Constance. The tone of voice is unclear. It appears to be compassionate, but there is an undertone of weariness as well. He goes on to scold the two women for wasting their lives on 'folly'. Yeats seems angry that their innocence and beauty have been sacrificed for nothing. It is as though he feels **they have betrayed both their own femininity and their social class**. If they had only known it, their one and only enemy was time.

In the final lines of the poem, Yeats dramatises his feelings by turning all his **resentment against time** itself. He associates the failed lives of the women with the decay of the Anglo-Irish Ascendancy. The energetic rhythm and repetition reflect his fury as he imagines striking match after match ('And strike another till time catch') and is consumed in a great 'conflagration'. The poet imagines that the significance of this inferno will eventually be understood by those who are wise, the 'sages'. In the last sentence, Yeats considers how 'They' (the enemies of the Anglo-Irish Ascendancy) hastened the end of a grand cultural era in Ireland. The 'great gazebo' is a symbol of the fine houses and gracious living that were slowly disappearing. The poem ends on a defiant note ('Bid me strike a match and blow'), with Yeats inviting the ghosts of Eva and Constance to help him resist the devastating effects of time.

✒ Writing About the Poem

'Many of Yeats's most evocative poems lament the loss of youth and beauty.' Discuss this view with reference to 'In Memory of Eva Gore-Booth and Con Markiewicz'.

Sample Paragraph

'In Memory of Eva Gore-Booth and Con Markiewicz' is largely focused on time as a destructive force. Yeats begins by describing the aristocratic sisters as 'Two girls in silk kimonos', the gentle sibilant sounds suggesting their elegance. The poem is really an elegy for the past and Yeats's nostalgic portrayal of the time he shared with the young women at Lissadell is filled with regret. The tone becomes more wistful as he remembers summer evenings 'and the talk of youth'. Yeats illustrates the effects of age when he contrasts the girls in their graceful refinement in their later years – 'withered old and skeleton-gaunt'. The image is startling, evidence of how he views the ravages of time. It is all the more shocking when compared with the delicate kimonos – symbols of lost beauty.

EXAMINER'S COMMENT

A well-focused top-grade standard which directly addresses the question. Good discussion of the poem's mood of regret ('nostalgic portrayal', 'tone becomes more wistful'). Excellent use of contrasting images to illustrate the poet's theme. The references and quotes are carefully chosen and show clear engagement with the poem. Expression is also impressive.

It's obvious that Yeats is also regretful of his own lost youth – similar to how he felt in 'Sailing to Byzantium'.

✒ Class/Homework Exercises

1. 'W. B. Yeats makes effective use of contrasting moods and atmospheres to express his strongly held ideas and heartfelt feelings.' Discuss this statement with reference to 'In Memory of Eva Gore-Booth and Con Markiewicz'.

2. 'Yeats frequently combines both a sensitive romantic nature and a fiercely critical voice.' Discuss this view with reference to both to the subject matter and style of 'In Memory of Eva Gore-Booth and Con Markiewicz'.

⊙ Points to Consider

- Elegy for a lost world of great beauty, style and sophistication.

- The poem reveals Yeats's own attitudes to the two sisters.

- Life's transience sharply contrasted with the longevity of art.

- Various tones – nostalgic, reflective, scornful, critical.

- Striking imagery of light and shade and seasonal change.

10 Swift's Epitaph

Title: Jonathan Swift, satirist and clergyman, author of *Gulliver's Travels* and dean of St Patrick's Cathedral. The original inscription in Latin is on his memorial in the cathedral. Yeats liked to spend time there.
Epitaph: inscription for a tomb or memorial.

Swift has sailed into his rest;
Savage indignation there
Cannot lacerate his breast.
Imitate him if you dare,
World-besotted traveller; he   5
Served human liberty.

his rest: suggestion of afterlife; death is not an end.
Savage indignation: the driving force of Swift's satirical work. He believed in a society where wrong was punished and good rewarded.
lacerate: cut; tear.
World-besotted: obsessed with travelling or with material concerns rather than spiritual matters.
he/Served human liberty: Yeats believed Swift served the liberty of the intellect, not liberty for the common people. Yeats associated democracy with organised mobs of ignorant people.

'Swift's Epitaph'

👤 Personal Response

1. How would you describe the tone of this poem?
2. Comment on the poet's use of the verb 'lacerate'. What do you think Yeats is trying to convey?

👁 Critical Literacy

'Swift's Epitaph' is a translation from the original Latin epitaph composed by Swift for himself. Yeats adds a new first line to the original. He regarded this epitaph as the 'greatest … in history'.

W. B. Yeats admired Swift, who was proud and solitary and belonged to the Anglo-Irish tradition, as did Yeats himself. He regarded the Anglo-Irish as superior. He once said, 'We have created most of the modern literature of this country. We have created the best of its political intelligence.' Yeats's additional first line to the epitaph conveys a dignified sailing into the spiritual afterlife by the deceased Swift. The rest of the poem is a **translation** from the Latin original. Swift is now free from all the negative reactions he was subjected to when alive: 'Savage indignation there/Cannot lacerate his breast.' Swift's self-portrait conveys the impression of a man of fierce **independence and pride**. 'Imitate him if you dare' is the challenge thrown down like a gauntlet to the reader to try to be like him. 'World-besotted traveller' can be read as a man who has travelled extensively in his imagination as well as in reality. His contribution to humanity is summed up in the final sentence: 'he/Served human liberty'. **He freed the artist** from the masses so that the artist could 'make liberty visible'. The tone of this short, compressed poem is proud and defiant, like Swift.

🖋 Writing About the Poem

'W. B. Yeats frequently confronts the painful reality of death in fierce, challenging poetry.' Discuss this view with particular reference to 'Swift's Epitaph'.

Sample Paragraph

Yeats wrote two provocative epitaphs – his own in 'Under Ben Bulben' and this translation of Swift's self-composed epitaph in Latin. Both show a disregard for life as a permanent end in itself. Yeats reveals a fearless, confident Swift departing this life for the next in the sibilant line, 'Swift has sailed into his rest'. The metaphor highlights the natural progression of the soul returning to its eternal rest. Death provides a sanctuary from this world. Death is a reality of life's circle. Swift's 'Savage indignation' was directed at the two great evils of contemporary society, starvation and emigration. But 'there', in paradise, he is able to 'leave aside his life's work and all the criticism he received. The verb 'lacerate' suggests the public backlash he suffered as a result. Yeats challenges readers, asking if we are brave enough to stand up (like Swift) for what is right, 'Imitate him if you dare'. The final comment – that he 'Served human liberty' – asks us to join him in demanding a world where good is rewarded and wickedness punished.

✒ Class/Homework Exercises

1. 'Yeats uses dramatic and forceful language to express his passionate views on ageing and the passing of time.' Discuss this statement with reference to 'Swift's Epitaph'.
2. 'W. B. Yeats often chooses confrontation when exploring universal themes in thought-provoking poetry.' Discuss this view with reference to 'Swift's Epitaph'.

⊙ Points to Consider

- **The satirist Jonathan Swift has made a strong impact on Yeats's imagination.**

- **Sibilant metaphor of sailing suggests the ease of passage from this life to the next.**

- **Emphatic language highlights Swift's efforts to improve the human condition and the resulting response.**

- **Poem offers a direct provocative challenge to readers.**

11 An Acre of Grass

Picture and book remain,
An acre of green grass
For air and exercise,
Now strength and body goes;
Midnight, an old house   5
Where nothing stirs but a mouse.

My temptation is quiet.
Here at life's end
Neither loose imagination,
Nor the mill of the mind   10
Consuming its rag and bone,
Can make the truth known.

Grant me an old man's frenzy,
Myself must I remake
Till I am Timon and Lear   15
Or that William Blake
Who beat upon the wall
Till Truth obeyed his call;

A mind Michael Angelo knew
That can pierce the clouds,   20
Or inspired by frenzy
Shake the dead in their shrouds;
Forgotten else by mankind,
An old man's eagle mind.

acre: the secluded garden of Yeats's home, where he spent his final years.

an old house: the house was in Rathfarnham, Co. Dublin.

loose imagination: vague, unfocused ideas.

frenzy: wildly excited state.

Timon and Lear: two of Shakespeare's elderly tragic heroes, both of whom raged against the world.
William Blake: English visionary poet and painter (1757–1827).

Michael Angelo: Michelangelo, Italian Renaissance artist (1475–1564).

shrouds: burial garments.

'An acre of green grass'

👤 Personal Response

1. How does Yeats create a mood of calm and serenity in the opening stanza?
2. Briefly explain the change of tone in stanza three.

👁 Critical Literacy

Written in 1936 when Yeats was 71, the poet expresses his resentment towards ageing gracefully. Instead, he will dedicate himself to seeking wisdom through frenzied creativity. People sometimes take a narrow view of the elderly and consider them completely redundant. In Yeats's case, he is determined not to let old age crush his spirit.

Stanza one paints a picture of retirement as a surrender to death. Yeats's life has been reduced to suit his basic needs. 'Picture and book' might refer to the poet's memories. Physically weak, he feels like a prisoner whose enclosed garden area is for 'air and exercise'. There is an underlying **feeling of alienation and inactivity**: 'nothing stirs'.

In stanza two, the poet says that it would be easy to give in to the stereotypical image of placid contentment: 'My temptation is quiet', especially since old age ('life's end') has weakened his creative powers. **Yeats admits that his 'loose imagination' is not as sharp as it was when he was in his prime.** He no longer finds immediate inspiration ('truth') in everyday experiences, which he compares to life's 'rag and bone'.

The third stanza opens on a much more dramatic and forceful note as the poet confronts his fears: 'Grant me an old man's frenzy'. Yeats's personal prayer is totally lacking in meekness. Instead, he urges himself to focus enthusiastically on his own creative purpose – 'frenzy'. **He pledges to 'remake' himself** in the image of such heroic figures as Timon, Lear and William Blake. The passionate tone and run-on lines add to his sense of commitment to his art.

In stanza four, Yeats develops **his spirited pursuit of meaningful old age** by reflecting on 'A mind Michael Angelo knew'. The poet is stimulated and encouraged to follow the great artist's example and 'pierce the clouds'. The image suggests the daring power of imagination to lift the spirit in the search for truth and beauty. The final lines build to a climax as Yeats imagines the joys of 'An old man's eagle mind'. Such intense creativity can 'Shake the dead' and allow the poet to continue experiencing life to its fullest.

✒ Writing About the Poem

'W. B. Yeats uses powerful language and imagery to express his personal views.' Discuss this statement with reference to 'An Acre of Grass'.

Sample Paragraph

Yeats takes a highly unusual approach to ageing in 'An Acre of Grass'. To begin with, his subdued tone suggests that he is happy in his quiet 'acre of green grass'. Everything seems organised, yet a little too organised for his liking. In the first few lines, we get a picture of someone close to second childhood, engrossed in his 'picture and book'. Acutely aware of his advancing years, he resents being at 'life's end' and is quick to rebel against it. Clearly, he still yearns for renewed energy and inspiration. The irony of returning to childhood and lacking 'loose imagination' appals him. His forceful language emerges in the second half of the poem when he demands 'an old man's frenzy'. His need to be creative again is illustrated by the references to Lear (the tragic king in Shakespeare's play who fought to the bitter end) and to William Blake and Michelangelo. Like them, Yeats wants to live a productive life – with an 'eagle mind'. The dramatic metaphor typifies his startling imagery. In these final lines, his tone is defiant. He will not fade away.

EXAMINER'S COMMENT

There is some very good discussion in this paragraph and a clear sense of engagement. Informed points focused on the subdued tone and irony in the early stanzas. Accurate quotations are integrated effectively into the commentary. Expression is impressive also: varied sentence length, ranging vocabulary ('yearns for renewed energy and inspiration', 'dramatic metaphor typifies his startling imagery') and good control of syntax. A top-grade standard.

Class/Homework Exercises

1. 'Some of Yeats's most thought-provoking poems combine his personal concerns with public issues.' Discuss this view with reference to 'An Acre of Grass'.

2. 'Yeats uses simple and direct language in exploring his concerns about ageing and death.' Discuss this statement with reference to 'An Acre of Grass'.

Points to Consider

- Confessional poem addresses familiar themes of old age and artistic revitalisation.

- Striking contrast between his initial acceptance of age and his final determination to renew himself.

- Effective use of imagery to show that the house has also been engulfed by old age.

- References to Blake, Timon of Athens and King Lear focus on Yeats's desired poetic-frenzy.

12 *from* **Under Ben Bulben**

V

Irish poets, learn your trade,
Sing whatever is well made,
Scorn the sort now growing up
All out of shape from toe to top,
Their unremembering hearts and heads   5
Base-born products of base beds.
Sing the peasantry, and then
Hard-riding country gentlemen,
The holiness of monks, and after
Porter-drinkers' randy laughter;   10
Sing the lords and ladies gay
That were beaten into the clay
Through seven heroic centuries;
Cast your mind on other days
That we in coming days may be   15
Still the indomitable Irishry.

VI

Under bare Ben Bulben's head
In Drumcliff churchyard Yeats is laid,
An ancestor was rector there
Long years ago, a church stands near,   20
By the road an ancient cross.
No marble, no conventional phrase;
On limestone quarried near the spot
By his command these words are cut:
   Cast a cold eye   25
   On life, on death.
   Horseman, pass by!

whatever is well made: great art.

base: low; unworthy.

indomitable: invincible; unbeatable.

Under bare Ben Bulben's head: defiant symbol of the famous mountain.

ancestor: the poet's great-grandfather.

Horseman: possibly a symbolic figure from local folklore; or possibly any passer-by.

'Under bare Ben Bulben's head'

409 |

👤 Personal Response

1. Comment on the tone used by Yeats in giving advice to other writers. Refer to the text in your answer.

2. From your reading of the poem, explain the kind of 'Irishry' that Yeats wishes to see celebrated in poetry. Support the points you make with reference or quotation.

3. Describe the mood of Drumcliff churchyard as visualised by the poet. Use close reference to the text to show how Yeats uses language to create this mood.

👁 Critical Literacy

This was one of Yeats's last poems. Sections V and VI of the elegy sum up his personal views on the future of Irish poetry and also include the enigmatic epitaph he composed for his own gravestone. Using art as a gateway to spiritual fulfilment is characteristic of the poet.

Section V is a hard-hitting address by Yeats to his contemporaries and all the poets who will come after him. He encourages them to set the highest 'well-made' standards for their work. His uncompromisingly negative view of contemporary writing ('out of shape from toe to top') is quickly clarified. The reason why modern literature is in such a state of confusion is that the poets' 'unremembering hearts and heads' **have lost touch with tradition**. The formality and discipline of great classic poetry have been replaced by unstructured writing and free verse. The authoritative tone becomes even more scathing as Yeats castigates the inferiority of his peers as 'Base-born products'.

It is not only intellectual artistic tradition that the poet admires; he finds another valuable tradition in the legends and myths of old Ireland. Yeats urges his fellow writers to 'Sing the peasantry'. But he also advises them to **absorb other cultural traditions**. Here he includes the 'Hard-riding country gentlemen' of his own Anglo-Irish class and the 'holiness of monks' – those who seek truth through ascetic or spiritual means. Even the more sensuous 'randy laughter' of 'Porter-drinkers' can be inspirational. For Yeats, the peasant and aristocratic traditions are equally worth celebrating. Irish history is marked by a combination of joy, heroism, defeat and resilience. Yet despite (or perhaps because of) his harsh criticism of the present generation, there is little doubt about the poet's passionate desire to encourage new writing that would reflect the true greatness of 'indomitable Irishry'.

Section VI is a great deal less dogmatic. Writing in the third person, Yeats describes his final resting place in Drumcliff. The voice is **detached and dignified**. Using a series of unadorned images, he takes us to the simple churchyard at the foot of Ben Bulben. The mountain stands as a proud symbol of how our unchanging silent origins outlive human tragedy. It is to his Irish roots that the poet ultimately wants to return. His wishes are modest but curt – 'No marble'. Keen to avoid the well-worn headstone inscriptions, Yeats provides his own incisive epitaph. The three short lines are enigmatic and balance opposing views, typical of so much of his poetry. The poet's last warning ('Cast a cold eye') reminds us to live measured lives based on a realistic understanding of the cycle of life and death. The beautiful Christian setting, subdued tone and measured rhythm all contribute to the quiet dignity of Yeats's final farewell.

✒ Writing About the Poem

'W. B. Yeats's inspired poetry gives expression to the spirit of a whole nation through his mastery of form.' Discuss this view with reference to 'Under Ben Bulben'.

Sample Paragraph

'Under Ben Bulben' addresses themes close to Yeats's heart – the perfection of art, Irish nationalism and the reality of death. The poet's views are evident throughout – expressed in an imperative voice: 'Irish poets, learn your trade'. Yeats believed strongly in traditional verse, spending hours shaping a poem. He is bitterly opposed to the type of free verse of contemporary poets, 'Scorn the sort now growing up/All out of shape from toe to top'. His use of enjambed lines and the inverted phrase ('toe to top') mimics the ugliness of modern poetry. Instead he offers readers the crafted perfection of couplets and a succinct three-line conclusion, 'Cast a cold eye/On life, on death./Horseman, pass by!' He also makes being Irish something to be desired, a race, undefeated after years of oppression, 'Still the indomitable Irishry', even inventing a new word to express our unique culture. The modern poets he is addressing are urged to remember this, 'Cast your minds on other days'. Yeats's poetry actually practises what he preaches, presenting a 'well-made' poem with a vision of what it means to be Irish.

EXAMINER'S COMMENT

A top-grade response that explores the form and structure of the poem alongside the central theme of Irishness. Points are aptly illustrated with accurate quotation. Some impressive discussion regarding the poet's critical tone in mocking aspects of contemporary poetry. Expression throughout is clear and well-controlled.

✒ Class/Homework Exercises

1. 'W. B. Yeats has remarked that his poetry is generally written out of despair.' Discuss this statement referring to both the subject matter and style of 'Under Ben Bulben'.
2. 'Yeats's forceful language and vivid imagery convey his intense vision of life and death.' Discuss this view with reference to 'Under Ben Bulben'.

⊙ Points to Consider

- Self-epitaph achieving his aim 'to hammer my thoughts into unity'.

- Formal vision of integrated spiritual reality, natural cycle of life and death.

- Revitalised use of traditional rhyme scheme and metered poetry (strict four-beat rhythm).

- Use of colloquial language. Short lines give a modern quality to the poem.

- Distinctive poetic voice, authoritative, compelling, direct and exhilarating.

13 Politics

W. B. YEATS

Title: winning and using power to govern society.

'*In our time the destiny of man presents its meanings in political terms.*'
Thomas Mann

How can I, that girl standing there,
My attention fix
On Roman or on Russian
Or on Spanish politics?
Yet here's a travelled man that knows   5
What he talks about,
And there's a politician
That has read and thought,
And maybe what they say is true
Of war and war's alarms,   10
But O that I were young again
And held her in my arms.

Thomas Mann was a German novelist who argued that the future of man was determined by states and governments.

On Roman or on Russian/ Or on Spanish politics: a reference to the political upheavals of Europe in the 1930s.

'But O that I were young again/
And held her in my arms'

413

👤 Personal Response

1. This poem suggests that politics are not important. Does the poet convince you? Write a paragraph in response, with reference to the text.
2. Where does the language used in the poem convey a sense of deep longing? How effective is this?

👁 Critical Literacy

'Politics' is a satire written in 1939, when Yeats was 73, in response to a magazine article. He said it was based on 'a moment of meditation'.

A **satire** uses ridicule to expose foolishness. A magazine article praised Yeats for his 'public' work. The poet was delighted with this word, as one of his aims had always been to 'move the common people'. However, the article went on to say that Yeats should have used this 'public' voice to address public issues such as politics. Yeats disagreed, as he had always regarded politics as dishonest and superficial. He thought professional politicians manipulated through 'false news'. This is evident from the ironic comment, 'And maybe what they say is true'. Here we see the poet's indifference to these matters.

This poem addresses **real truths**, the proper material for poems, the universal experience of **human relationships**, not the infinite abstractions that occupied politicians ('war and war's alarms'). Big public events, Yeats is suggesting, are not as important as love. The girl in the poem is more important than all the politics in the world: 'How can I ... My attention fix/On Roman or on Russian/Or on Spanish politics'? So Yeats is overthrowing the epigraph at the beginning of the poem, where the novelist Thomas Mann is stating that people should be concerned with political matters. Politics is the winning and using of power to govern the state. Yeats is adopting the persona of the distracted lover who is unable to focus on the tangled web of European politics in the 1930s. This poem was to be placed in his last poetry collection, almost like a farewell, as he states again that what he desires is youth and love.

But this poem can also give another view. Is the 'she' in the poem Ireland? Yeats has addressed public issues in poems such as 'Easter 1916' and 'September 1913' and he was already a senator in the Irish government. As usual, he leaves us with questions as he draws us through this deceptively simple poem with its **ever-changing tones** that range from the questioning opening to mockery, doubt and finally longing. The **steady rhyme** (the second line rhymes with the fourth and so on) drives the poem forward to its emphatic **closing wish**, the cry of an old man who wishes to recapture his youth and lost love.

🖋 Writing About the Poem

'Yeats's final poems are particularly poignant because all that matters to him is youth and love.' Discuss this view with reference to 'Politics'.

Sample Paragraph

It's thought that 'Politics' is Yeats's last poem – and it expresses his belief in the importance of emotions over everything else. Although written in 1938 when Europe was edging towards war, the poet is unable to focus on public affairs – 'Roman or on Russian/Or on Spanish politics'. Instead, he is much more interested in a beautiful girl who is nearby. His tone is tender and filled with longing – 'O that I were young again/ And held her in my arms'. As in 'Sailing to Byzantium', he is well aware of the impossibility of reversing time – and that is what makes the poem so moving. The exclamation 'O' is all the more touching because the poet understands how hopeless his desires are. The reality is that he can never regain youth or experience love with a young woman again. For me, this old man's bittersweet realisation makes 'Politics' one of Yeats's most poignant poems.

> **EXAMINER'S COMMENT**
>
> *A short but insightful high-grade response that engages loosely with the poem. Points are clearly focused on Yeats's reluctant acceptance that youth and love can only be memories. Good focus on the poet's mood and tone ('tender', 'touching', 'bittersweet'). The cross-reference broadens the discussion and expression is well-controlled throughout.*

✒ Class/Homework Exercises

1. 'W. B. Yeats frequently writes simple but beautiful poems that have universal significance.' Discuss this statement with reference to 'Politics'.
2. 'Despite his intense disappointment with reality, Yeats can often find hope in his imagination.' Discuss this view with reference to 'Politics'.

⊙ Points to Consider

- **Central focus on the poet's nostalgia for his younger days.**
- **Yeats is preoccupied with private human interaction rather than public or political situations.**
- **The poet expresses little optimism or even interest in the future.**
- **Various tones – reflective, sceptical, ironic, nostalgic, resigned.**
- **Effective use of contrasts: intellect and emotion, age and youth, male and female.**

Understanding the Prescribed Poetry Question

Marks are awarded using the PCLM Marking Scheme:
P = 15; C = 15; L = 15; M = 5
Total = 50

- **P** (Purpose = 15 marks) refers to the set question and is the launch pad for the answer. This involves engaging with all aspects of the question. Both theme and language must be addressed, although not necessarily equally.
- **C** (Coherence = 15 marks) refers to the organisation of the developed response and the use of accurate, relevant quotation. Paragraphing is essential.
- **L** (Language = 15 marks) refers to the student's skill in controlling language throughout the answer.
- **M** (Mechanics = 5 marks) refers to spelling and grammar.
- Although no specific number of poems is required, students usually discuss at least 3 or 4 in their written responses.
- Aim for at least 800 words, to be completed within 45–50 minutes.

NOTE

In keeping with the PCLM approach, the student has to take a stance by agreeing, disagreeing or partially agreeing with the statement:

- **Yeats's reflective poetry** (conflict, disappointment, loss, mortality, ageing, escape, perfection of art, immortality, eternity, etc.)

... largely defined through:

- **the tension between idealism and reality** (contrasting imagery, compelling symbols, dramatic language, powerful rhetoric, intense paradoxes, conflicting moods and tones, etc.)

Sample Leaving Cert Questions on Yeats's Poetry

1. 'W. B. Yeats's reflective poetry is defined largely by the tension between his search for an ideal world and the failure to escape reality.' To what extent do you agree or disagree with this statement? In developing your answer, discuss both the themes and poetic language of the poetry of W. B. Yeats on your course.

2. 'Yeats's poetry can sometimes seem obscure and challenging, but his powerful language has enduring appeal.' Discuss this view, developing your answer with reference to both the themes and poetic style of the poetry of W. B. Yeats on your course.

3. From your study of the poetry of W. B. Yeats on your course, select the poems that, in your opinion, best demonstrate his effective use of rich symbolism and vivid imagery to explore a range of poetic themes. Justify your response, developing your answer with reference to the poetry of W. B. Yeats on your course.

How do I organise my answer?

(Sample question 1)

'W. B. Yeats's reflective poetry is defined largely by the tension between his search for an ideal world and the failure to escape reality.' To what extent do you agree or disagree with this statement? In developing your answer, discuss both the themes and poetic language of the poetry of W. B. Yeats on your course.

Sample Plan 1

Intro: (*Stance: agree with viewpoint in the question*) Yeats's poetry is distinguished by a powerful strain between his pursuit of an ideal state and the inability to flee the harsh reality of everyday life. Effective use of forceful imagery, dramatic language and a variety of compelling tones.

Point 1: (*Elegy – world of beauty and grace/ugly reality – contrast*) 'In Memory of Eva Gore-Booth and Con Markievicz' nostalgically recalls an elegant world juxtaposing it against the ravages of time. Contemptuous tone conveys Yeats's resentment at real life choices made by Gore-Booth sisters ('gazelle' transforms into 'skeleton-gaunt').

Point 2: (*Confession – ageing/renewal – vivid imagery, allusions*) 'An Acre of Grass' presents Yeats's resentful attitude to the reality of ageing ('Now strength and body goes'). He yearns for the artistic world ('an old man's frenzy'). Startling imagery captures the poet's intense desire for artistic activity and productivity ('Shake the dead in their shrouds').

Point 3: (*Self-epitaph – inferior modern literature/perfection of classical literature – imperative, contrast*) '*from* Under Ben Bulben' contrasts ugliness of modern verse ('Base-born products') with perfection of heroic couplets ('learn your trade,/Sing whatever is well made').

Point 4: (*Satire – ageing/renewal – contrasts*) 'Politics' ironically comments on reality of politicians' false promises ('And maybe what they say is true') with his deeply-held belief in the power of the emotions ('O that I were young again/And held her in my arms').

Conclusion: Yeats frequently reveals his inner struggle in confronting human realities. He creates poetry bringing his ideal world to life to enable us to see beyond what meets the eye while acknowledging but never fully accepting the harsh truths of everyday experience.

Sample Paragraph: Point 2

'An Acre of Grass' is Yeats's defiant confession that he refuses to grow old gracefully. While he acknowledges the reality that he is 'Here at life's end', he despises old age's inactivity, 'nothing stirs'. Instead, he desires 'an old man's frenzy'. Yeats's internal struggle with the reality of ageing causes him to turn to his great role models. These include characters from Shakespeare, 'Timon and Lear', who railed against this unjust world. His desperate tone is evident in his prayer for help, 'Grant me'. But the poet is determined to continue with his artistic pursuits, despite his acknowledgement that his 'loose imagination' no longer finds inspiration in the dull 'rag and bone' of 'everyday routine. Dramatic verbs ('pierce', 'inspired') describe the creative vigour of this 'old man's eagle mind'. Yeats will even disturb the 'dead in their shrouds'. His tone reflects his inner conflict.

EXAMINER'S COMMENT

Sustained top-grade response that addresses the question. Analytical points show a clear understanding of the poem. There is close engagement with the text, particularly in the discussion of how the poet's turmoil is conveyed through vivid imagery, intense tones, rhythm and contrasts. Impressive expression throughout and excellent use of supportive quotes.

(Sample question 2)

'Yeats's poetry can sometimes seem obscure and challenging, but his powerful language has enduring appeal.' Discuss this view, developing your answer with reference to both the themes and poetic style of the poetry of W.B. Yeats on your course.

Sample Plan 2

Intro: (*Stance: partially agree with viewpoint in the question*) Yeats challenges readers to consider challenging concepts – transience,

NOTE

In keeping with the PCLM approach, the student has to take a stance by agreeing and/or disagreeing that Yeats's poetry can sometimes seem

– **obscure and challenging** (complex philosophical themes – materialism/idealism, ageing/regeneration, nature/mysticism, art/beauty, political conflict/patriotism, unclear references/allusions, etc.)

… but there is enduring appeal in:

– **powerful language** (evocative imagery, startling sound effects, dramatic verbs, striking comparisons, engaging tones, compelling rhythms, etc.)

creativity, the breakdown of civilisation, political change, heroism, the immortality of art. His powerful language has enduring appeal – forceful metaphors, vivid images and symbols, dramatic quality repetition.

Point 1: (*Apocalyptic vision – chilling imagery, foreboding tone*) 'The Second Coming' presents compelling imagery – a falcon spiralling out of control ('turning and turning'). Interesting Biblical imagery ('rough beast') lends authority and dramatic verbs emphasise the turbulent mood.

Point 2: (*Transience/eternity – absorbing symbols, compound words*) 'Sailing to Byzantium' tackles the eternal problem of mortality/immortality. Vigorous phrases ('salmon-falls', 'mackerel-crowded') evoke fertility. Poet regards ageing man as worthless ('paltry thing') presenting a haunting image of frailty and decay ('dying animal'). Using emphatic language, Yeats addresses this stimulating theme.

Point 3: (*Destruction/nurturing – rich metaphor, repetition, contrasts*) '*from* Meditations in Time of Civil War: The Stare's Nest By My Window' introduces nature's regenerative power ('bees build') to expose the horrific damage wreaked by conflict ('A man is killed, or a house burned'). Repetitive image of political vacuum ('empty house of the stare') contrasted with maternal nurturing ('mother birds bring grubs and flies').

Point 4: (*Provocative challenge – sibilant language, defiant tone*) 'Swift's Epitaph' opens with an evocative metaphor describing Swift's death ('sailed into his rest'). This serene image contrasts with reality of hostile reaction ('Savage indignation') to Swift's efforts for improving humanity.

Conclusion: Yeats defiantly confronts his readers with challenging, but clearly defined themes, including the future, transience and conflict. Attractive writing style, inspiring visual and aural effects, innovative language and a rich variety of tones all excite the reader.

Sample Paragraph: Point 1

'The Second Coming' presents another challenging idea – the apocalyptic vision of society's collapse. This is seen in the central image of the falcon spiralling out of control, 'Turning and turning and in the widening gyre'. Yeats involves readers by confronting them directly with an uncomfortable truth. He believes that fanatics are taking control, 'the worst/Are full of passionate intensity'. Although he presents us with a disturbing image of humanity's spirit rising in a shocking 'Second Coming', he vividly describes it – 'blank and pitiless as the sun'. As always, the poet's expression is memorable, e.g. his use of alliteration, 'darkness drops', strikes a foreboding note. Vigorous visual imagery, 'blood-dimmed tide', reinforces the hectic scene. For Yeats, the era of innocence and order symbolised by the 'rocking cradle in Bethlehem is disappearing. In its place, is a new era where a savage god will be 'moving its slow thighs'. A difficult subject is brought to life by the power of the poet's language.

Leaving Cert Sample Essay

'W. B. Yeats makes effective use of rich symbolism and vivid imagery to explore a range of poetic themes.' Discuss this statement, developing your answer with reference to both the themes and poetic style of the poetry of W. B. Yeats on your course.

Sample Essay

1. The passing of time, political change and the search for spiritual meaning are recurring themes in Yeats's poetry. He is often angry about ageing and the limits of human existence. He offers his personal opinions on public and universal themes in poems such as 'The Lake Isle of Innisfree', 'September 1913', 'The Wild Swans at Coole' and 'Easter 1916'. Yeats communicates his views in a powerful display of vibrant symbolism and vivid imagery.

2. In 'The Lake Isle of Innisfree', Yeats addresses a personal yet public theme, the longing of exiled emigrants to return to the peace of their homeland. Beautiful images describe the idyllic existence on Innisfree. The intensity of noonday heat on the heather is suggested by the broad-vowelled phrase 'purple glow'. The serenity of this magical place is evoked through slow broad vowels, alliterative 'l' sounds and onomatopoeia, 'I hear lake water lapping with low sounds by the shore'. This hypnotic vision – and Yeats's deep sense of longing – is interrupted by the startling reality of impersonal urban life, 'I stand on the roadway, or on the pavements grey'. Insistent monosyllable sounds emphasise the poet's deep desire to escape, 'I hear it in the deep heart's core'.

3. 'The Wild Swans at Coole' uses equally contrasting images. The swans are a powerful symbol of youthful vigour. Alliteration and onomatopoeia convey the dynamism of the noisy swans 'wheeling in great broken rings'. The swans' strong relationship, 'Lover by lover', is noted. Swans usually mate for life. This serene image is interrupted, as in the previous poem, with the bitter reality of Yeats's personal anguish. Unlike these 'brilliant creatures', he is ageing. He has been disappointed in life, 'now my heart is sore'. Yet, it is the dream which lingers in the reader's mind due to the poet's technical brilliance. The swans 'still drift on the still water,/ Mysterious, beautiful'. Yeats, again has combined personal and universal concerns, lost love and transience in haunting language.

4. In contrast to such lyrical beauty, the hard-hitting political poem, 'September 1913', attacks Irish citizens who focus on materialistic gain. Their servile attitude to religion is also mocked – they count 'prayer to shivering prayer'. Yeats was furious at the Dublin merchant classes of early 20th century Dublin who refused to fund the Hugh Lane Gallery and who were partly responsible for the trade union lockout. In contrast,

INDICATIVE MATERIAL

• **Yeats's effective use of rich symbolism and vivid imagery** (powerful metaphors, colourful similes, vibrant descriptive details, striking references and allusions, lively aural imagery, etc.)

… that explore:

• **a range of poetic themes** (public and private – reality/ escape, transience/ immortality, exhilaration/ tragedy of conflict, materialistic present/ romanticised past, creativity, culture, etc.)

Yeats communicates the idealistic dream which these merchants do not understand. He reminds them that there were once patriotic heroes who 'stilled your childish play'. The price they paid was the 'hangman's rope' or exile from their homeland, 'The grey wing upon every tide'. Yeats has taken a local conflict and given it a global application through powerful visual and aural imagery.

5. 'Easter 1916' is another political poem highlighting Yeats's ambivalent feelings. He is condescending towards those who fought for Irish freedom. He is barely civil, exchanging 'polite meaningless words' with them. The poet thought of Ireland as a land of fools who wore the clothes of clowns, 'where motley is worn'. Yet another paradox, 'A terrible beauty', acknowledges the pain and suffering of the rebels of 1916. Their devotion to a cause made their hearts 'Enchanted to a stone'. Yeats believed that radical dedication to an ideal resulted in men losing their humanity. This is indeed 'terrible'. However, the purity of their devotion also made it 'beautiful'.

6. Yeats addresses the conflict between mortality and immortality in 'Sailing to Byzantium'. The poet belittles an old man through the use of the telling symbol, 'at tattered coat upon a stick'. Alienated from a youthful Ireland, described in dynamic images, 'salmon-falls', 'mackerel-crowded seas', he lists the inescapable cycle of life, 'begotten, born, and dies'. He will fight against old age through art. Yeats rejects the decaying mortal body, 'A dying animal', and decides to become a golden bird 'set upon a golden bough' to continue his trade as poet, singing of 'what is past or passing or to come'. But this time the dream does not work. The Emperor is 'drowsy', inattentive. Byzantium, this mythical symbol of 'artifice' does not satisfy. Instead, it is the realistic image of the 'young/in one another's arms' which lingers in the reader's mind. The poet poses the problem of mortality and immortality and leaves it to the reader to consider.

7. Yeats repeatedly considers public and private themes, including escape, transience, conflict and death. These are carefully shaped, resulting in poems that reverberate 'like a ringing bell' due to forceful symbolism and compelling imagery.

EXAMINER'S COMMENT

Following the clear overview in the brief introduction, this focused top-grade response engages enthusiastically with both the question and selected illustrative poems. Some excellent critical discussion of the visual and aural imagery in 'The Lake Isle of Innisfree' and 'The Wild Swans at Coole'. While there was impressive focus on symbolism in 'Sailing to Byzantium', this element of the question might also have been developed more in paragraphs 4 and 5. Overall, confident expression and effective use of suitable quotation throughout contribute much to this highly commendable essay.

GRADE: H1
P = 15/15
C = 13/15
L = 13/15
M = 5/5
Total = 46/50

(765 words)

◠◠ Revision Overview

'The Lake Isle of Innisfree'
In this beautiful poem, filled with sensual images, Yeats dreams of escaping the modern world to find peace in the countryside.

'September 1913'
Disenchanted with materialism, Yeats contrasts Ireland's past with the self-serving values of modern society.

'The Wild Swans at Coole'
A persistent sense of failure and regret underlies this poem in which Yeats explores the transience of human life.

'An Irish Airman Foresees his Death'
In this presentation of the power of the human spirit, Yeats addresses Irish national identity.

'Easter 1916'
The force of political passion is central to this poem in which Yeats expresses his conflicted emotions regarding the Easter Rising.

'The Second Coming'
Yeats's longing for order leads him to envision some sort of Second Coming. This was traditionally associated with the return of Christ to Earth.

'Sailing to Byzantium'
Yeats yearns for meaning in this complex poem which addresses the reality of ageing.

'The Stare's Nest By My Window'
Yeats returns to the subject of moral and social collapse, and the search for renewal. The desire for freedom is central to the poem.

'In Memory of Eva Gore-Booth and Con Markiewicz'
Yeats laments time's effects on beauty and youthful idealism. The poem also considers the contribution that artists make to society.

'Swift's Epitaph'
Yeats's high regard for Swift can be seen as part of his commitment to Anglo-Irish cultural politics.

'An Acre of Grass'
Another confessional poem. The loss of poetic vision makes Yeats long for insight into the mystery of life and death.

'from "Under Ben Bulben"'
Facing death, Yeats embraces the spiritual world of eternity. He urges Irish poets to share his vision for fulfilment through art.

'Politics'
In this nostalgic poem, Yeats acknowledges human weakness. He believed love was more important than politics in shaping destiny.

💬 Last Words

'Yeats's poetry is simple and eloquent to the heart.'
Robert Louis Stevenson

'He had this marvellous gift of beating the scrap metal of the day-to-day life into a ringing bell.'
Seamus Heaney

'All that is beautiful in art is laboured over.'
W. B. Yeats

 CREATIVITY   TRANSIENCE   MEANING OF LIFE   LOVE   IRELAND   NATURE   HISTORY/ MEMORY   LONGING   ART   HEROISM

The Unseen Poem

'Students should be able ... to read poetry conscious of its specific mode of using language as an artistic medium.'
(DES English Syllabus, 4.5.1)

Note that responding to the unseen poem is an exercise in aesthetic reading. It is especially important, in assessing the responses of the candidates, to guard against the temptation to assume a 'correct' reading of the poem.

Reward the candidates' awareness of the patterned nature of the language of poetry, its imagery, its sensuous qualities, and its suggestiveness.

SEC Marking Scheme

In the Unseen Poem 20-mark question, you will have 20 minutes to read and respond to a short poem that you are unlikely to have already studied. Targeted reading is essential. **Read over the questions** first to focus your thoughts and feelings.

In your **first reading** of the poem:
- Aim to get an initial sense of what the poet is saying and think about why the poet is writing about that particular subject.
- What is happening? Who is involved? Is there a sense of place and atmosphere?
- Underline interesting words or phrases that catch your attention. Avoid wasting time worrying about any words that you don't understand. Instead, **focus on what makes sense** to you.

Read through the poem **a second time:**
- Who is speaking in the poem? Is it the poet or another character?
- Is the poet describing a scene?
- Or remembering an experience?
- What point is the poet making?
- What do you notice about the poet's language use?
- How does the poem make you feel?
- Did it make you wonder? Trust your own reaction.

Check the **'Glossary of Common Literary Terms'** on GillExplore.ie

- **Theme** (the central idea or message in a poem. There may be more than one theme)
- **Imagery** (includes similes, metaphors, symbols and personification)
- **Sound (aural) effects** – often referred to as onomatopoeia (includes alliteration, assonance, sibilance, rhyme and repetition)
- **Tone** (nostalgic, happy, sad, reflective, angry, optimistic, etc.)
- **Mood** (atmosphere can be relaxed, mysterious, poignant, uneasy, etc.)
- **Rhythm** (the pace or movement of lines, similar to the musical 'beat' of a song. Rhythm often reflects mood and can be slow, regular, rapid, uneven, etc.)
- **Language** (the poet's choice and order of words, including imagery and poetic devices)
- **Style** (the use of language. Poets choose various techniques, such as imagery, tone, etc. to convey meaning and emotion)
- **Lyric** (poem that expresses the poet's thoughts and feelings. Lyric poems are often short and sometimes resemble a song in form or style)
- **Rhyme** (the occurrence of the same or similar sounds – usually at the end of a line. Rhyme often adds emphasis)
- **Stanza** (two or more lines of poetry that together form a section of a poem)
- **Persona** (the speaker or 'voice' in the poem ... This may or may not be the poet)
- **Personification** (where a thing is treated as a living being, e.g. 'his brown skin hung in strips' – Elizabeth Bishop's description of the fish she caught)
- **Enjambment** (when a line doesn't have punctuation at the end. The resulting run-on lines usually add emphasis)
- **Irony** (when there is a different meaning to what is stated, e.g. the title of Plath's poem, 'The Times Are Tidy')
- **Emotive language** (language that affects the reader's feelings, e.g. 'our times have robbed your cradle' in Eavan Boland's 'Child of Our Time')
- **Contrasts**
- **Structure and layout**

REMEMBER!

'This section [Unseen Poetry] was often not answered, resulting in a loss of 20 marks. Omitting questions or parts of questions has a deleterious effect and is often due to poor time management.'
Chief Examiner's Report

Unseen Poem – Practice 1

Read the following poem by Alan Bold and answer **either** Question 1
or Question 2 which follow.

1   Autumn

Autumn arrives
Like an experienced robber
Grabbing the green stuff
Then cunningly covering his tracks
With a deep multitude
Of colourful distractions.
And the wind,
The wind is his accomplice
Putting an air of chaos
Into the careful diversions
So branches shake
And dead leaves are suddenly blown
In the faces of inquisitive strangers.
The theft chills the world,
Changes the temper of the earth
Till the normally placid sky
Glows red with a quiet rage.

Alan Bold

1. (a) What do you learn about the poet's attitude to autumn in
the above poem? Support your answer with reference to the
poem. (10)

   (b) Identify two images from the poem that make an impact on you
and give reasons for your choice. (10)

OR

2. Discuss the appeal of this poem, commenting on its theme, tone and
the poet's use of language and imagery. Support your answer with
reference to the poem. (20)

Sample Answer 1

Q1. (a) (Poet's attitude to autumn)
(Basic response)

The poet's attitude to autumn is not good at all because he calls autumn an experienced robber which is a negative thing. Alan does not compare the beauty in which nature is full of descriptive scenery of leaves falling in countryside areas. I think he's wrong about autumn to call it a theif in the night because this is not the whole picture at all and he only sees the negative side like storms and trees shaking. There is another story to the beauty of autumn's nature other than the dead leaves which are a reminder of death which is a totally negative side. Alan has a pesimmistic attitude and this is too narrow to be true to life.

EXAMINER'S COMMENT

- *Makes one valid point about negativity.*
- *Little development or use of reference.*
- *No focus on the varied aspects of autumn.*
- *Expression is awkward and repetitive.*
- *Incorrect spellings ('theif', 'pesimmistic').*
Marks awarded: 3/10

Sample Answer 2

Q1. (a) (Poet's attitude to autumn)
(Top-grade response)

Alan Bold has a very playful outlook towards the season of autumn. In comparing it to a cunning 'experienced' robber who sneaks in every year to steal 'the green stuff' that grows in summer, he seems fascinated by the way nature changes so secretively. Bold develops the metaphor throughout the poem, closely observing how the wind (autumn's 'accomplice') creates chaos, tossing colourful leaves across the ground. Autumn is depicted as a powerful natural force which not only changes the landscape, but also affects how people feel. This is evident in the poem's final lines where he suggests that autumn marks the transition into winter and is a reminder that nature can be destructive – and even something to be feared. The poet's overall attitude is that the season of autumn warns human beings about our fragile relationship with the natural world.

EXAMINER'S COMMENT

- *Insightful answer that engages closely with the poem.*
- *Interesting final point about nature's destructive power.*
- *Good use made of supportive quotations throughout.*
- *Varied sentence length, fluent expression.*
- *Grammar and spellings are excellent.*
Marks awarded: 10/10

Sample Answer 3

Q1. (b) (Two images that make an impact)
(Basic response)

'the faces of inquisitive strangers' This is the first image that makes an impact on me and my reasons for my choice is that it is just as it would happen in reality when people are in parks. This when we see the leaves are blown around into your face during October. If people have young children with them they never stop asking questions about the weather and everything.

'normally placid sky' The second image from the poem that made an impact on me and my reason for my choice is because this is that it is pure Irish weather in which the clouds are grey. It is usually about to rain in Ireland just like the calm before the storm. It does not exactly stay placid for long in this country. This image is detailed and true to life.

EXAMINER'S COMMENT
- *Little engagement with the poem's language.*
- *Limited point about the realism of both images.*
- *Needs more developed discussion.*
- *Drifted into general commentary.*
- *Repetitive, flawed expression throughout.*
Marks awarded: 4/10

Sample Answer 4

Q1. (b) (Two images that make an impact)
(Top-grade response)

I thought the 'experienced robber' image was powerful. The simile suggests that autumn is sly – disturbing the peace of summer. Bold cleverly develops the comparison, emphasising the criminal image of the season, with associated words, such as 'covering his tracks' and 'cunningly'. The effect is playful – autumn is fooling everyone into a false sense of security by disguising the changes that are happening to the climate. This lively colourful season is not to be fully trusted.

In a second striking image, the poet personifies the wind, describing it as autumn's 'accomplice' in creating widespread havoc. It creates an air of chaos – literally. This gives nature a human characteristic, which only strengthens its awesome power. The wind shows autumn to be even more terrifying because something so strong is merely its accomplice.

EXAMINER'S COMMENT
- *Perceptive analysis of the poet's inventive language.*
- *Good understanding of the extended metaphor.*
- *Effective use of apt textual reference.*
- *Excellent expression throughout.*
Marks awarded: 9/10

Unseen Poem – Practice 2

Read the following poem by Grace Nichols and answer **either** Question 1
or Question 2 which follow.

Roller-Skaters

Flying by
on the winged-wheels
of their heels

Two teenage earthbirds
zig-zagging
down the street

Rising
unfeathered –
in sudden air-leap

Defying law
death and gravity
as they do a wheely

Landing back
in the smooth swoop
of youth

And faces gaping
gawking, impressed
and unimpressed

Only mother watches – heartbeat in her mouth

Grace Nichols

1. **(a)** What do you think the poet is saying about the relationships between parents and their children in 'Roller-Skaters'? Support your answer with reference to the poem. (10)

    (b) Identify two images from the poem that make an impact on you and give reasons for your choice. (10)

    OR

2. Discuss the language, including the imagery, used by the poet throughout this poem. Make detailed reference to the poem in support of your answer. (20)

Sample Answer 1

Q2. (Poet's language use)
(Basic response)

The poet's language including the imagry used by the poet is very detailed. It shows a street where roller skaters are taking place. The details show they are brave doing the wheely and zig zags as they are actually risking their lives for the sport they love. I myself have mixed feelings about the imagry because it shows how they jump in the air and amazing tricks. Like leaps but on the other hand their mother is afraid that he will be hurt. The language describes the danger involved in this sport.

People out in the street are looking at the image of these skaters. This is an image of risking life or just to show off to attract attention. The language and images make me think of the danger involved behind the first impressions of an exciting sport that attracts kids in every city. At the start of the poem it is very exciting because no one is injured so far but as Grace protrays the skaters more in a detailed way the language becomes more dangerous for example when she says there is a risk of death during the wheely. No wonder the mother watching has an image of her heart in her mouth because it is a dangerous situation and she is not too impressed.

EXAMINER'S COMMENT

- *Makes some points about detailed description.*
- *Little development or use of close reference to language.*
- *Minimal focus on the effectiveness of imagery.*
- *Expression is awkward and repetitive at times.*
- *Mechanical errors ('imagry', 'protrays').*
Marks awarded: 6/20

Sample Answer 2

Q2. (Poet's language use)
(Top-grade response)

Vivid imagery and energetic language are key features in this poem. Nichols describes the young roller skaters 'Flying by' and having 'winged-wheels'. Both these descriptions are metaphors as the skaters are not actually 'flying' nor do they have real 'wings'. The poem can be seen as one developed metaphor that suggests the breakneck actions of the skaters who seek excitement. Short lines and dynamic verbs, such as 'zig-zagging' and 'Rising' suggest their speed.

The skaters are compared to 'earthbirds' which is very effective. I can almost imagine that they will take off into the air at any minute. Later on, they are described as 'unfeathered', which links back to the same idea that they are defying 'death and gravity'. Towards the end, the poet mentions the 'smooth sweep of youth' and suggests that the skaters are enjoying their freedom.

The poem's rhythm is lively throughout and not interrupted by punctuation. This highlights the reckless moves the skaters make. Run-on lines (enjambment) create a sense of continuous movement. Sound effects play a huge part in the poem. There is a pattern of slender 'i' and 'e' vowels – e.g. 'winged-wheels' – in the opening lines which increases the pace. The alliteration suggests the repeated actions of the skaters.

The layout is arranged in a series of short lines and this highlights the skaters' lively movement. The final separate line cleverly suggests how the mother is outside of the action and can only watch from a distance as her child takes risks.

EXAMINER'S COMMENT

- *Focused on the effectiveness of language throughout.*
- *Ranges over various aspects, including imagery and sound.*
- *Well-developed discussion of the bird metaphor.*
- *Insightful comments on rhythm and structure.*
- *Good expression (although 'suggests' is overused).*
  Marks awarded: 18/20

REMEMBER!

There is no single 'correct' reading of the poem. Respond to the poem honestly. How does it make you feel? Trust your own reaction.

Unseen Poem – Practice 3

Read the following poem by David Harmer and answer **either** Question 1 **or** Question 2 which follow.

At Cider Mill Farm

I remember my uncle's farm
Still in mid-summer
Heat hazing the air above the red roof tops
Some cattle sheds, a couple of stables
Clustered round a small yard
Lying under the hills that stretched their long back
Through three counties.

I rolled with the dogs
Among the hay bales
Stacked high in the barn he built himself
During a storm one autumn evening
Tunnelled for treasure or jumped with a scream
From a pirate ship's mast into the straw
Burrowed for gold and found he'd buried
Three battered Ford cars deep in the hay.

He drove an old tractor that sweated oil
In long black streaks down the rusty orange
It chugged and whirred, coughed into life
Each day as he clattered across the cattle grids
I remember one night my cousin and I
Dragging back cows from over the common
We prodded them homeward through the rain
And then drank tea from huge tin mugs
Feeling like farmers.

He's gone now, he sold it
But I have been back for one last look
To the twist in the lane that borders the stream
Where Mary, Ruth and I once waded
Water sloshing over our wellies
And I showed my own children my uncle's farm
The barn still leaning over the straw
With for all I know three battered Ford cars
Still buried beneath it.

David Harmer

1. **(a)** What is your impression of the poet's experiences on the farm in 'At Cider Hill Farm'? Support your answer with reference to the poem. (10)

   (b) Select two images from the poem that appeal to you and give reasons for your choice. (10)

   OR

2. Discuss the language used by the poet, commenting on imagery, tone and sound effects. Support your answer with reference to the poem. (20)

Sample Answer 1

Q1. (a) (Poet's experiences on the farm)

(Basic response)

My first impression of David harmer is that he remembers spending a lot of happy times on his school holidays in cider mill farm. It belonged to his uncle who was the farm owner during his childhood, so he would have been there in the holidays. He had a lot of happy experiences splashing in the river and messing with the dogs but his best experience is of the one time he drank tea from the big tin mugs belonging to the proper farmers after working with the cattle one evening. But the boy was dissapointed after the farm was sold, any child would naturally suffer from dissapointment by loosing their freedom. Up to then the farm life was very appealing, a good break away from school during the holidays.

> **EXAMINER'S COMMENT**
> - Some references to the poet's happy experiences.
> - These could have been more effectively supported by quotes.
> - Lacks discussion on stylistic features, e.g. nostalgic tone.
> - Capital letter errors and misspellings ('dissapointed', 'loosing').
> Marks awarded: 4/10

Sample Answer 2

Q1. (a) (Poet's experiences on the farm)

(Top-grade response)

David Harmer's reminiscences are of exciting childhood days on his uncle's farm. From the start, his tone is nostalgic, 'Heat hazing the air above the red roof tops'. The vowel sounds and gentle alliteration emphasise the poet's happy memories of far-off times. He uses little punctuation, suggesting that the memories are distant and all grouped together. The images of rural scenes show the impact that the countryside 'under the hills' had on him. I think it's almost as if the changing seasons matched the change in the poet's life as he grew up. The poem's mood is enthusiastic, however. The boy's sense of adventure is seen when exploring new sensations among the farm animals, 'We prodded them homeward through the rain'.

> **EXAMINER'S COMMENT**
> - Intuitive response focusing on the poet's idyllic childhood.
> - Good range of discussion points.
> - Well-supported by suitable quotations.
> - Effective reference to imagery, tone and sound effects.
> - Confident expression and excellent mechanics.
> Marks awarded: 10/10

He seems fascinated by the 'rusty orange' tractor – and its unusual noises which still excite his imagination, 'It chugged and whirred'. As a child, he delighted in creating his own world of pirates and buried treasure. It's clear that the time on the farm was important, so much so that he wants to pass on his memories to his own children.

Sample Answer 3

Q1. (b) (Two appealing images)
(Basic response)

The first appealing image is of 'one night dragging back cows' because this shows cows don't hurry and have to be prodded with sticks to make them move. They nearly have to get dragged along as the image says, so this is the reason why this is a good image as it really shows that farmers totally have their hands full trying to get animals to go anywhere. It's just the way cows are. The next image is 'three battered Ford cars'. This is the second appealing image of cars rusting in a field like a scrapyard. This can be seen in parts of the country where cars are dumped without a second thought and they are a complete and total eyesore to the public who have to look at them, day and night. So in one way this is not appealing as an image because some people just dump rubbish anywhere. It's not a very appealing thing either for the public to have to put up with in this day and age, is it?

Sample Answer 4

Q1. (b) (Two appealing images)
(Top-grade response)

There are many appealing images in this poem. I liked the ones that focused on the poet's carefree childhood, such as 'Heat hazing the air above the red roof tops'. The summer setting has strong associations with warmth and happiness. The poet remembers the haze of bright sunlight and the vivid red colours of the farm buildings. This vibrant imagery suggests an exaggerated childlike memory which is reinforced by the 'h' and 'r' alliteration. The line has a dreamlike quality, suggesting the wonder of the experience.

Some of the feelings the poet recalls are reinforced by sound images, for example, 'Water sloshing over our wellies'. The onomatopoeic effect of 'sloshing' echoes the squelching noises made by the children as they splashed through the water. Again, the repetition of sound in 'Water' and 'wellies' mimics their repeated actions as they stomped in the stream. This all contributes to the upbeat mood of the poem. Harmer is re-living a moment when he was totally happy-go-lucky on his uncle's farm.

Unseen Poem – Practice 4

Read the following poem by Rosita Boland and answer **either** Question 1 **or** Question 2 which follow.

Lipstick

Home from work one evening,
I switched the radio on as usual,
chose a knife and started to slice
red peppers, scallions, wild mushrooms.

I started listening to a programme about Iran.
After the Shah fled, Revolutionary Guards
patrolled the streets of Teheran
looking for stray hairs, exposed ankles
and other signs of female disrespect.

The programme ended.
I was left standing in my kitchen
looking at the chopped vegetables on the table;
the scarlet circles of the peppers
delicate mouths, scattered at random.

When they discovered a woman wearing lipstick
they razor-bladed it off:
replaced one red gash with another.

Rosita Boland

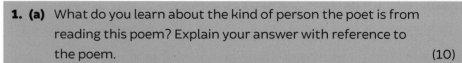

1. (a) What do you learn about the kind of person the poet is from reading this poem? Explain your answer with reference to the poem. **(10)**

(b) Identify a mood or feeling evoked in 'Lipstick' and explain how the poet creates this mood or feeling. Support your answer with reference to the poem. **(10)**

OR

2. What impact did this poem make on you? Refer closely to the text in discussing its theme, tone and the poet's use of language and imagery. **(20)**

Sample Answer 1

Q2. (Impact of the poem)
(Basic response)

This was a hard to understand poem about a worker who comes home to make a meal. But she starts to listen to the radio news about what is happening in the war. I think she imagines the soilders running wild attacking people. One soilder uses a knife and attacks an innocent woman who is just dressed up and wearing lipstick which is her basic human right and just out for the evening. 'They patrolled the street'. This guard should of known better. This is the part of the poem that made the most impact on me personally. I am totally against armies running wild out of control.

This is the theme of war and the tone of this poem is showing up what happens on the back streets in some parts of the world. If your not doing any harm you should be left in peace. There is a big difference between the image of the innocent woman out to enjoy herself on a night out as she is intitled and the angry language of the soilder out on patrol who attacks her for no good reason. This is also at the end of the poem where I think there is a big difference between the two women. Unfortunately it is not a state of peace everywhere else which is the main impact of the poem.

EXAMINER'S COMMENT

- *Makes one reasonable point about the impact of violence.*
- *Only slight engagement with the poem.*
- *No convincing analysis of the poet's language use.*
- *Expression could have been much more controlled.*
- *Mechanical errors ('soilder', 'intitled', 'should of', 'your').*

Marks awarded: 6/20

Sample Answer 2

Q2. (Impact of the poem)

(Top-grade response)

Although the language is simple in this poem, it actually makes the point that routine violence against women is still common in some societies, such as Iran. This makes a greater impact as the poem develops because the poet's tone is almost relaxed in the first stanza – 'I switched the radio on as usual'. The radio programme is truly shocking. Boland points out the stark difference between what we take for granted as normality here at home and the grotesque reality of life in conflict areas, such as the Middle East.

The vivid image of the attack on the civilian is horrific. The poet creates a dramatic effect by contrasting the girl's fragile beauty and the brutal violence she experiences. There are also some subtle echoes within the poem. The guard's vicious action is foreshadowed by the earlier image of the poet herself using a kitchen knife to slice vegetables. I can relate to her sense of revulsion as she imagines the Iranian policeman's use of a razor blade to replace 'one red gash with another'.

I was also struck by the emphasis on the innocence of victims and the helplessness the poet feels. The quiet tone of the final stanza reflects her sense of failure, 'left standing there in my kitchen'. Vivid images of the half-chopped vegetables, particularly the 'scarlet circles of the peppers', are closely associated with the 'Delicate mouths' of vulnerable women who suffer vicious abuse and injustice. The ending has a clarity that sums up the savage regime in Tehran.

EXAMINER'S COMMENT

- *Convincing personal response to the question.*
- *Points are clear, incisive and aptly supported.*
- *Links theme and stylistic features very well.*
- *Perceptive analysis of tone, imagery and contrast.*
- *Excellent expression, fluent and varied.*

Marks awarded: 20/20

REMEMBER!

Avoid wasting time worrying about any words in an Unseen Poem that you don't understand. Instead, focus on what makes sense to you.

Unseen Poem Revision Points

- **Study the wording of questions** to identify the task that you have to do.

- Express your **key points** clearly.

- Include **supportive reference or quotation** (correctly punctuated).

- Refer to both the poet's **style** (how the poem is written) as well as the **themes** (what the poet is writing about).

- **Select interesting phrases** that give you an opportunity to discuss subject matter and use of language.

- **Avoid summaries** that simply repeat the text of the poem.

- **Engage with the poem** by responding genuinely to what the poet has written.

Unseen Poem – Practice 5

Read the following poem by Pat Boran and answer **either** Question 1
or Question 2 which follow. (Allow 20 minutes to complete the answer.)

5 Stalled Train

In the listening carriage, someone's phone
cries out for help. A student frisks himself,
a woman weighs her handbag
then stares into space. Our train
is going nowhere. We've stood here
so long now the cattle in this field
have dared come right up close
to chew and gaze. We tell ourselves
that somewhere down the line
things we cannot understand
are surely taking place — the future
almost within reach — and into each
small telephone that rings
or shudders now, like doubt,
we commit (if still in whispers)
our hopes and fears, our last known
whereabouts.

Pat Boran

1. (a) In your opinion, is the dominant mood in the poem positive or
negative? Explain your answer with reference to the poem. (10)

(b) Identify two images from the poem that you find interesting
and give reasons for your choice. (10)

OR

2. Discuss the impact of this poem, with reference to
its theme and the poet's use of language and
imagery. Refer closely to the text in support
of your answer. (20)

PROMPT!

- *Think about the poet's attitude to modern life.*
- *Imagery is vivid, graphic, cinematic.*
- *Surreal, mysterious, dreamlike atmosphere.*
- *Effective use of personification and symbols.*
- *Final lines are disturbing.*
- *Poem raises many interesting questions.*

Acknowledgements

The authors and publisher are grateful to the following for permission to reproduce copyrighted material:

'The Fish', 'The Bight', 'At the Fishhouses', 'The Prodigal', 'Questions of Travel', 'The Armadillo', 'Sestina', 'First Death in Nova Scotia', 'Filling Station', and 'In the Waiting Room' from *The Completed Poems*, 1927–1979 by Elizabeth Bishop. Published by Chatto and Windus. Reprinted by permission of The Random House Group Limited;

'Lipstick' from *Dissecting the Heart* by Rosita Boland. Copyright © Rosita Boland, 2013, reproduced by kind permission of the author and The Gallery Press, Loughcrew, Oldcastle, County Meath, Ireland;

'Autumn' by Alan Bold. Copyright © Alan Bold. Reprinted with permission of Alice Bold;

'Stalled Train' from *Then Again* by Pat Boran, 2019, Dedalus Press. Copyright © Pat Boran, reproduced by kind permission of Dedalus Press;

'There's a certain Slant of light', 'I felt a Funeral, in my Brain', 'A Bird came down the Walk', 'I Heard a fly buzz – when I died', 'The Soul has Bandaged moments', 'I could bring You Jewels – had I a mind to', 'A narrow Fellow in the Grass', 'I taste a liquor never brewed', 'After great pain, a formal feeling comes' by Emily Dickinson. T*he Poems of Emily Dickinson: Reading Edition*, edited by Ralph W. Franklin, Cambridge, Mass.: The Belknap Press of Harvard University Press, Copyright © 1998, 1999 by the President and Fellows of Harvard College. Copyright © 1951, 1955 by the President and Fellows of Harvard College. Copyright © renewed 1979, 1983 by the President and Fellows of Harvard College. Copyright © 1914, 1918, 1919, 1924, 1929, 1930, 1932, 1935, 1937, 1942 by Martha Dickinson Bianchi. Copyright © 1952, 1957, 1958, 1963, 1965 by Mary L. Hampson;

'At Cider Mill Farm' by David Harmer, from *The Works 3* chosen by Paul Cookson, Macmillan Children's Books, 2004. Copyright © David Harmer. Used by permission of the author;

'Begin', 'Bread', '"Dear Autumn Girl"', 'Poem from a Three Year Old', 'Oliver to his Brother', 'I See You Dancing, Father', 'A Cry for Art O'Leary', 'Things I Might Do', 'A Great Day', 'Fragments', 'The soul's loneliness', 'Saint Brigid's Prayer' by Brendan Kennelly, from *Familiar Strangers: New and Selected Poems 1960–2004* (Bloodaxe Books, 2004). Reproduced with permission of Bloodaxe Books;

'Roller-Skaters' from *Give Yourself a Hug* © Grace Nichols, 1994. Reproduced with permission of Curtis Brown Group Limited, London on behalf of Grace Nichols;

'Aunt Jennifer's Tigers', 'The Uncle Speaks in the Drawing Room', 'Power', 'Storm Warnings', 'Living in Sin', 'The Roofwalker', 'Our Whole Life', 'Trying to Talk with a Man', 'Diving into the Wreck', 'From a Survivor', from *Collected Poems: 1950–2012* by Adrienne Rich. Copyright © 2016, 2013 by Adrienne Rich Literary Trust. Copyright © 2011, 2007, 2004, 2001, 1999, 1995, 1991, 1989, 1986, 1984, 1981, 1967, 1963, 1962, 1961, 1960, 1959, 1958, 1957, 1956, 1955, 1954, 1953, 1952, 1951 by Adrienne Rich. Copyright © 1984, 1978, 1975, 1973, 1971, 1969, 1966 by W.W. Norton & Company, Inc.

The authors and publisher have made every effort to trace all copyright holders, but if any have been inadvertently overlooked we would be pleased to make the necessary arrangement at the first opportunity.